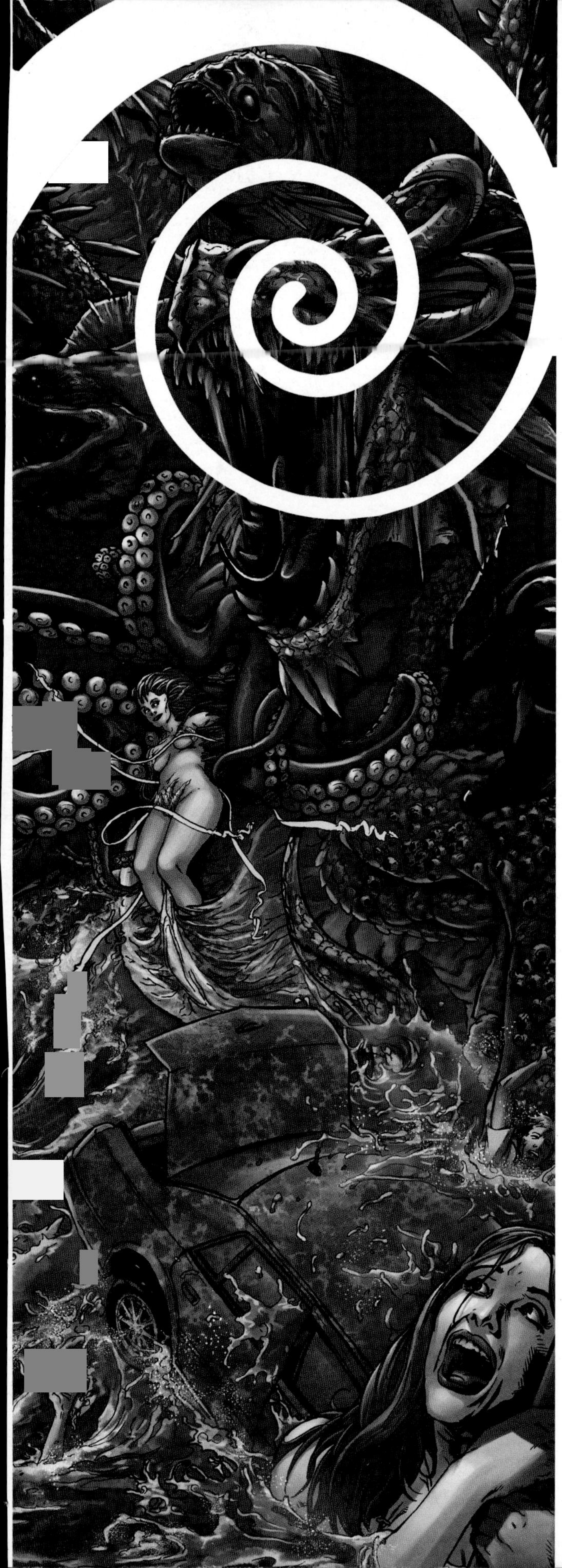

**Justin Jordan**
story



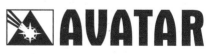

**German Erramouspe**
**Michael DiPascale**
artwork

**Christian Zanier**
cover

**Christian Zanier**
**Michael DiPascale**
chapter breaks & gallery

**Digikore Studios**
Erramouspe interior color
cover color

**Kurt Hathaway**
letters

**William Christensen**
editor-in-chief

**Mark Seifert**
creative director

**Jim Kuhoric**
managing editor

**David Marks**
director of events

**Ariana Osborne**
production assistant

**Dark Gods Volume 1**
July 2015. Published by Avatar Press, Inc., 515 N. Century Blvd. Rantoul, IL 61866.  Printed in Canada.

AVATAR

www.avatarpress.com
www.twitter.com/avatarpress
www.facebook.com/avatarpresscomics

**CHAPTER 1**

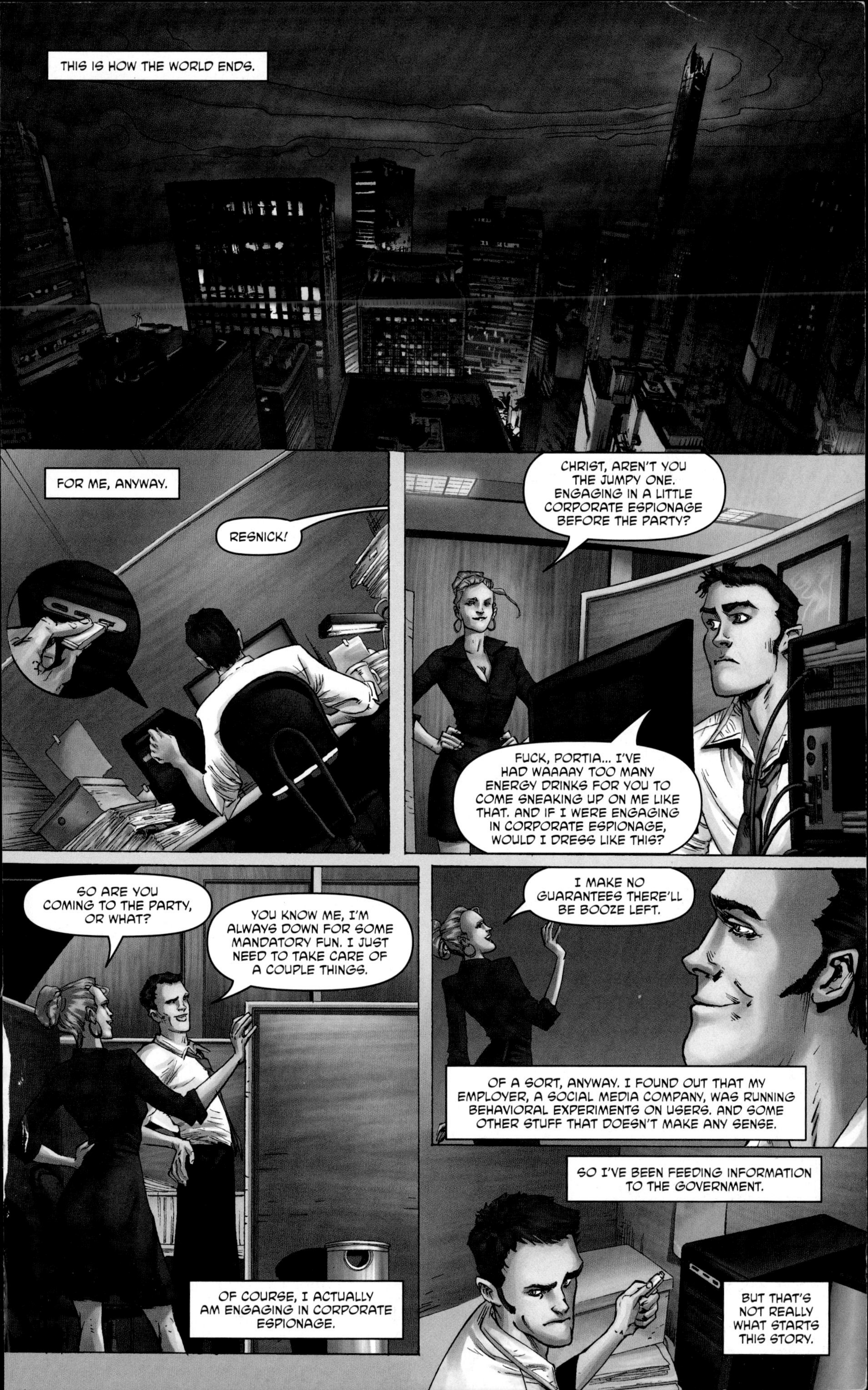
THIS IS HOW THE WORLD ENDS.
FOR ME, ANYWAY.
RESNICK!
CHRIST, AREN'T YOU THE JUMPY ONE. ENGAGING IN A LITTLE CORPORATE ESPIONAGE BEFORE THE PARTY?
FUCK, PORTIA... I'VE HAD WAAAAY TOO MANY ENERGY DRINKS FOR YOU TO COME SNEAKING UP ON ME LIKE THAT. AND IF I WERE ENGAGING IN CORPORATE ESPIONAGE, WOULD I DRESS LIKE THIS?
SO ARE YOU COMING TO THE PARTY, OR WHAT?
YOU KNOW ME, I'M ALWAYS DOWN FOR SOME MANDATORY FUN. I JUST NEED TO TAKE CARE OF A COUPLE THINGS.
I MAKE NO GUARANTEES THERE'LL BE BOOZE LEFT.
OF COURSE, I ACTUALLY AM ENGAGING IN CORPORATE ESPIONAGE.
OF A SORT, ANYWAY. I FOUND OUT THAT MY EMPLOYER, A SOCIAL MEDIA COMPANY, WAS RUNNING BEHAVIORAL EXPERIMENTS ON USERS. AND SOME OTHER STUFF THAT DOESN'T MAKE ANY SENSE.
SO I'VE BEEN FEEDING INFORMATION TO THE GOVERNMENT.
BUT THAT'S NOT REALLY WHAT STARTS THIS STORY.

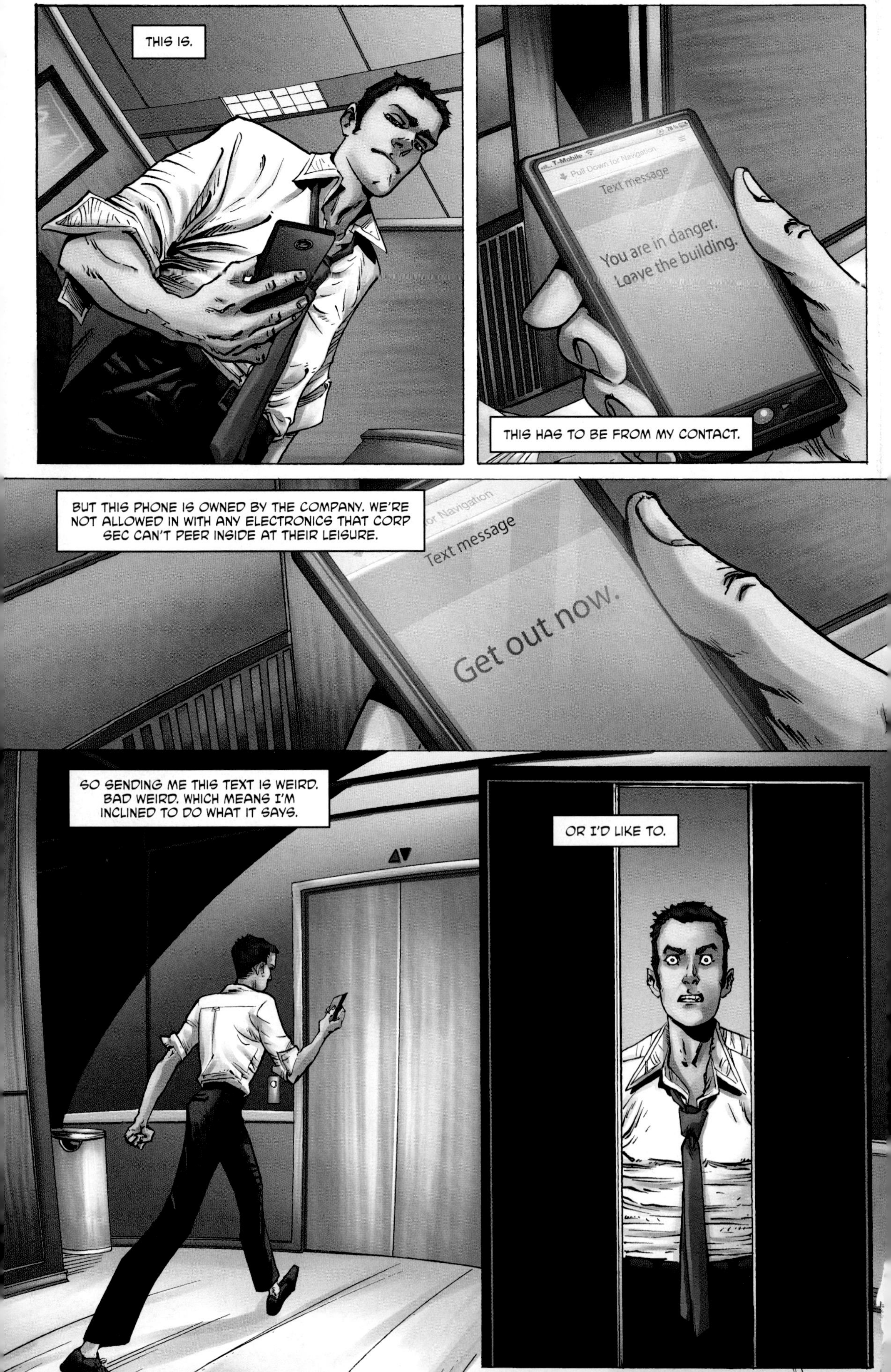
THIS IS.
T-Mobile
Pull Down for Navigation
Text message
You are in danger.
Leave the building.
THIS HAS TO BE FROM MY CONTACT.
BUT THIS PHONE IS OWNED BY THE COMPANY. WE'RE NOT ALLOWED IN WITH ANY ELECTRONICS THAT CORP SEC CAN'T PEER INSIDE AT THEIR LEISURE.
Text message
Get out now.
SO SENDING ME THIS TEXT IS WEIRD. BAD WEIRD. WHICH MEANS I'M INCLINED TO DO WHAT IT SAYS.
OR I'D LIKE TO.

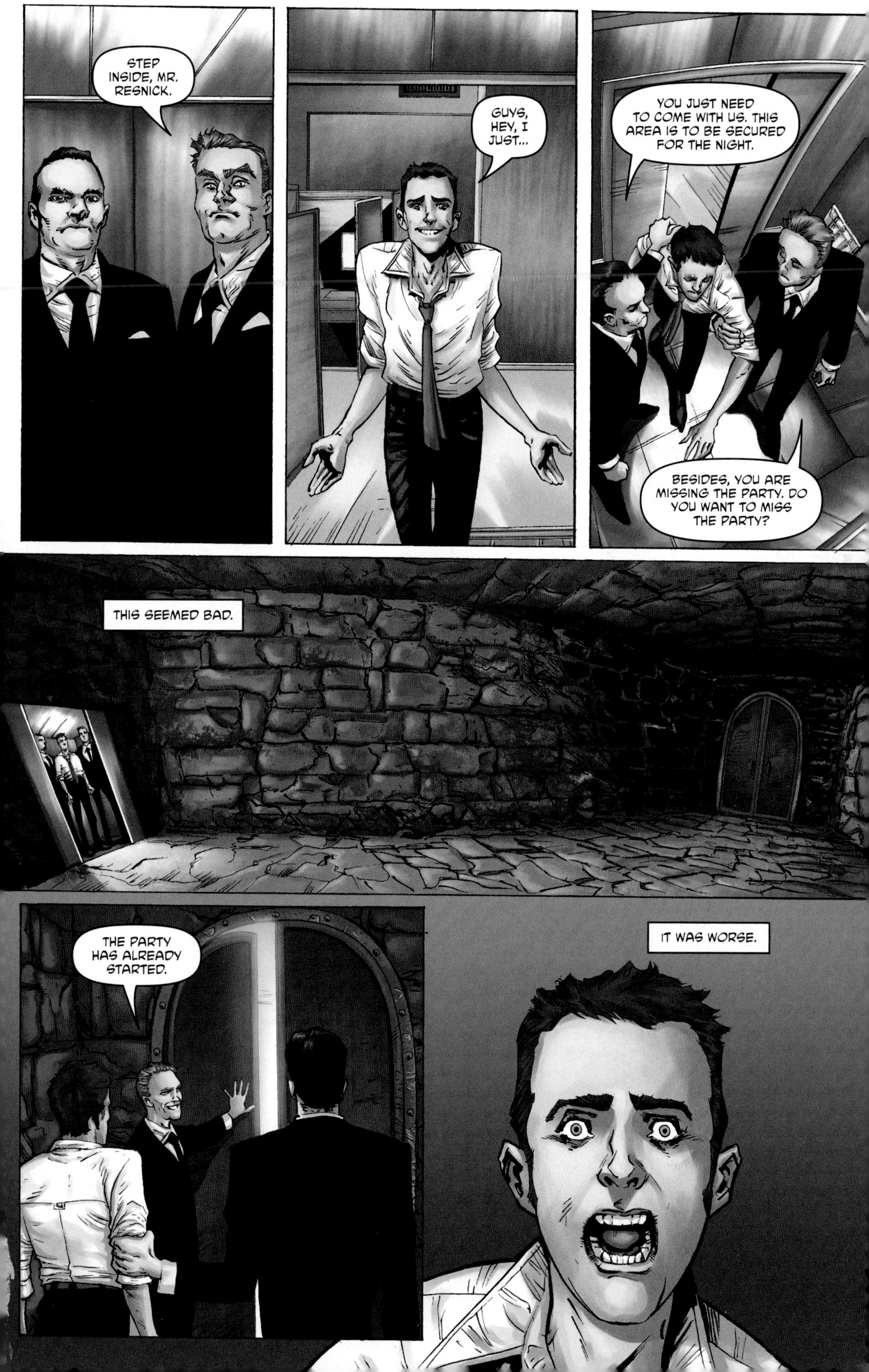
STEP INSIDE, MR. RESNICK.
GUYS, HEY, I JUST...
YOU JUST NEED TO COME WITH US. THIS AREA IS TO BE SECURED FOR THE NIGHT.
BESIDES, YOU ARE MISSING THE PARTY. DO YOU WANT TO MISS THE PARTY?
THIS SEEMED BAD.
THE PARTY HAS ALREADY STARTED.
IT WAS WORSE.

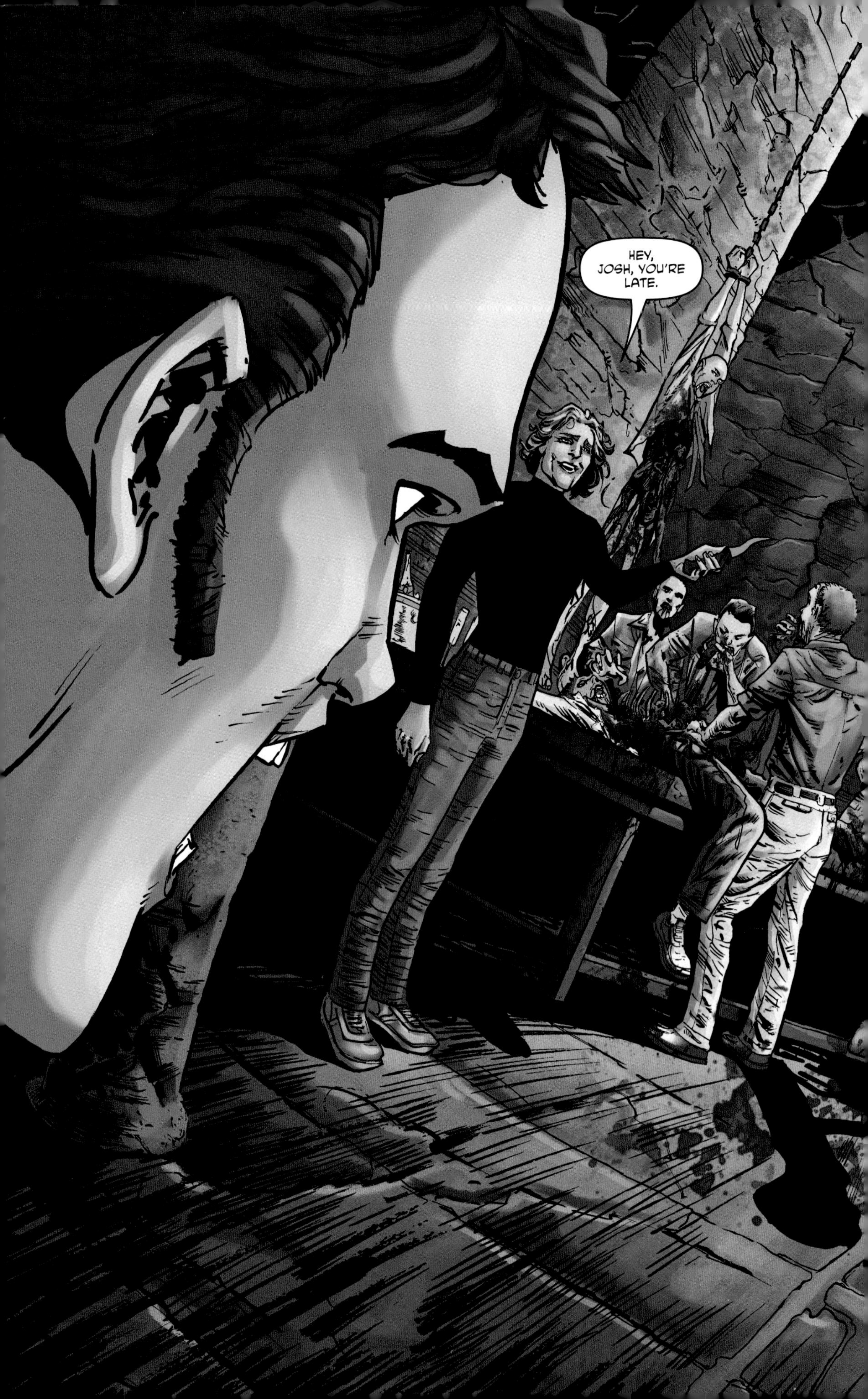
HEY, JOSH, YOU'RE LATE.

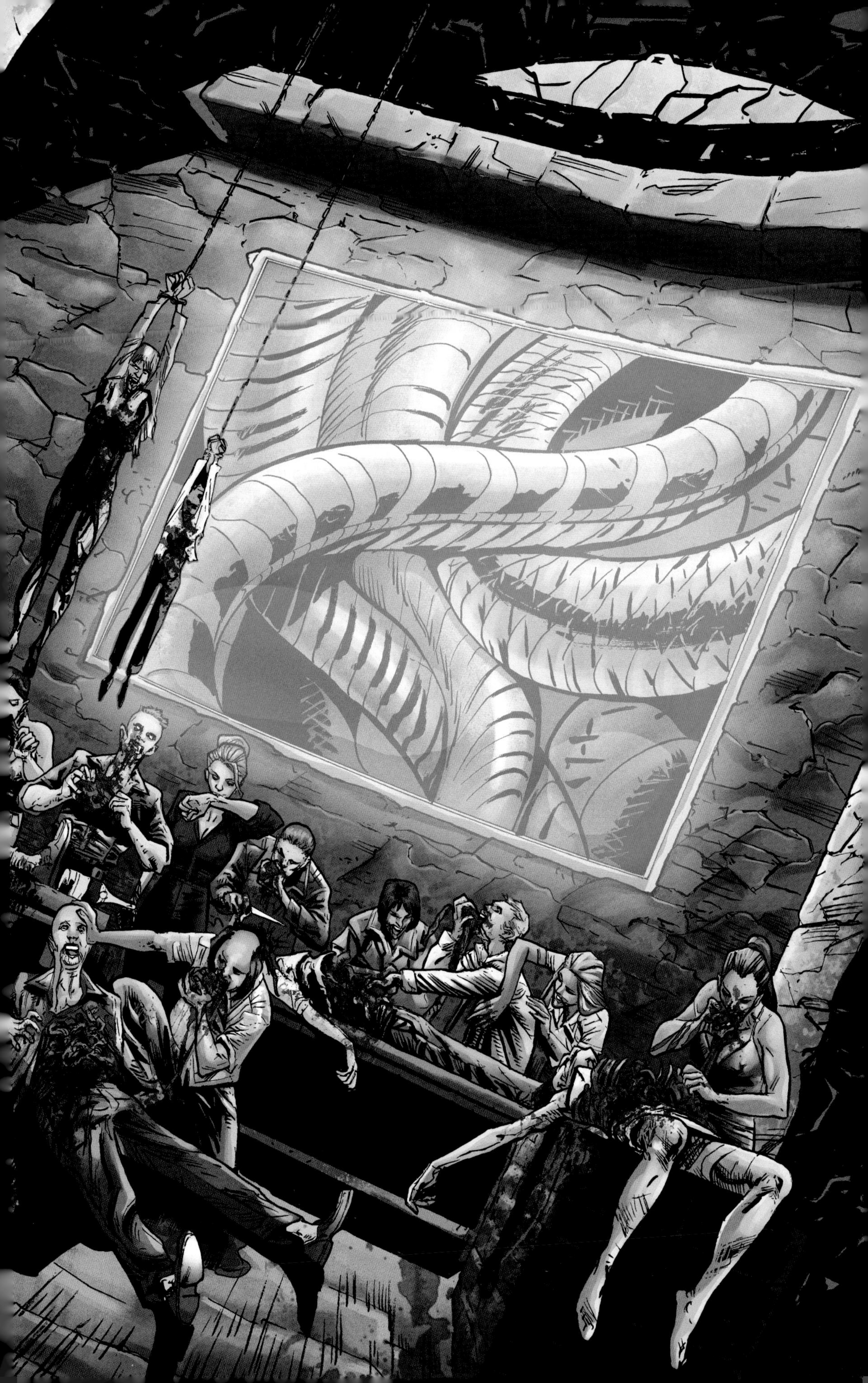

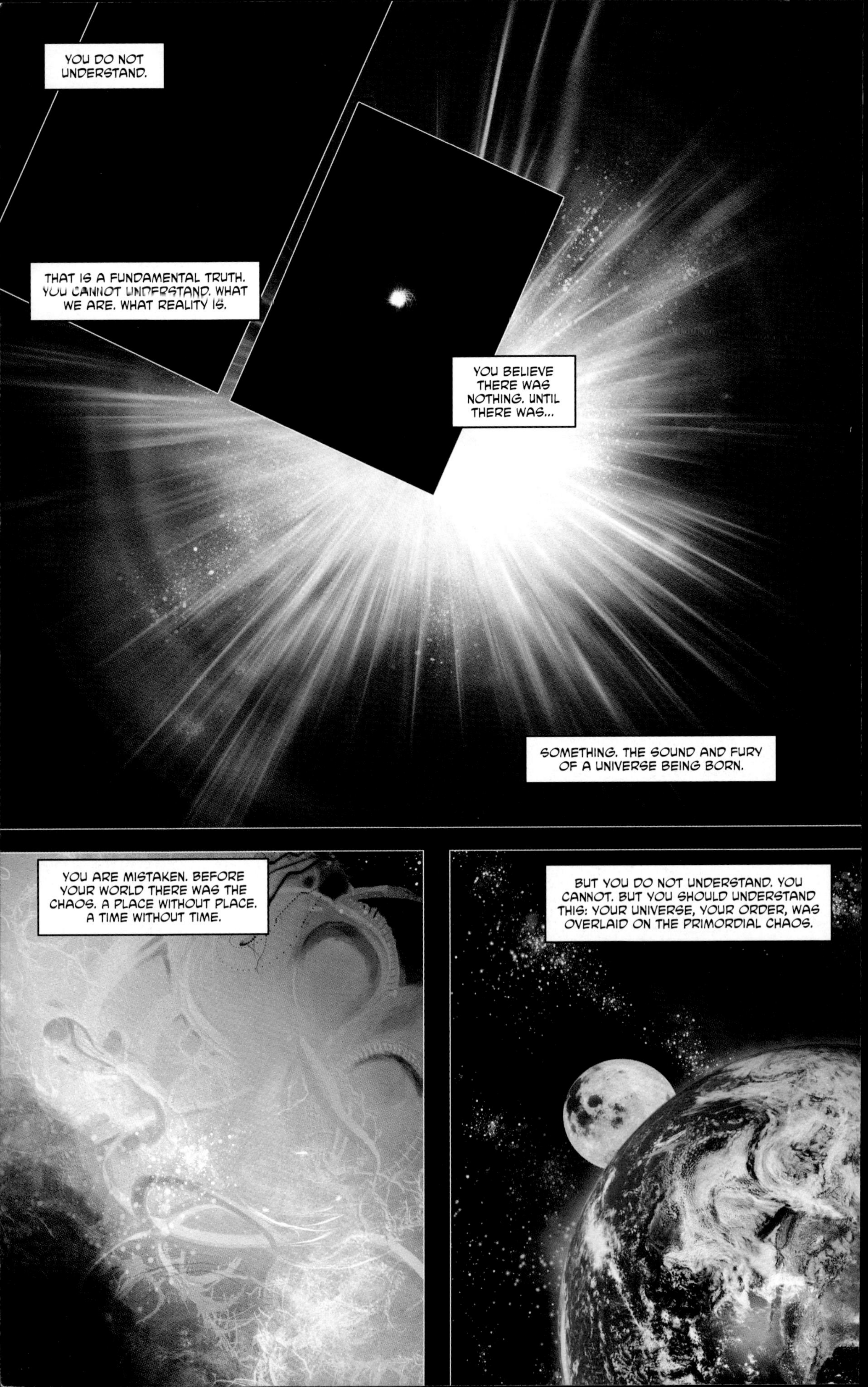
YOU DO NOT UNDERSTAND.
THAT IS A FUNDAMENTAL TRUTH. YOU CANNOT UNDERSTAND. WHAT WE ARE. WHAT REALITY IS.
YOU BELIEVE THERE WAS NOTHING. UNTIL THERE WAS...
SOMETHING. THE SOUND AND FURY OF A UNIVERSE BEING BORN.
YOU ARE MISTAKEN. BEFORE YOUR WORLD THERE WAS THE CHAOS. A PLACE WITHOUT PLACE. A TIME WITHOUT TIME.
BUT YOU DO NOT UNDERSTAND. YOU CANNOT. BUT YOU SHOULD UNDERSTAND THIS: YOUR UNIVERSE, YOUR ORDER, WAS OVERLAID ON THE PRIMORDIAL CHAOS.

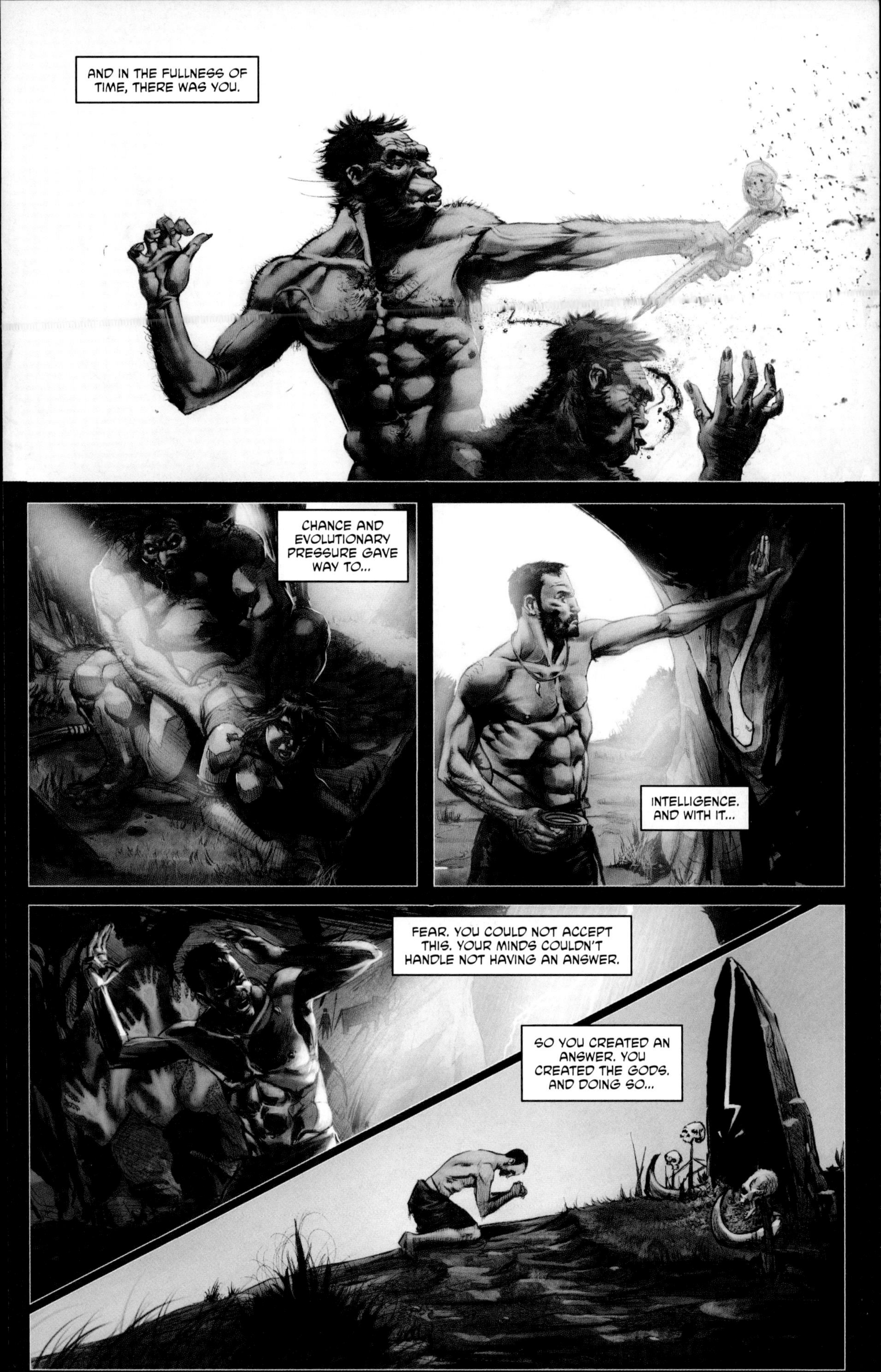
AND IN THE FULLNESS OF TIME, THERE WAS YOU.
CHANCE AND EVOLUTIONARY PRESSURE GAVE WAY TO...
INTELLIGENCE. AND WITH IT...
FEAR. YOU COULD NOT ACCEPT THIS. YOUR MINDS COULDN'T HANDLE NOT HAVING AN ANSWER.
SO YOU CREATED AN ANSWER. YOU CREATED THE GODS. AND DOING SO...

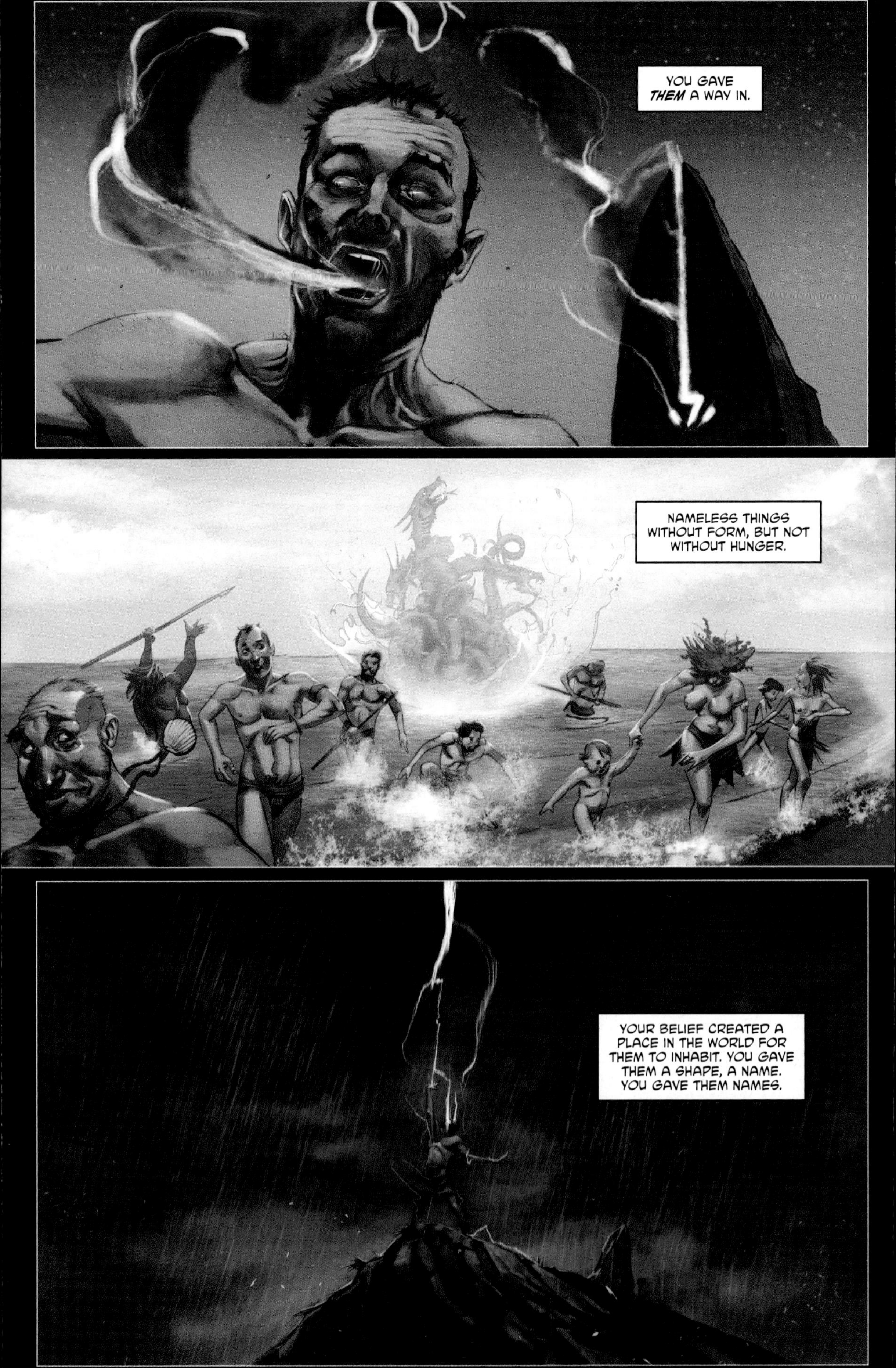
YOU GAVE *THEM* A WAY IN.
NAMELESS THINGS WITHOUT FORM, BUT NOT WITHOUT HUNGER.
YOUR BELIEF CREATED A PLACE IN THE WORLD FOR THEM TO INHABIT. YOU GAVE THEM A SHAPE, A NAME. YOU GAVE THEM NAMES.

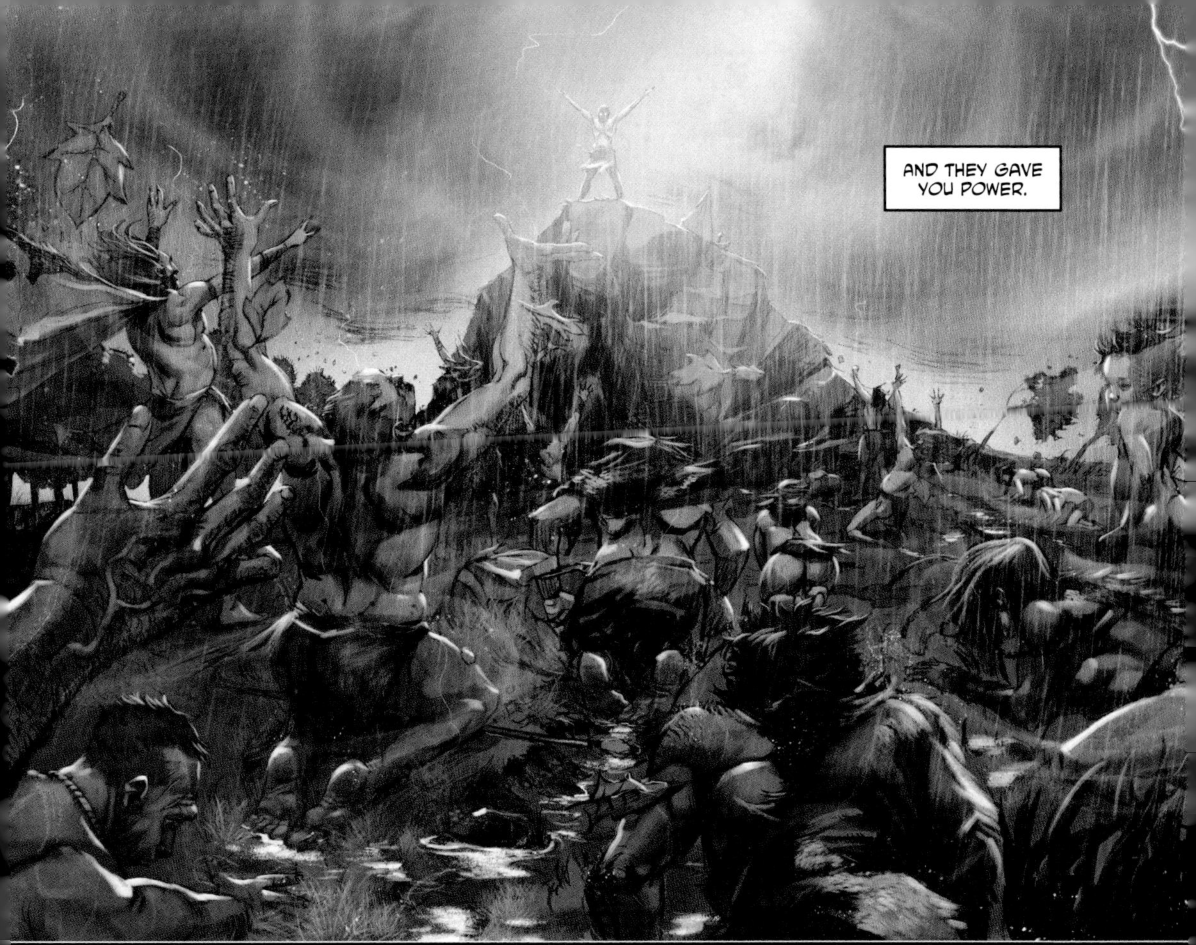
AND THEY GAVE YOU POWER.

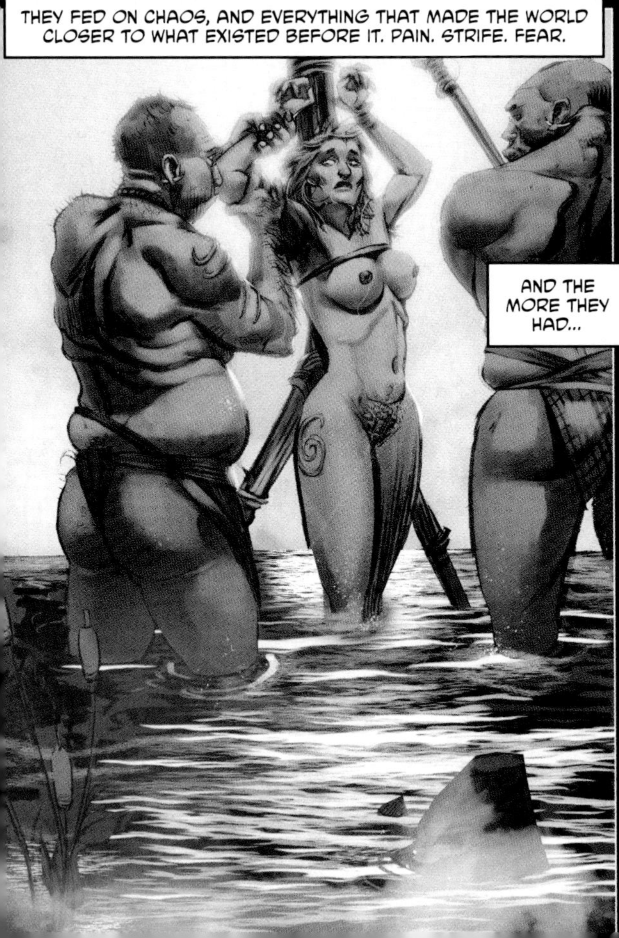
THEY FED ON CHAOS, AND EVERYTHING THAT MADE THE WORLD CLOSER TO WHAT EXISTED BEFORE IT. PAIN. STRIFE. FEAR.
AND THE MORE THEY HAD...

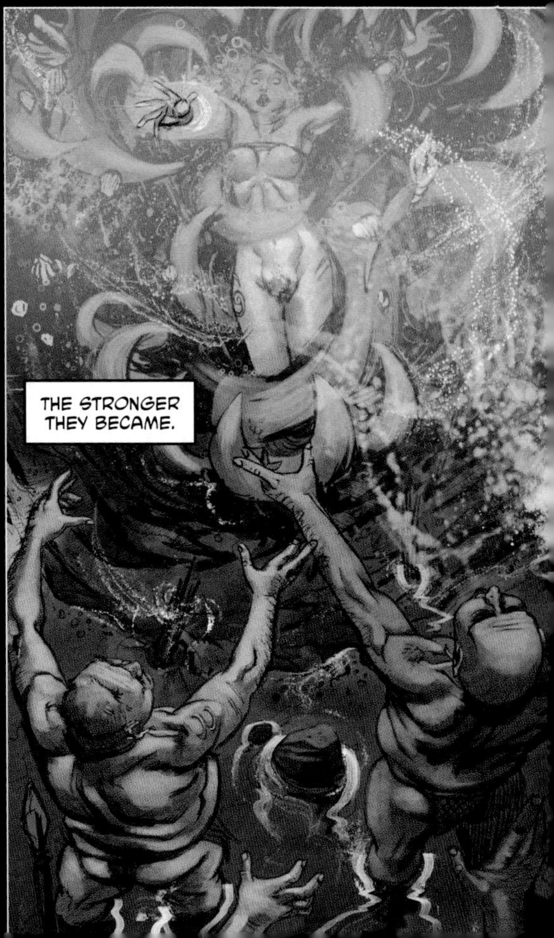
THE STRONGER THEY BECAME.

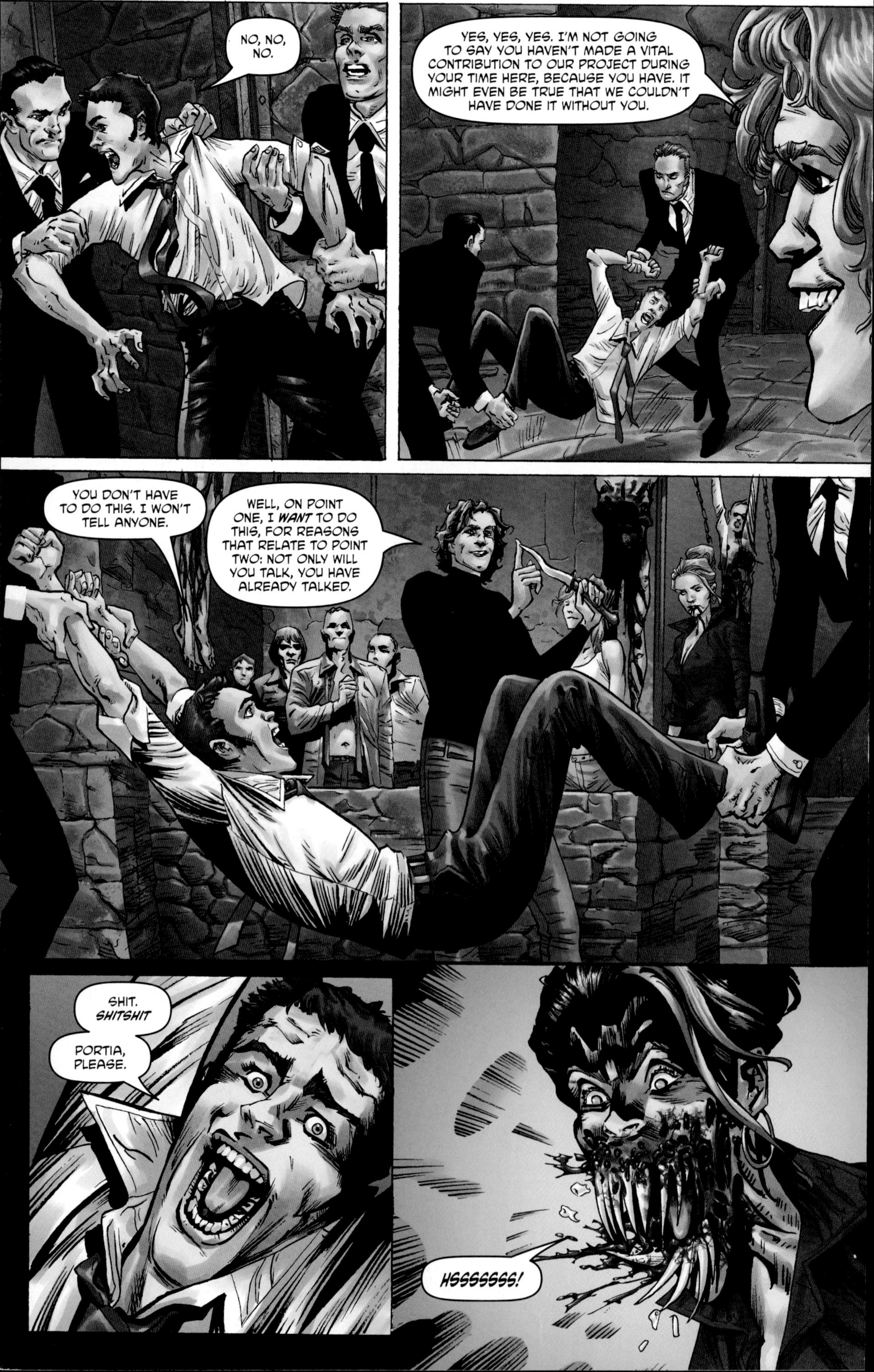
NO, NO, NO.
YES, YES, YES. I'M NOT GOING TO SAY YOU HAVEN'T MADE A VITAL CONTRIBUTION TO OUR PROJECT DURING YOUR TIME HERE, BECAUSE YOU HAVE. IT MIGHT EVEN BE TRUE THAT WE COULDN'T HAVE DONE IT WITHOUT YOU.
YOU DON'T HAVE TO DO THIS. I WON'T TELL ANYONE.
WELL, ON POINT ONE, I *WANT* TO DO THIS, FOR REASONS THAT RELATE TO POINT TWO: NOT ONLY WILL YOU TALK, YOU HAVE ALREADY TALKED.
SHIT. *SHITSHIT*
PORTIA, PLEASE.
*HSSSSSSS!*

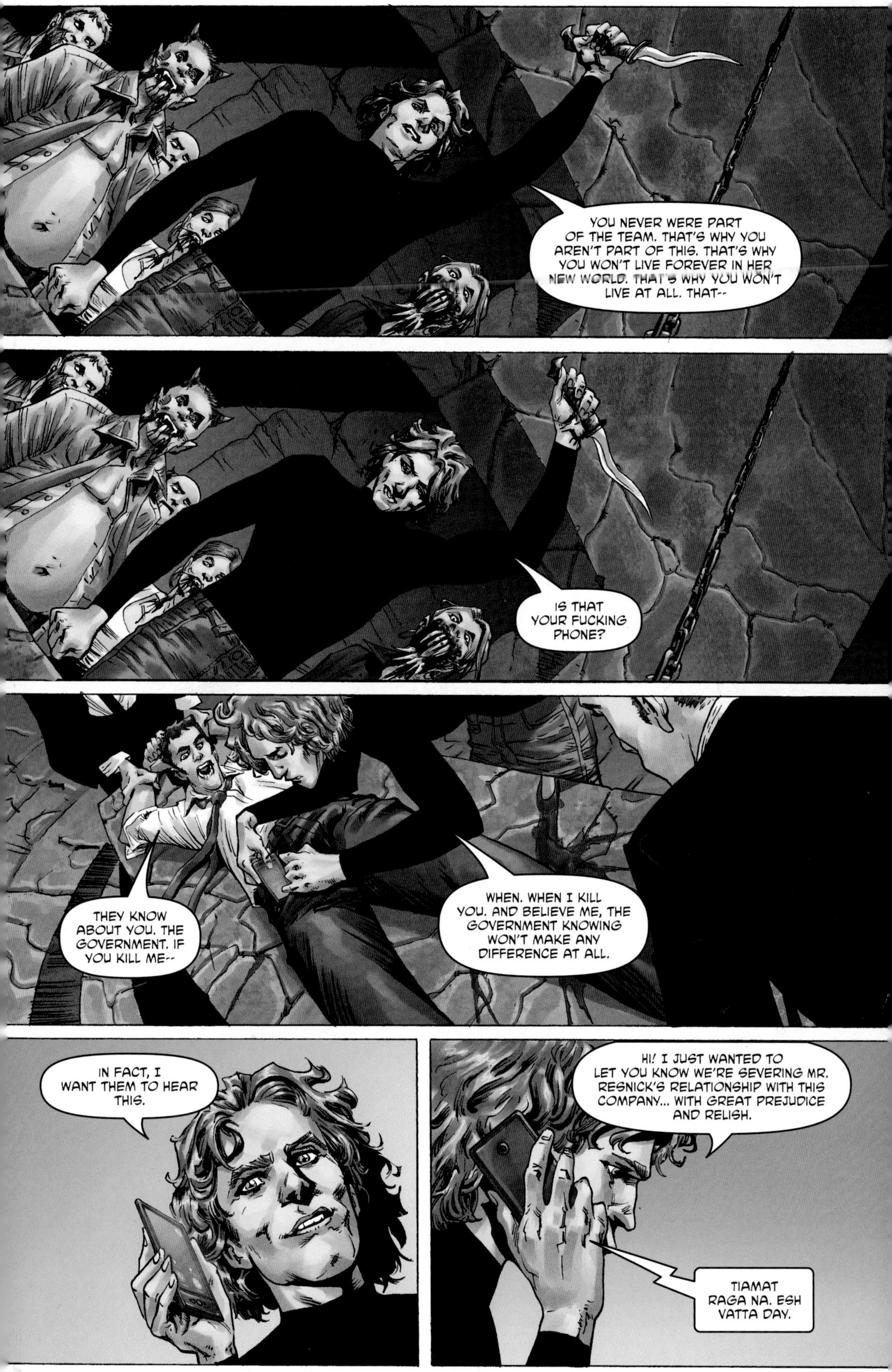
YOU NEVER WERE PART OF THE TEAM. THAT'S WHY YOU AREN'T PART OF THIS. THAT'S WHY YOU WON'T LIVE FOREVER IN HER NEW WORLD. THAT'S WHY YOU WON'T LIVE AT ALL. THAT--
IS THAT YOUR FUCKING PHONE?
THEY KNOW ABOUT YOU. THE GOVERNMENT. IF YOU KILL ME--
WHEN. WHEN I KILL YOU. AND BELIEVE ME, THE GOVERNMENT KNOWING WON'T MAKE ANY DIFFERENCE AT ALL.
IN FACT, I WANT THEM TO HEAR THIS.
HI! I JUST WANTED TO LET YOU KNOW WE'RE SEVERING MR. RESNICK'S RELATIONSHIP WITH THIS COMPANY... WITH GREAT PREJUDICE AND RELISH.
TIAMAT RAGA NA. ESH VATTA DAY.

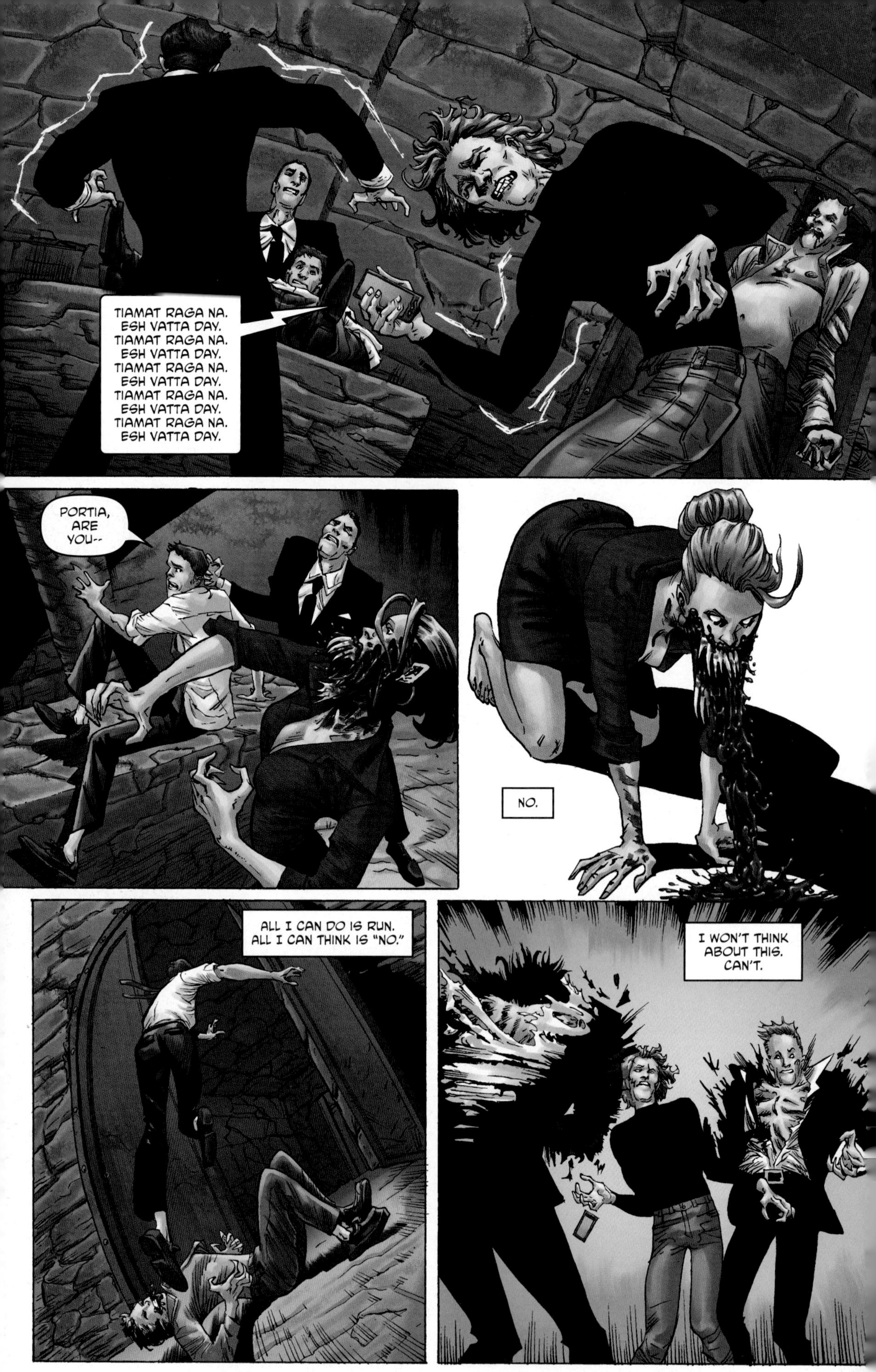
TIAMAT RAGA NA. ESH VATTA DAY. TIAMAT RAGA NA. ESH VATTA DAY. TIAMAT RAGA NA. ESH VATTA DAY. TIAMAT RAGA NA. ESH VATTA DAY. TIAMAT RAGA NA. ESH VATTA DAY.
PORTIA, ARE YOU--
NO.
ALL I CAN DO IS RUN. ALL I CAN THINK IS "NO."
I WON'T THINK ABOUT THIS. CAN'T.

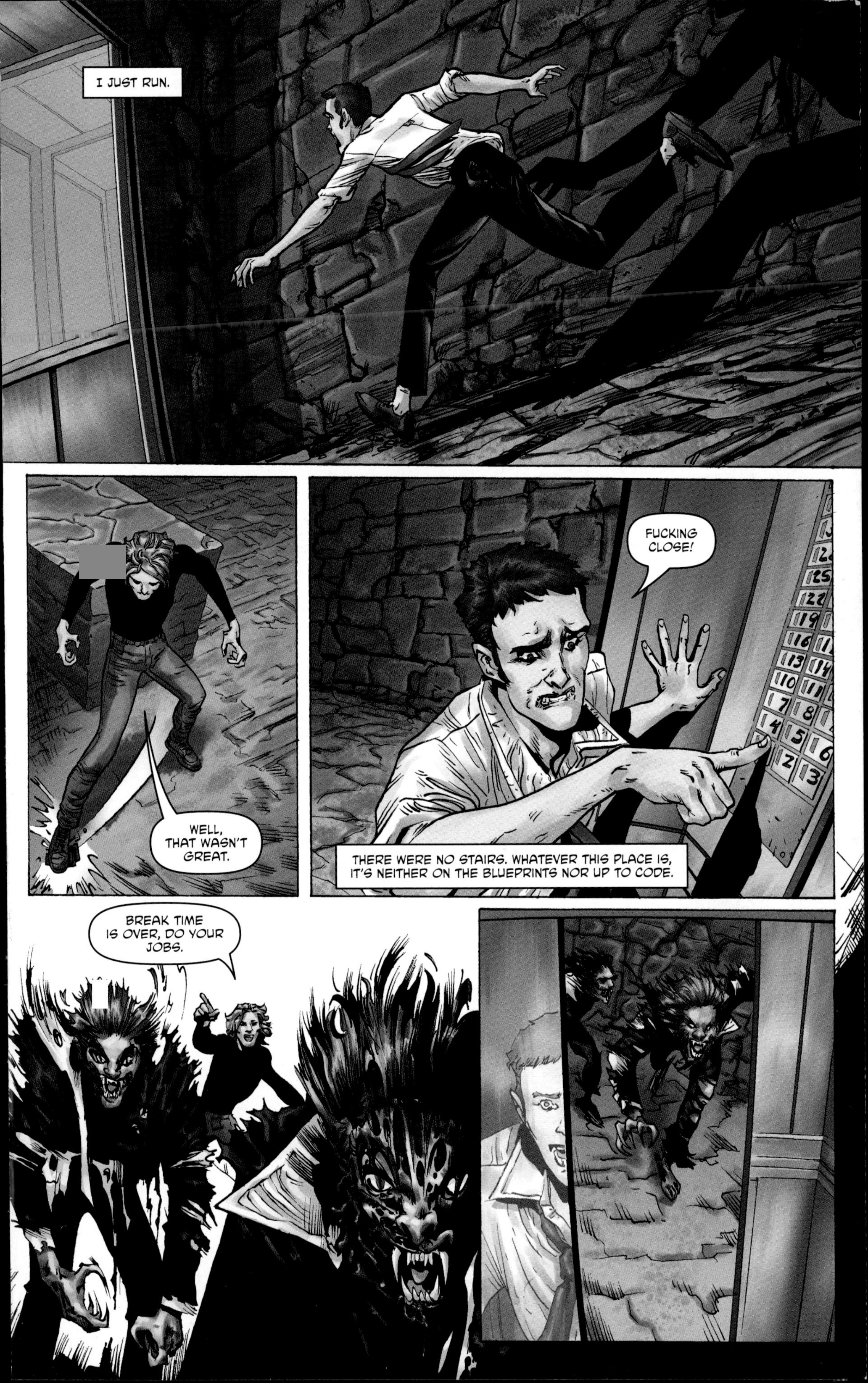
I JUST RUN.
WELL, THAT WASN'T GREAT.
FUCKING CLOSE!
THERE WERE NO STAIRS. WHATEVER THIS PLACE IS, IT'S NEITHER ON THE BLUEPRINTS NOR UP TO CODE.
BREAK TIME IS OVER, DO YOUR JOBS.

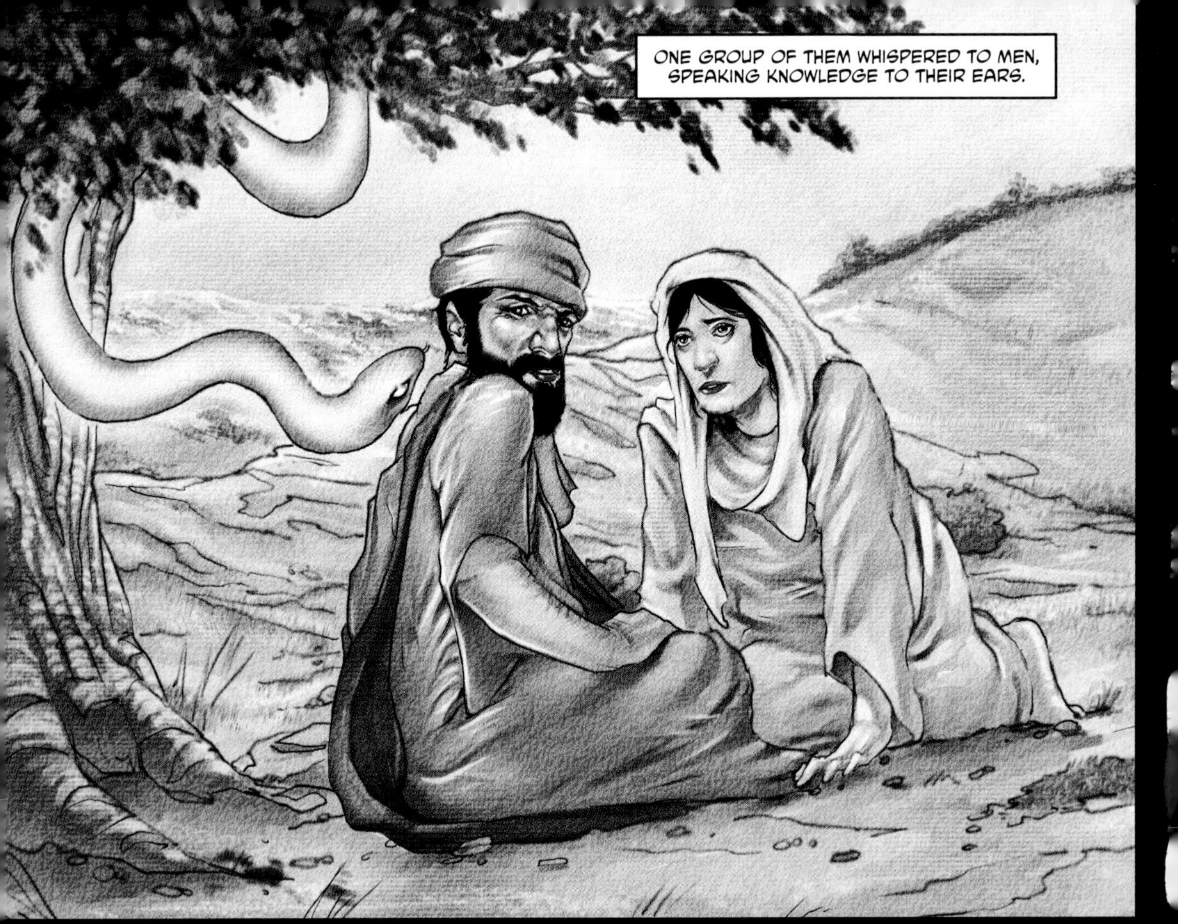
ONE GROUP OF THEM WHISPERED TO MEN, SPEAKING KNOWLEDGE TO THEIR EARS.

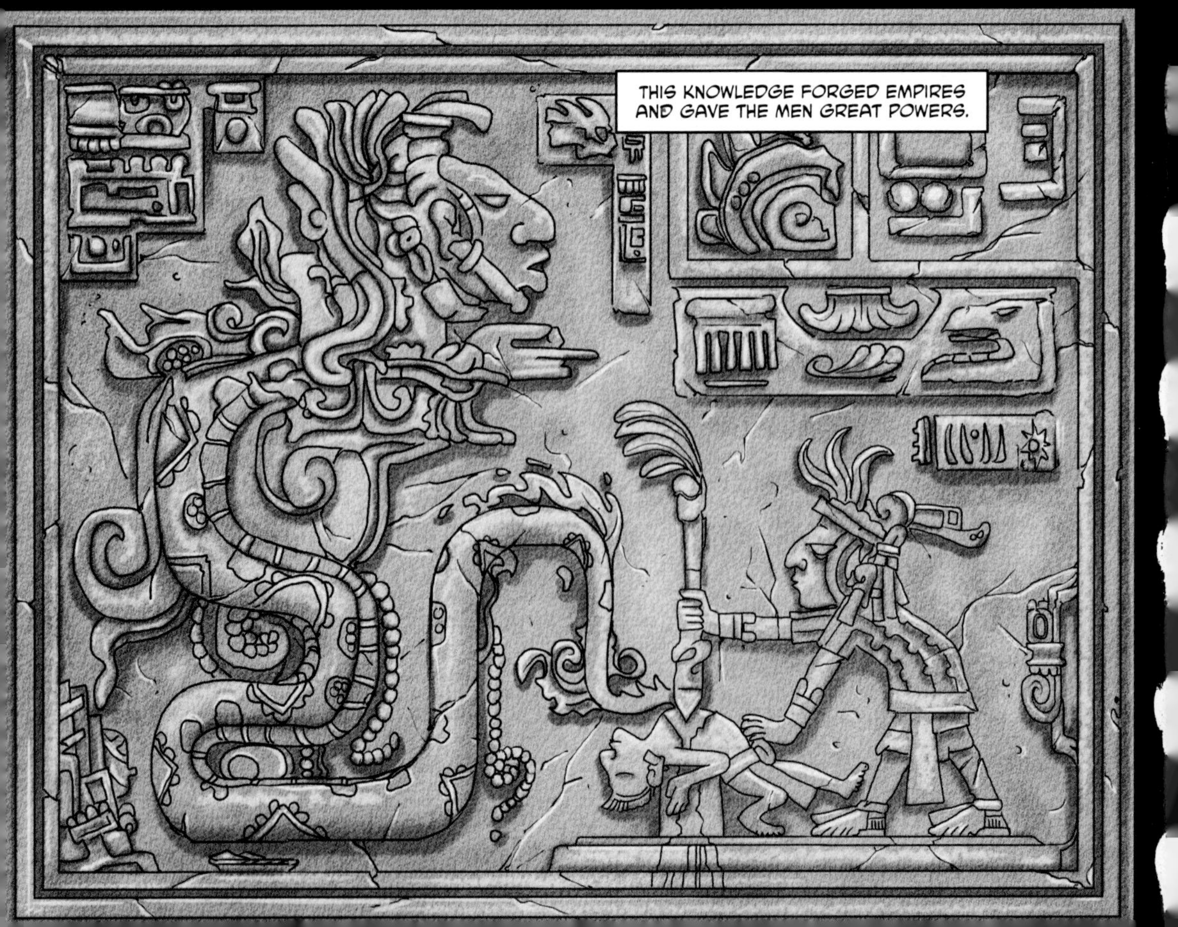
THIS KNOWLEDGE FORGED EMPIRES AND GAVE THE MEN GREAT POWERS.

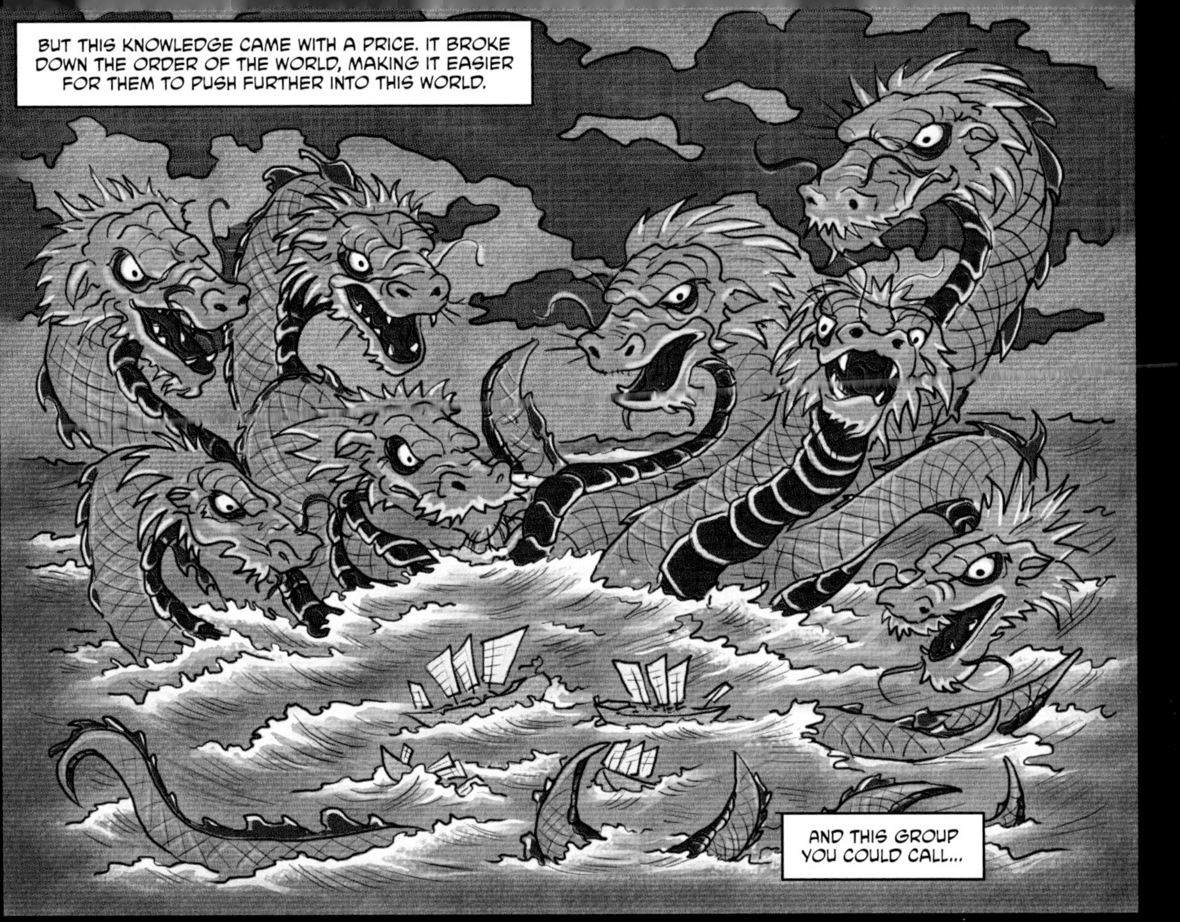
BUT THIS KNOWLEDGE CAME WITH A PRICE. IT BROKE DOWN THE ORDER OF THE WORLD, MAKING IT EASIER FOR THEM TO PUSH FURTHER INTO THIS WORLD.
AND THIS GROUP YOU COULD CALL...

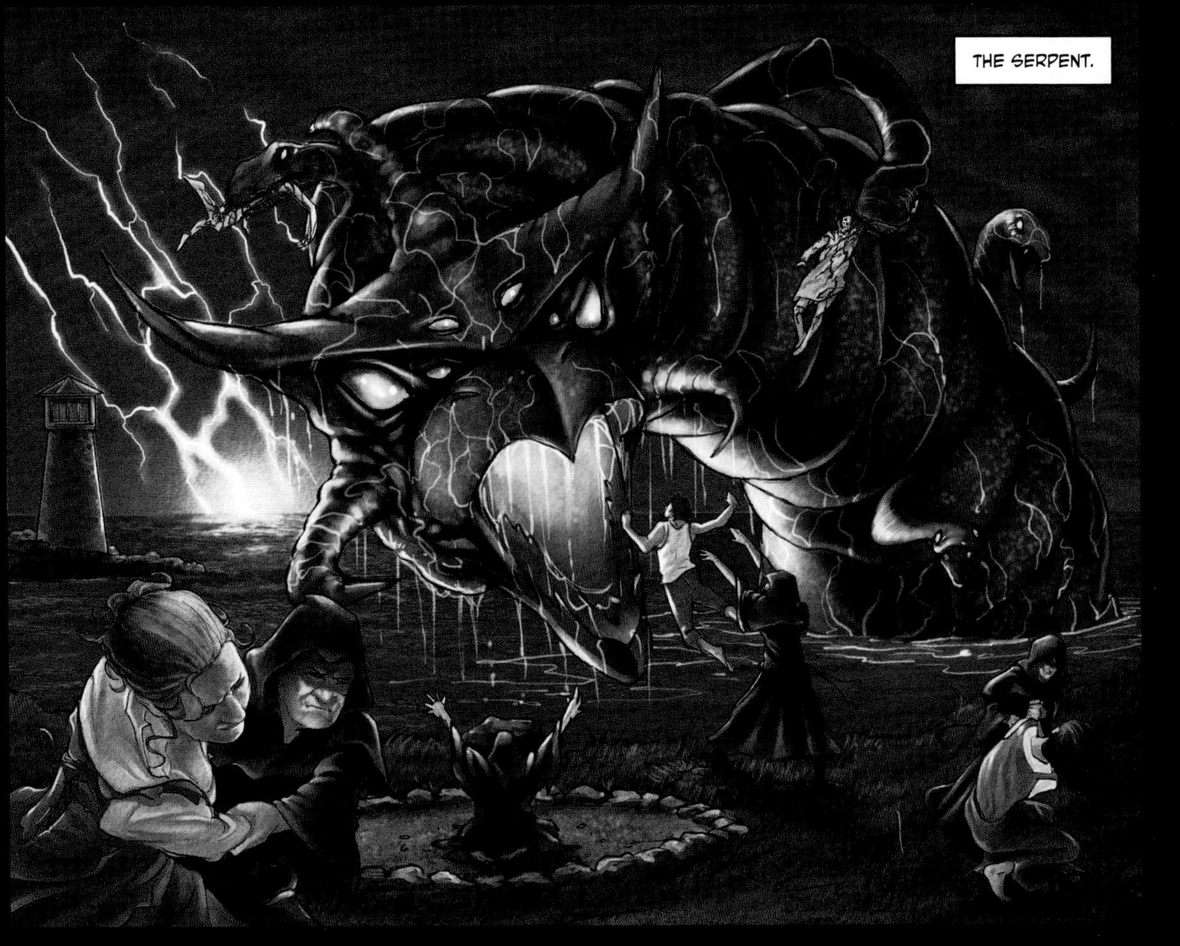
THE SERPENT.

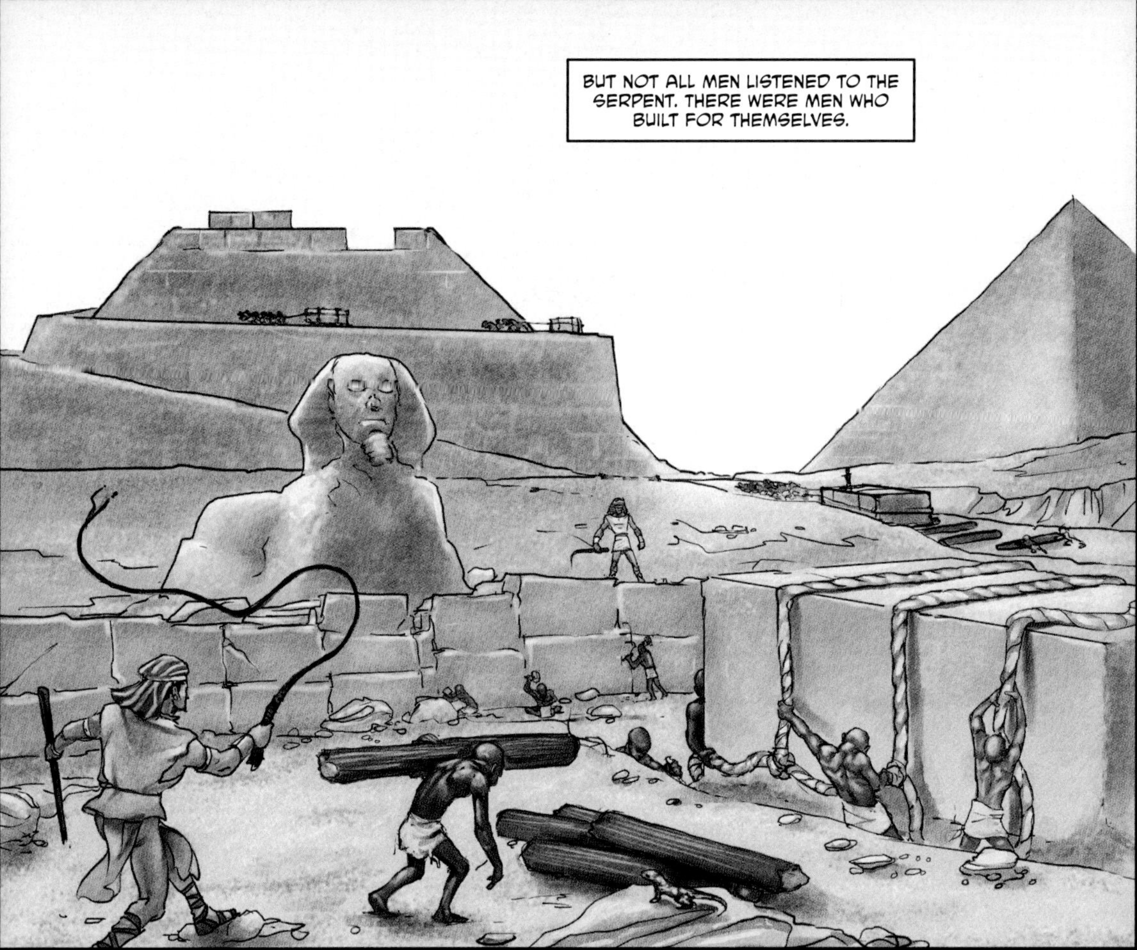
BUT NOT ALL MEN LISTENED TO THE SERPENT. THERE WERE MEN WHO BUILT FOR THEMSELVES.

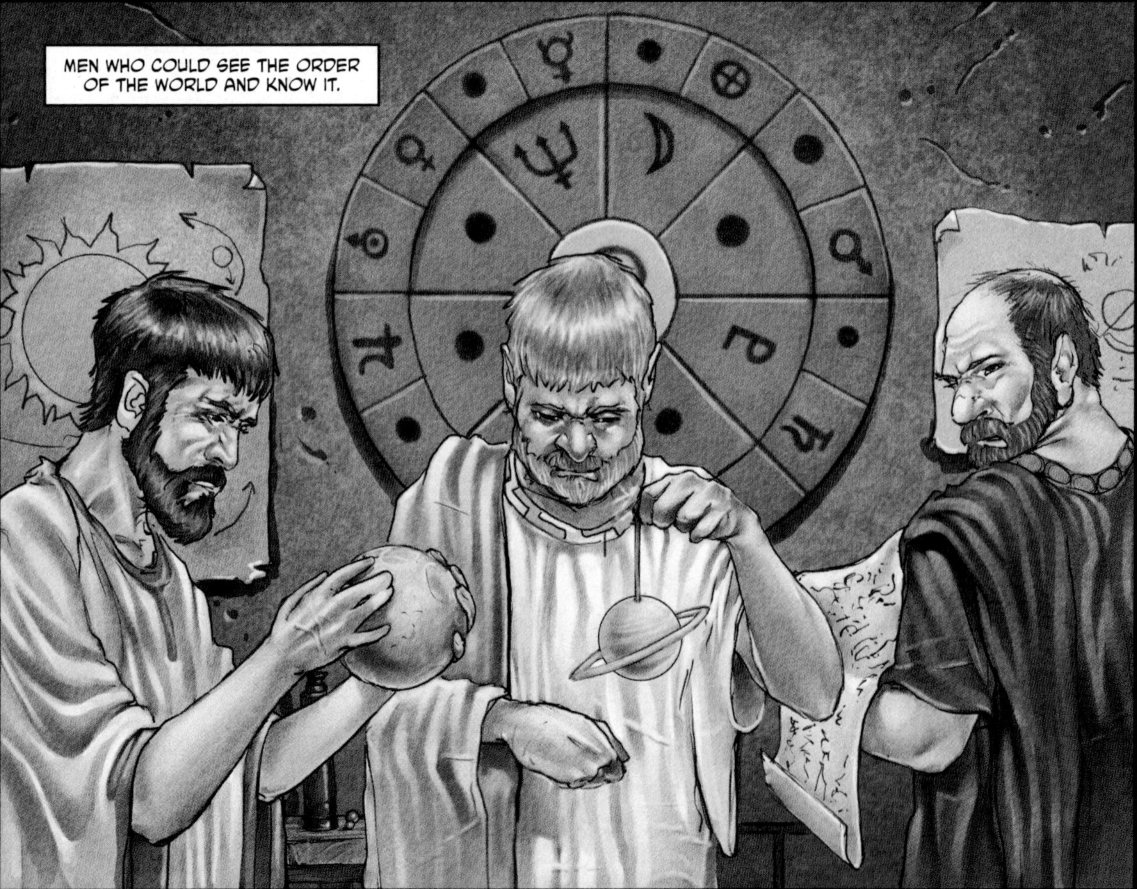
MEN WHO COULD SEE THE ORDER OF THE WORLD AND KNOW IT.

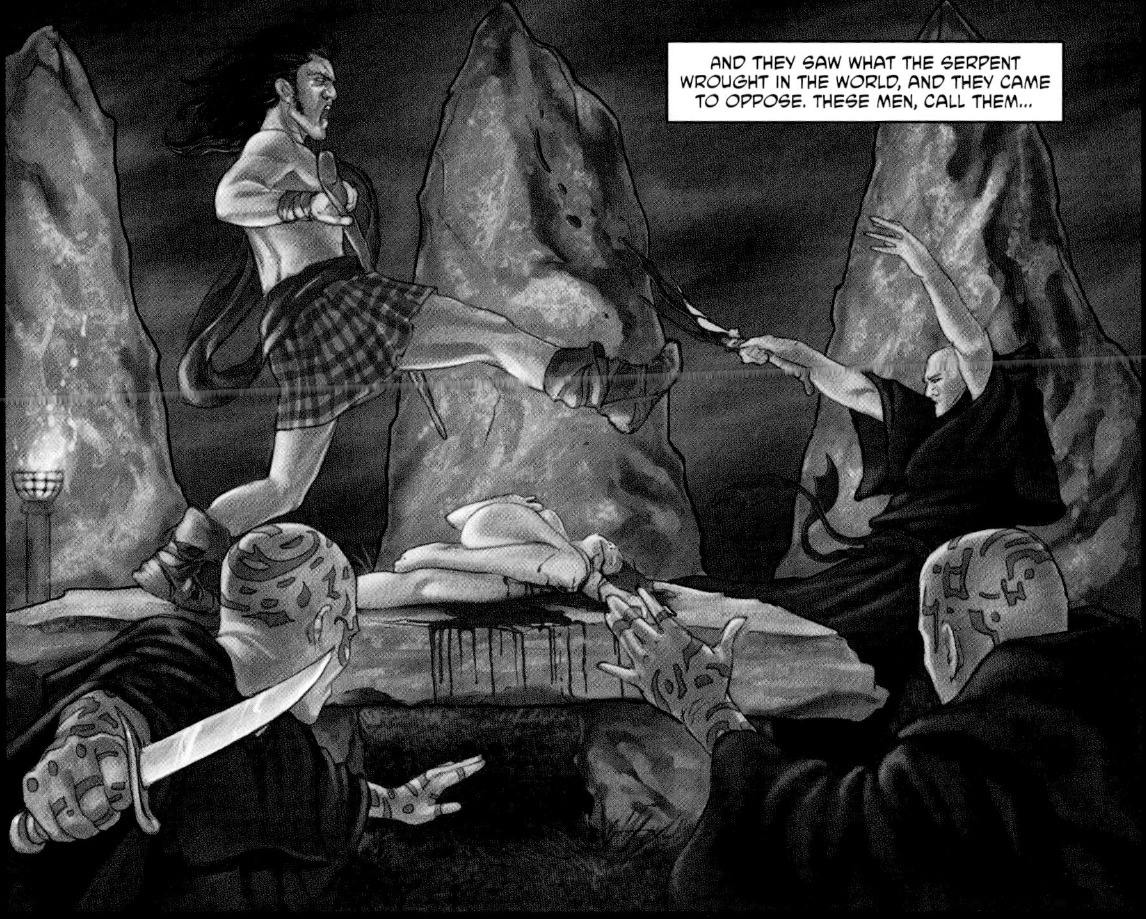
AND THEY SAW WHAT THE SERPENT WROUGHT IN THE WORLD, AND THEY CAME TO OPPOSE. THESE MEN, CALL THEM...

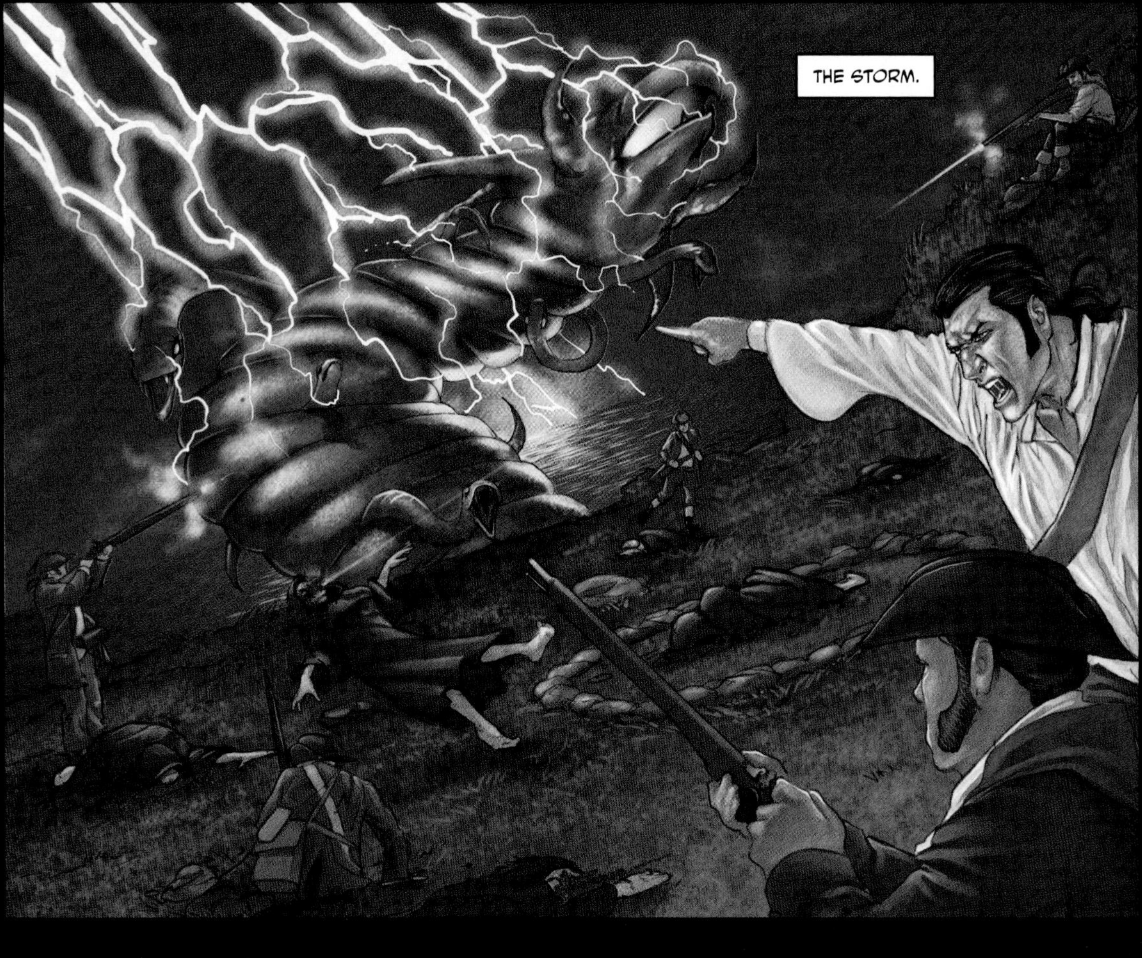
THE STORM.

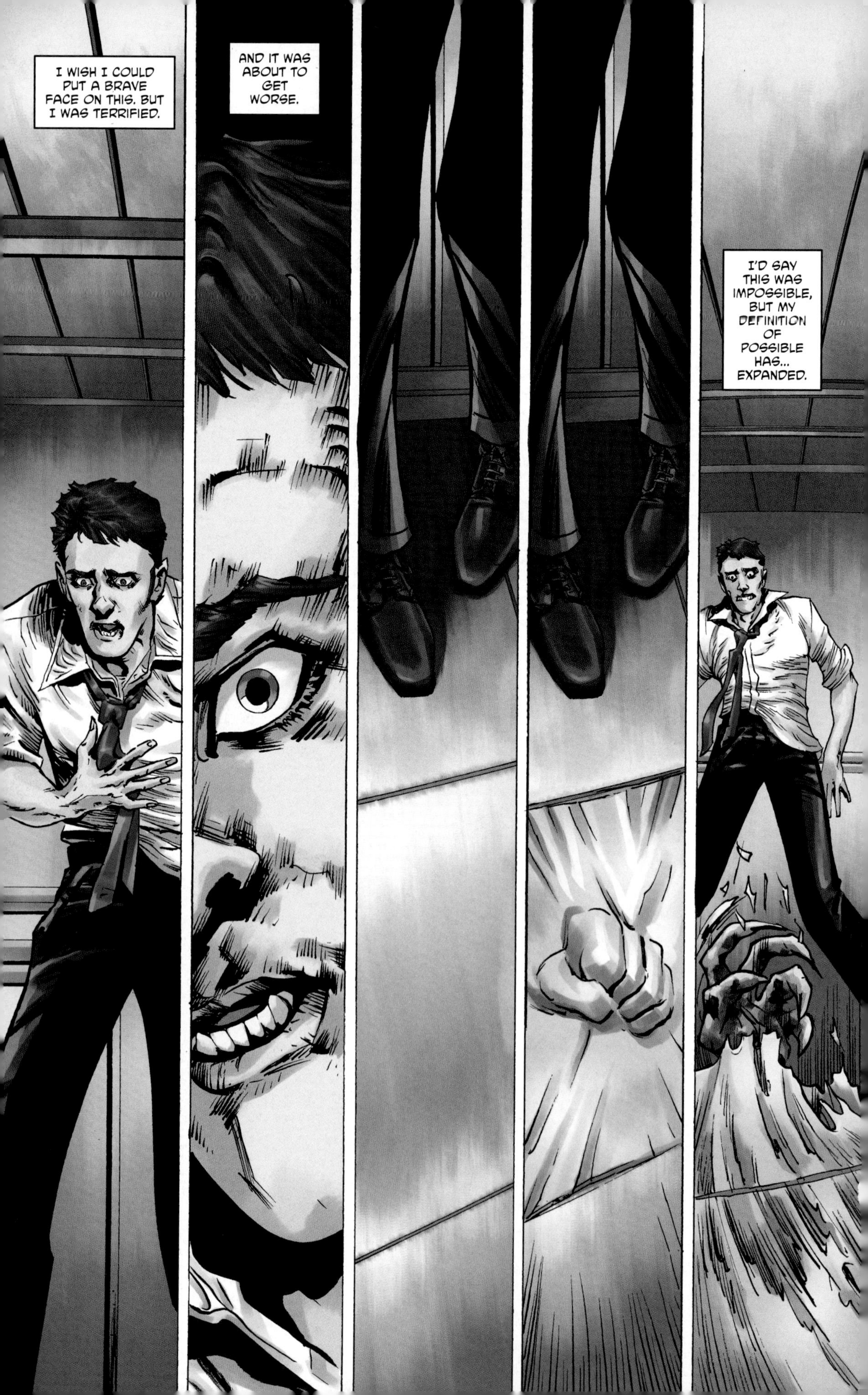
I WISH I COULD PUT A BRAVE FACE ON THIS. BUT I WAS TERRIFIED.
AND IT WAS ABOUT TO GET WORSE.
I'D SAY THIS WAS IMPOSSIBLE, BUT MY DEFINITION OF POSSIBLE HAS... EXPANDED.

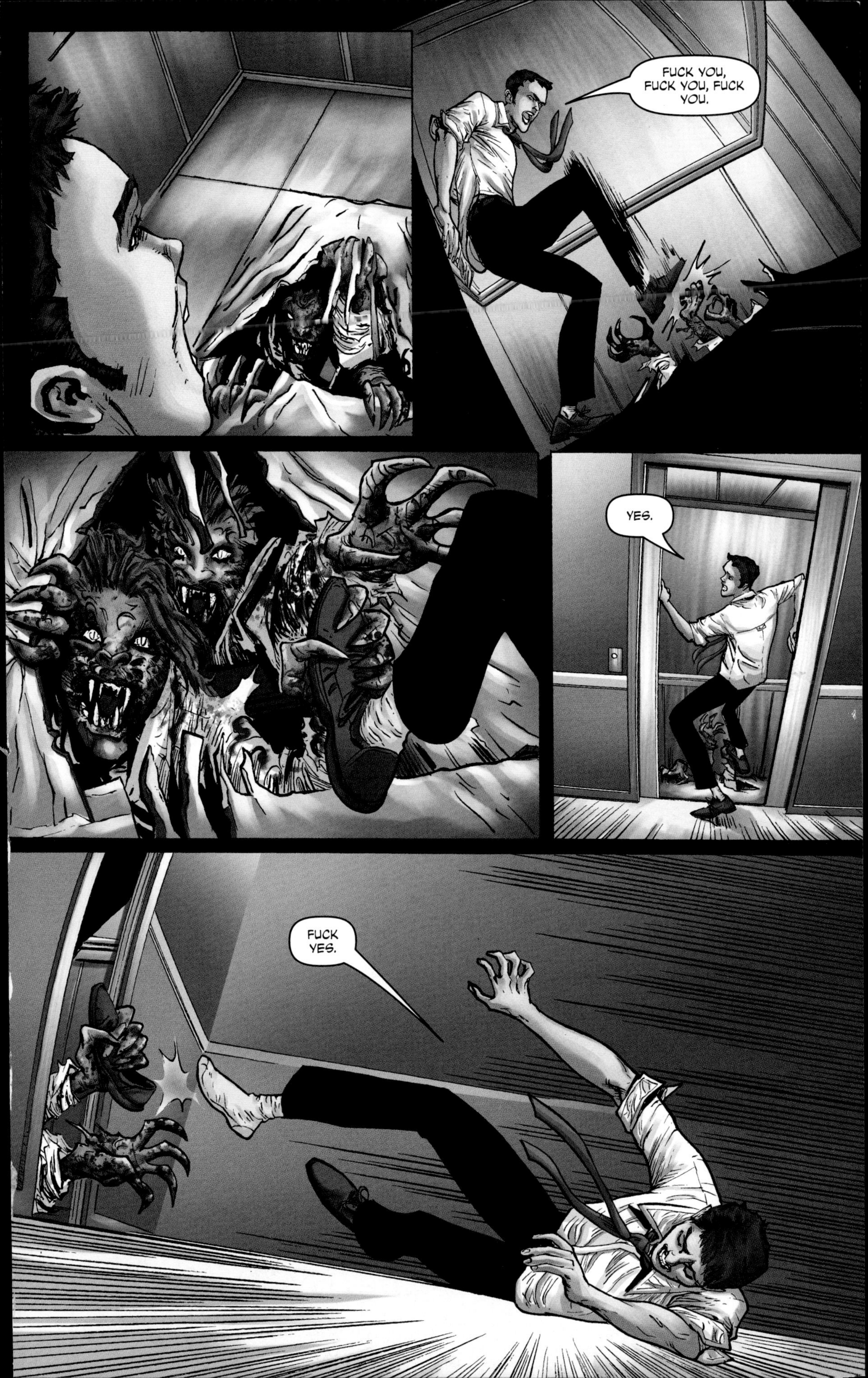
FUCK YOU, FUCK YOU, FUCK YOU.
YES.
FUCK YES.

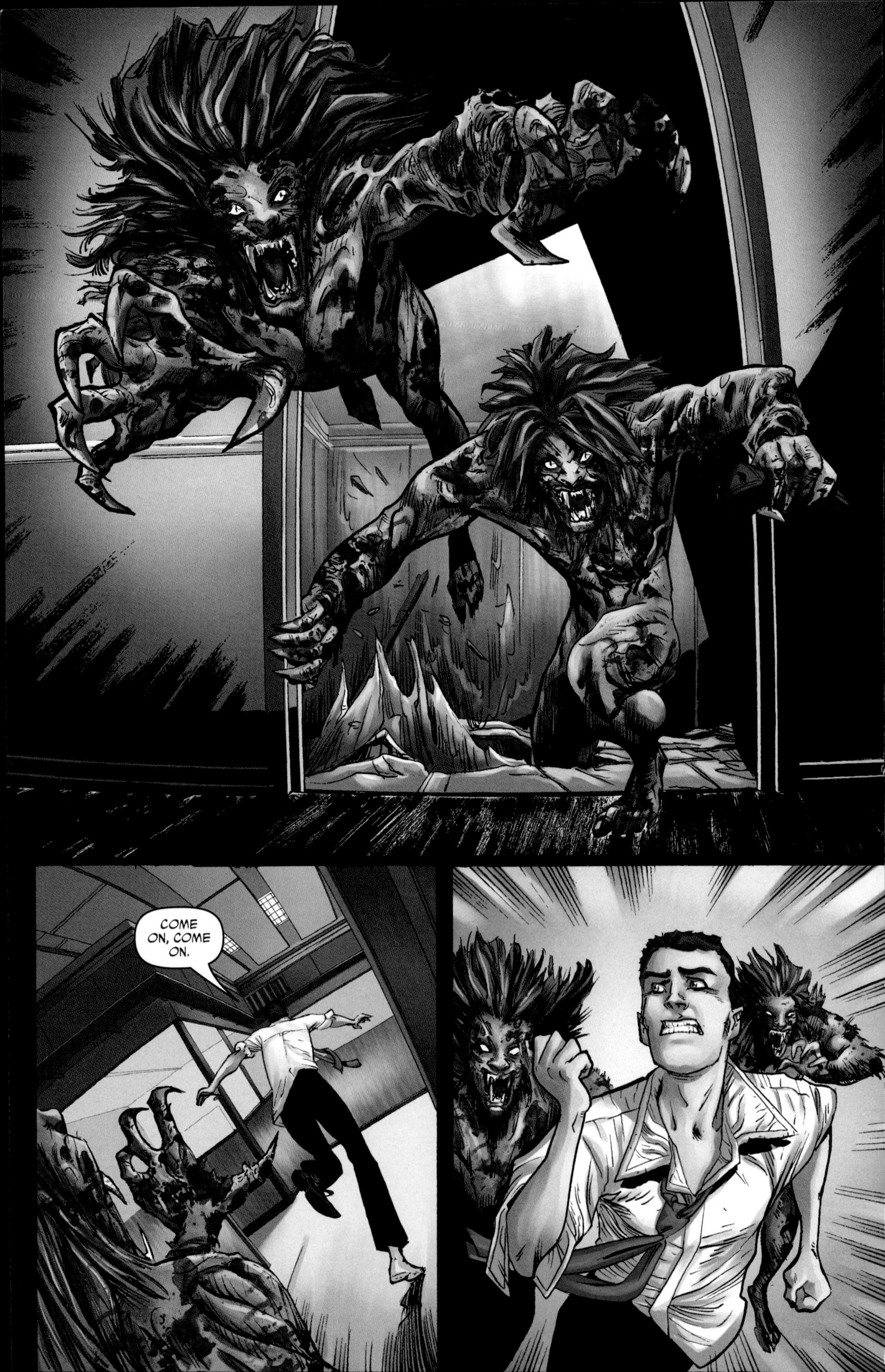
COME ON, COME ON.

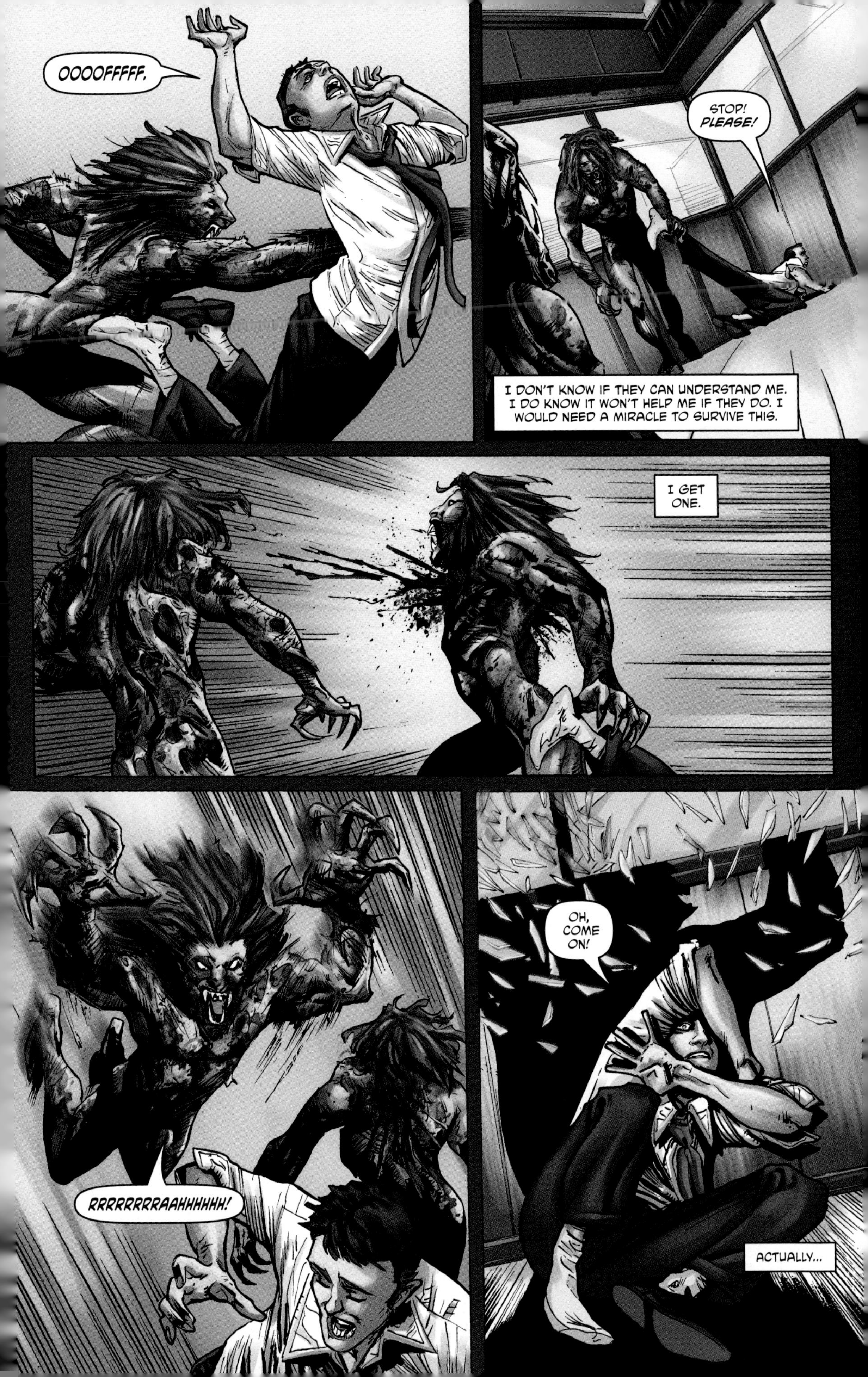
OOOOFFFFF.
STOP! PLEASE!
I DON'T KNOW IF THEY CAN UNDERSTAND ME. I DO KNOW IT WON'T HELP ME IF THEY DO. I WOULD NEED A MIRACLE TO SURVIVE THIS.
I GET ONE.
RRRRRRRRAAHHHHHH!
OH, COME ON!
ACTUALLY...

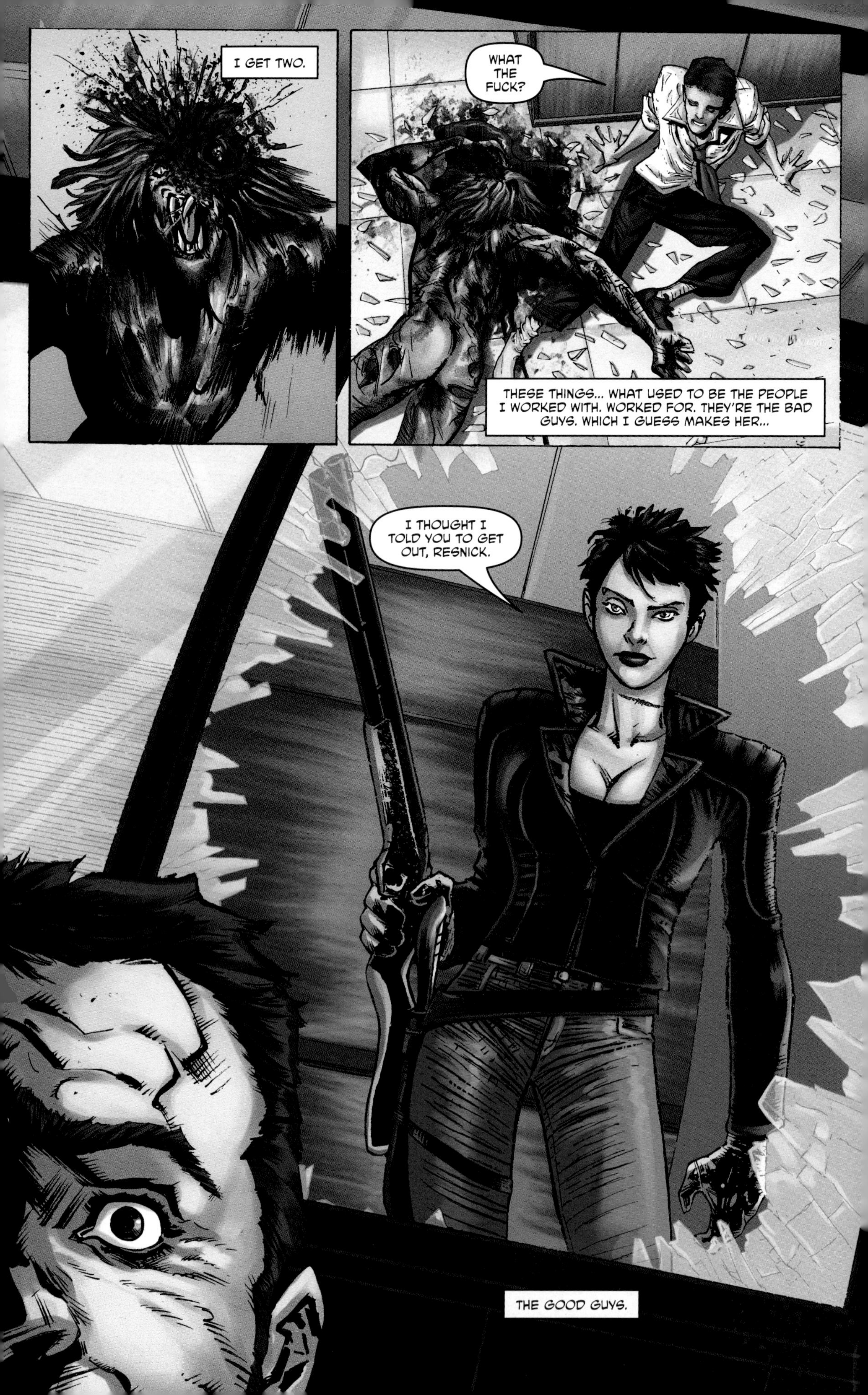
I GET TWO.
WHAT THE FUCK?
THESE THINGS... WHAT USED TO BE THE PEOPLE I WORKED WITH. WORKED FOR. THEY'RE THE BAD GUYS. WHICH I GUESS MAKES HER...
I THOUGHT I TOLD YOU TO GET OUT, RESNICK.
THE GOOD GUYS.

**CHAPTER 2**

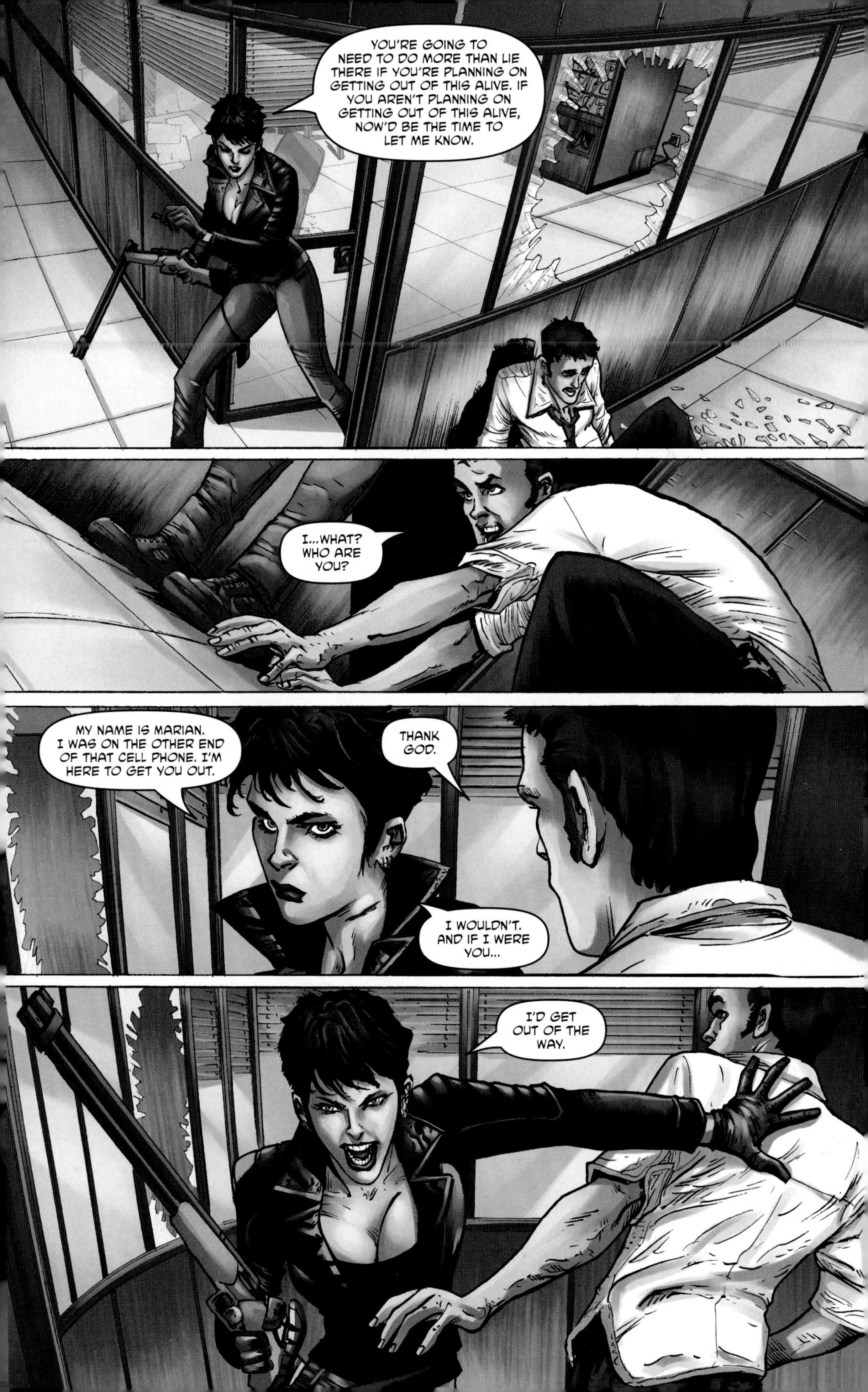
YOU'RE GOING TO NEED TO DO MORE THAN LIE THERE IF YOU'RE PLANNING ON GETTING OUT OF THIS ALIVE. IF YOU AREN'T PLANNING ON GETTING OUT OF THIS ALIVE, NOW'D BE THE TIME TO LET ME KNOW.
I...WHAT? WHO ARE YOU?
MY NAME IS MARIAN. I WAS ON THE OTHER END OF THAT CELL PHONE. I'M HERE TO GET YOU OUT.
THANK GOD.
I WOULDN'T. AND IF I WERE YOU...
I'D GET OUT OF THE WAY.

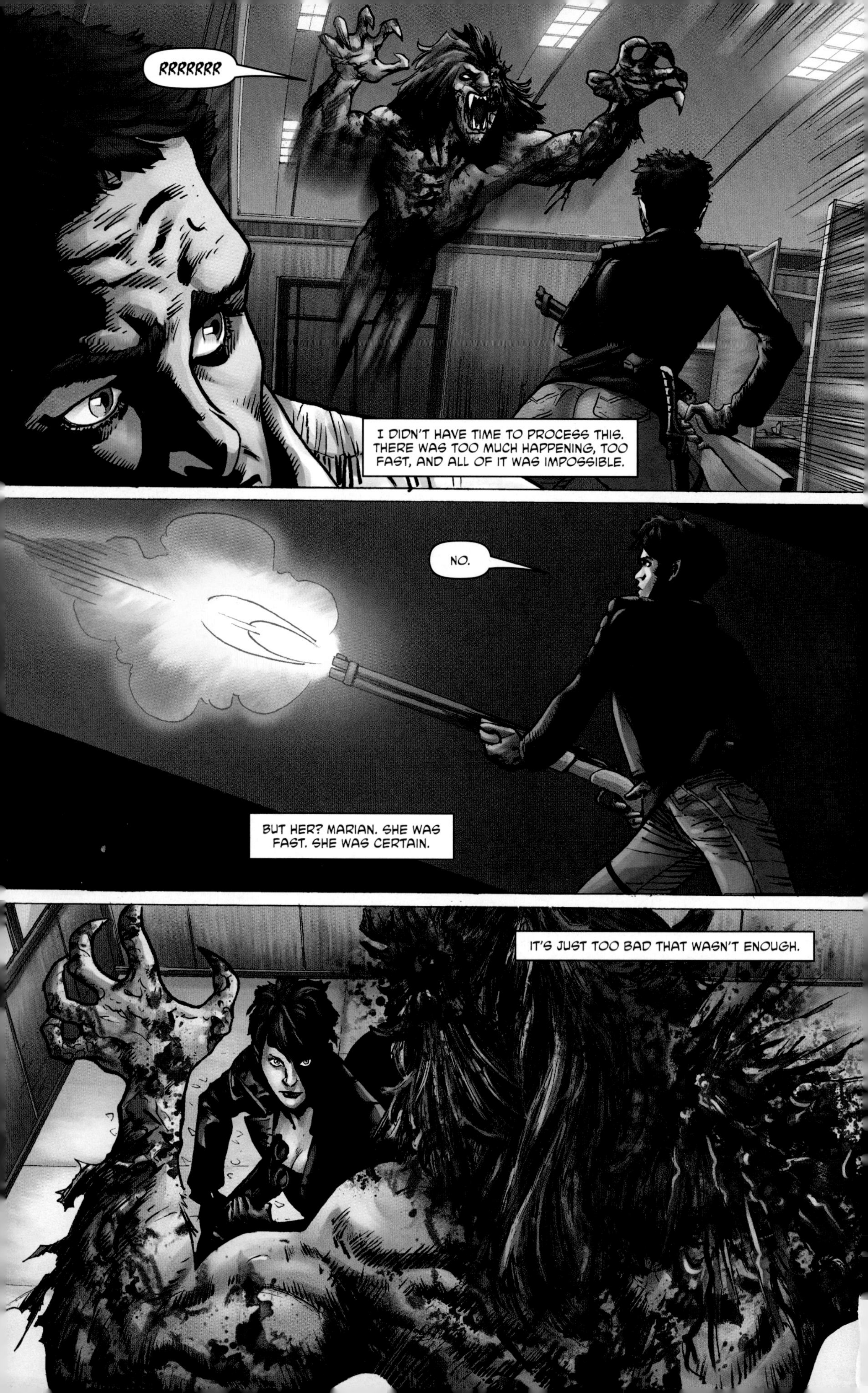
RRRRRRR
I DIDN'T HAVE TIME TO PROCESS THIS. THERE WAS TOO MUCH HAPPENING, TOO FAST, AND ALL OF IT WAS IMPOSSIBLE.
NO.
BUT HER? MARIAN. SHE WAS FAST. SHE WAS CERTAIN.
IT'S JUST TOO BAD THAT WASN'T ENOUGH.

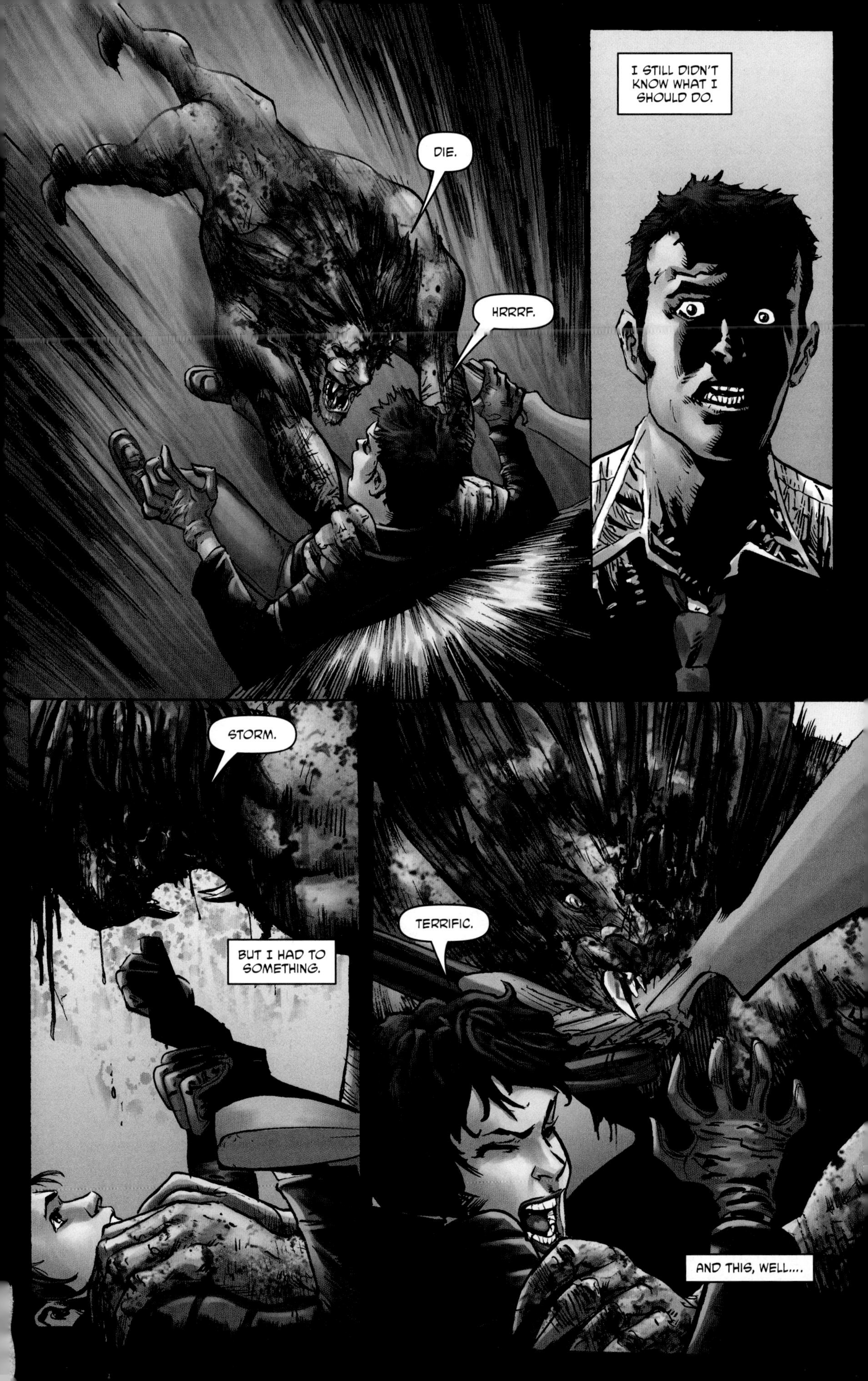
DIE.
HRRRF.
I STILL DIDN'T KNOW WHAT I SHOULD DO.
STORM.
BUT I HAD TO SOMETHING.
TERRIFIC.
AND THIS, WELL....

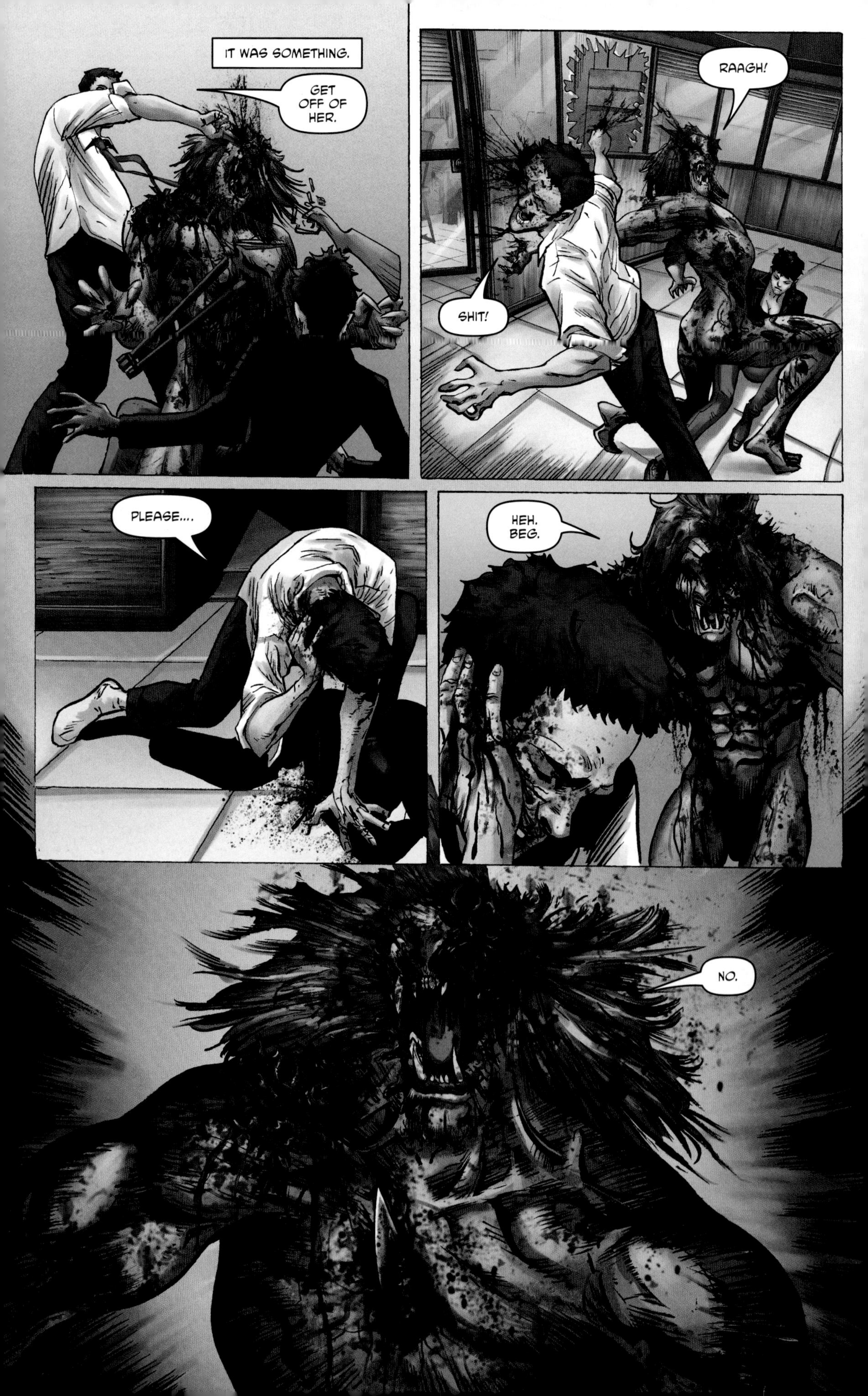
IT WAS SOMETHING.
GET OFF OF HER.
RAAGH!
SHIT!
PLEASE....
HEH. BEG.
NO.

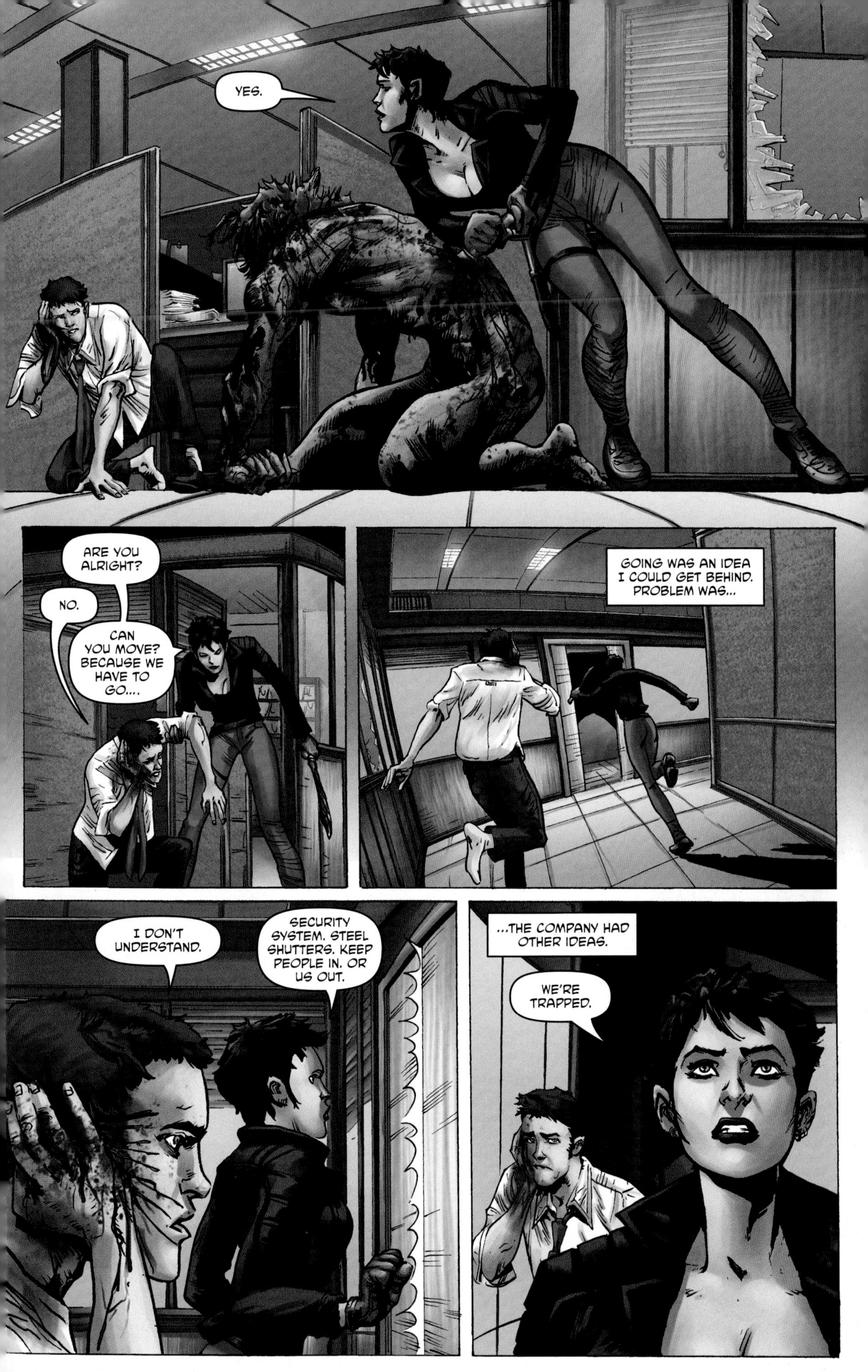
YES.
ARE YOU ALRIGHT?
NO.
CAN YOU MOVE? BECAUSE WE HAVE TO GO....
GOING WAS AN IDEA I COULD GET BEHIND. PROBLEM WAS...
I DON'T UNDERSTAND.
SECURITY SYSTEM. STEEL SHUTTERS. KEEP PEOPLE IN. OR US OUT.
...THE COMPANY HAD OTHER IDEAS.
WE'RE TRAPPED.

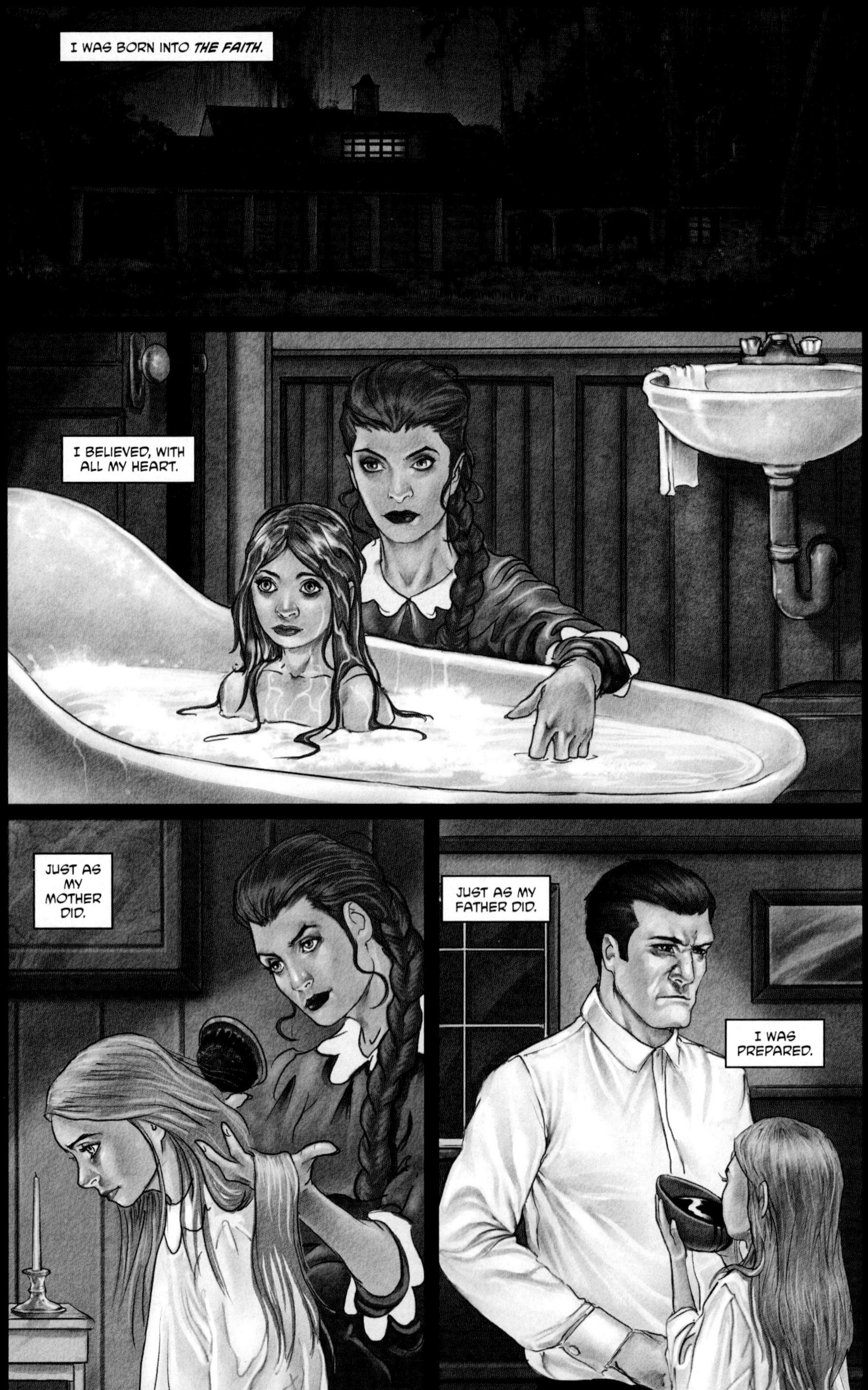
I WAS BORN INTO THE FAITH.
I BELIEVED, WITH ALL MY HEART.
JUST AS MY MOTHER DID.
JUST AS MY FATHER DID.
I WAS PREPARED.

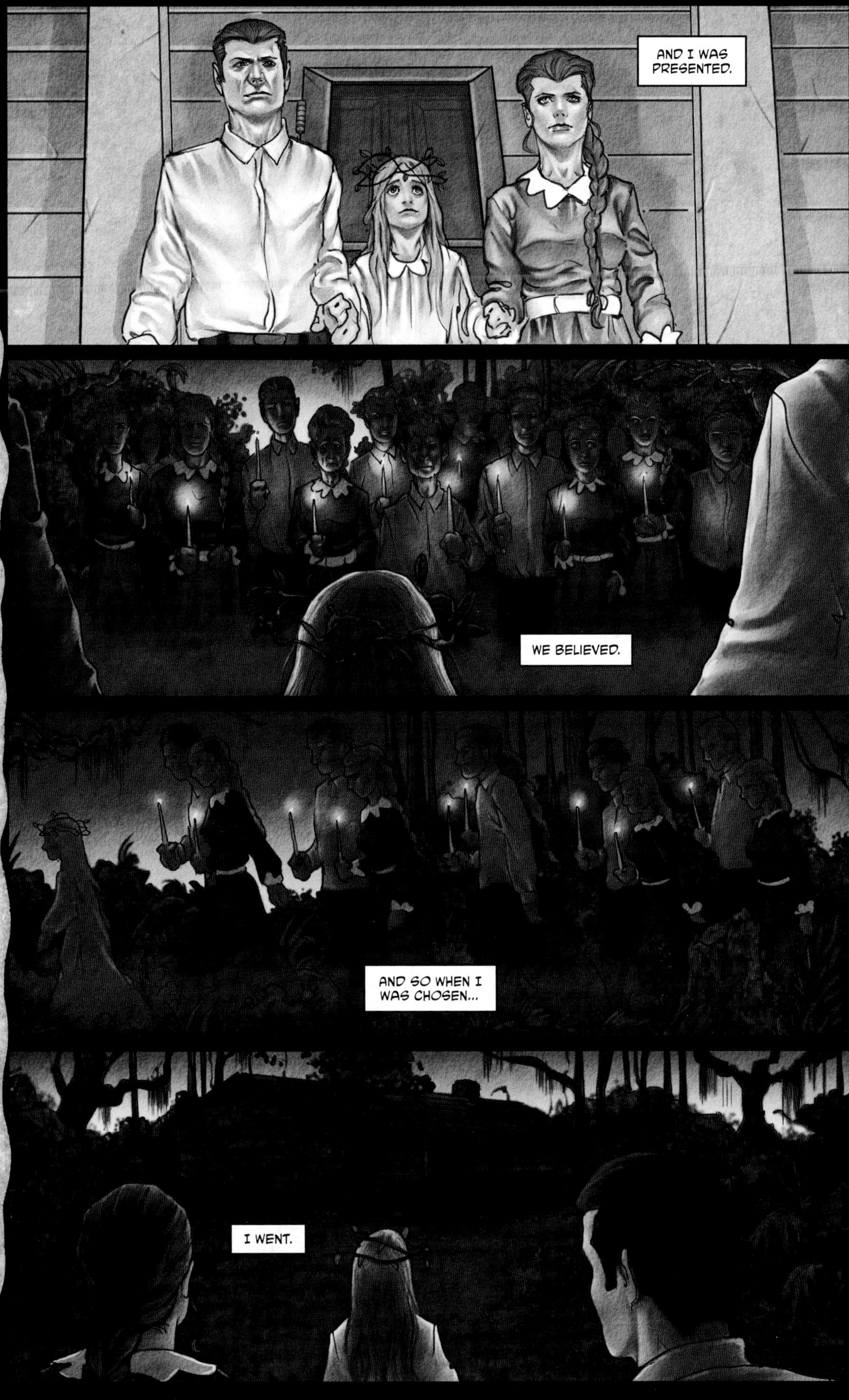
AND I WAS PRESENTED.
WE BELIEVED.
AND SO WHEN I WAS CHOSEN...
I WENT.

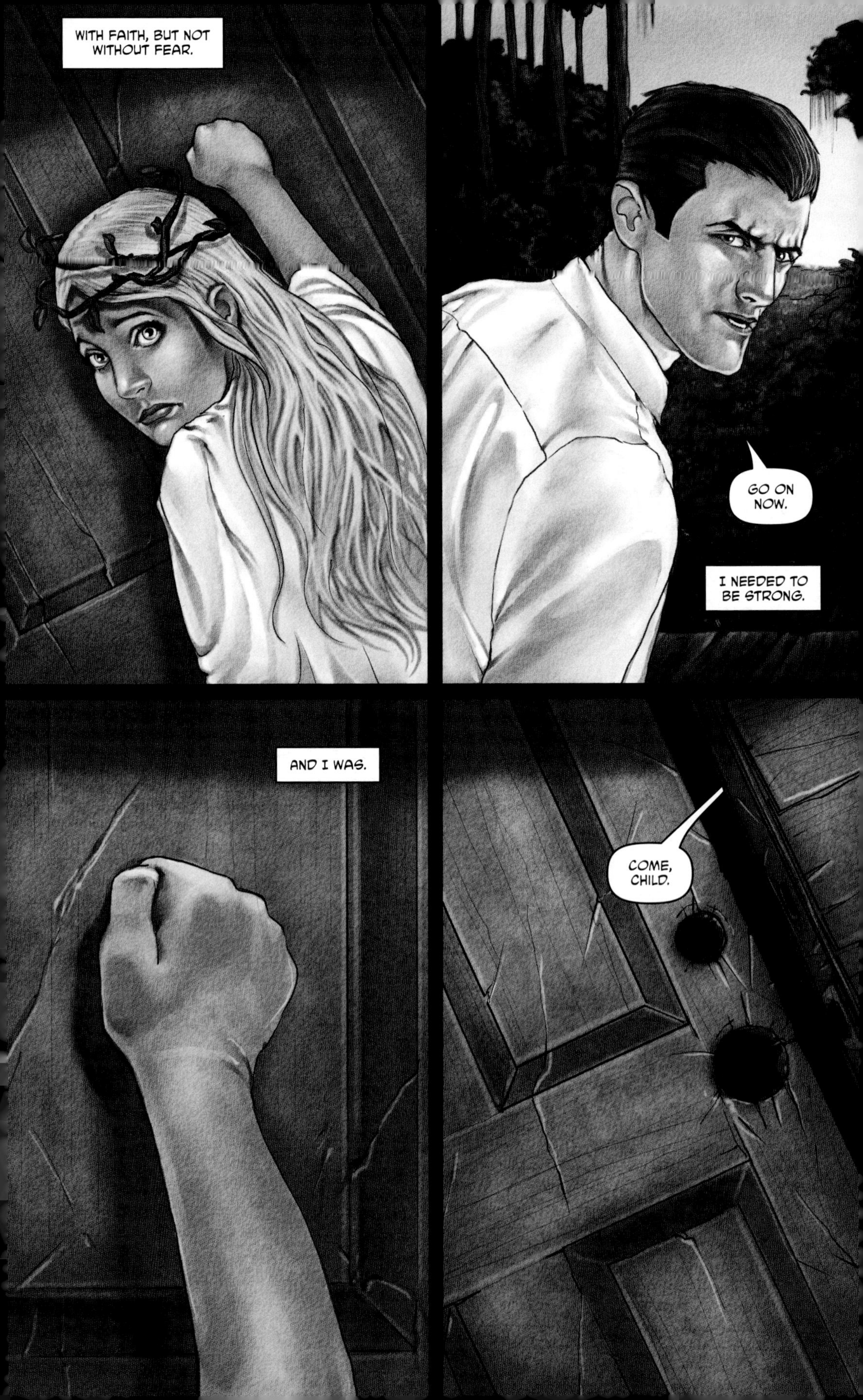
WITH FAITH, BUT NOT WITHOUT FEAR.
GO ON NOW.
I NEEDED TO BE STRONG.
AND I WAS.
COME, CHILD.

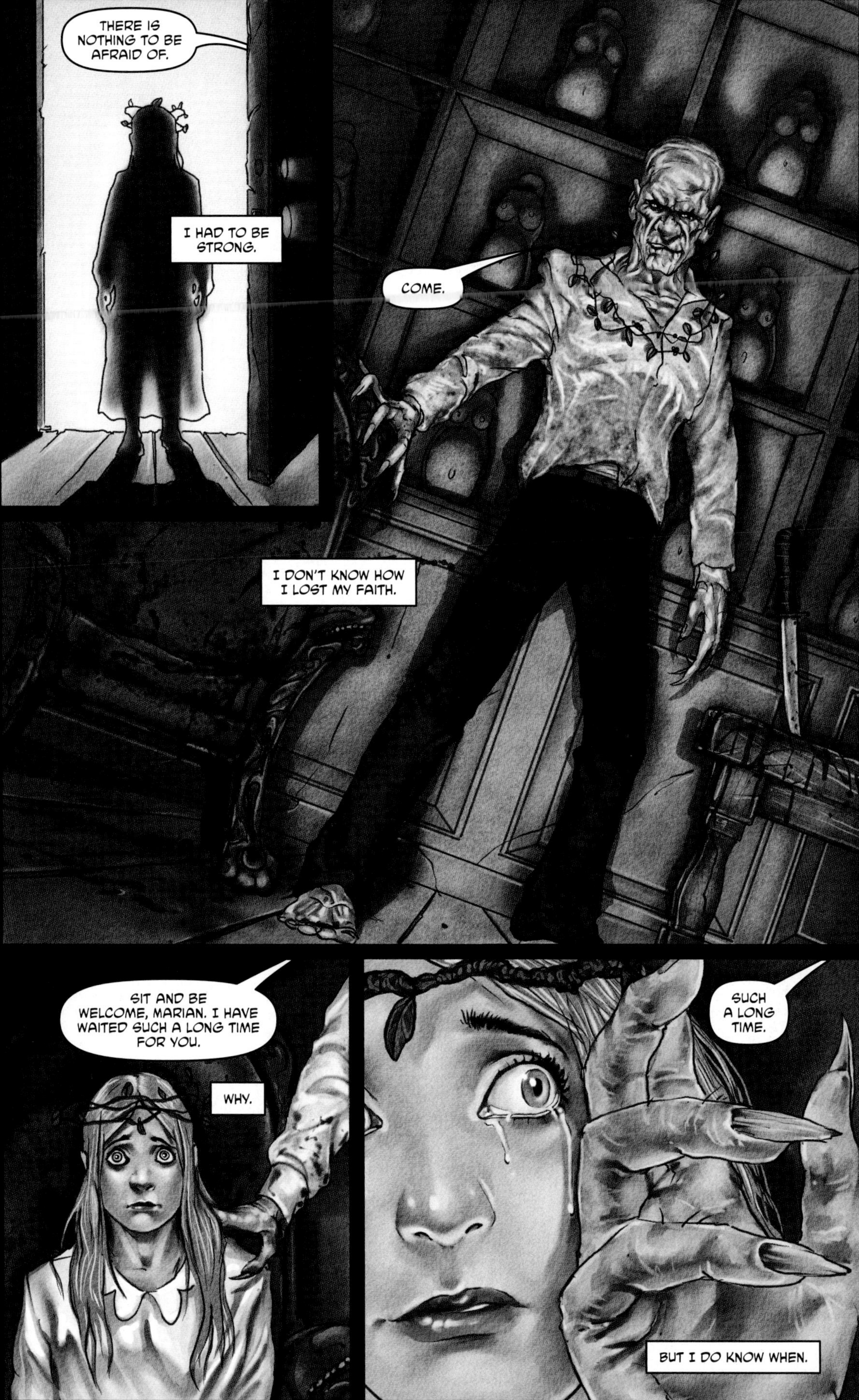
THERE IS NOTHING TO BE AFRAID OF.
I HAD TO BE STRONG.
COME.
I DON'T KNOW HOW I LOST MY FAITH.
SIT AND BE WELCOME, MARIAN. I HAVE WAITED SUCH A LONG TIME FOR YOU.
WHY.
SUCH A LONG TIME.
BUT I DO KNOW WHEN.

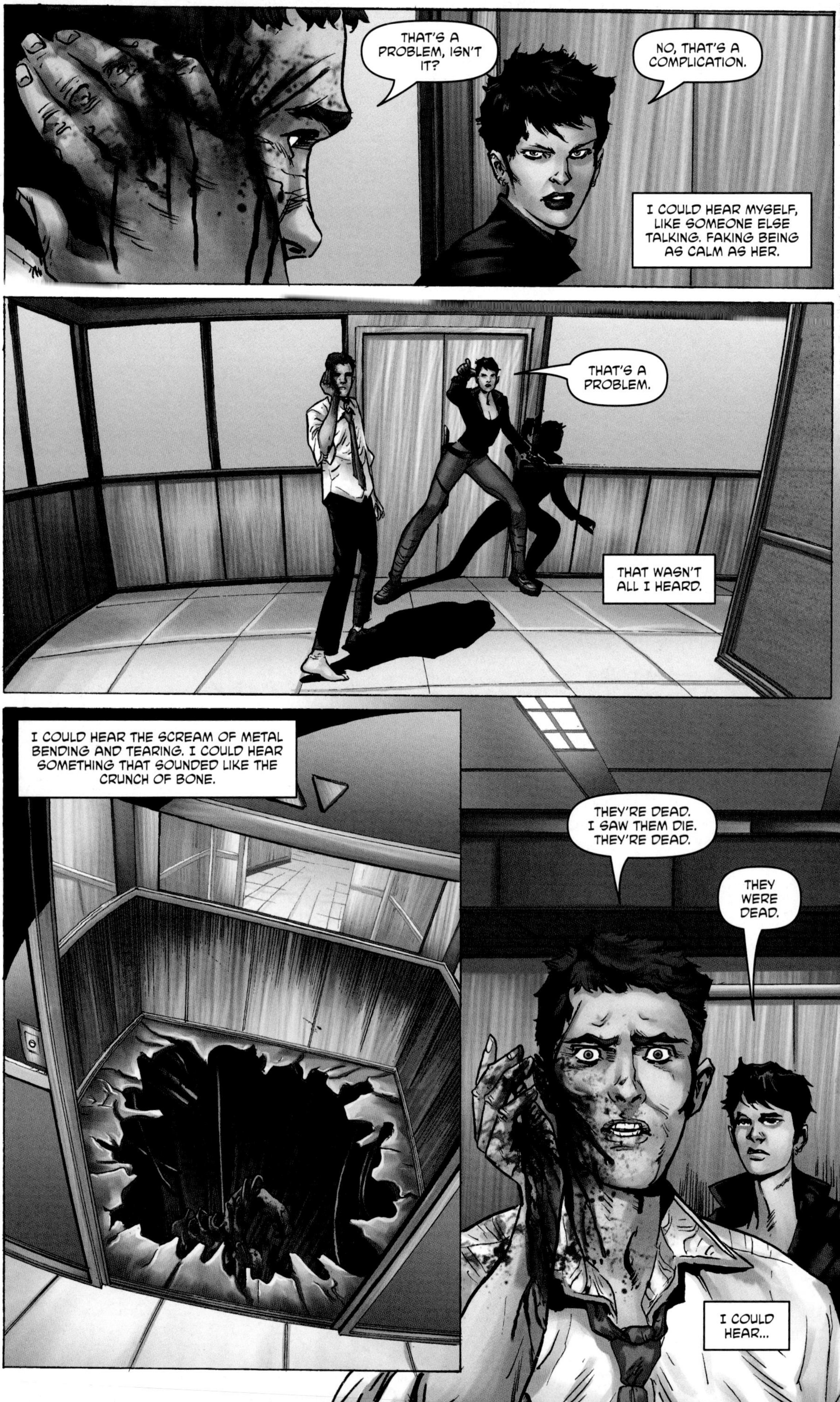
THAT'S A PROBLEM, ISN'T IT?
NO, THAT'S A COMPLICATION.
I COULD HEAR MYSELF, LIKE SOMEONE ELSE TALKING. FAKING BEING AS CALM AS HER.
THAT'S A PROBLEM.
THAT WASN'T ALL I HEARD.
I COULD HEAR THE SCREAM OF METAL BENDING AND TEARING. I COULD HEAR SOMETHING THAT SOUNDED LIKE THE CRUNCH OF BONE.
THEY'RE DEAD. I SAW THEM DIE. THEY'RE DEAD.
THEY WERE DEAD.
I COULD HEAR...

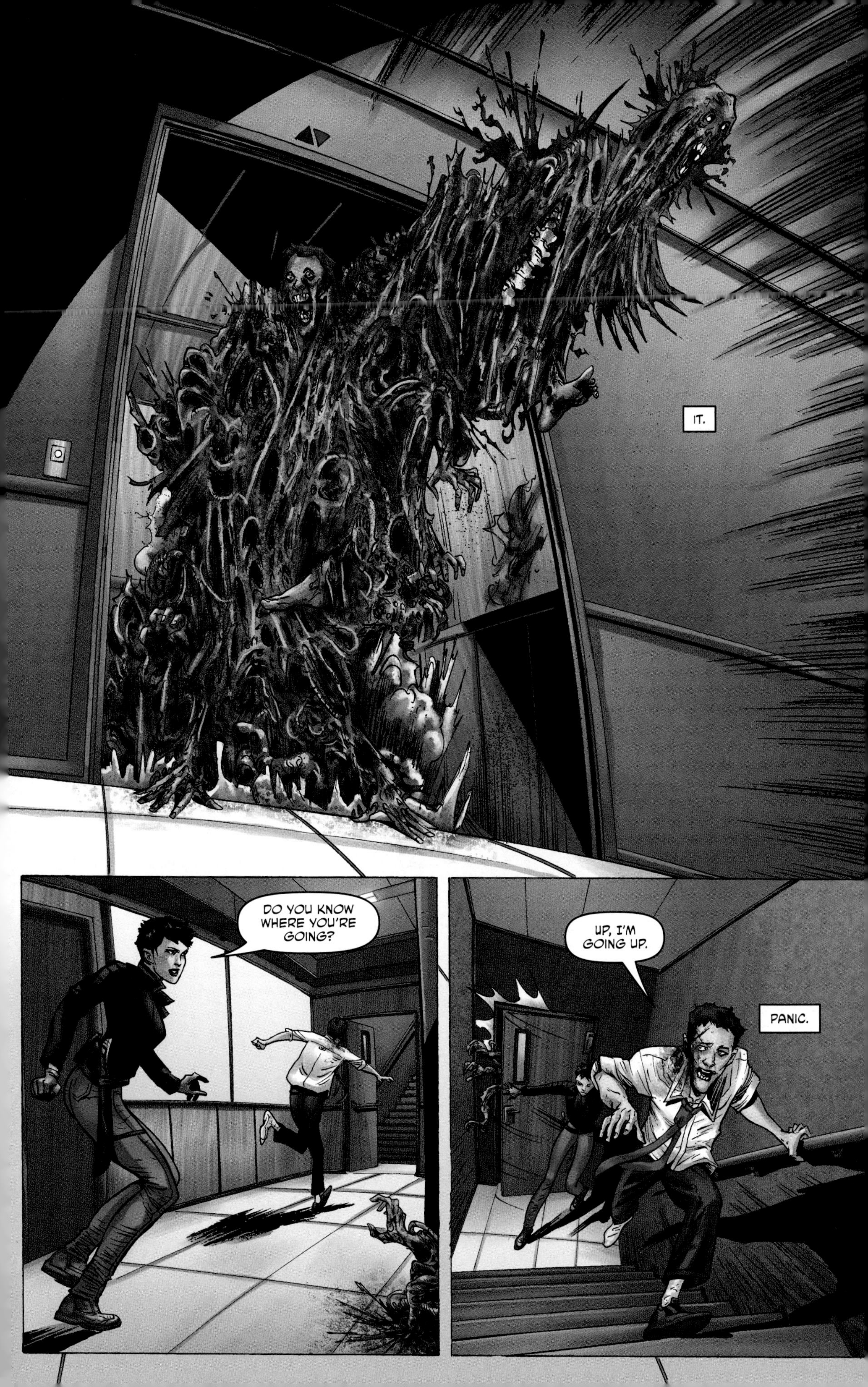
IT.
DO YOU KNOW WHERE YOU'RE GOING?
UP, I'M GOING UP.
PANIC.

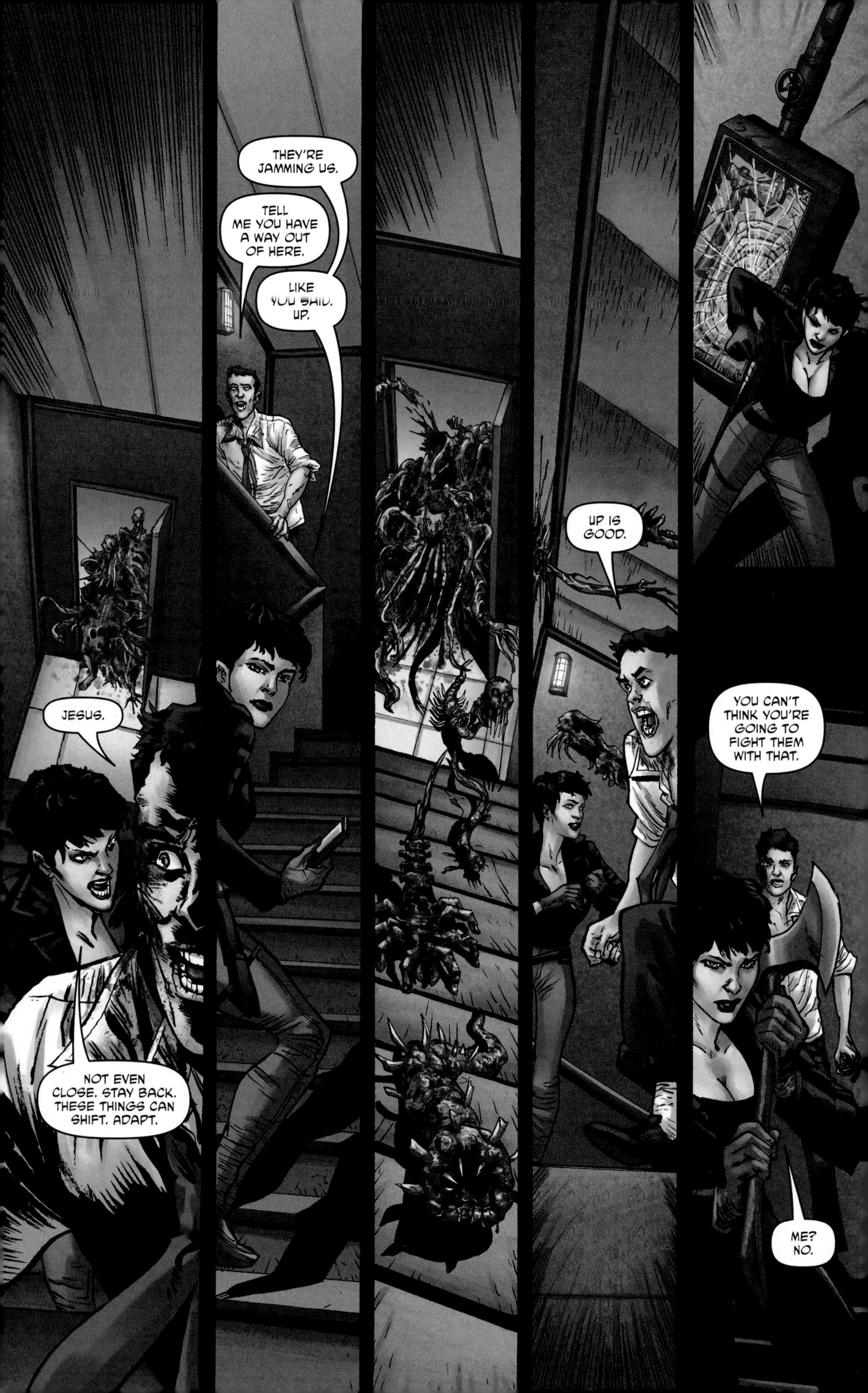
JESUS.
NOT EVEN CLOSE. STAY BACK. THESE THINGS CAN SHIFT. ADAPT.
THEY'RE JAMMING US.
TELL ME YOU HAVE A WAY OUT OF HERE.
LIKE YOU SAID. UP.
UP IS GOOD.
YOU CAN'T THINK YOU'RE GOING TO FIGHT THEM WITH THAT.
ME? NO.

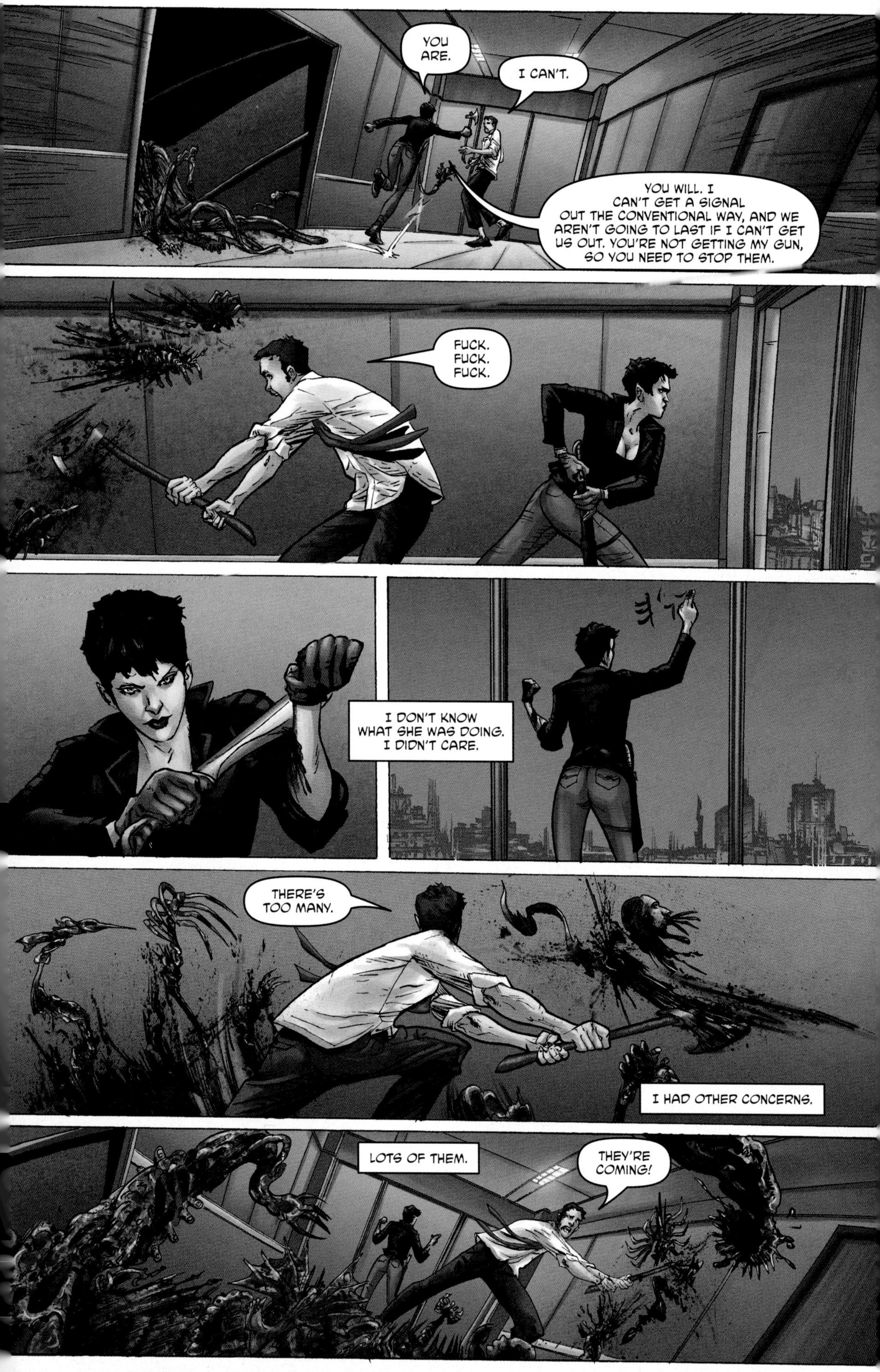
YOU ARE.
I CAN'T.
YOU WILL. I CAN'T GET A SIGNAL OUT THE CONVENTIONAL WAY, AND WE AREN'T GOING TO LAST IF I CAN'T GET US OUT. YOU'RE NOT GETTING MY GUN, SO YOU NEED TO STOP THEM.
FUCK. FUCK. FUCK.
I DON'T KNOW WHAT SHE WAS DOING. I DIDN'T CARE.
THERE'S TOO MANY.
I HAD OTHER CONCERNS.
LOTS OF THEM.
THEY'RE COMING!

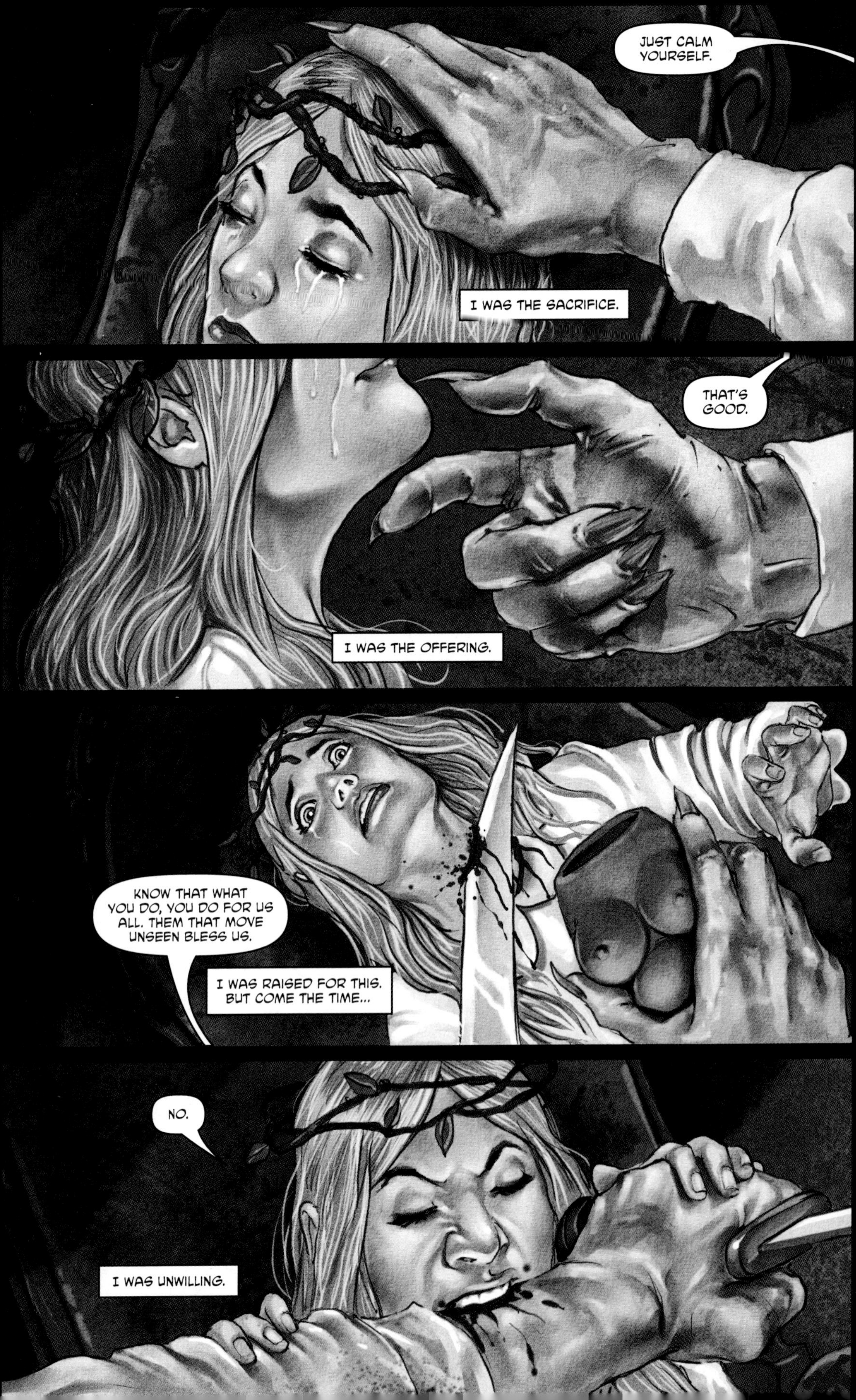
JUST CALM YOURSELF.
I WAS THE SACRIFICE.
THAT'S GOOD.
I WAS THE OFFERING.
KNOW THAT WHAT YOU DO, YOU DO FOR US ALL. THEM THAT MOVE UNSEEN BLESS US.
I WAS RAISED FOR THIS. BUT COME THE TIME...
NO.
I WAS UNWILLING.

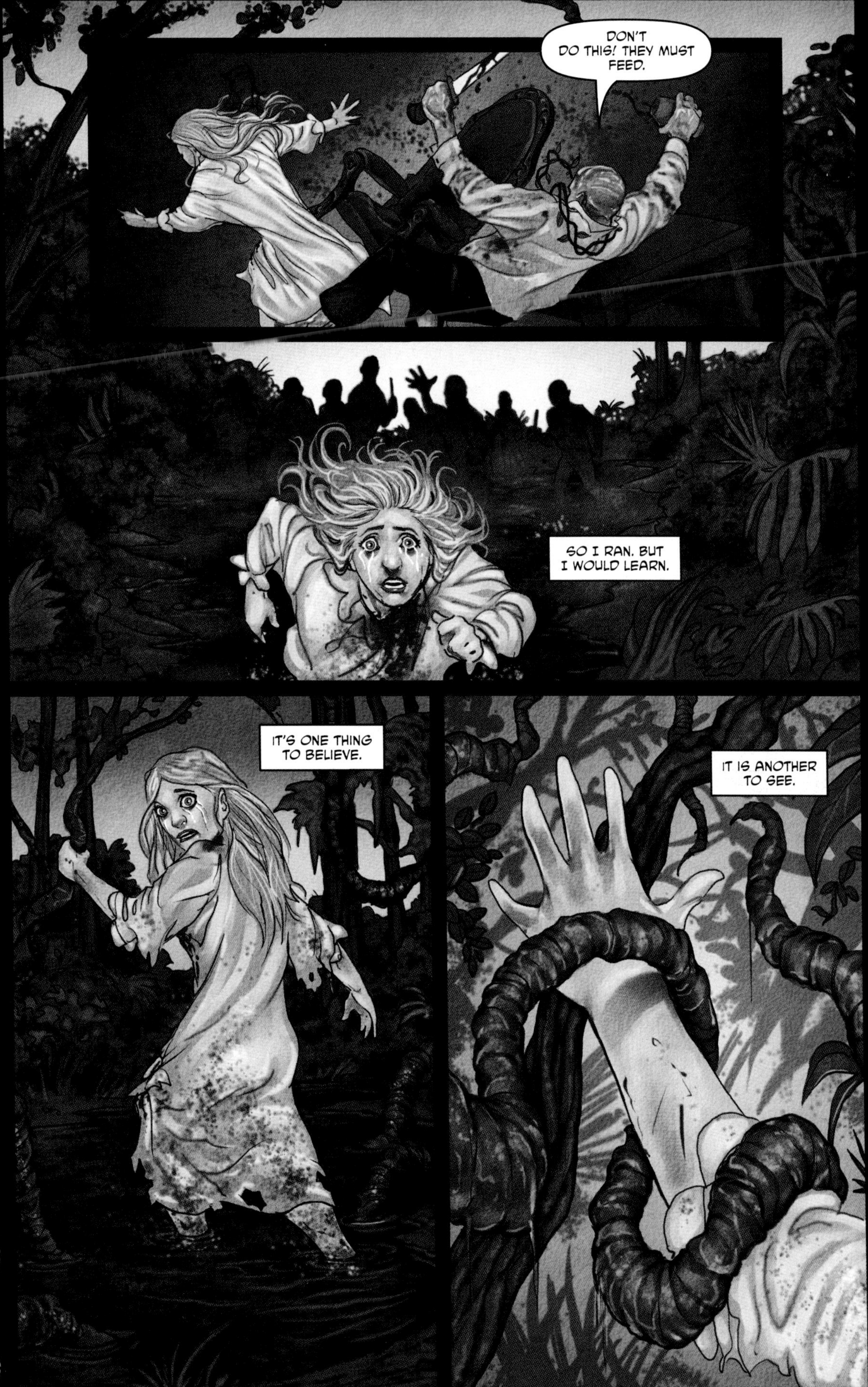
DON'T DO THIS! THEY MUST FEED.
SO I RAN. BUT I WOULD LEARN.
IT'S ONE THING TO BELIEVE.
IT IS ANOTHER TO SEE.

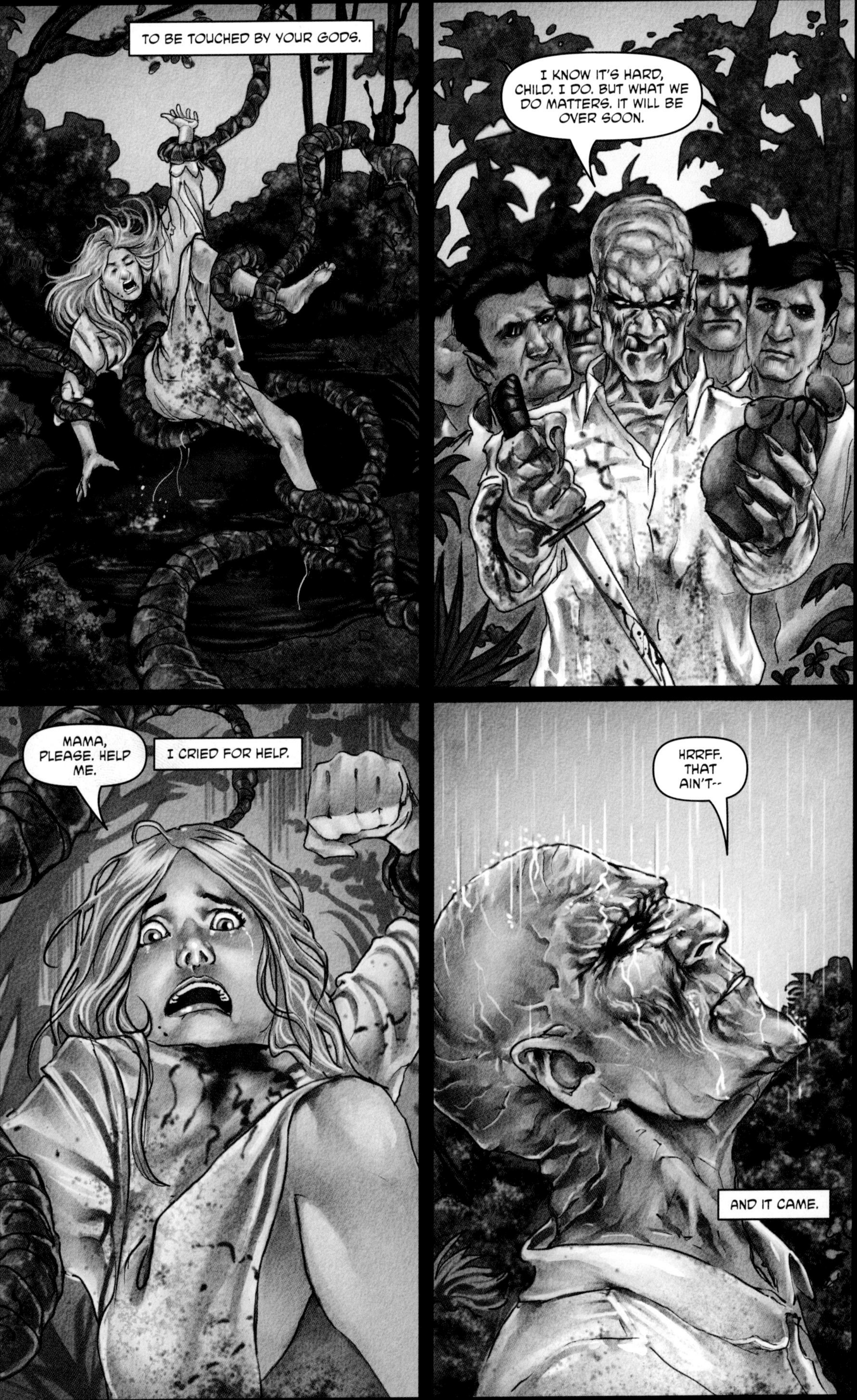
TO BE TOUCHED BY YOUR GODS.
I KNOW IT'S HARD, CHILD. I DO. BUT WHAT WE DO MATTERS. IT WILL BE OVER SOON.
MAMA, PLEASE. HELP ME.
I CRIED FOR HELP.
HRRFF. THAT AIN'T--
AND IT CAME.

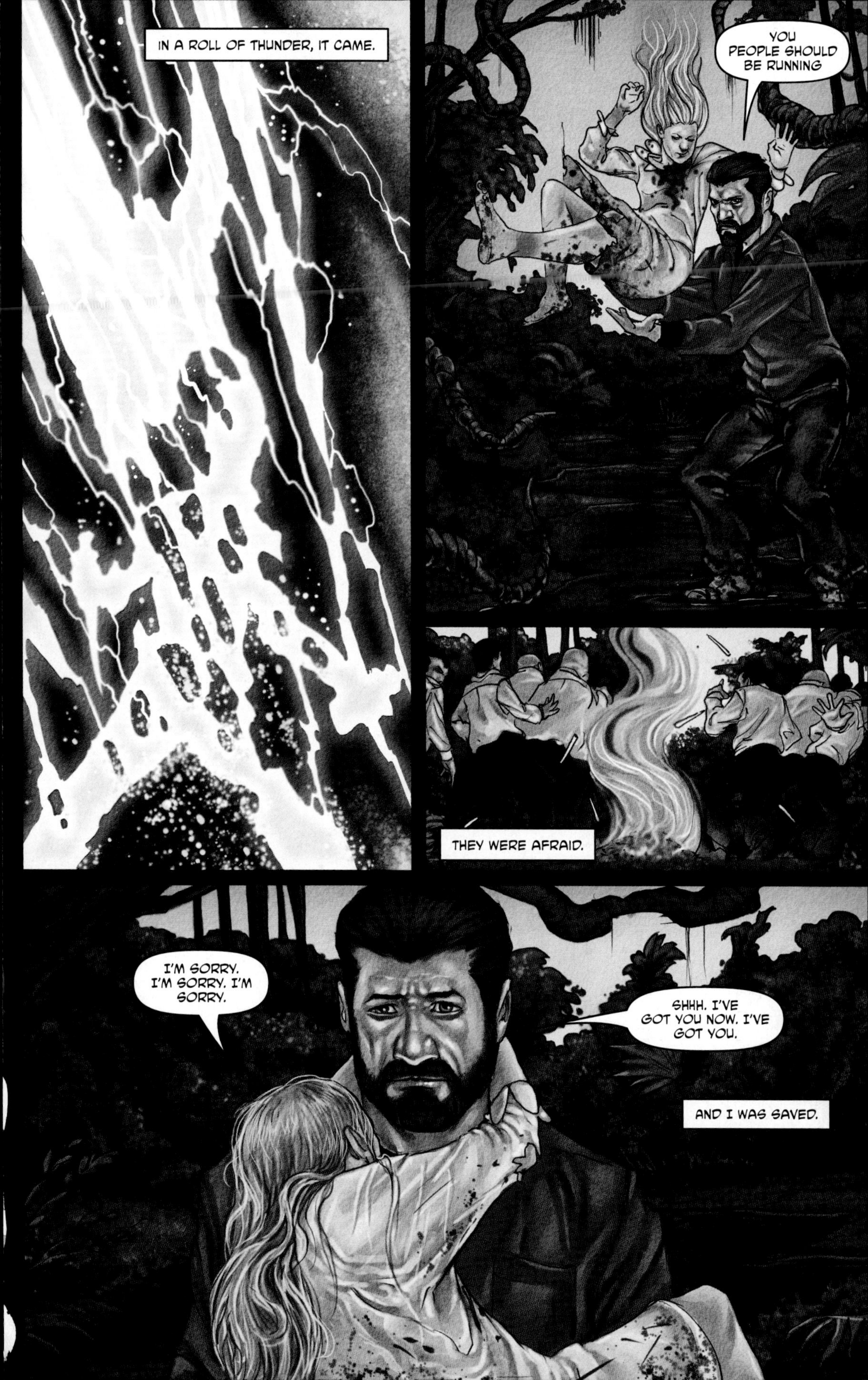
IN A ROLL OF THUNDER, IT CAME.
YOU PEOPLE SHOULD BE RUNNING
THEY WERE AFRAID.
I'M SORRY. I'M SORRY. I'M SORRY.
SHHH. I'VE GOT YOU NOW. I'VE GOT YOU.
AND I WAS SAVED.

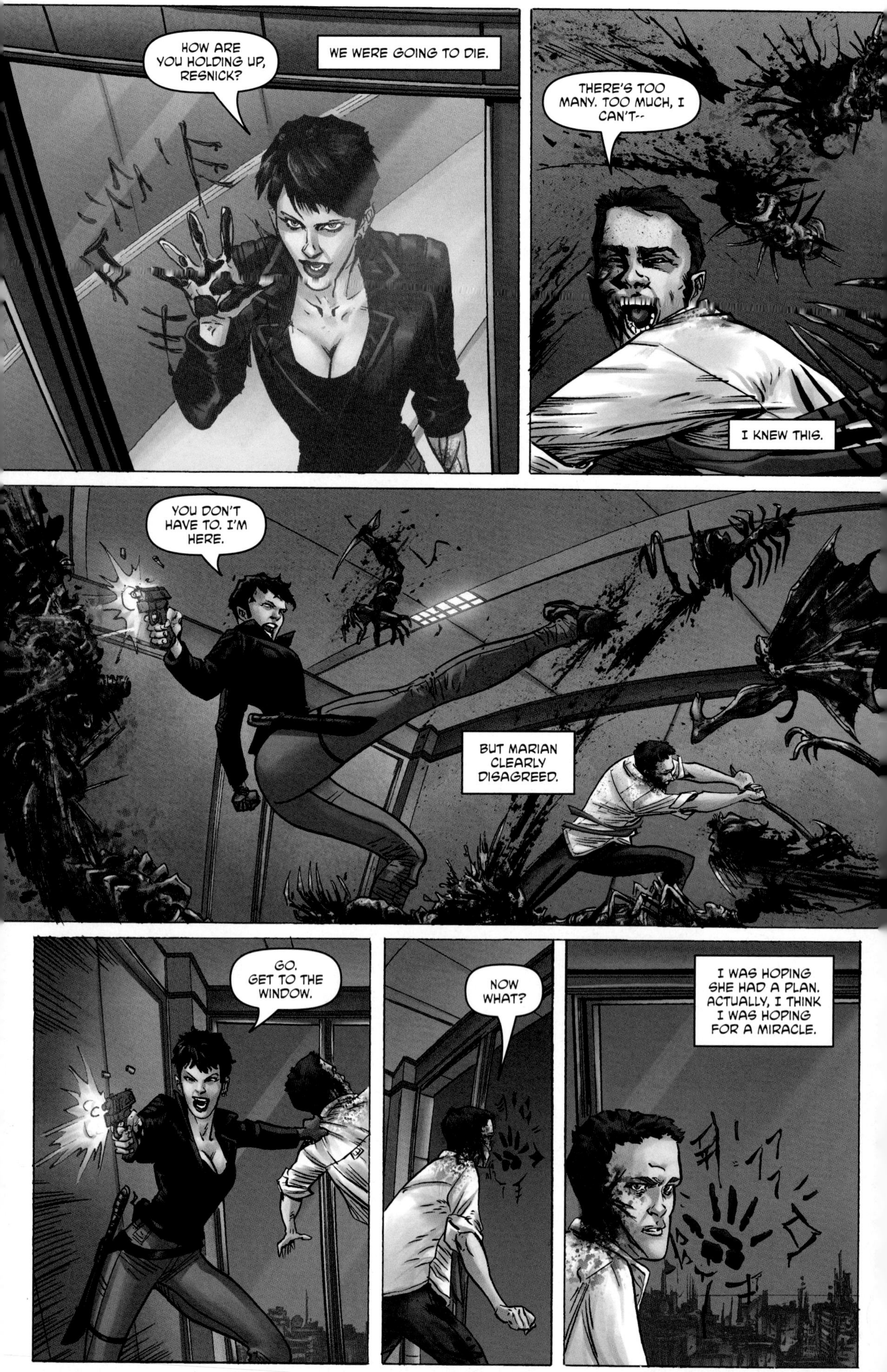
HOW ARE YOU HOLDING UP, RESNICK?
WE WERE GOING TO DIE.
THERE'S TOO MANY. TOO MUCH, I CAN'T--
I KNEW THIS.
YOU DON'T HAVE TO. I'M HERE.
BUT MARIAN CLEARLY DISAGREED.
GO. GET TO THE WINDOW.
NOW WHAT?
I WAS HOPING SHE HAD A PLAN. ACTUALLY, I THINK I WAS HOPING FOR A MIRACLE.

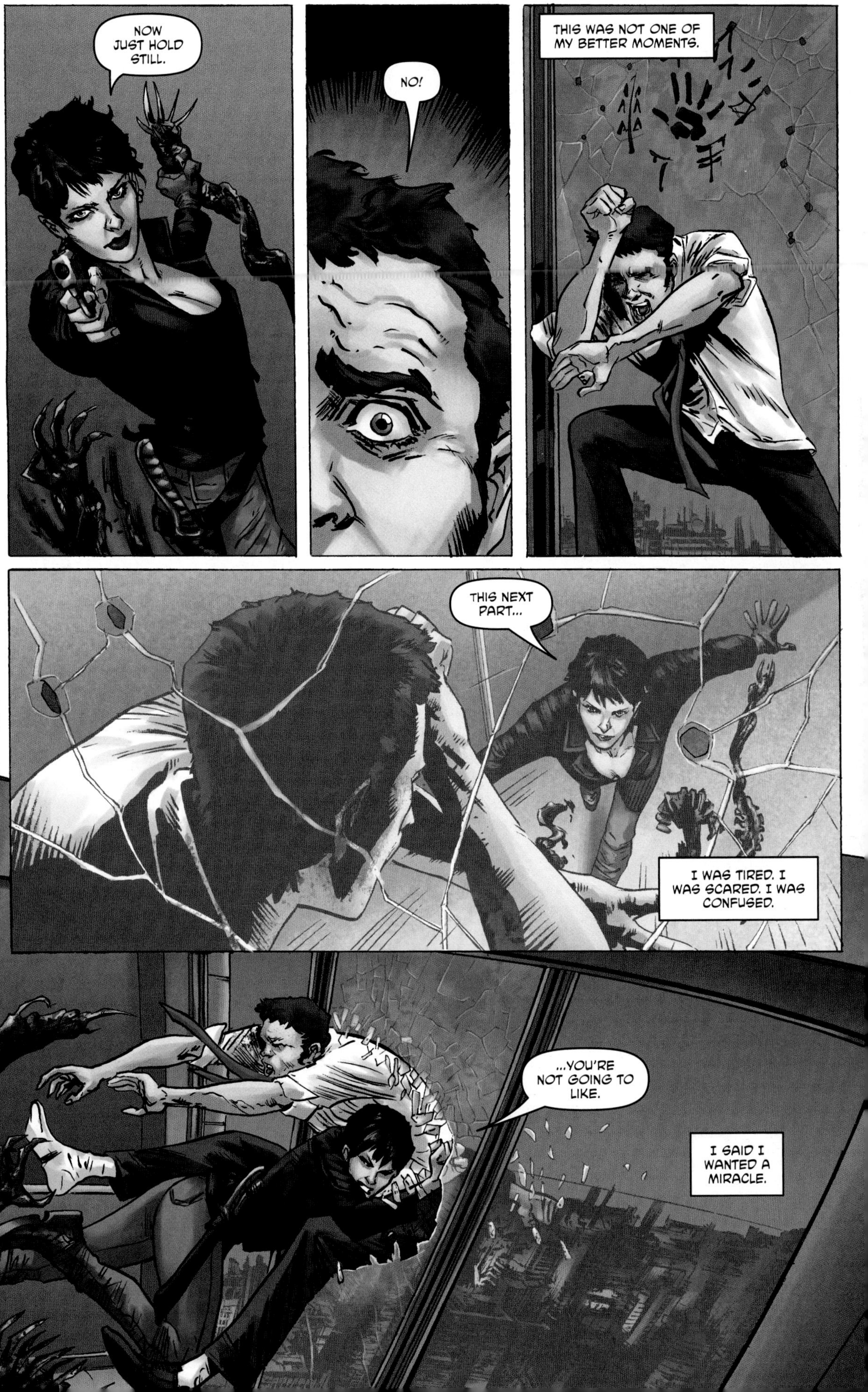
NOW JUST HOLD STILL.
NO!
THIS WAS NOT ONE OF MY BETTER MOMENTS.
THIS NEXT PART...
I WAS TIRED. I WAS SCARED. I WAS CONFUSED.
...YOU'RE NOT GOING TO LIKE.
I SAID I WANTED A MIRACLE.

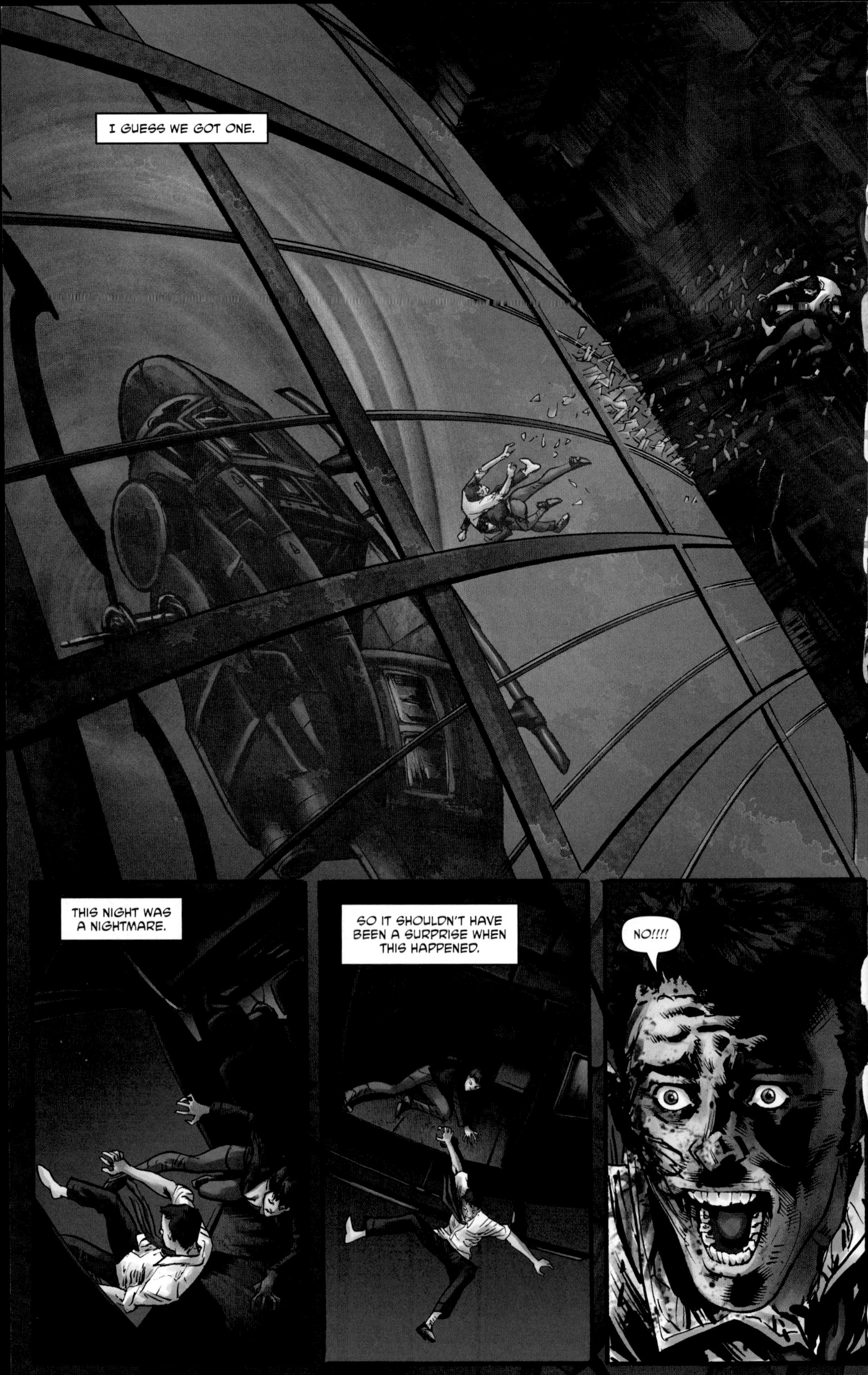
I GUESS WE GOT ONE.
THIS NIGHT WAS A NIGHTMARE.
SO IT SHOULDN'T HAVE BEEN A SURPRISE WHEN THIS HAPPENED.
NO!!!!

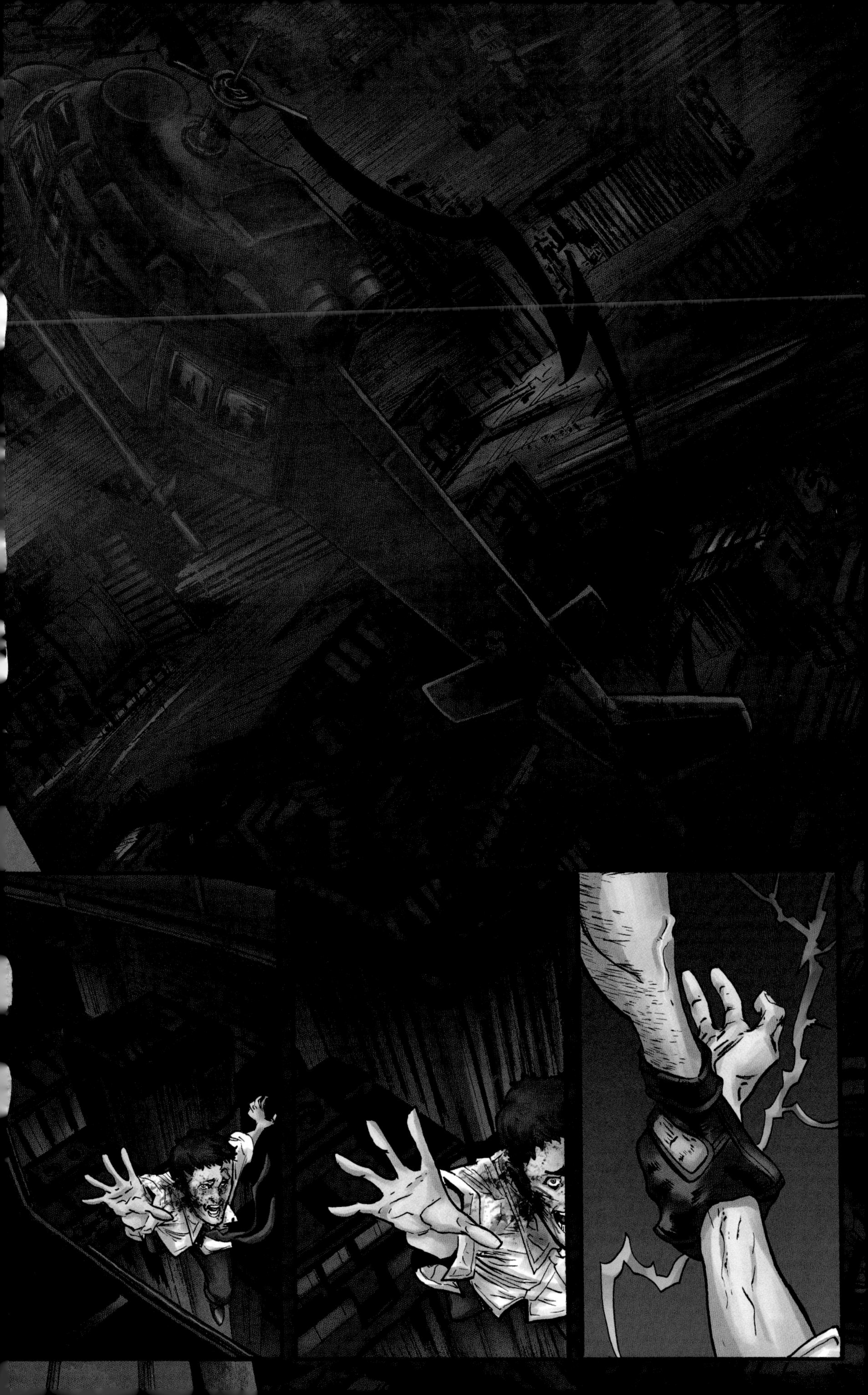

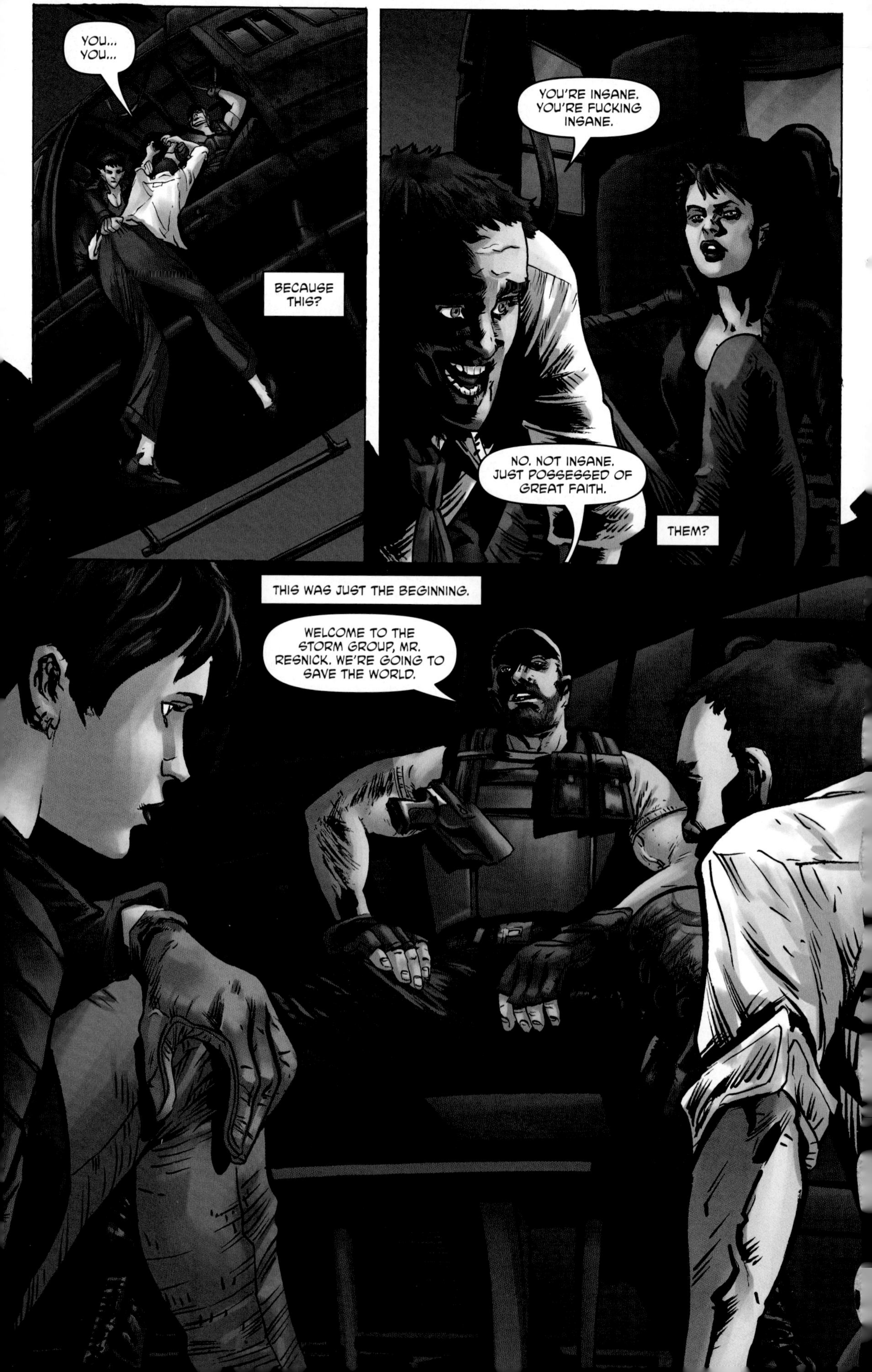
YOU... YOU...
BECAUSE THIS?
YOU'RE INSANE. YOU'RE FUCKING INSANE.
NO. NOT INSANE. JUST POSSESSED OF GREAT FAITH.
THEM?
THIS WAS JUST THE BEGINNING.
WELCOME TO THE STORM GROUP, MR. RESNICK. WE'RE GOING TO SAVE THE WORLD.

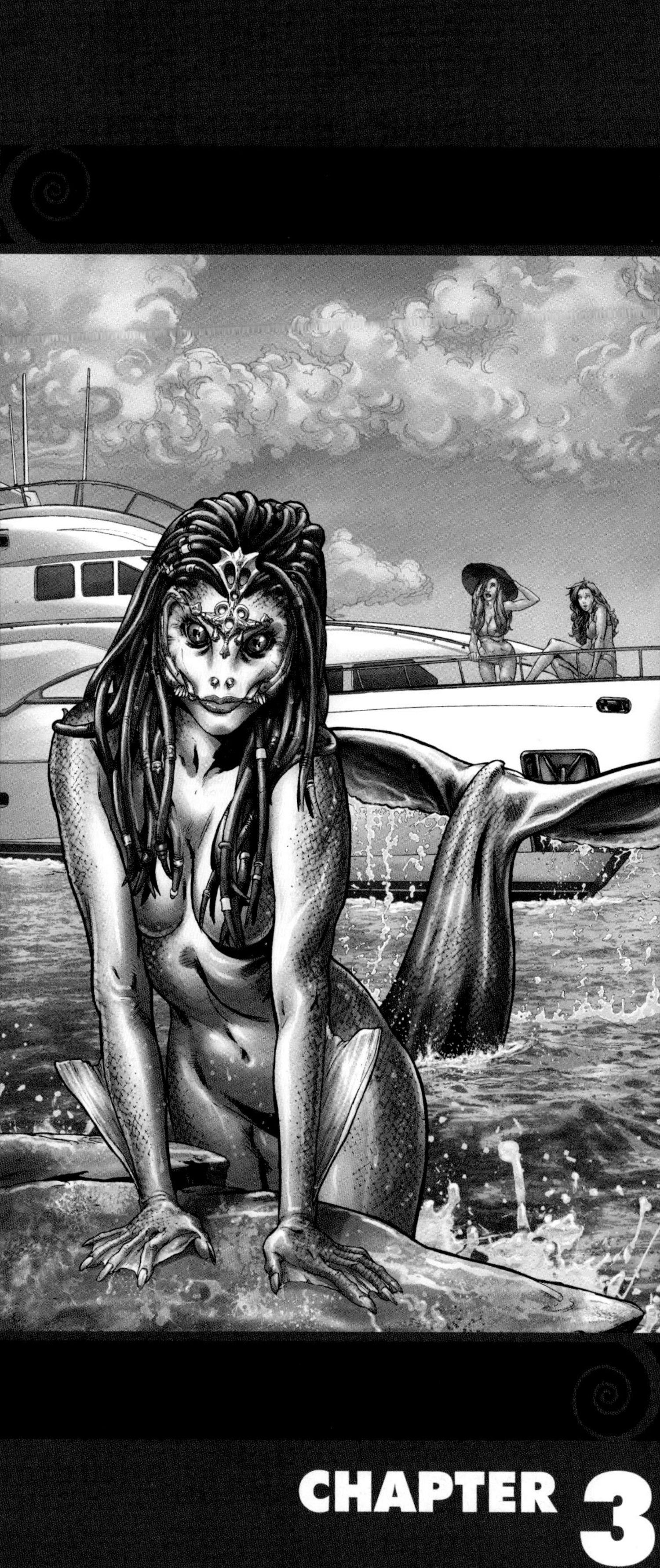

# CHAPTER 3

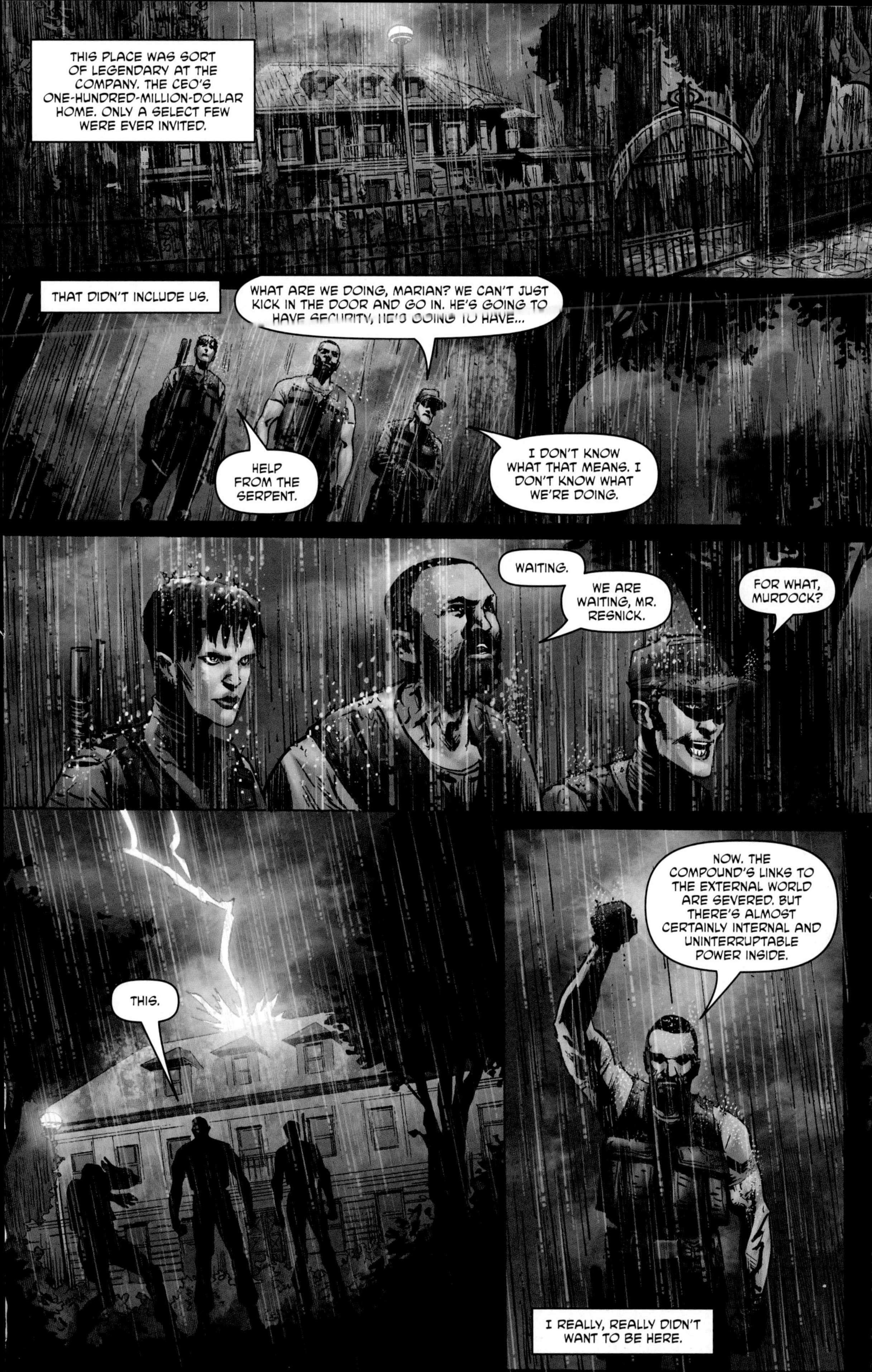
THIS PLACE WAS SORT OF LEGENDARY AT THE COMPANY. THE CEO'S ONE-HUNDRED-MILLION-DOLLAR HOME. ONLY A SELECT FEW WERE EVER INVITED.
THAT DIDN'T INCLUDE US.
WHAT ARE WE DOING, MARIAN? WE CAN'T JUST KICK IN THE DOOR AND GO IN. HE'S GOING TO HAVE SECURITY, HE'S GOING TO HAVE...
HELP FROM THE SERPENT.
I DON'T KNOW WHAT THAT MEANS. I DON'T KNOW WHAT WE'RE DOING.
WAITING.
WE ARE WAITING, MR. RESNICK.
FOR WHAT, MURDOCK?
THIS.
NOW. THE COMPOUND'S LINKS TO THE EXTERNAL WORLD ARE SEVERED. BUT THERE'S ALMOST CERTAINLY INTERNAL AND UNINTERRUPTABLE POWER INSIDE.
I REALLY, REALLY DIDN'T WANT TO BE HERE.

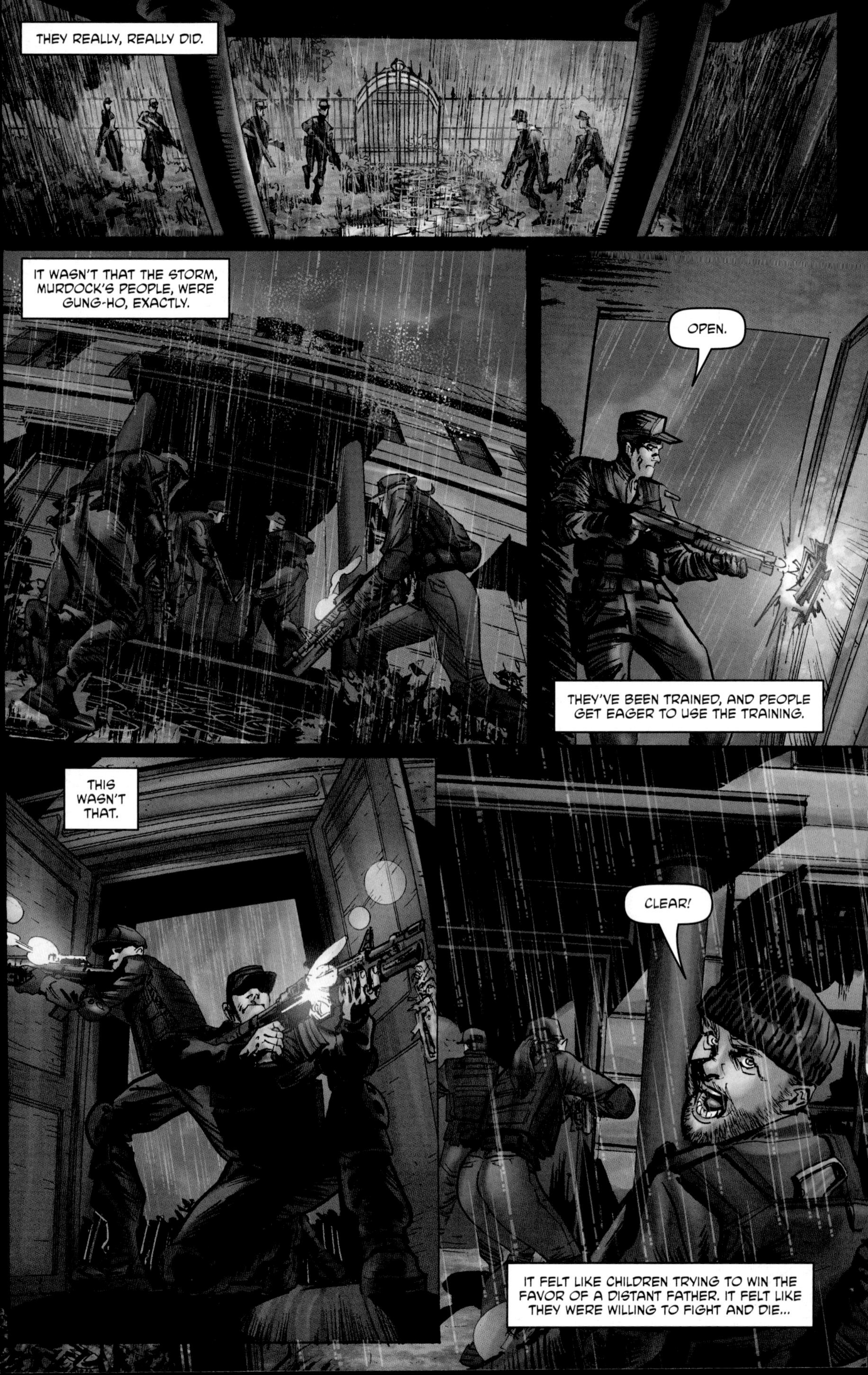
THEY REALLY, REALLY DID.
IT WASN'T THAT THE STORM, MURDOCK'S PEOPLE, WERE GUNG-HO, EXACTLY.
OPEN.
THEY'VE BEEN TRAINED, AND PEOPLE GET EAGER TO USE THE TRAINING.
THIS WASN'T THAT.
CLEAR!
IT FELT LIKE CHILDREN TRYING TO WIN THE FAVOR OF A DISTANT FATHER. IT FELT LIKE THEY WERE WILLING TO FIGHT AND DIE...

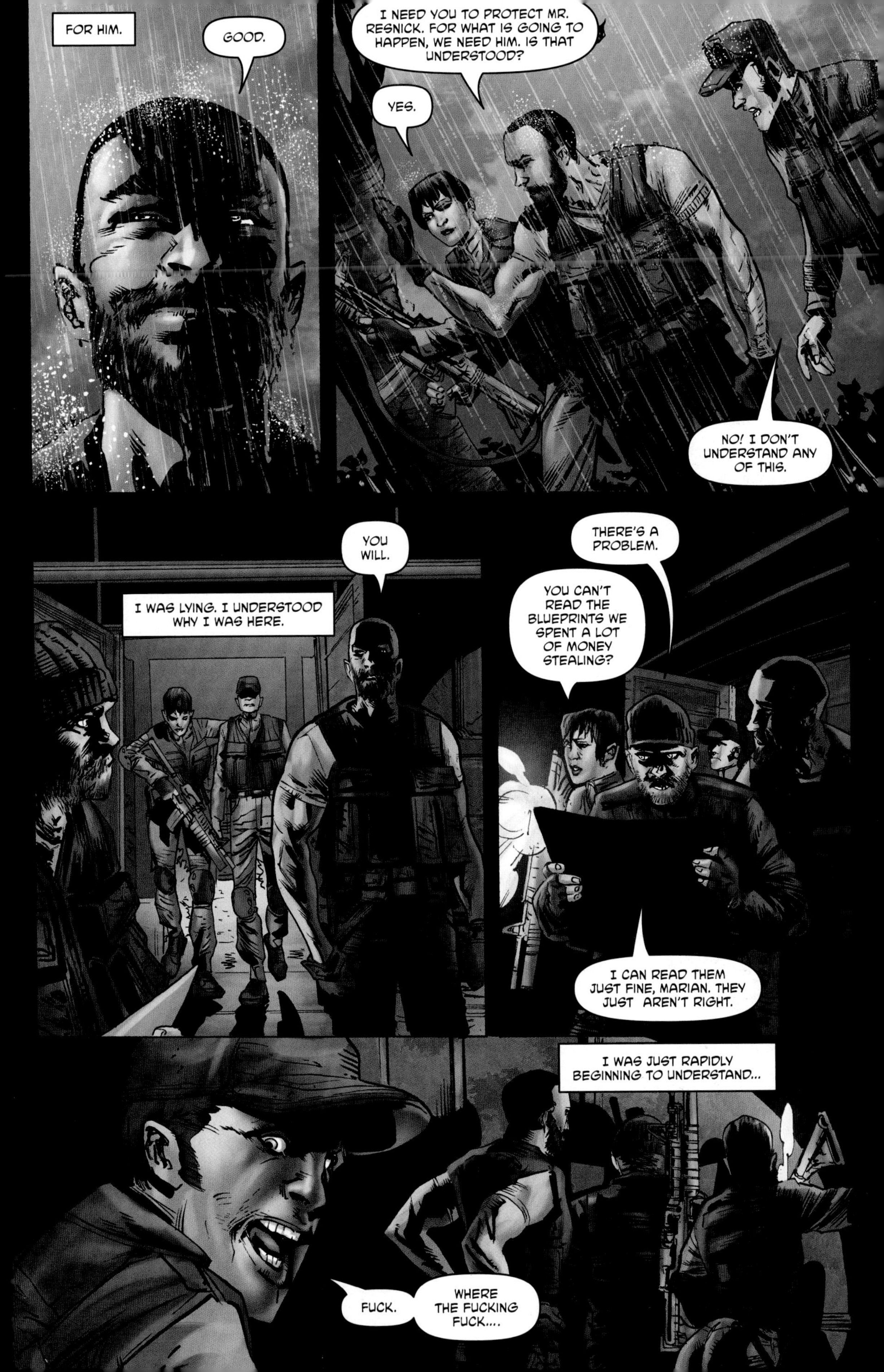

FOR HIM.
GOOD.
I NEED YOU TO PROTECT MR. RESNICK. FOR WHAT IS GOING TO HAPPEN, WE NEED HIM. IS THAT UNDERSTOOD?
YES.
NO! I DON'T UNDERSTAND ANY OF THIS.
YOU WILL.
I WAS LYING. I UNDERSTOOD WHY I WAS HERE.
THERE'S A PROBLEM.
YOU CAN'T READ THE BLUEPRINTS WE SPENT A LOT OF MONEY STEALING?
I CAN READ THEM JUST FINE, MARIAN. THEY JUST AREN'T RIGHT.
I WAS JUST RAPIDLY BEGINNING TO UNDERSTAND...
FUCK.
WHERE THE FUCKING FUCK....

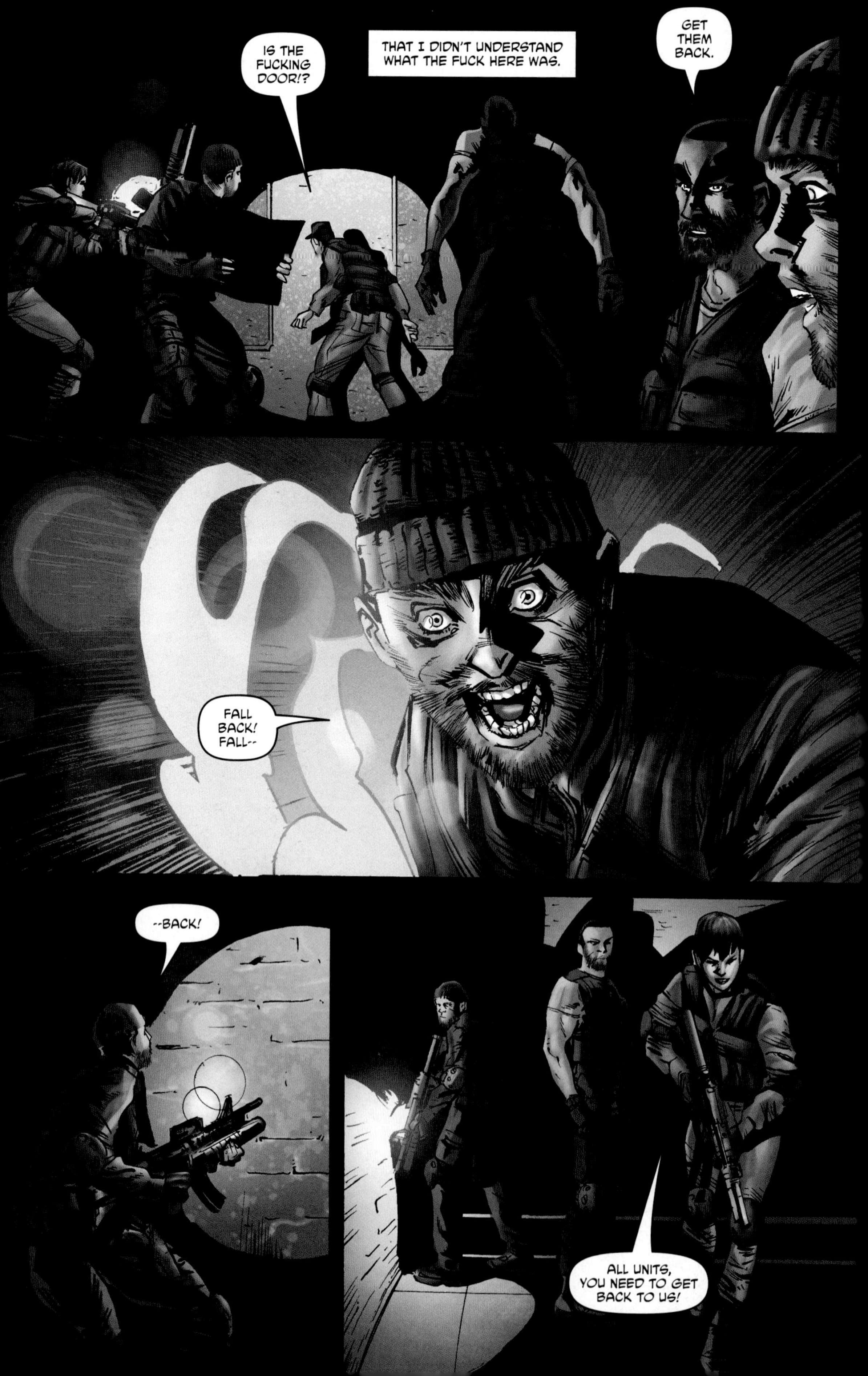
IS THE FUCKING DOOR!?
THAT I DIDN'T UNDERSTAND WHAT THE FUCK HERE WAS.
GET THEM BACK.
FALL BACK! FALL--
--BACK!
ALL UNITS, YOU NEED TO GET BACK TO US!

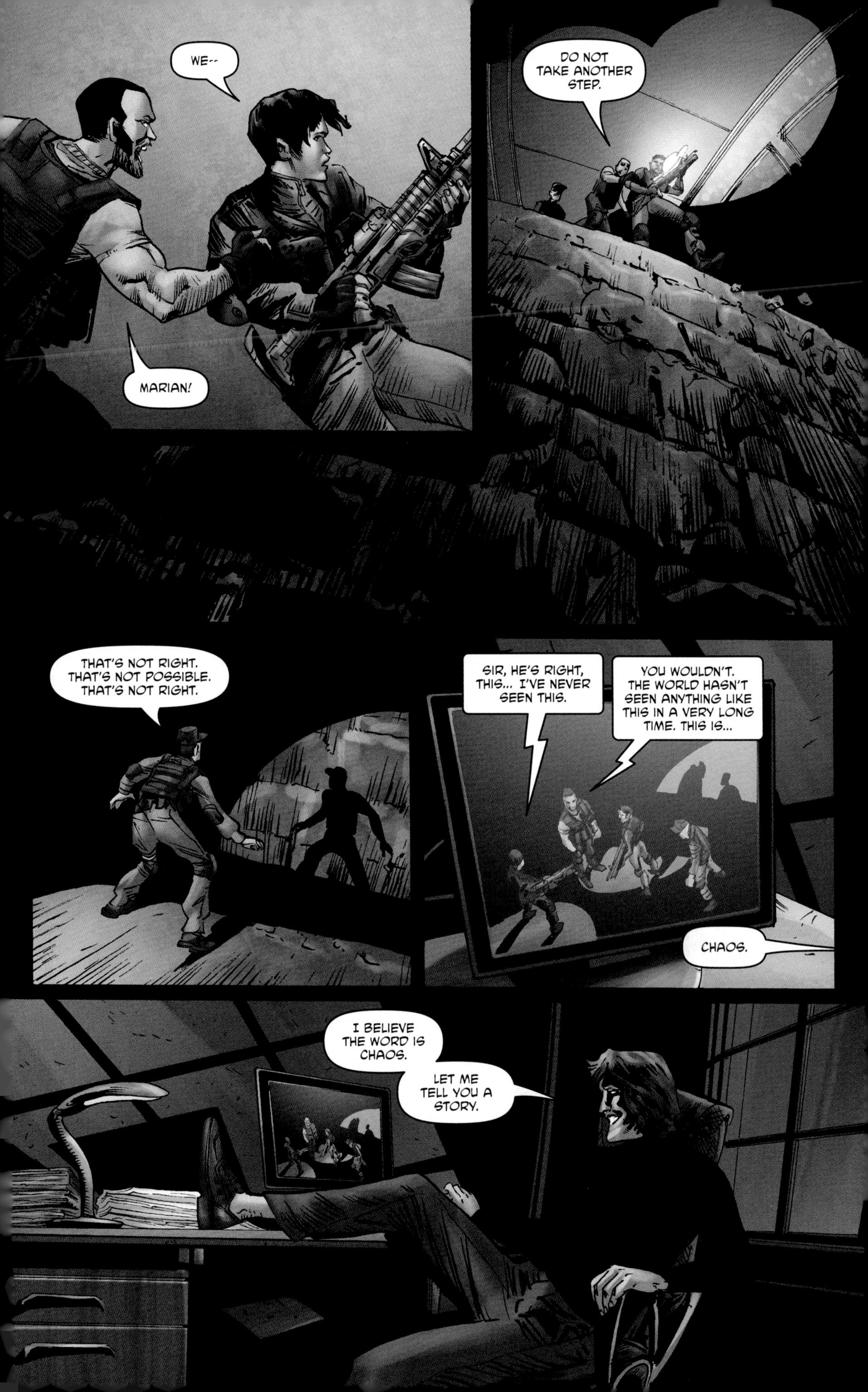
WE--
MARIAN!
DO NOT TAKE ANOTHER STEP.
THAT'S NOT RIGHT. THAT'S NOT POSSIBLE. THAT'S NOT RIGHT.
SIR, HE'S RIGHT, THIS... I'VE NEVER SEEN THIS.
YOU WOULDN'T. THE WORLD HASN'T SEEN ANYTHING LIKE THIS IN A VERY LONG TIME. THIS IS...
CHAOS.
I BELIEVE THE WORD IS CHAOS.
LET ME TELL YOU A STORY.

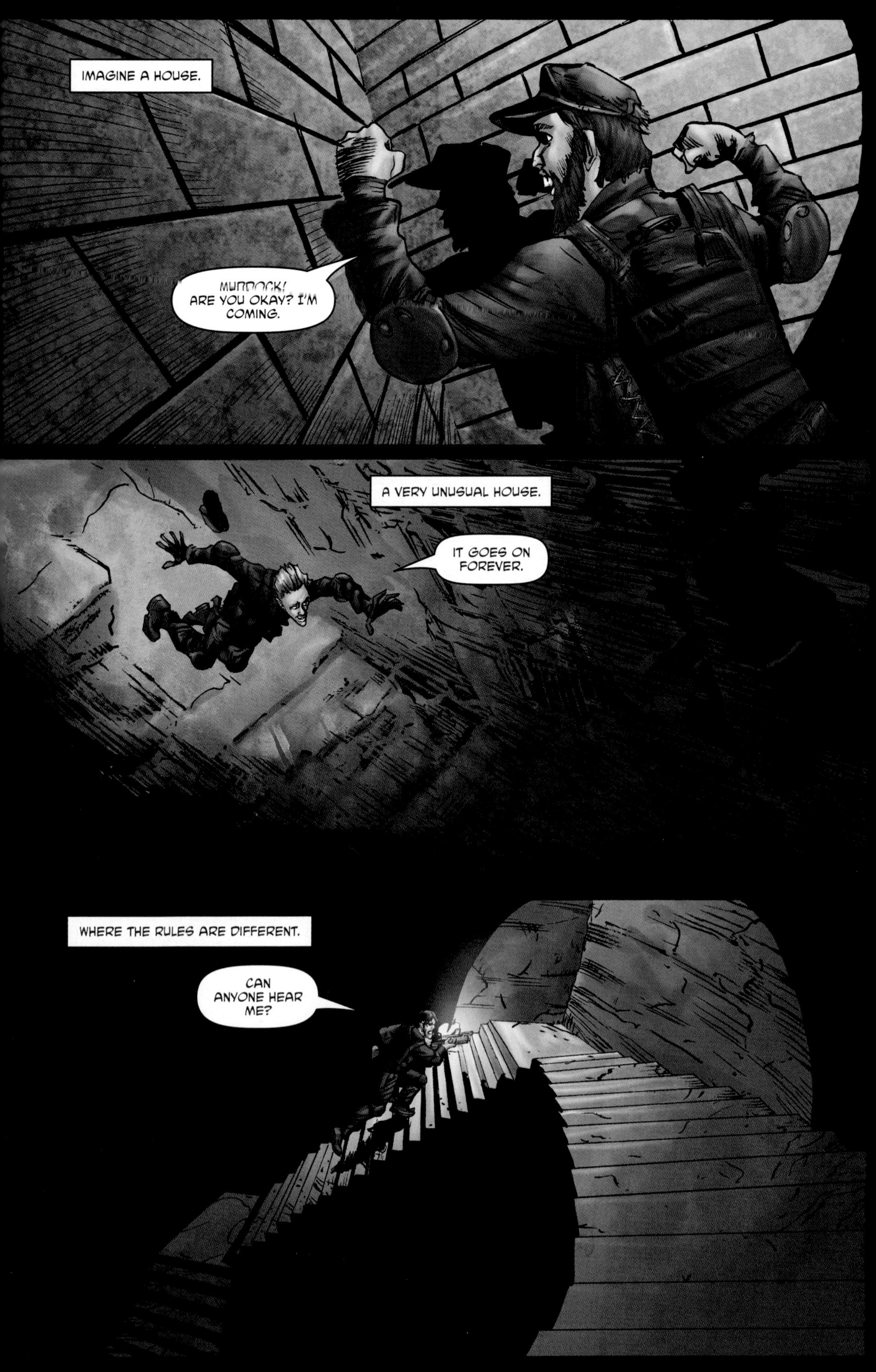
IMAGINE A HOUSE.
MURDOCK! ARE YOU OKAY? I'M COMING.
A VERY UNUSUAL HOUSE.
IT GOES ON FOREVER.
WHERE THE RULES ARE DIFFERENT.
CAN ANYONE HEAR ME?

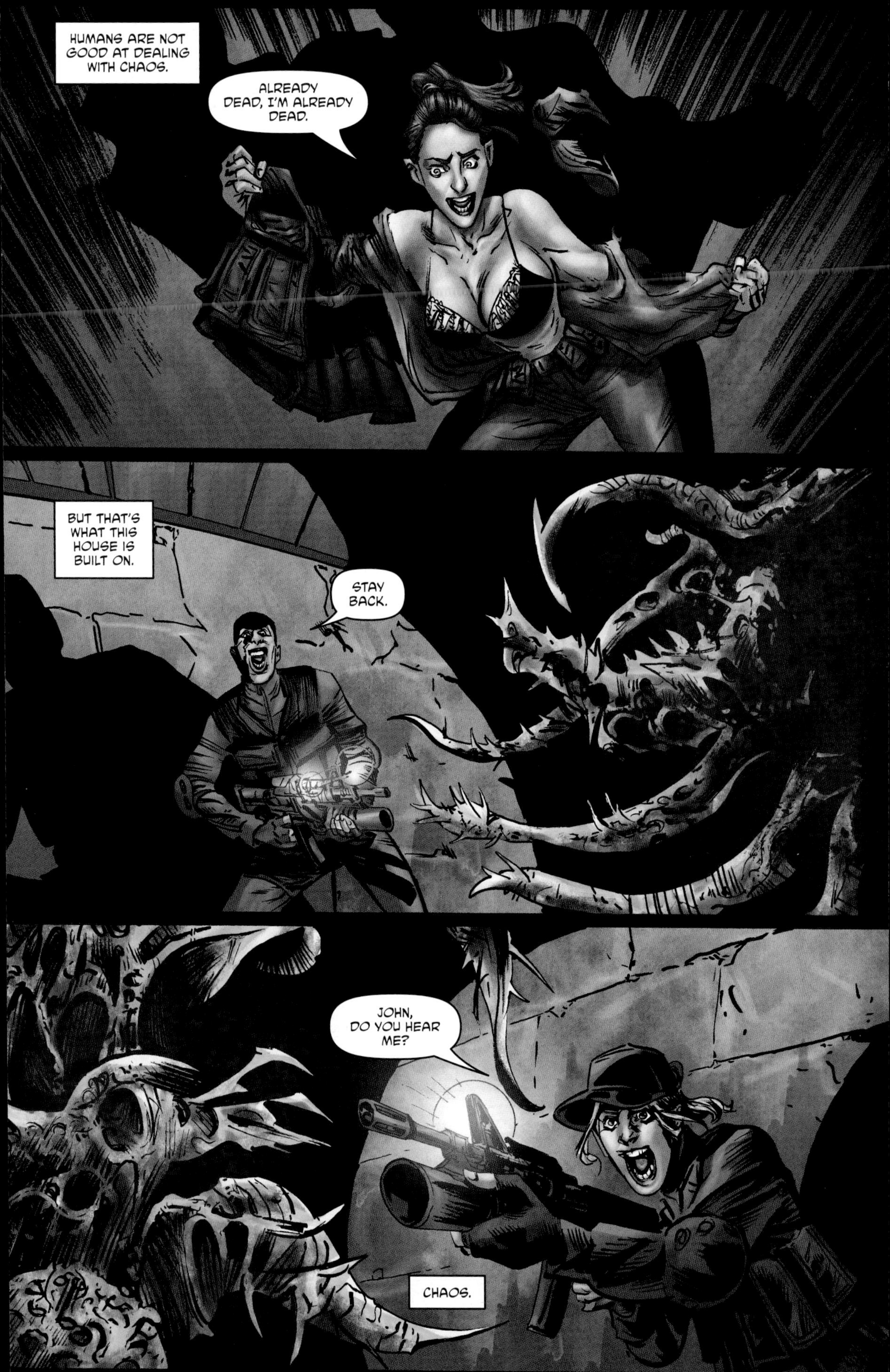
HUMANS ARE NOT GOOD AT DEALING WITH CHAOS.
ALREADY DEAD, I'M ALREADY DEAD.
BUT THAT'S WHAT THIS HOUSE IS BUILT ON.
STAY BACK.
JOHN, DO YOU HEAR ME?
CHAOS.

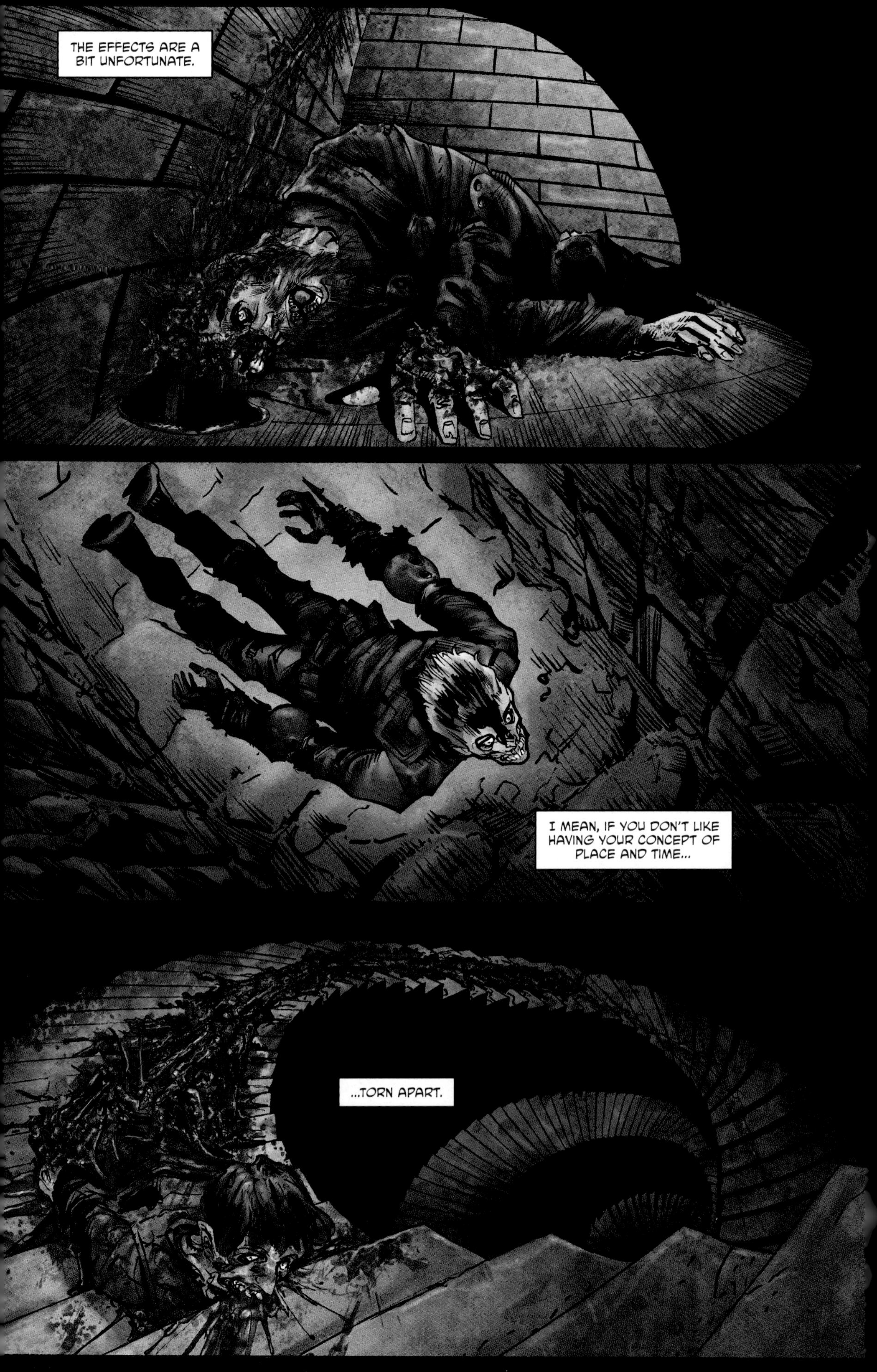
THE EFFECTS ARE A BIT UNFORTUNATE.
I MEAN, IF YOU DON'T LIKE HAVING YOUR CONCEPT OF PLACE AND TIME...
...TORN APART.

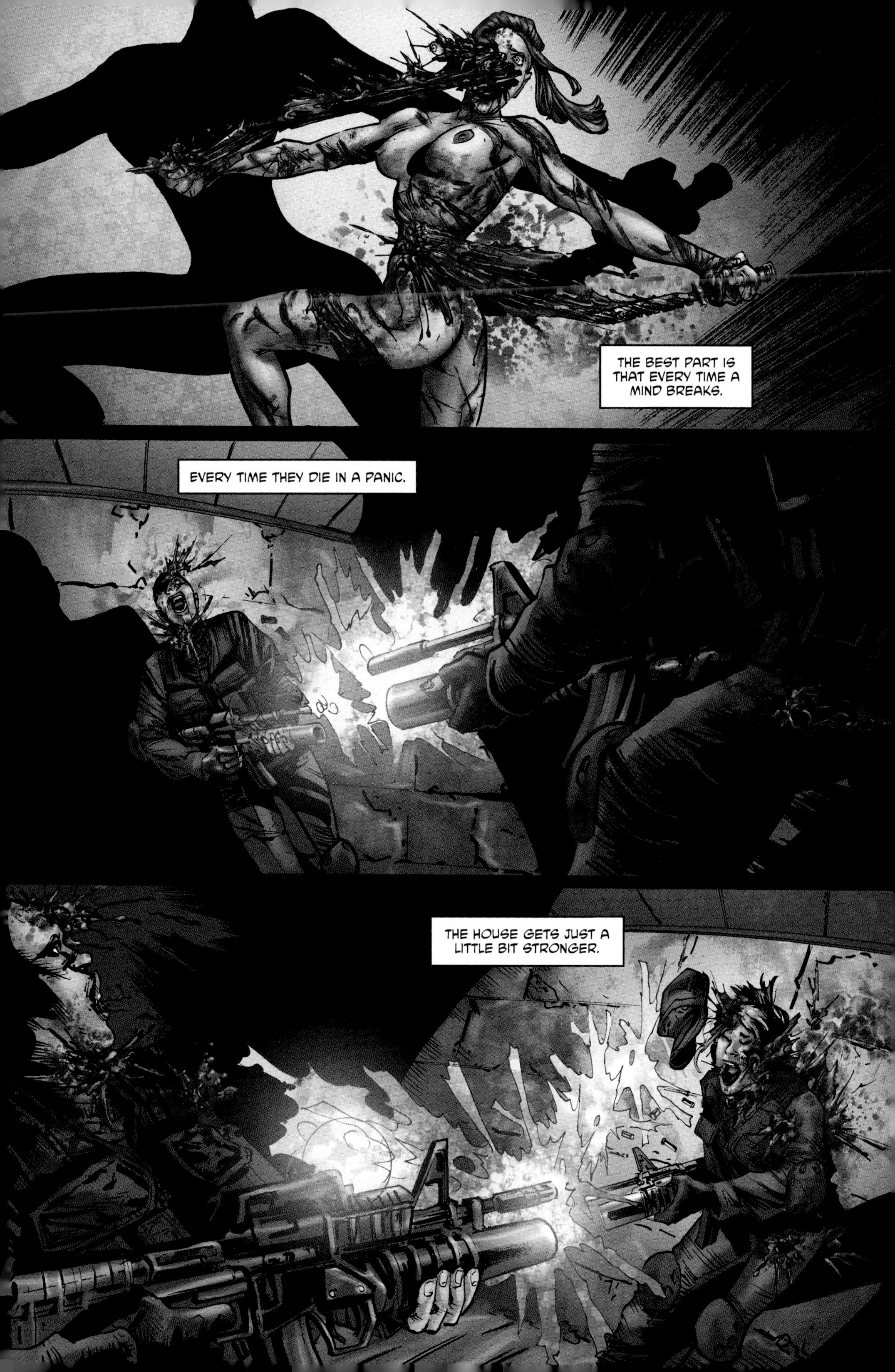
THE BEST PART IS THAT EVERY TIME A MIND BREAKS.
EVERY TIME THEY DIE IN A PANIC.
THE HOUSE GETS JUST A LITTLE BIT STRONGER.

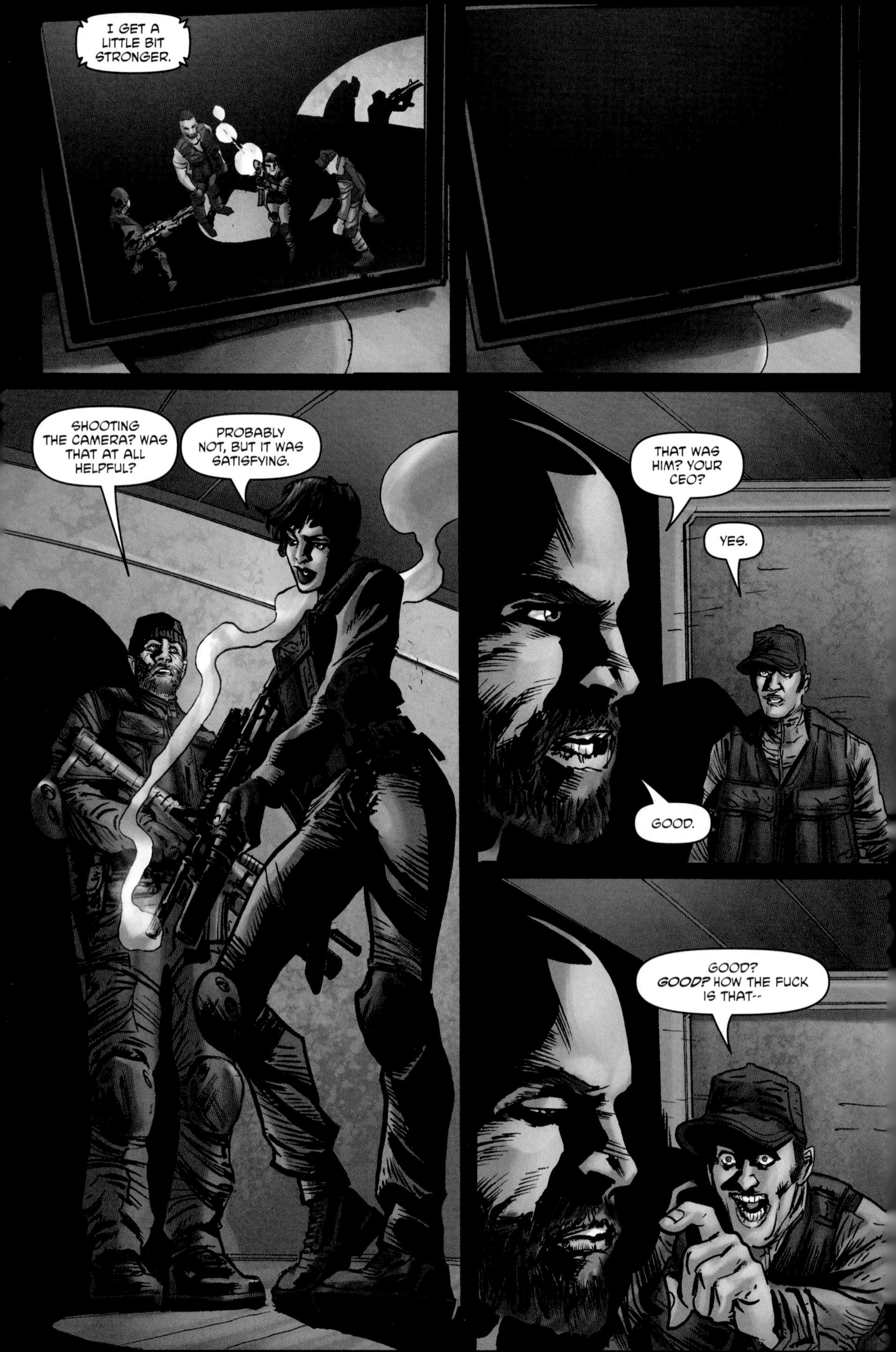
I GET A LITTLE BIT STRONGER.
SHOOTING THE CAMERA? WAS THAT AT ALL HELPFUL?
PROBABLY NOT, BUT IT WAS SATISFYING.
THAT WAS HIM? YOUR CEO?
YES.
GOOD.
GOOD? *GOOD?* HOW THE FUCK IS THAT--

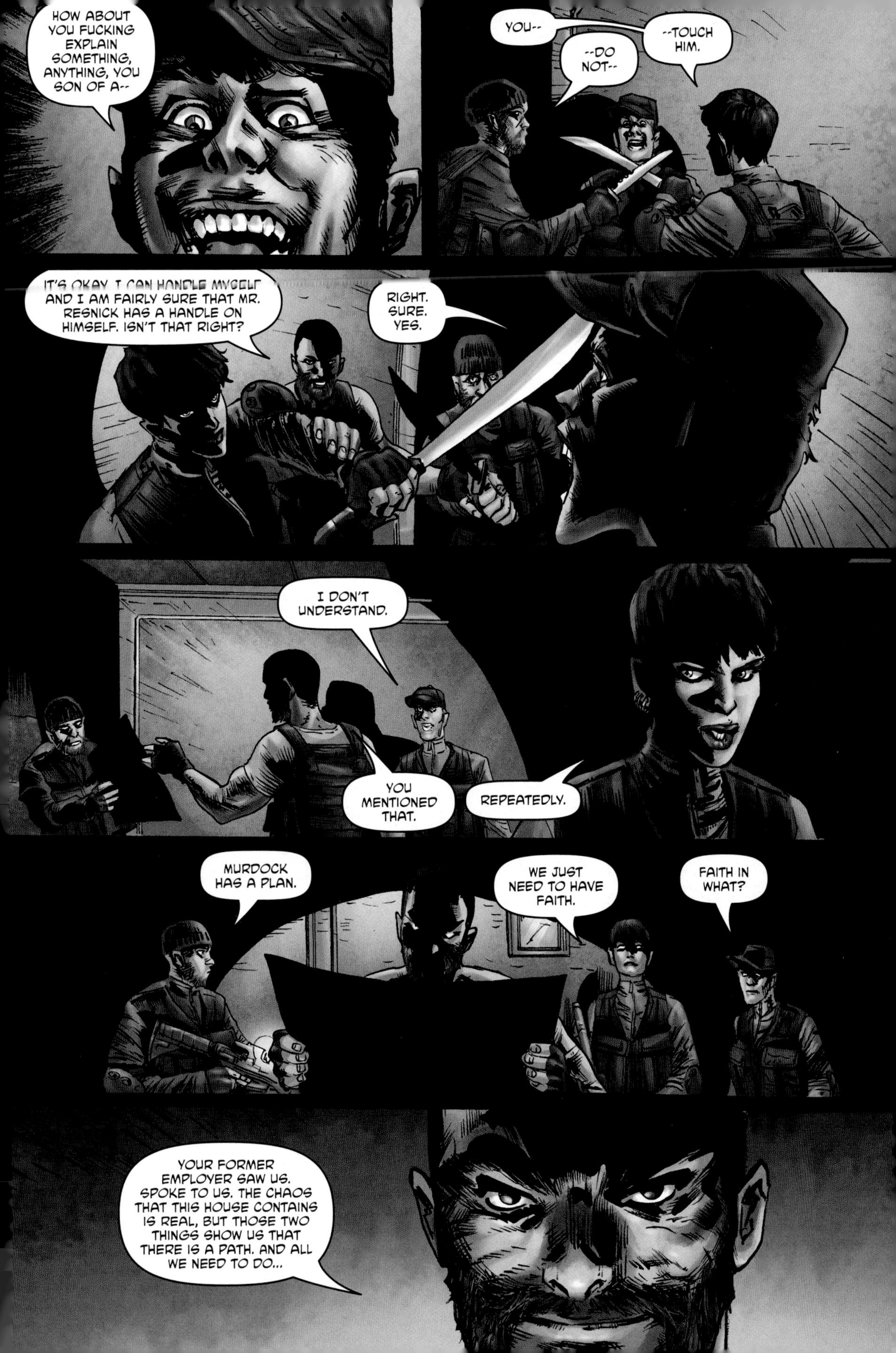
HOW ABOUT YOU FUCKING EXPLAIN SOMETHING, ANYTHING, YOU SON OF A--
YOU--
--DO NOT--
--TOUCH HIM.
IT'S OKAY. I CAN HANDLE MYSELF AND I AM FAIRLY SURE THAT MR. RESNICK HAS A HANDLE ON HIMSELF. ISN'T THAT RIGHT?
RIGHT. SURE. YES.
I DON'T UNDERSTAND.
YOU MENTIONED THAT.
REPEATEDLY.
MURDOCK HAS A PLAN.
WE JUST NEED TO HAVE FAITH.
FAITH IN WHAT?
YOUR FORMER EMPLOYER SAW US. SPOKE TO US. THE CHAOS THAT THIS HOUSE CONTAINS IS REAL, BUT THOSE TWO THINGS SHOW US THAT THERE IS A PATH. AND ALL WE NEED TO DO...

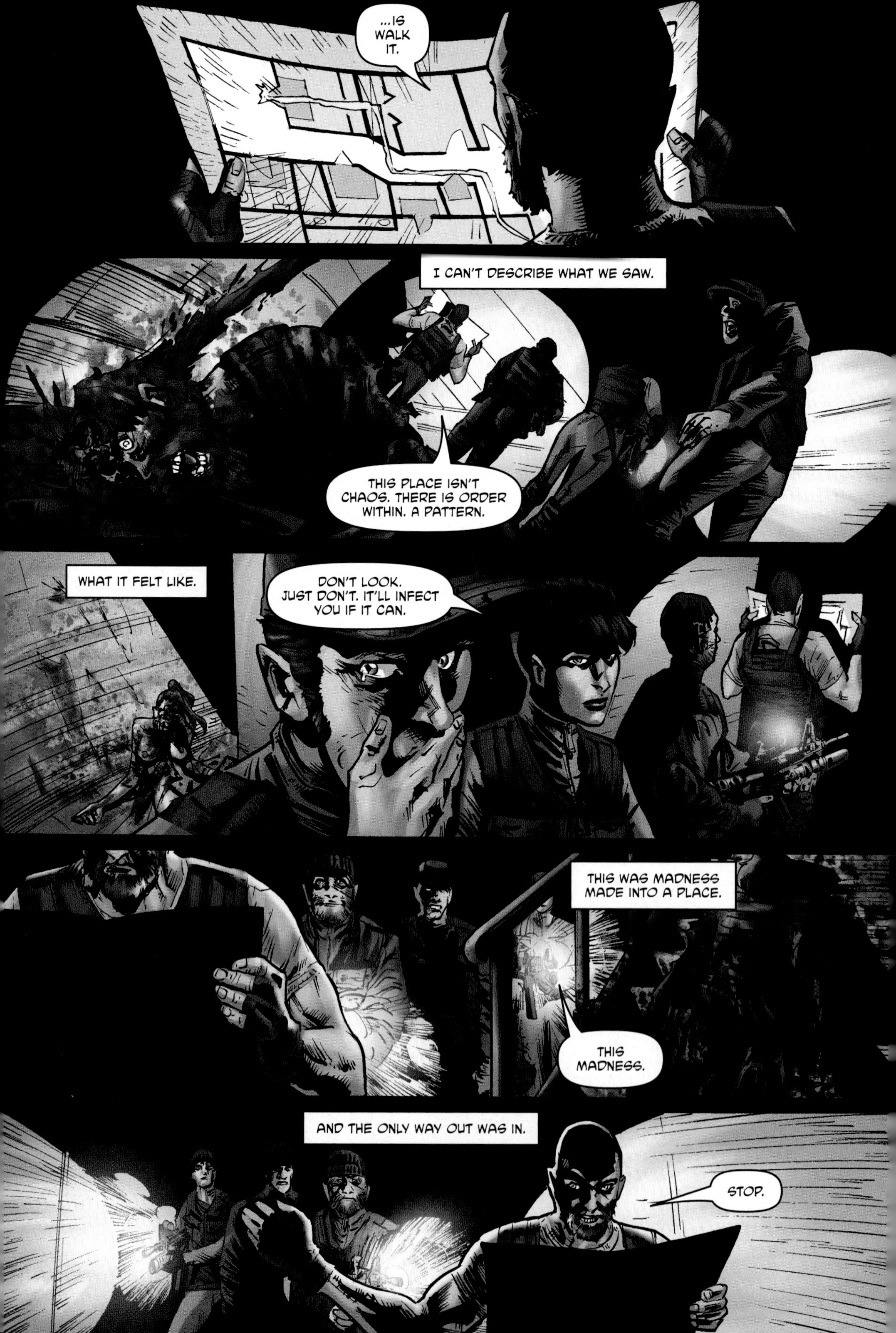

...IS WALK IT.
I CAN'T DESCRIBE WHAT WE SAW.
THIS PLACE ISN'T CHAOS. THERE IS ORDER WITHIN. A PATTERN.
WHAT IT FELT LIKE.
DON'T LOOK. JUST DON'T. IT'LL INFECT YOU IF IT CAN.
THIS WAS MADNESS MADE INTO A PLACE.
THIS MADNESS.
AND THE ONLY WAY OUT WAS IN.
STOP.

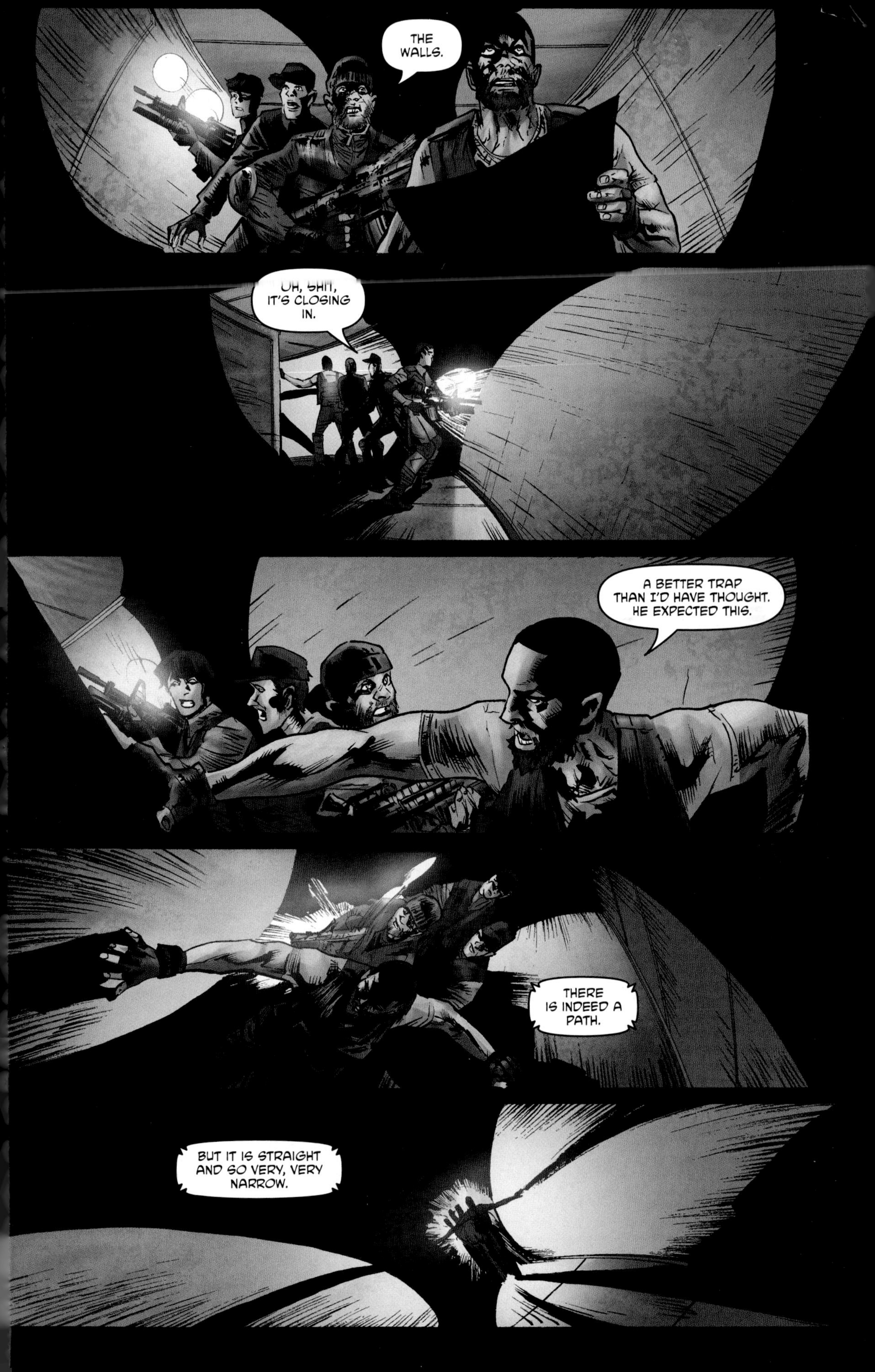
THE WALLS.
UH, SHIT, IT'S CLOSING IN.
A BETTER TRAP THAN I'D HAVE THOUGHT. HE EXPECTED THIS.
THERE IS INDEED A PATH.
BUT IT IS STRAIGHT AND SO VERY, VERY NARROW.

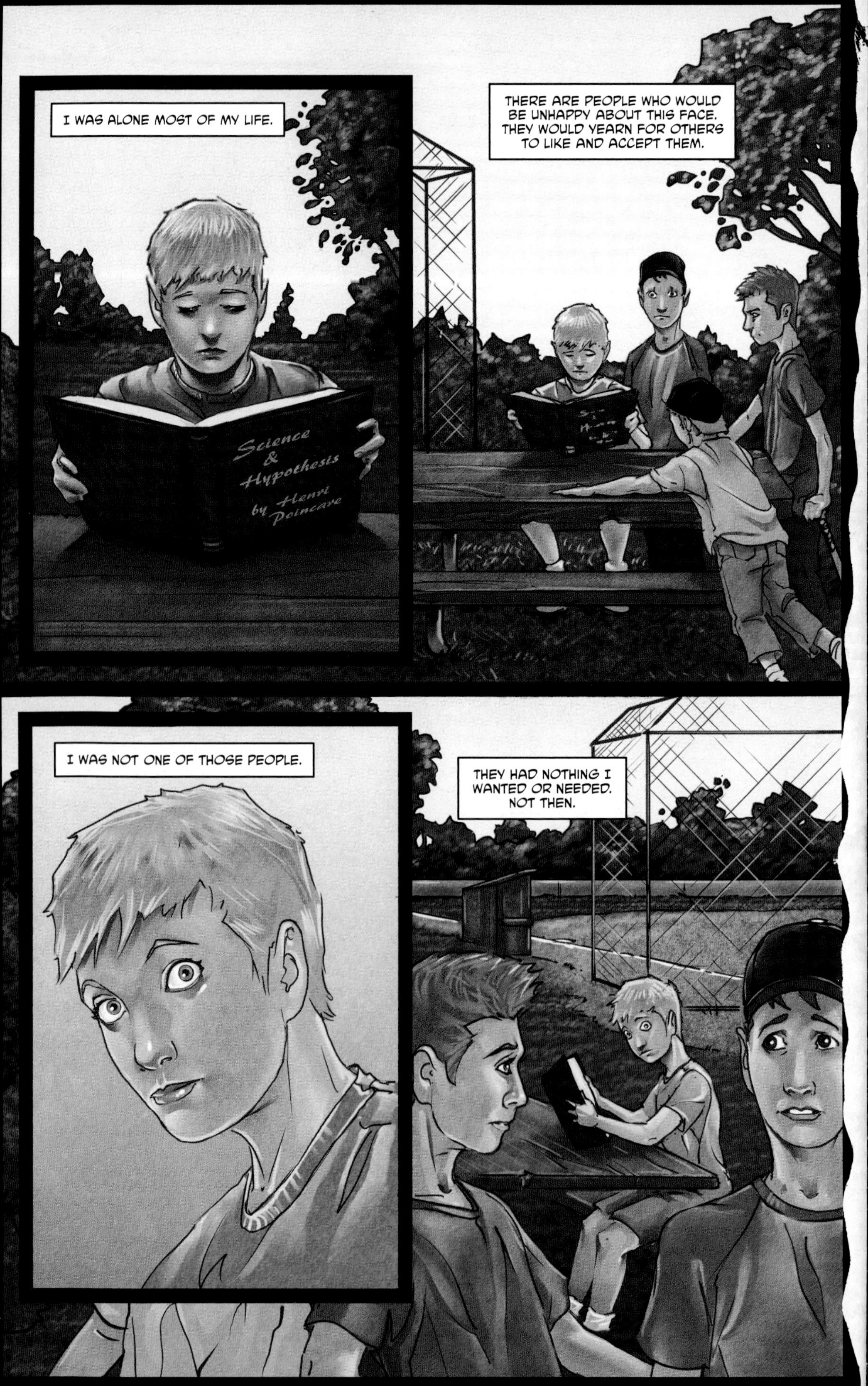
I WAS ALONE MOST OF MY LIFE.
Science & Hypothesis by Henri Poincare
THERE ARE PEOPLE WHO WOULD BE UNHAPPY ABOUT THIS FACE. THEY WOULD YEARN FOR OTHERS TO LIKE AND ACCEPT THEM.
I WAS NOT ONE OF THOSE PEOPLE.
THEY HAD NOTHING I WANTED OR NEEDED. NOT THEN.

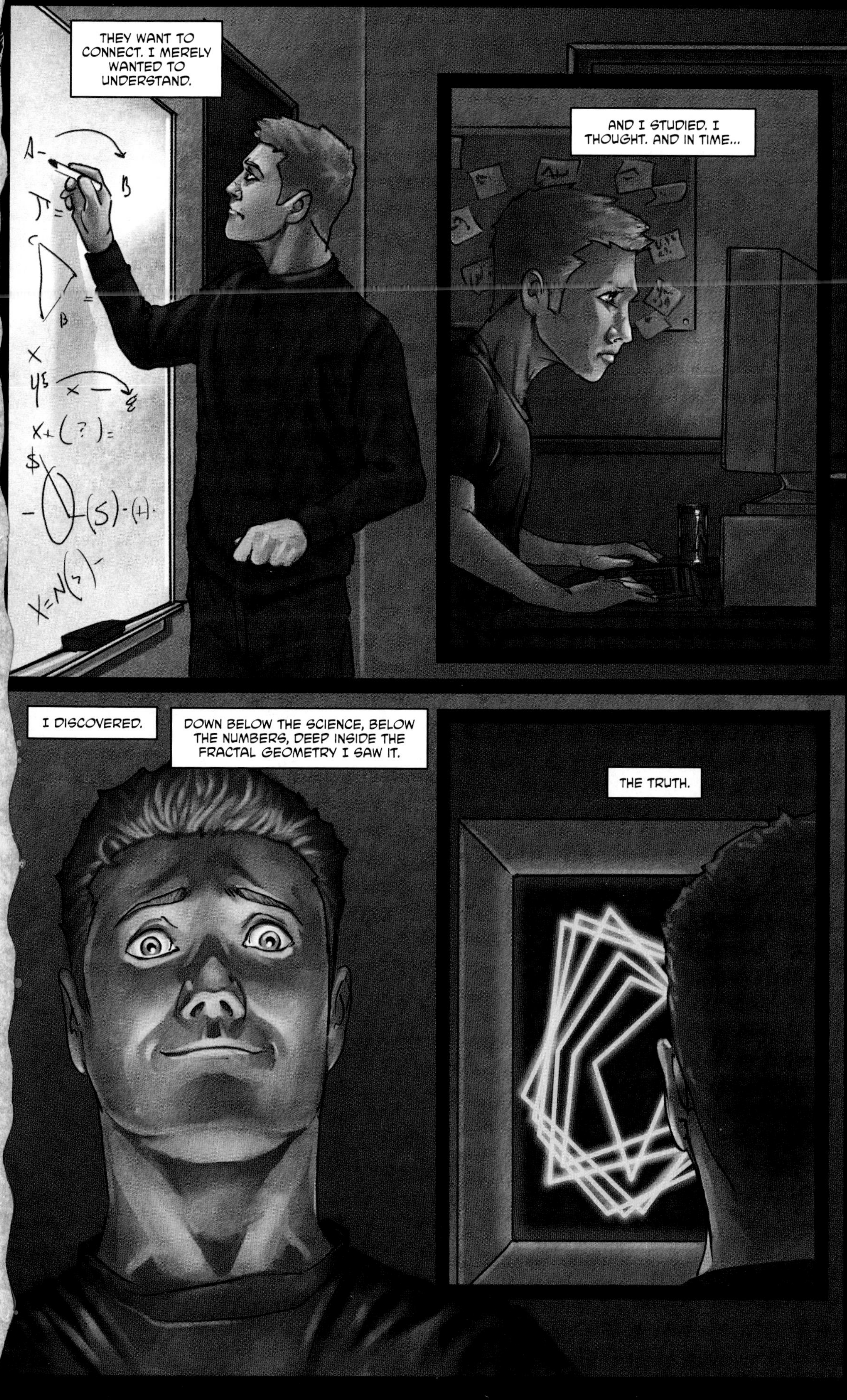
THEY WANT TO CONNECT. I MERELY WANTED TO UNDERSTAND.
AND I STUDIED. I THOUGHT. AND IN TIME...
I DISCOVERED.
DOWN BELOW THE SCIENCE, BELOW THE NUMBERS, DEEP INSIDE THE FRACTAL GEOMETRY I SAW IT.
THE TRUTH.

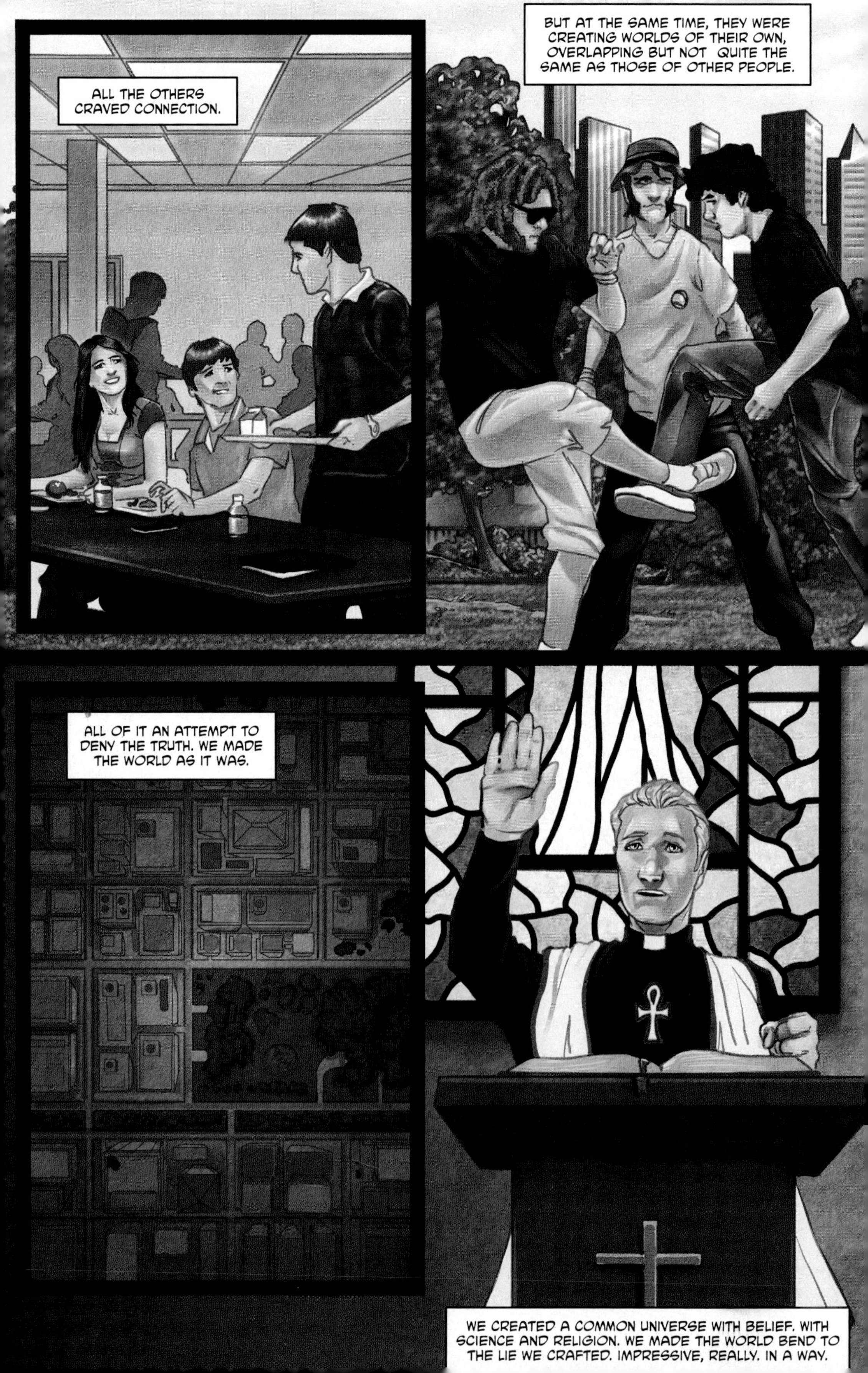
ALL THE OTHERS CRAVED CONNECTION.
BUT AT THE SAME TIME, THEY WERE CREATING WORLDS OF THEIR OWN, OVERLAPPING BUT NOT QUITE THE SAME AS THOSE OF OTHER PEOPLE.
ALL OF IT AN ATTEMPT TO DENY THE TRUTH. WE MADE THE WORLD AS IT WAS.
WE CREATED A COMMON UNIVERSE WITH BELIEF. WITH SCIENCE AND RELIGION. WE MADE THE WORLD BEND TO THE LIE WE CRAFTED. IMPRESSIVE, REALLY. IN A WAY.

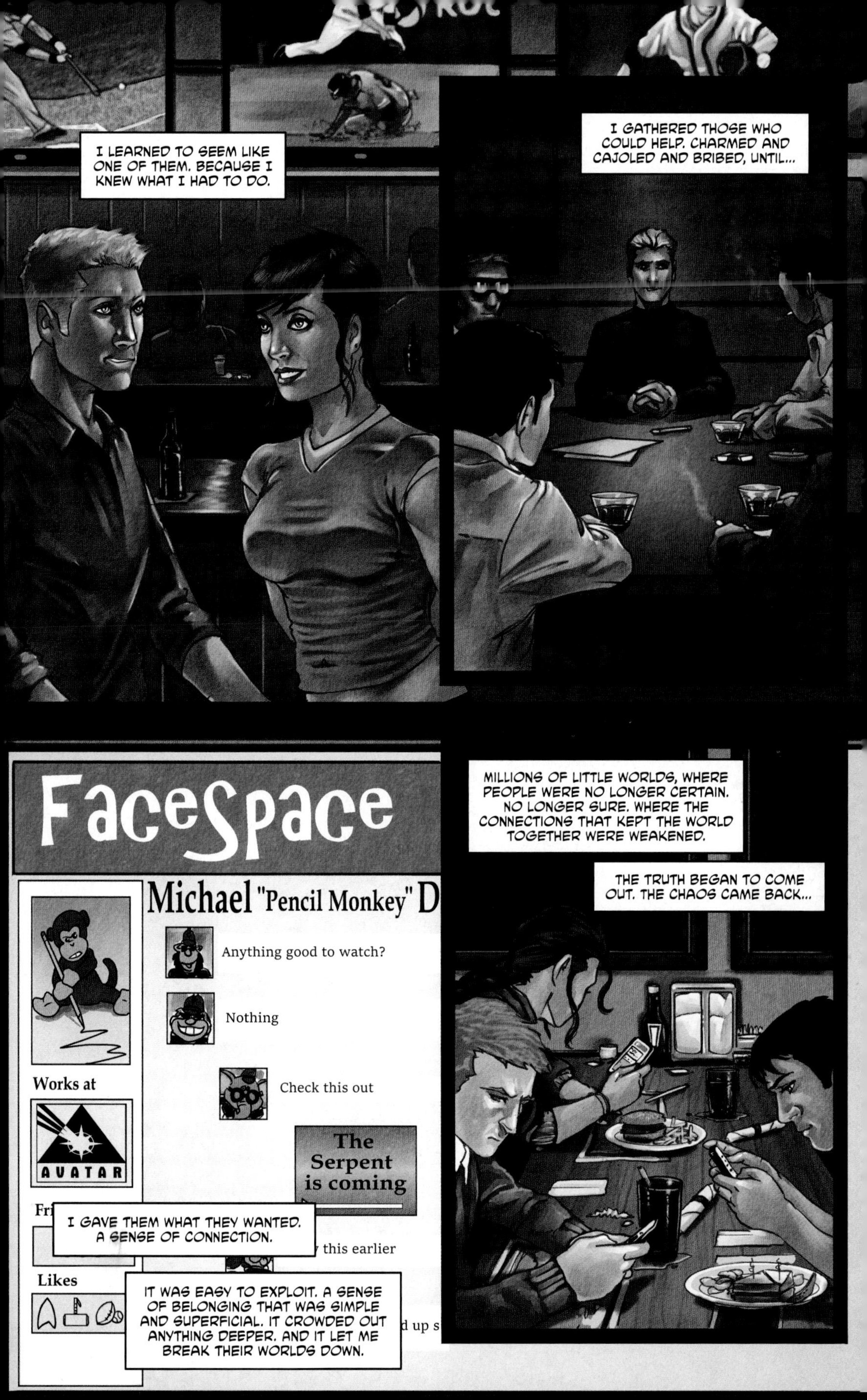
I LEARNED TO SEEM LIKE ONE OF THEM. BECAUSE I KNEW WHAT I HAD TO DO.
I GATHERED THOSE WHO COULD HELP. CHARMED AND CAJOLED AND BRIBED, UNTIL...
FaceSpace
Michael "Pencil Monkey" D
Anything good to watch?
Nothing
Check this out
The Serpent is coming
Works at
AVATAR
Likes
I GAVE THEM WHAT THEY WANTED. A SENSE OF CONNECTION.
IT WAS EASY TO EXPLOIT. A SENSE OF BELONGING THAT WAS SIMPLE AND SUPERFICIAL. IT CROWDED OUT ANYTHING DEEPER. AND IT LET ME BREAK THEIR WORLDS DOWN.
MILLIONS OF LITTLE WORLDS, WHERE PEOPLE WERE NO LONGER CERTAIN. NO LONGER SURE. WHERE THE CONNECTIONS THAT KEPT THE WORLD TOGETHER WERE WEAKENED.
THE TRUTH BEGAN TO COME OUT. THE CHAOS CAME BACK...

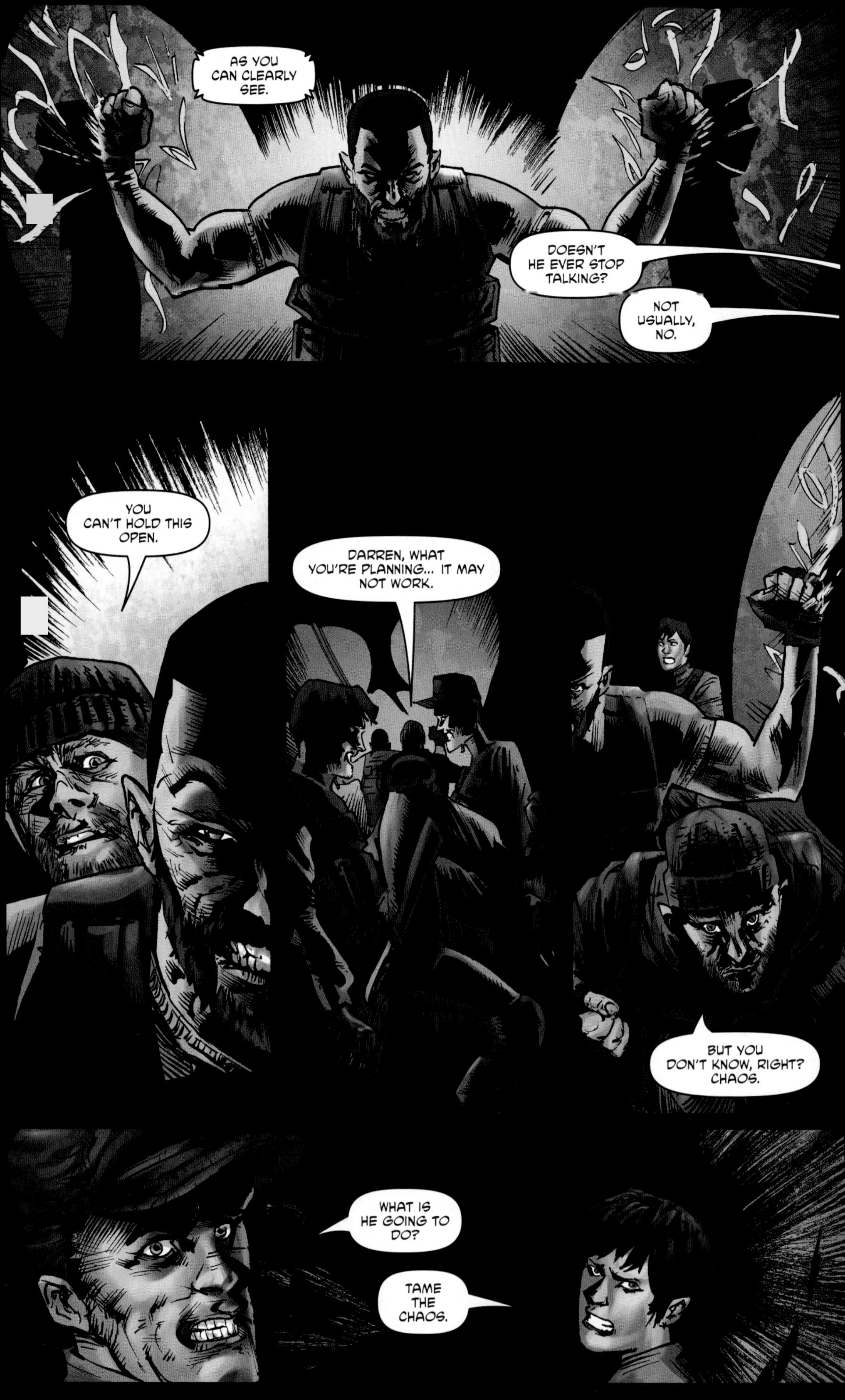
AS YOU CAN CLEARLY SEE.
DOESN'T HE EVER STOP TALKING?
NOT USUALLY, NO.
YOU CAN'T HOLD THIS OPEN.
DARREN, WHAT YOU'RE PLANNING... IT MAY NOT WORK.
BUT YOU DON'T KNOW, RIGHT? CHAOS.
WHAT IS HE GOING TO DO?
TAME THE CHAOS.

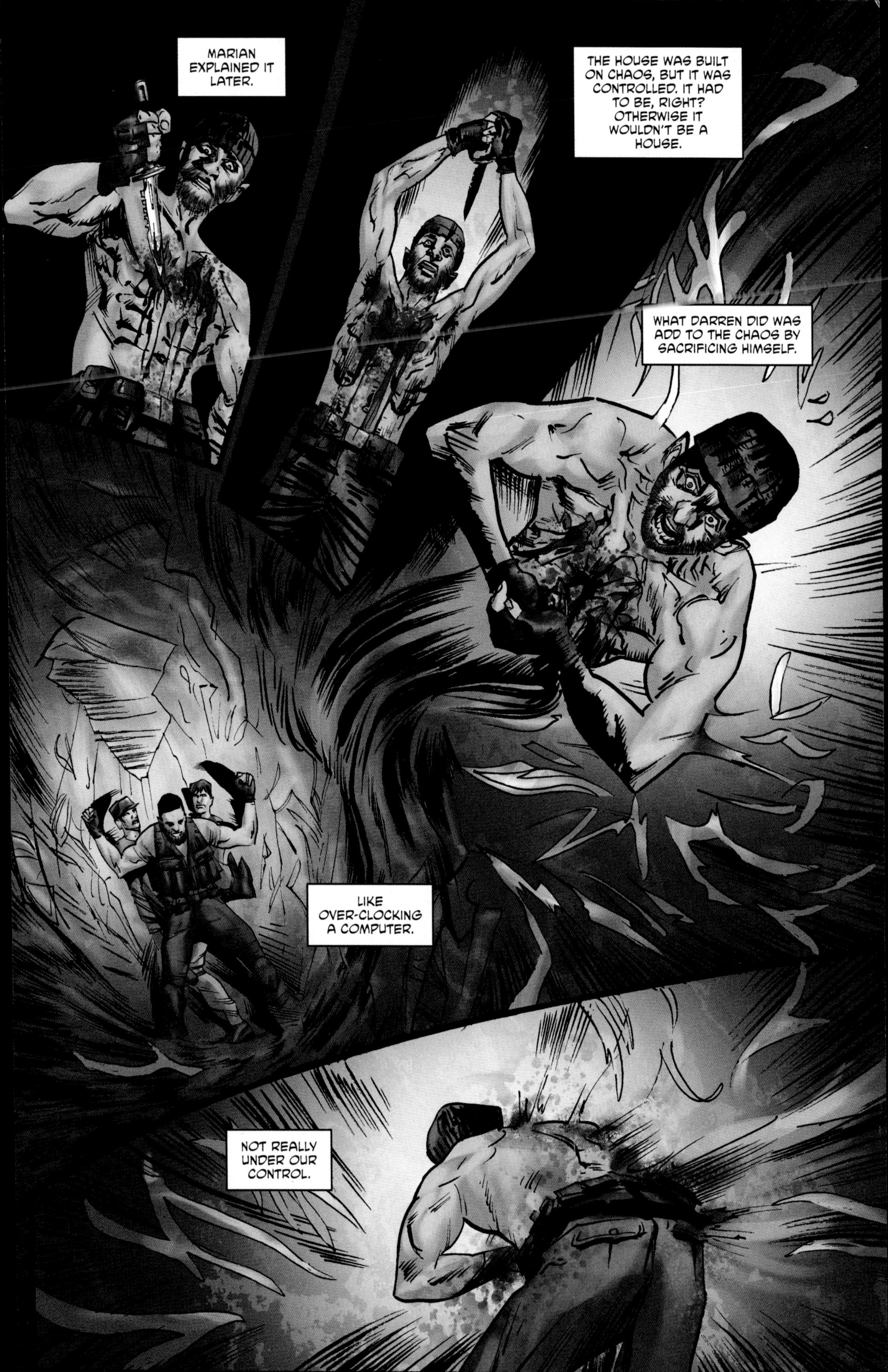
MARIAN EXPLAINED IT LATER.
THE HOUSE WAS BUILT ON CHAOS, BUT IT WAS CONTROLLED. IT HAD TO BE, RIGHT? OTHERWISE IT WOULDN'T BE A HOUSE.
WHAT DARREN DID WAS ADD TO THE CHAOS BY SACRIFICING HIMSELF.
LIKE OVER-CLOCKING A COMPUTER.
NOT REALLY UNDER OUR CONTROL.

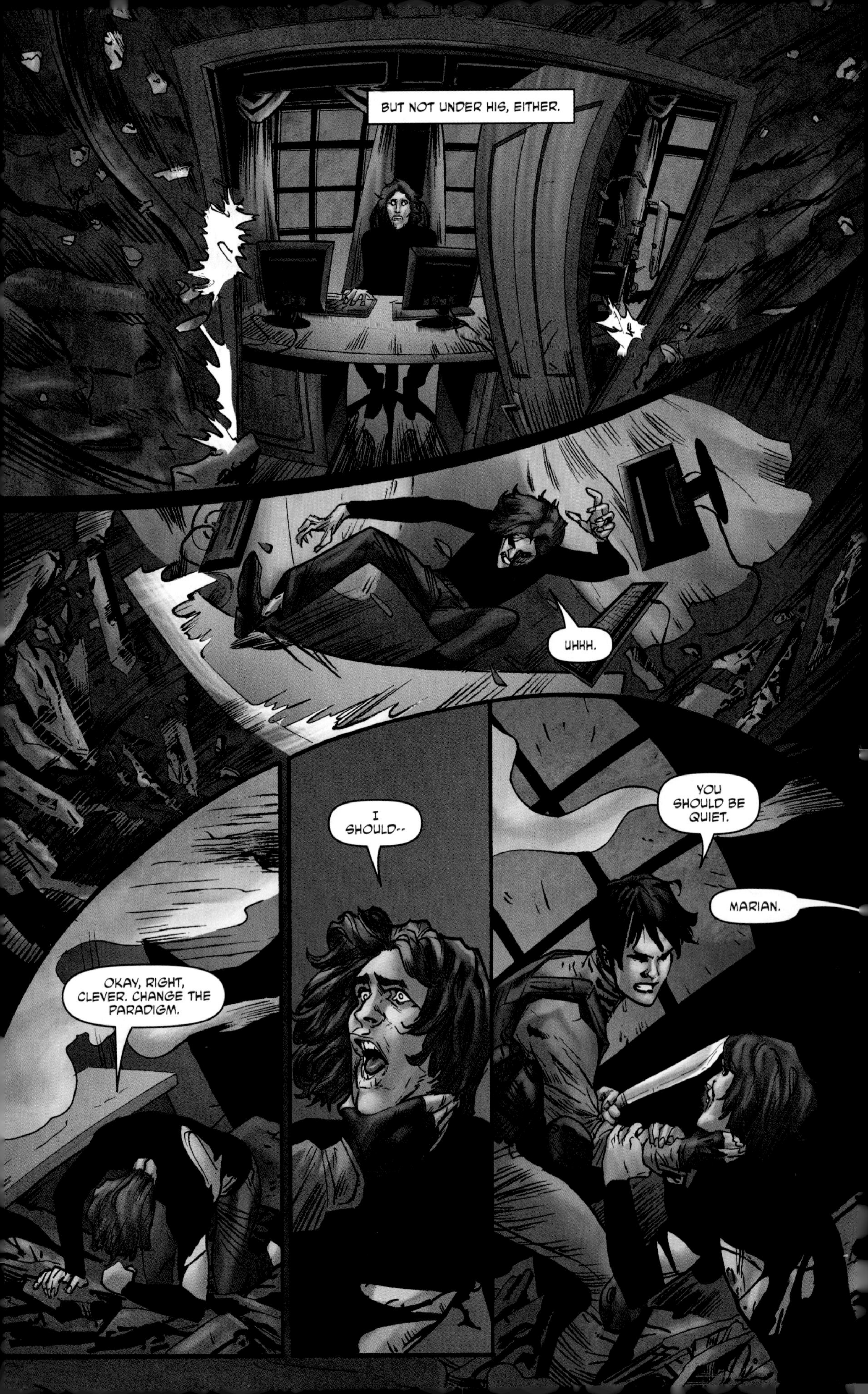
BUT NOT UNDER HIS, EITHER.
UHHH.
OKAY, RIGHT, CLEVER. CHANGE THE PARADIGM.
I SHOULD--
YOU SHOULD BE QUIET.
MARIAN.

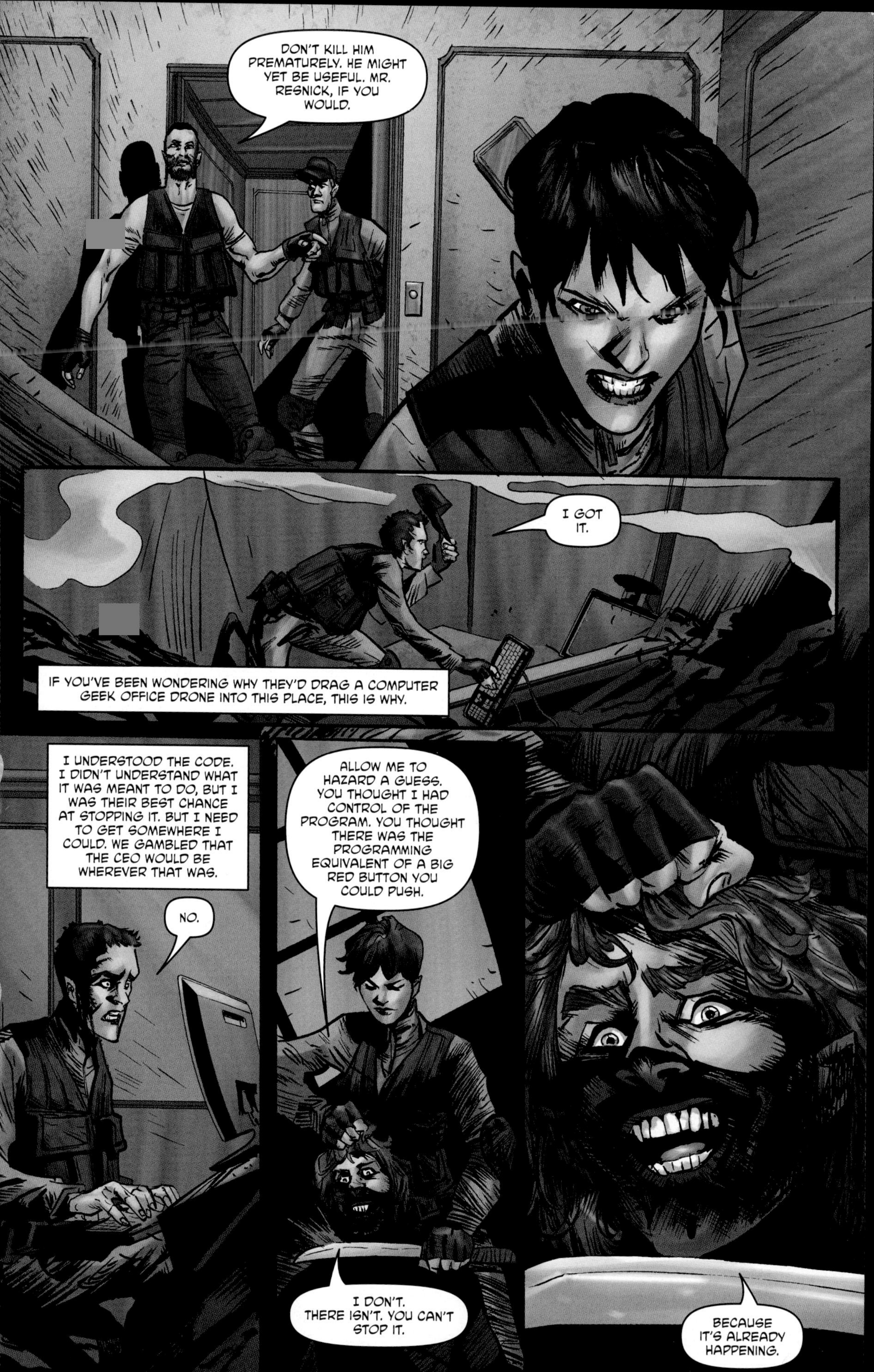
DON'T KILL HIM PREMATURELY. HE MIGHT YET BE USEFUL. MR. RESNICK, IF YOU WOULD.
I GOT IT.
IF YOU'VE BEEN WONDERING WHY THEY'D DRAG A COMPUTER GEEK OFFICE DRONE INTO THIS PLACE, THIS IS WHY.
I UNDERSTOOD THE CODE. I DIDN'T UNDERSTAND WHAT IT WAS MEANT TO DO, BUT I WAS THEIR BEST CHANCE AT STOPPING IT. BUT I NEED TO GET SOMEWHERE I COULD. WE GAMBLED THAT THE CEO WOULD BE WHEREVER THAT WAS.
NO.
ALLOW ME TO HAZARD A GUESS. YOU THOUGHT I HAD CONTROL OF THE PROGRAM. YOU THOUGHT THERE WAS THE PROGRAMMING EQUIVALENT OF A BIG RED BUTTON YOU COULD PUSH.
I DON'T. THERE ISN'T. YOU CAN'T STOP IT.
BECAUSE IT'S ALREADY HAPPENING.

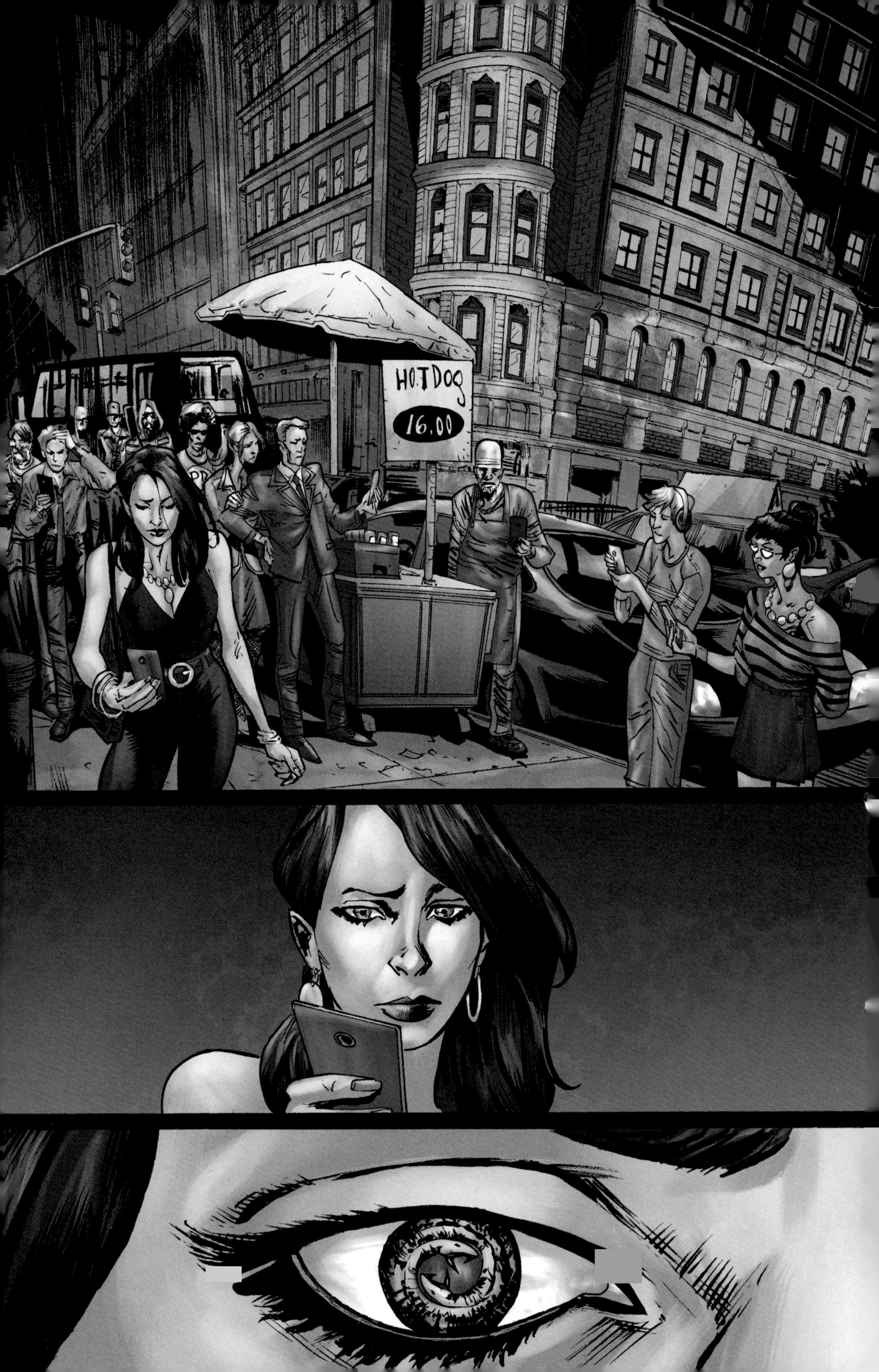
HOTDOG
16.00

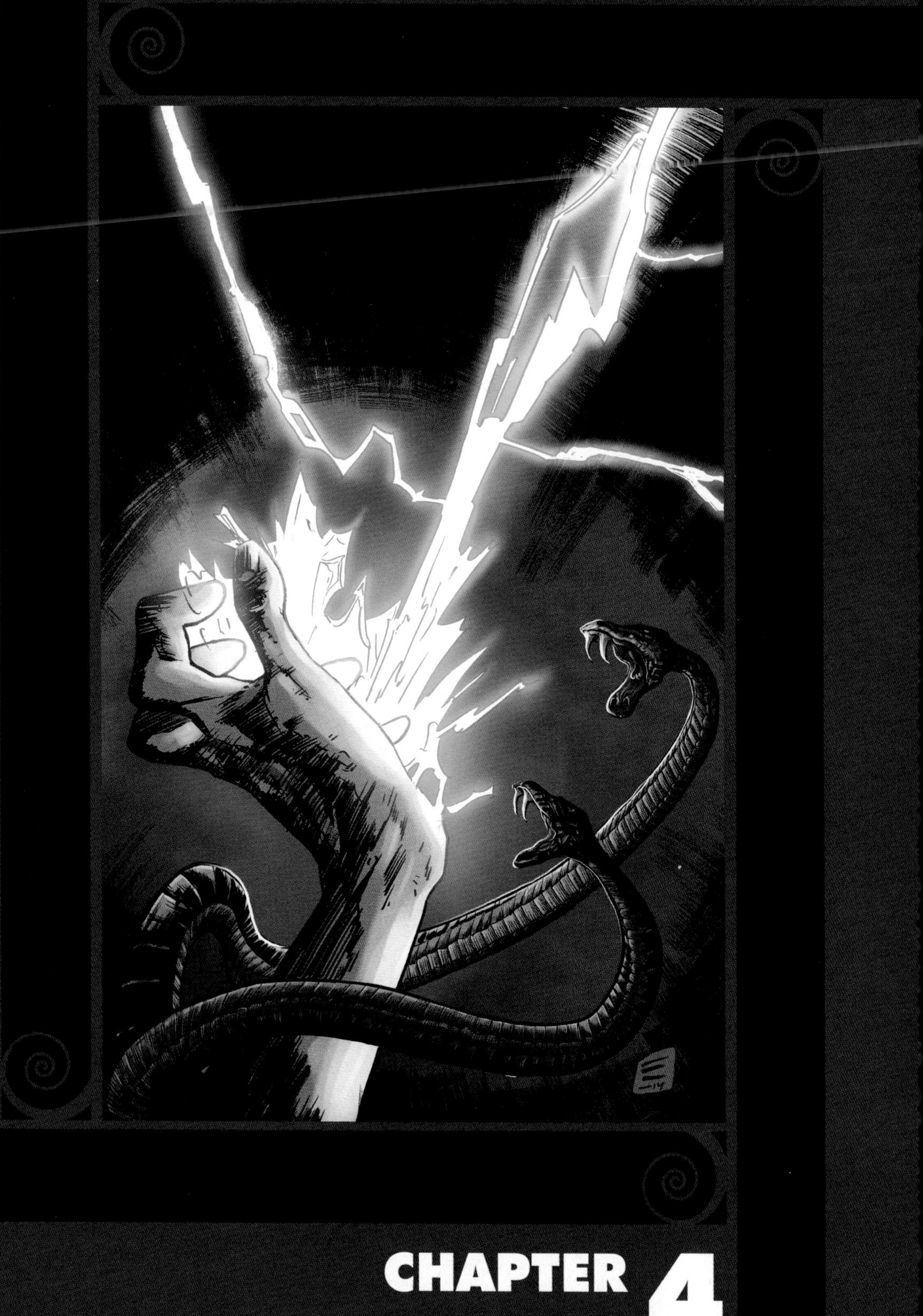

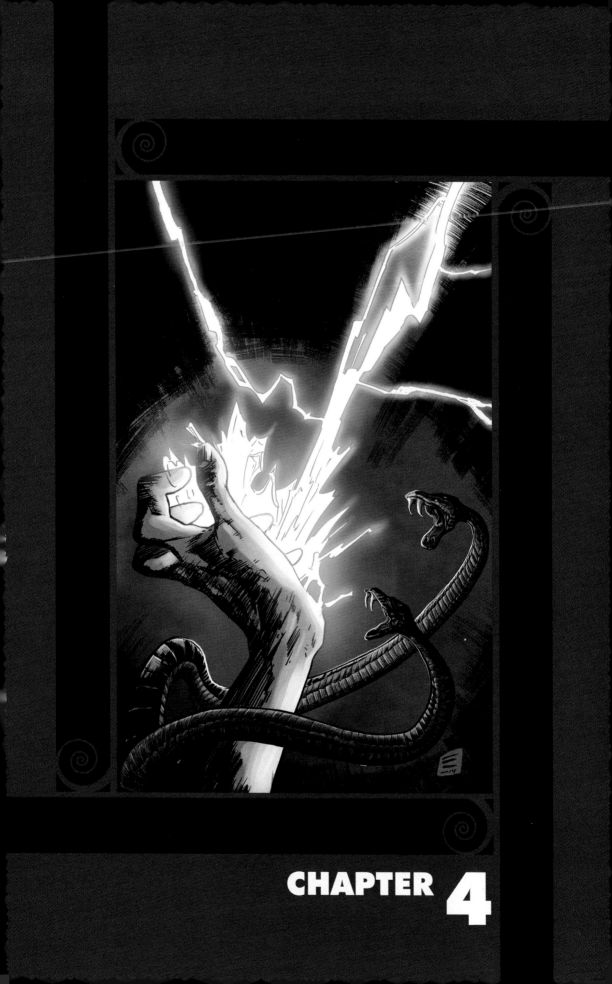

# CHAPTER 4

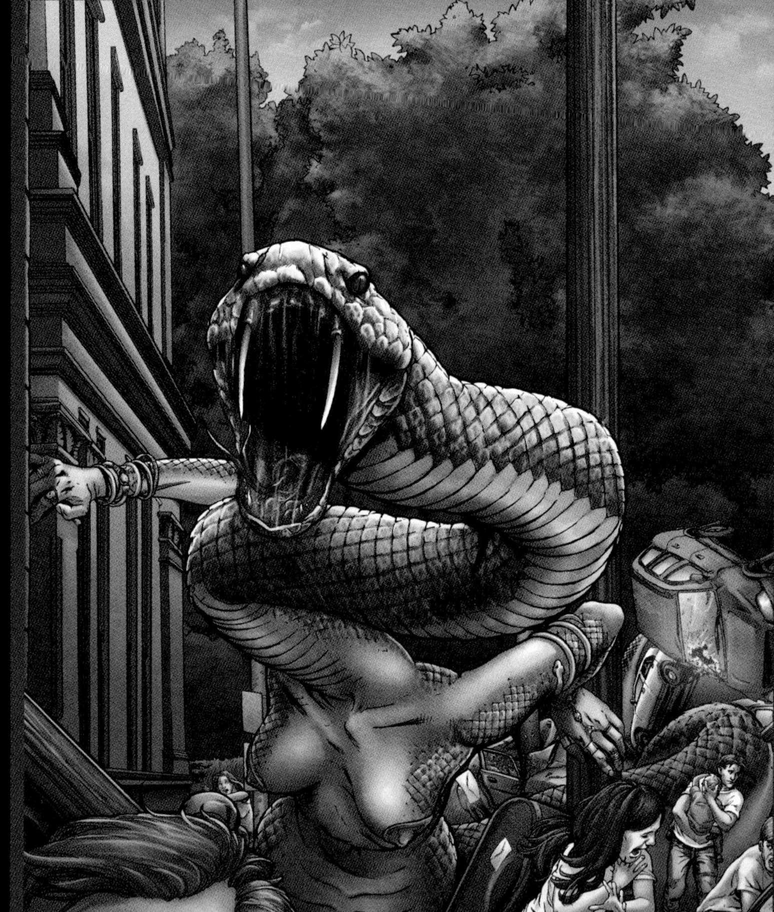

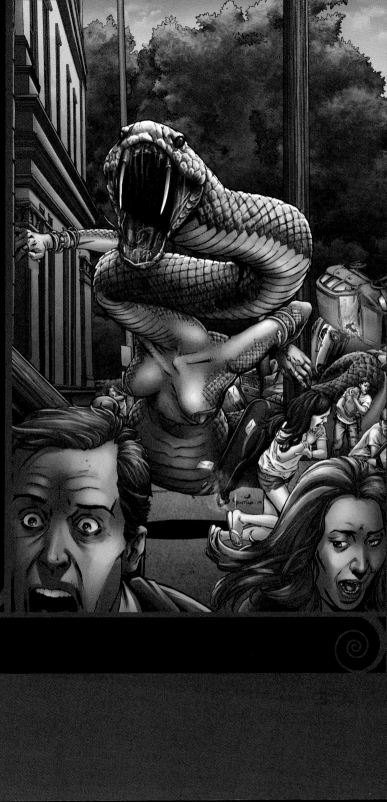

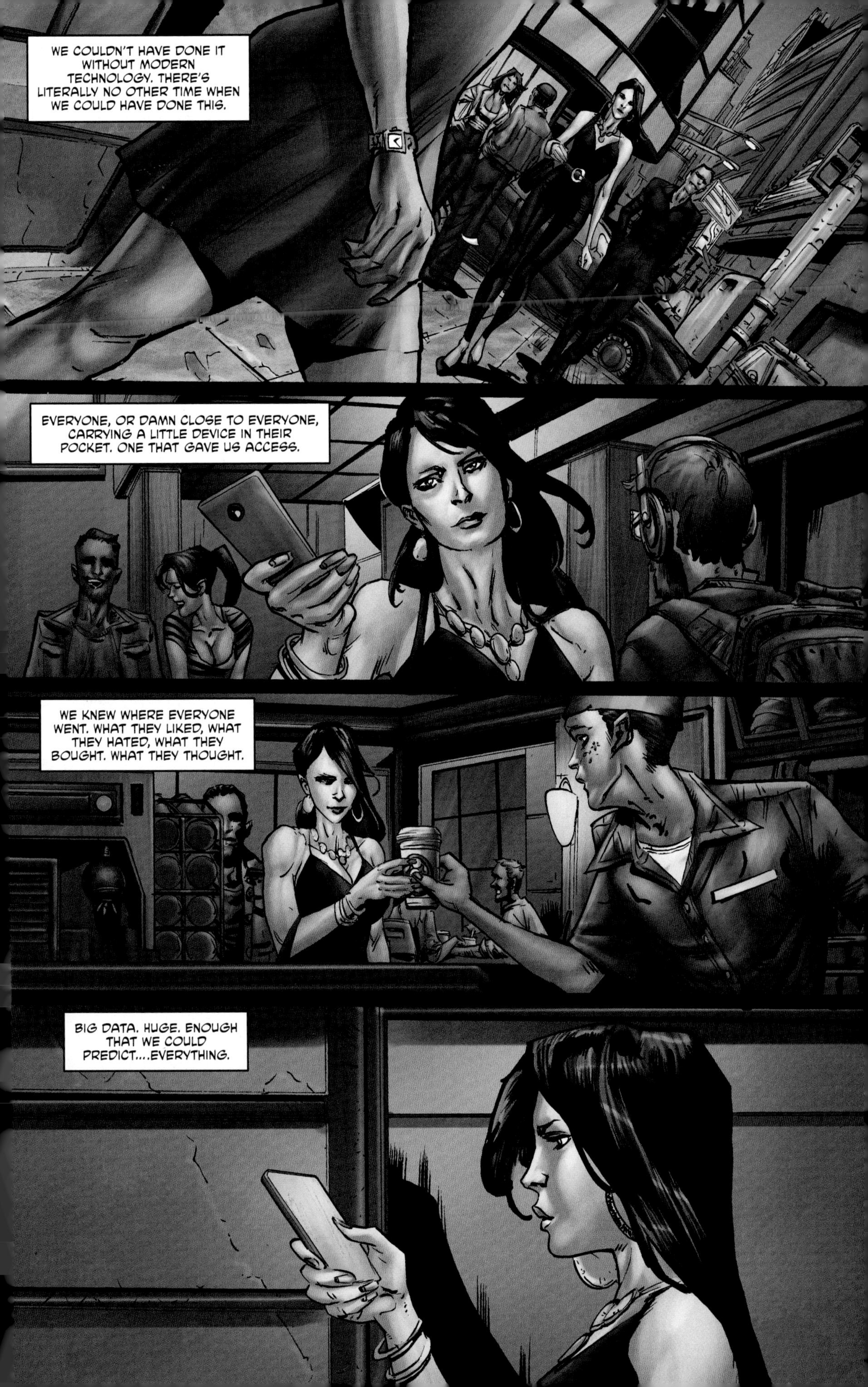
WE COULDN'T HAVE DONE IT WITHOUT MODERN TECHNOLOGY. THERE'S LITERALLY NO OTHER TIME WHEN WE COULD HAVE DONE THIS.
EVERYONE, OR DAMN CLOSE TO EVERYONE, CARRYING A LITTLE DEVICE IN THEIR POCKET. ONE THAT GAVE US ACCESS.
WE KNEW WHERE EVERYONE WENT. WHAT THEY LIKED, WHAT THEY HATED, WHAT THEY BOUGHT. WHAT THEY THOUGHT.
BIG DATA. HUGE. ENOUGH THAT WE COULD PREDICT....EVERYTHING.

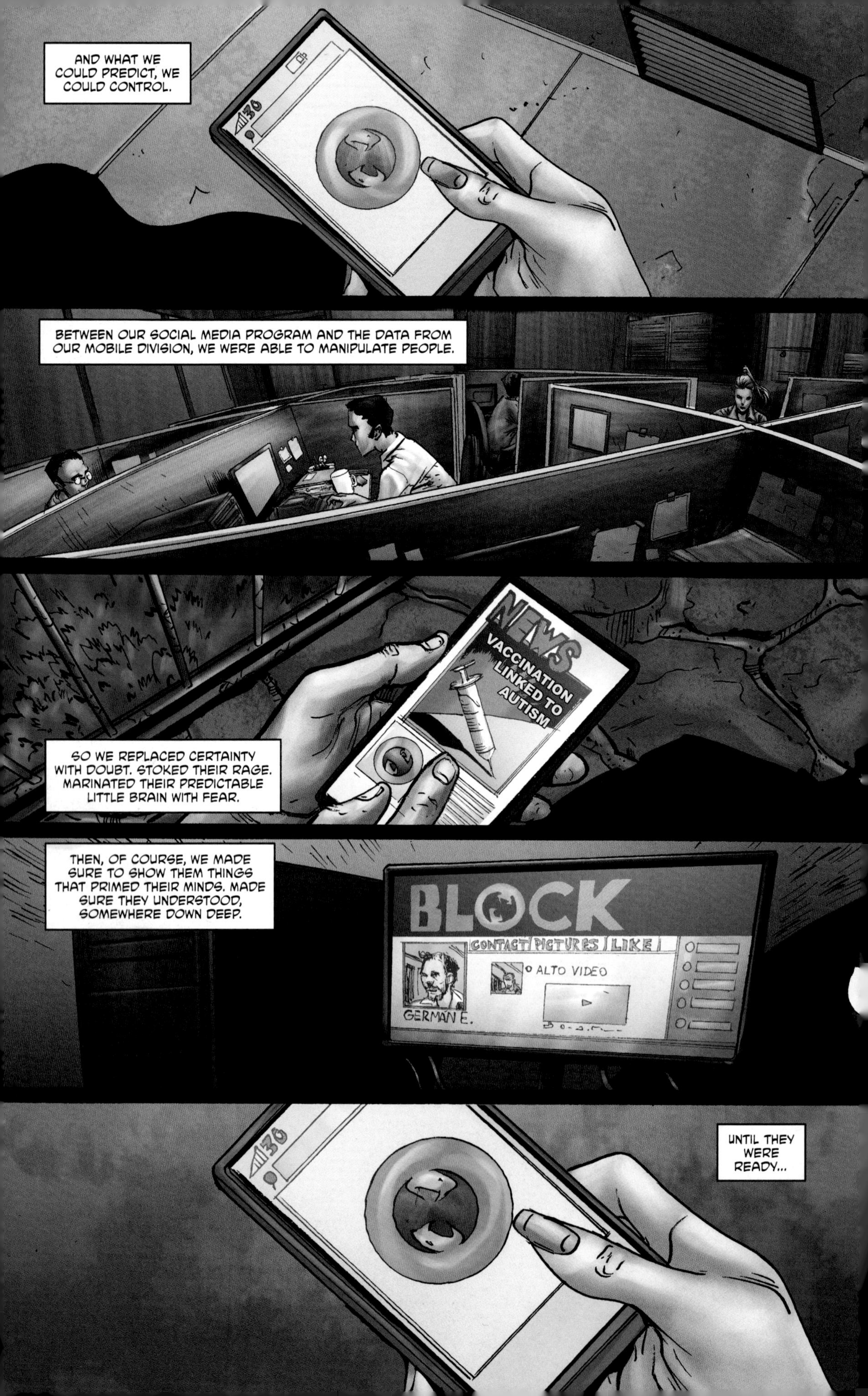
AND WHAT WE COULD PREDICT, WE COULD CONTROL.
BETWEEN OUR SOCIAL MEDIA PROGRAM AND THE DATA FROM OUR MOBILE DIVISION, WE WERE ABLE TO MANIPULATE PEOPLE.
NEWS
VACCINATION LINKED TO AUTISM
SO WE REPLACED CERTAINTY WITH DOUBT. STOKED THEIR RAGE. MARINATED THEIR PREDICTABLE LITTLE BRAIN WITH FEAR.
THEN, OF COURSE, WE MADE SURE TO SHOW THEM THINGS THAT PRIMED THEIR MINDS. MADE SURE THEY UNDERSTOOD, SOMEWHERE DOWN DEEP.
BLOCK
CONTACT PICTURES LIKE
ALTO VIDEO
GERMAN E.
UNTIL THEY WERE READY...

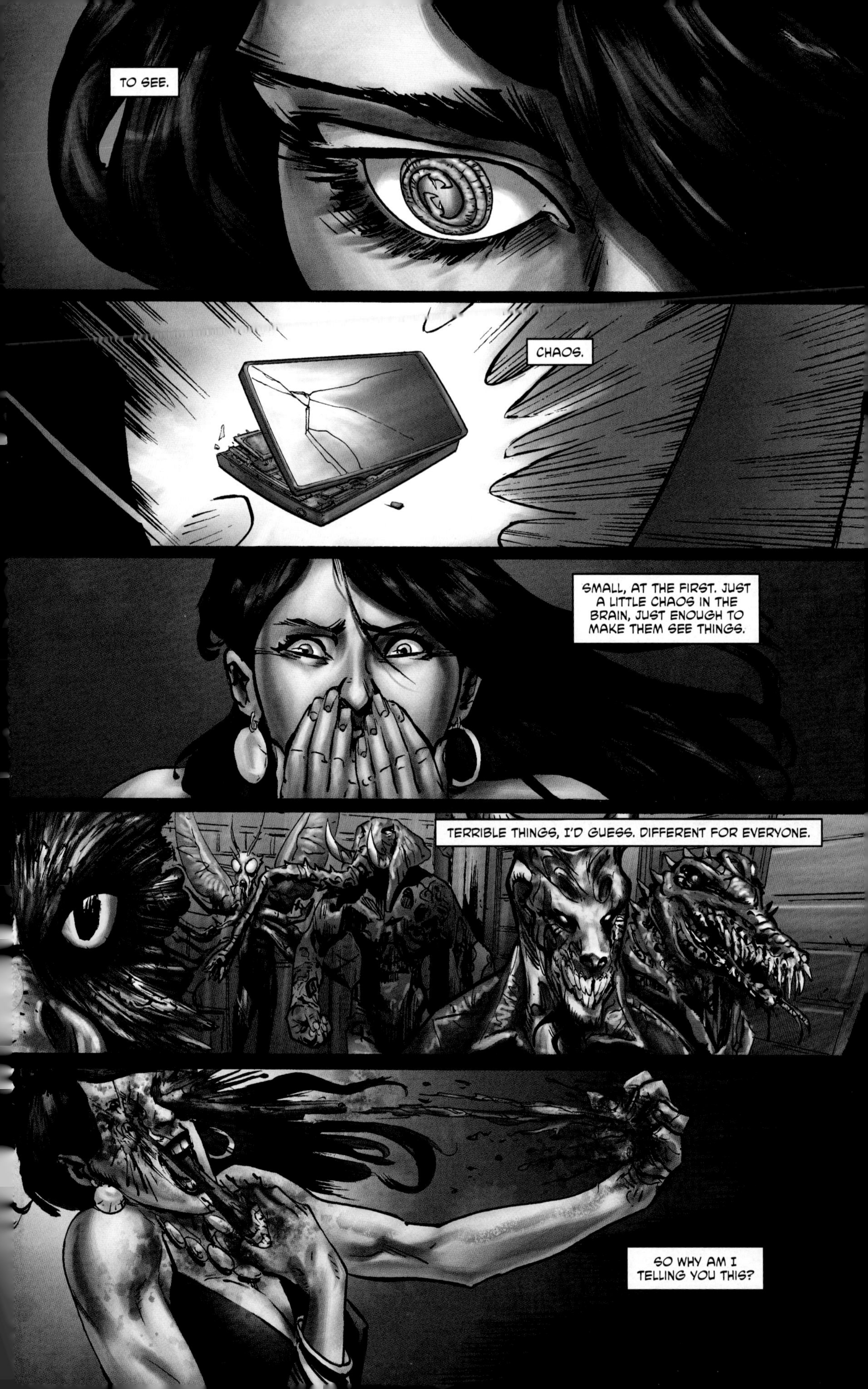
TO SEE.
CHAOS.
SMALL, AT THE FIRST. JUST A LITTLE CHAOS IN THE BRAIN, JUST ENOUGH TO MAKE THEM SEE THINGS.
TERRIBLE THINGS, I'D GUESS. DIFFERENT FOR EVERYONE.
SO WHY AM I TELLING YOU THIS?

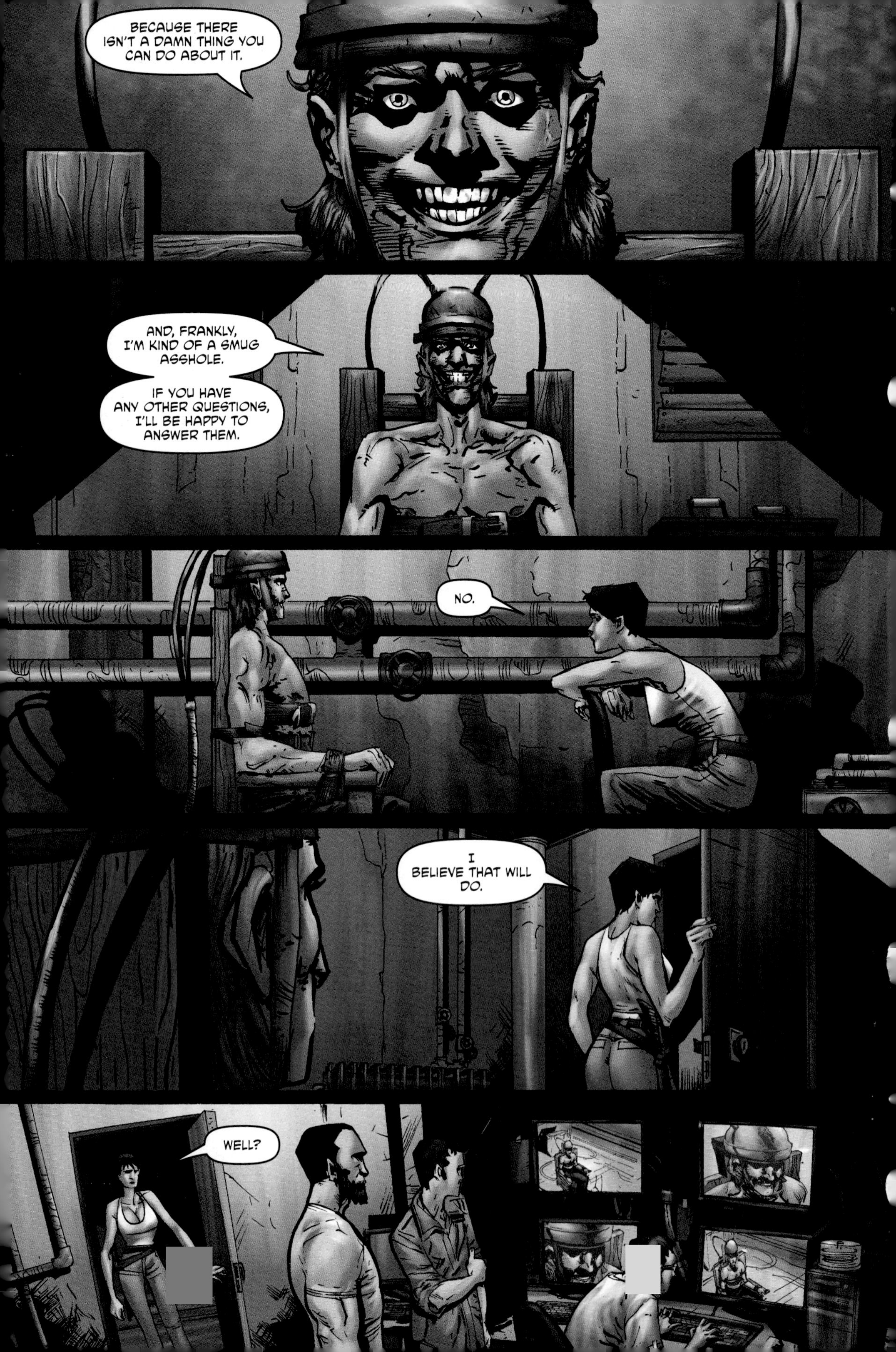
BECAUSE THERE ISN'T A DAMN THING YOU CAN DO ABOUT IT.
AND, FRANKLY, I'M KIND OF A SMUG ASSHOLE.
IF YOU HAVE ANY OTHER QUESTIONS, I'LL BE HAPPY TO ANSWER THEM.
NO.
I BELIEVE THAT WILL DO.
WELL?

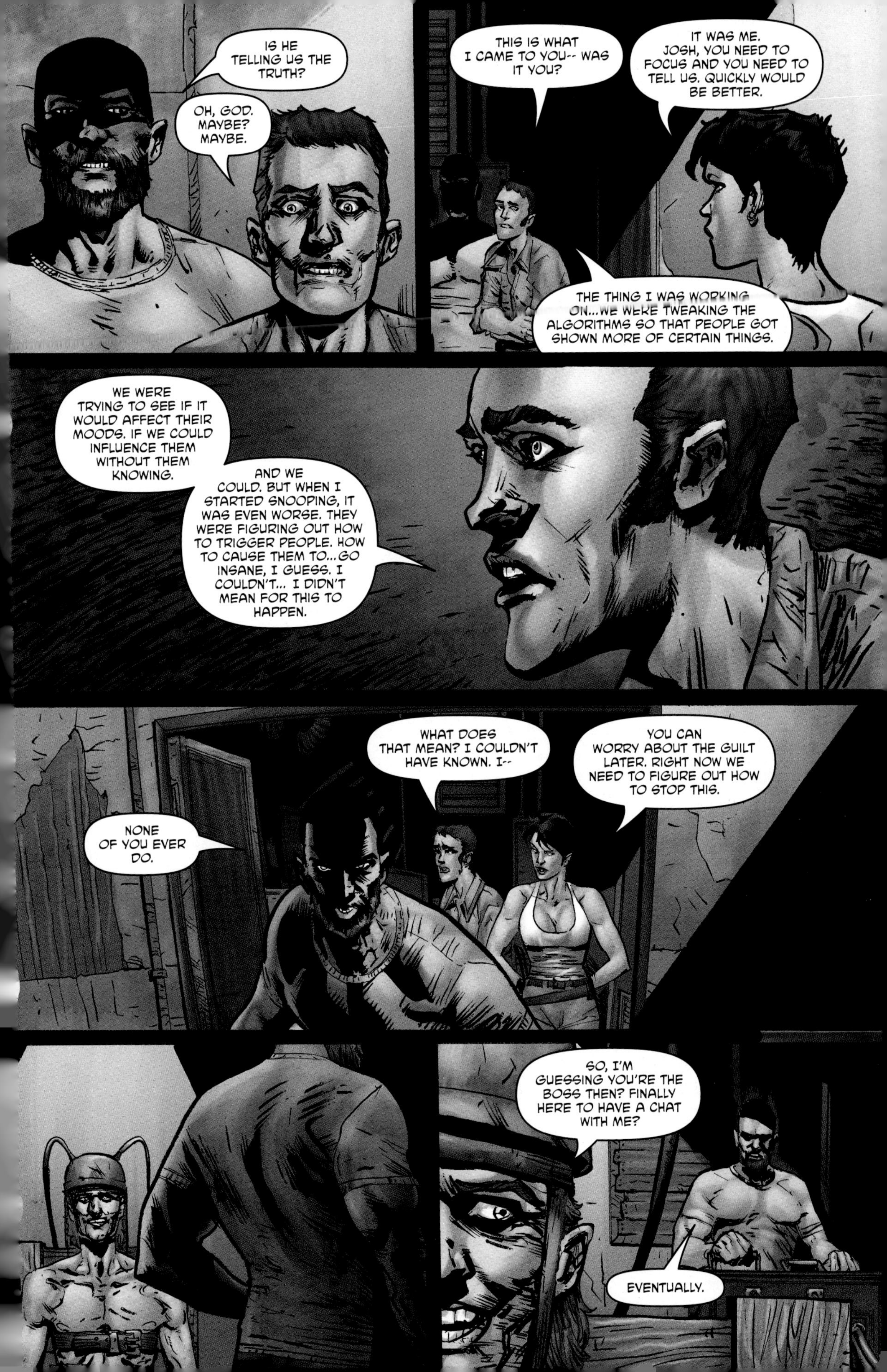
IS HE TELLING US THE TRUTH?
OH, GOD. MAYBE? MAYBE.
THIS IS WHAT I CAME TO YOU-- WAS IT YOU?
IT WAS ME. JOSH, YOU NEED TO FOCUS AND YOU NEED TO TELL US. QUICKLY WOULD BE BETTER.
THE THING I WAS WORKING ON...WE WERE TWEAKING THE ALGORITHMS SO THAT PEOPLE GOT SHOWN MORE OF CERTAIN THINGS.
WE WERE TRYING TO SEE IF IT WOULD AFFECT THEIR MOODS. IF WE COULD INFLUENCE THEM WITHOUT THEM KNOWING.
AND WE COULD. BUT WHEN I STARTED SNOOPING, IT WAS EVEN WORSE. THEY WERE FIGURING OUT HOW TO TRIGGER PEOPLE. HOW TO CAUSE THEM TO...GO INSANE, I GUESS. I COULDN'T... I DIDN'T MEAN FOR THIS TO HAPPEN.
NONE OF YOU EVER DO.
WHAT DOES THAT MEAN? I COULDN'T HAVE KNOWN. I--
YOU CAN WORRY ABOUT THE GUILT LATER. RIGHT NOW WE NEED TO FIGURE OUT HOW TO STOP THIS.
SO, I'M GUESSING YOU'RE THE BOSS THEN? FINALLY HERE TO HAVE A CHAT WITH ME?
EVENTUALLY.

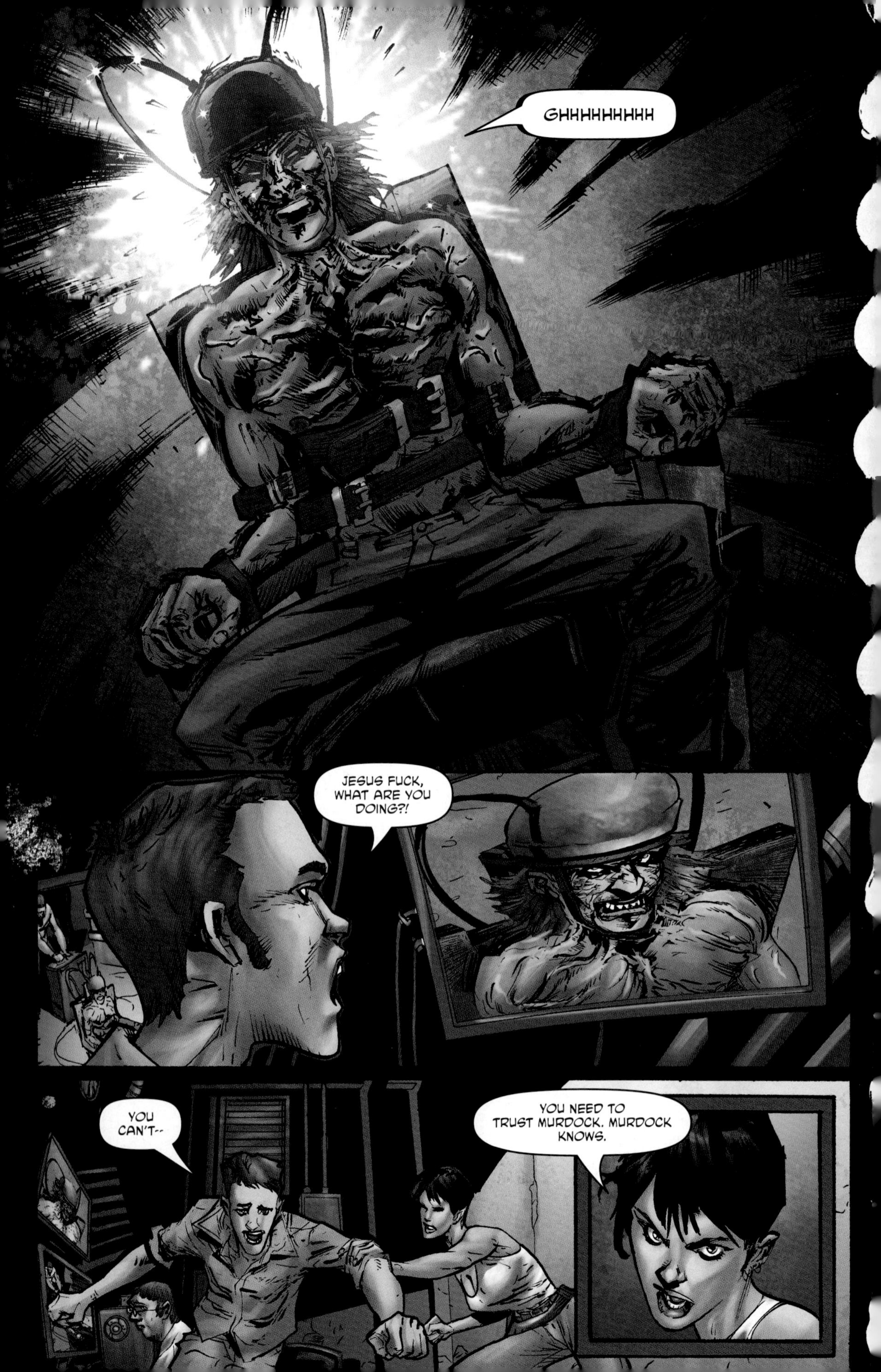
GHHHHHHHHH
JESUS FUCK, WHAT ARE YOU DOING?!
YOU CAN'T--
YOU NEED TO TRUST MURDOCK. MURDOCK KNOWS.

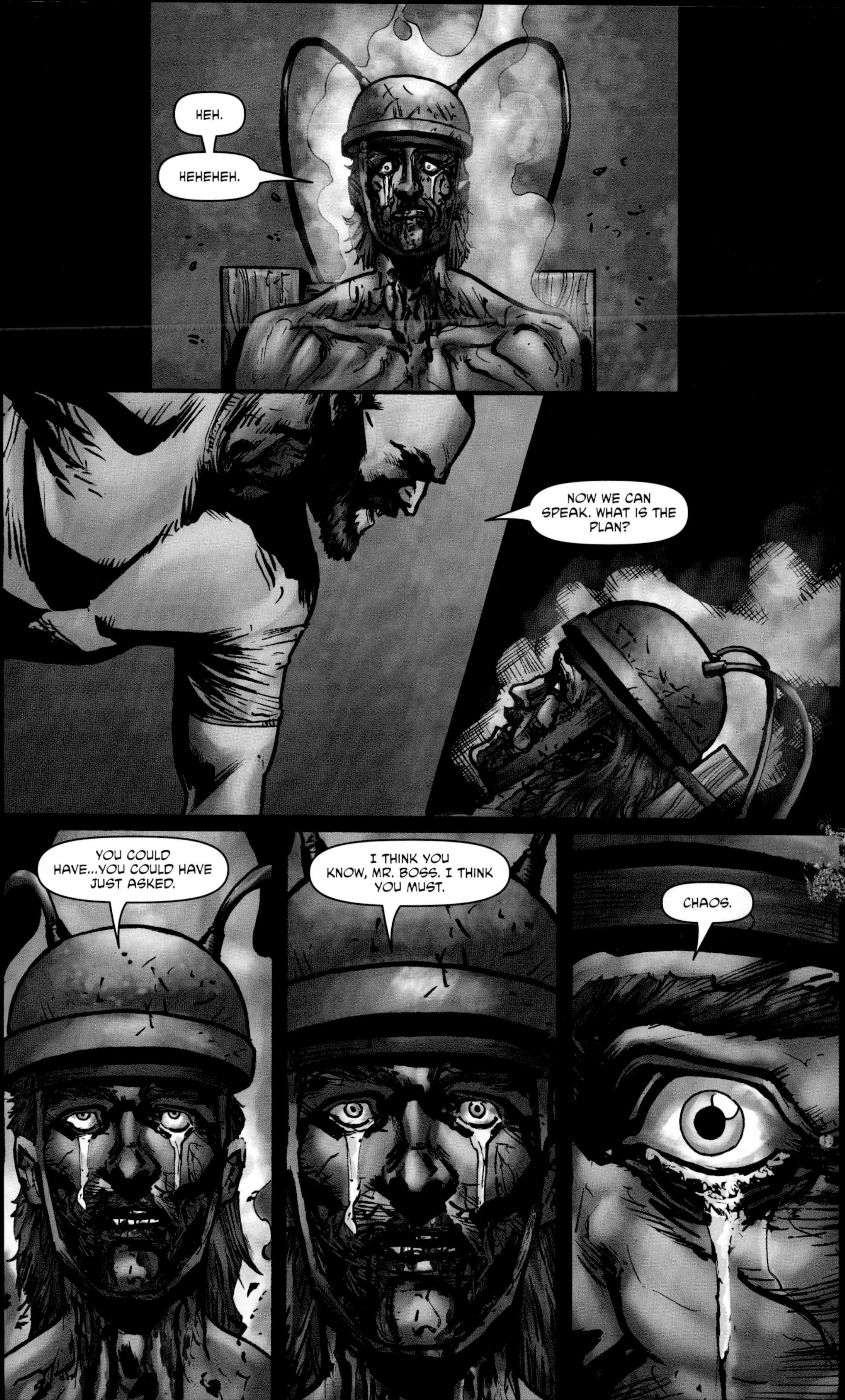
HEH.
HEHEHEH.
NOW WE CAN SPEAK. WHAT IS THE PLAN?
YOU COULD HAVE...YOU COULD HAVE JUST ASKED.
I THINK YOU KNOW, MR. BOSS. I THINK YOU MUST.
CHAOS.

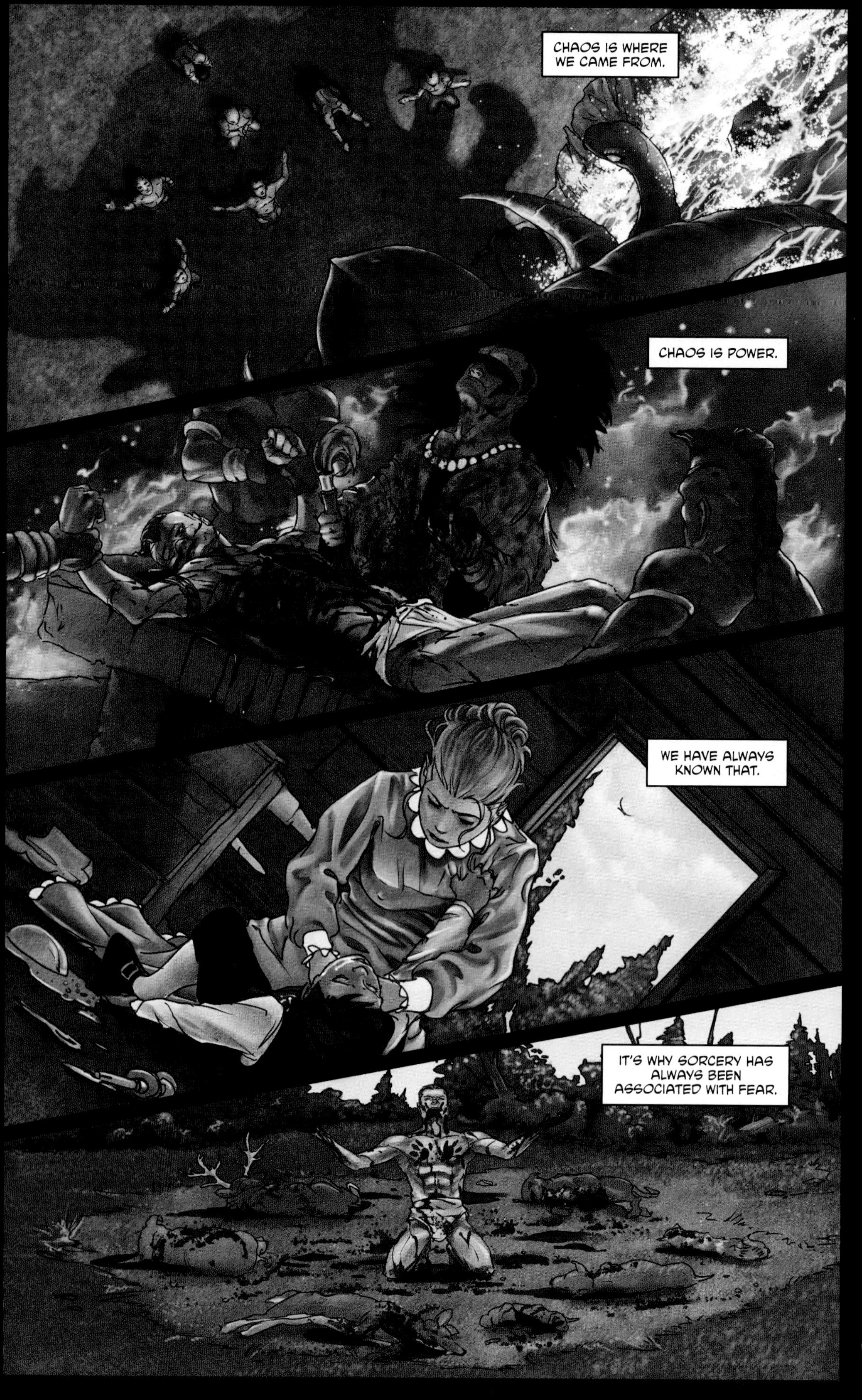
CHAOS IS WHERE WE CAME FROM.
CHAOS IS POWER.
WE HAVE ALWAYS KNOWN THAT.
IT'S WHY SORCERY HAS ALWAYS BEEN ASSOCIATED WITH FEAR.

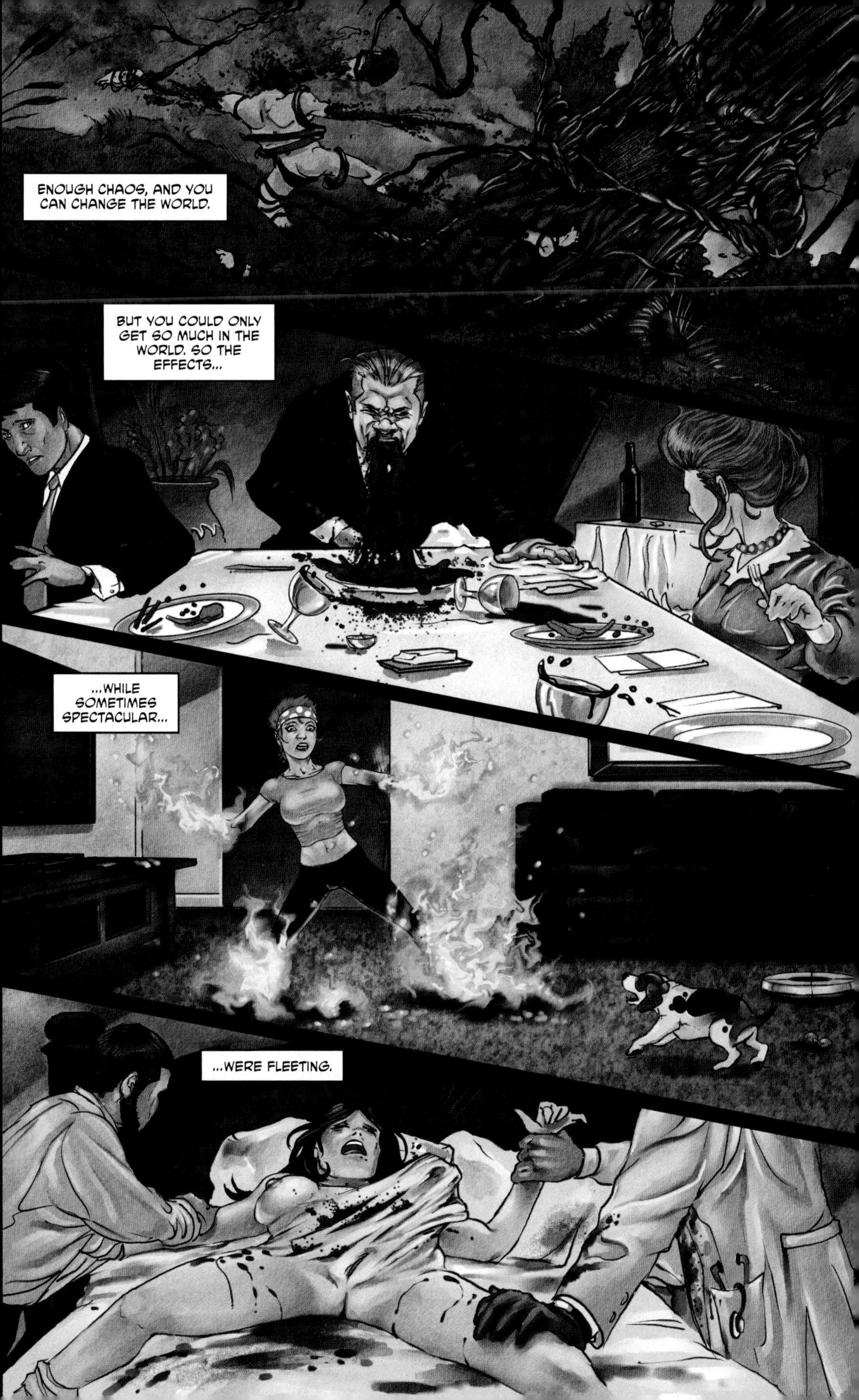
ENOUGH CHAOS, AND YOU CAN CHANGE THE WORLD.
BUT YOU COULD ONLY GET SO MUCH IN THE WORLD. SO THE EFFECTS...
...WHILE SOMETIMES SPECTACULAR...
...WERE FLEETING.

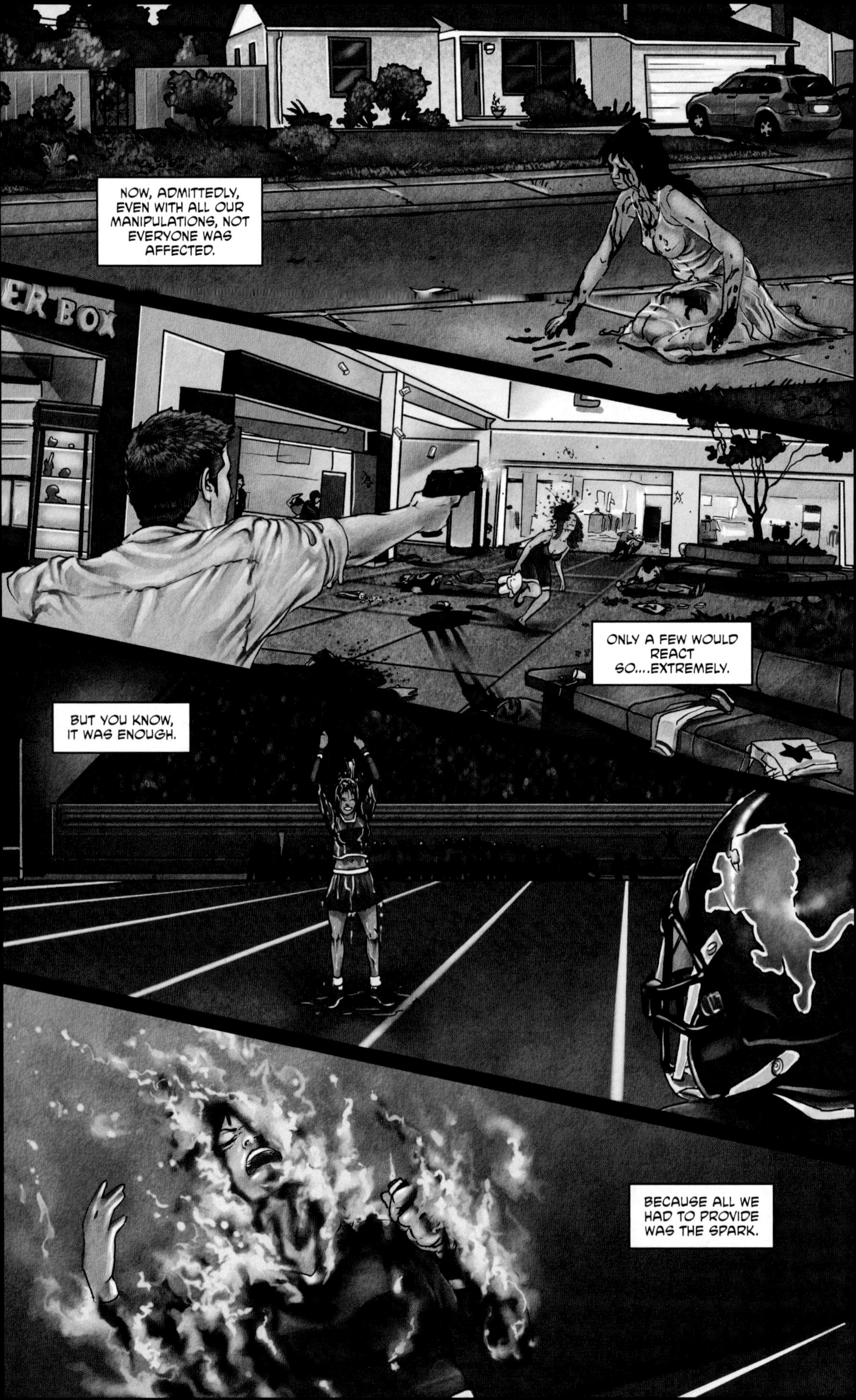
NOW, ADMITTEDLY, EVEN WITH ALL OUR MANIPULATIONS, NOT EVERYONE WAS AFFECTED.
ER BOX
ONLY A FEW WOULD REACT SO....EXTREMELY.
BUT YOU KNOW, IT WAS ENOUGH.
BECAUSE ALL WE HAD TO PROVIDE WAS THE SPARK.

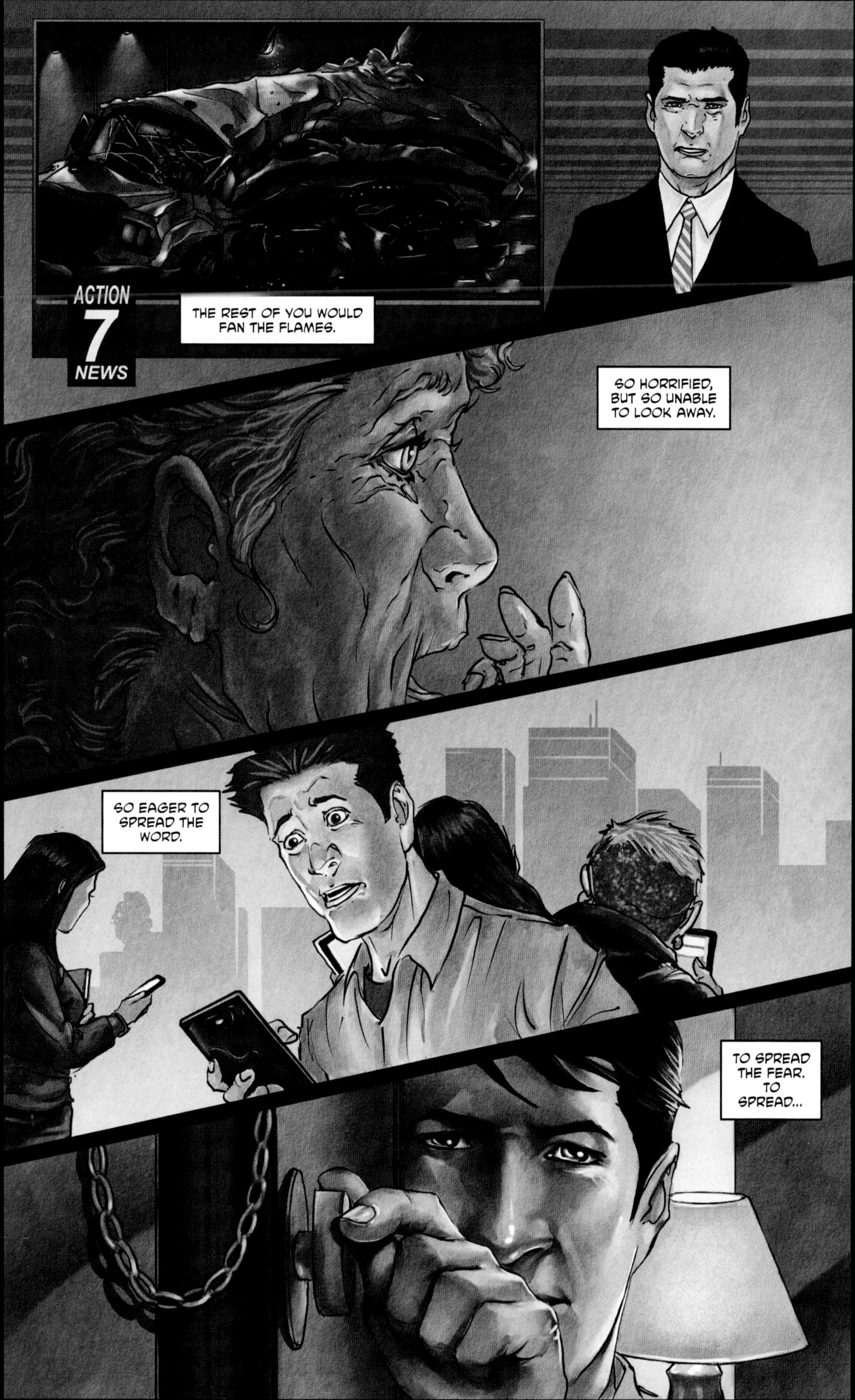
ACTION 7 NEWS
THE REST OF YOU WOULD FAN THE FLAMES.
SO HORRIFIED, BUT SO UNABLE TO LOOK AWAY.
SO EAGER TO SPREAD THE WORD.
TO SPREAD THE FEAR. TO SPREAD...

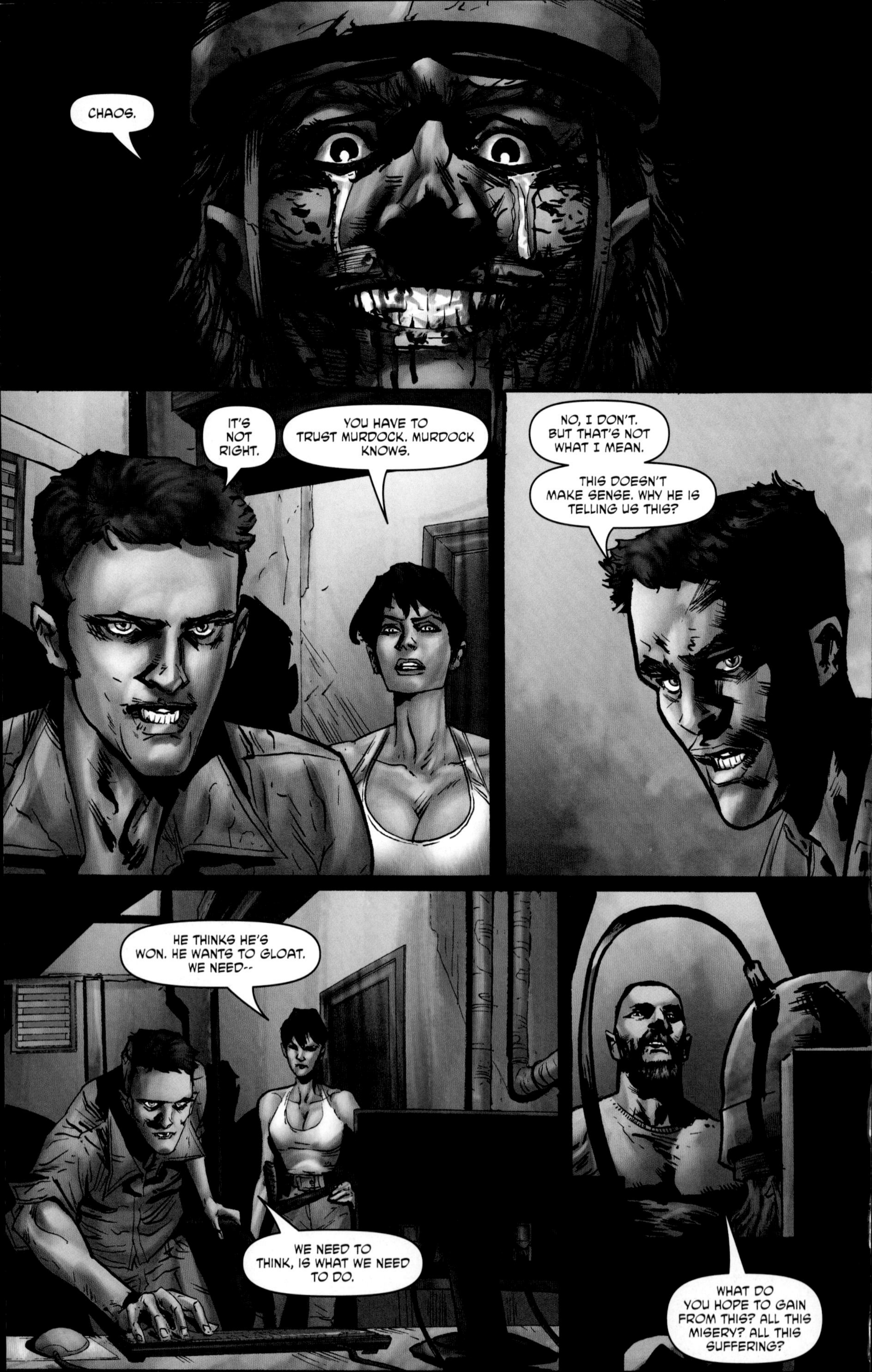
CHAOS.
IT'S NOT RIGHT.
YOU HAVE TO TRUST MURDOCK. MURDOCK KNOWS.
NO, I DON'T. BUT THAT'S NOT WHAT I MEAN.
THIS DOESN'T MAKE SENSE. WHY HE IS TELLING US THIS?
HE THINKS HE'S WON. HE WANTS TO GLOAT. WE NEED--
WE NEED TO THINK, IS WHAT WE NEED TO DO.
WHAT DO YOU HOPE TO GAIN FROM THIS? ALL THIS MISERY? ALL THIS SUFFERING?

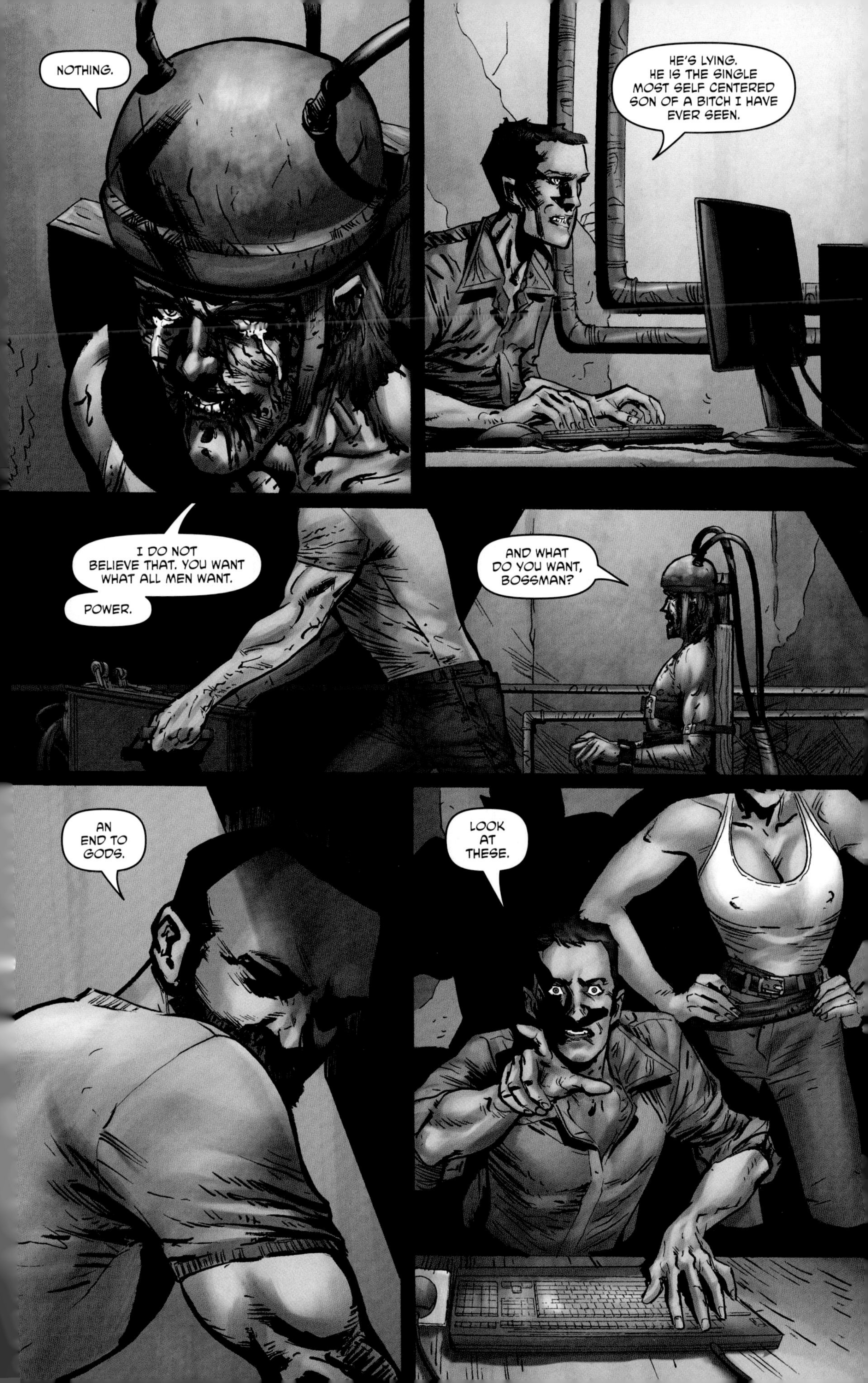
NOTHING.
HE'S LYING. HE IS THE SINGLE MOST SELF CENTERED SON OF A BITCH I HAVE EVER SEEN.
I DO NOT BELIEVE THAT. YOU WANT WHAT ALL MEN WANT.
POWER.
AND WHAT DO YOU WANT, BOSSMAN?
AN END TO GODS.
LOOK AT THESE.

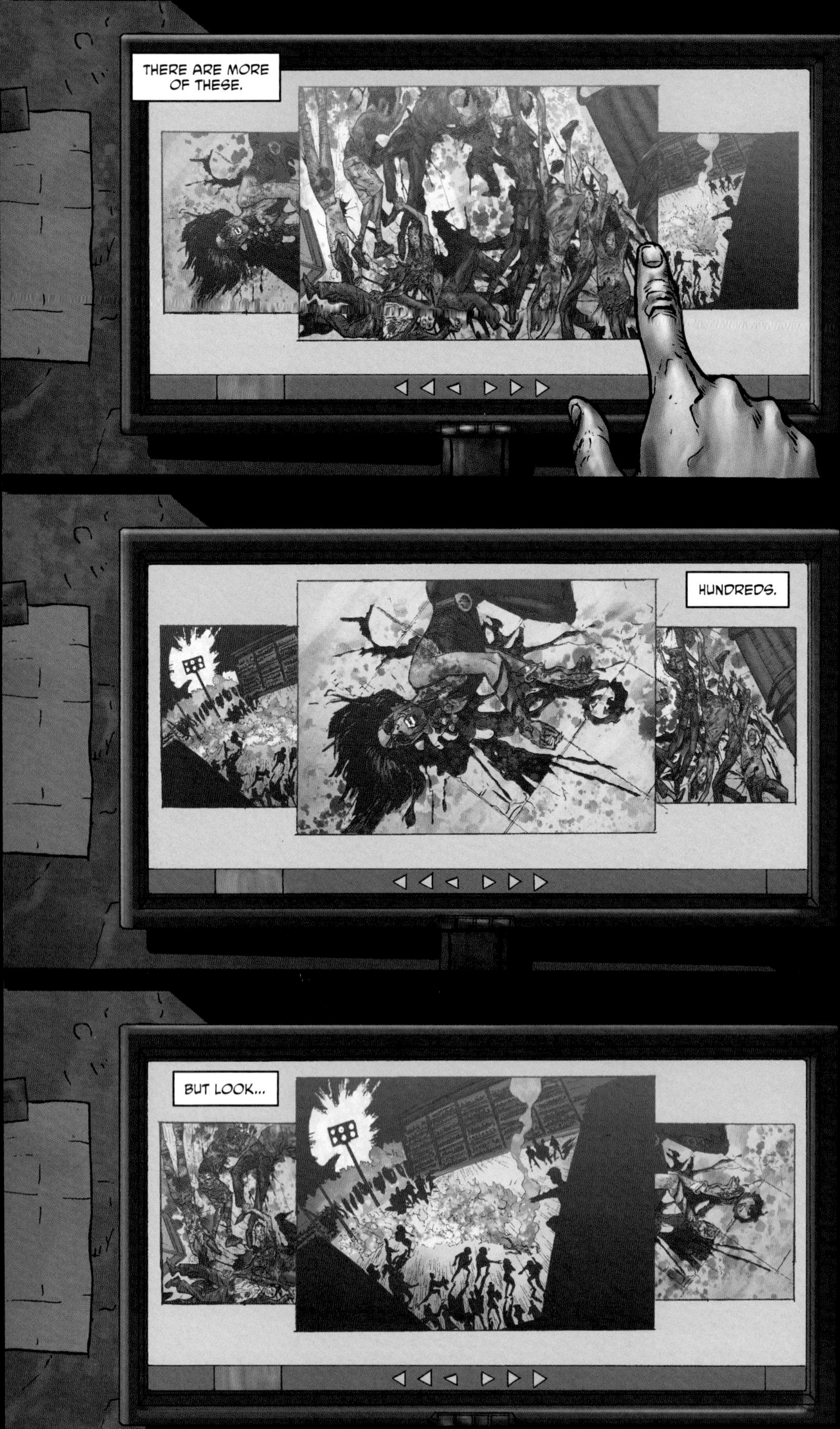
THERE ARE MORE OF THESE.
HUNDREDS.
BUT LOOK...

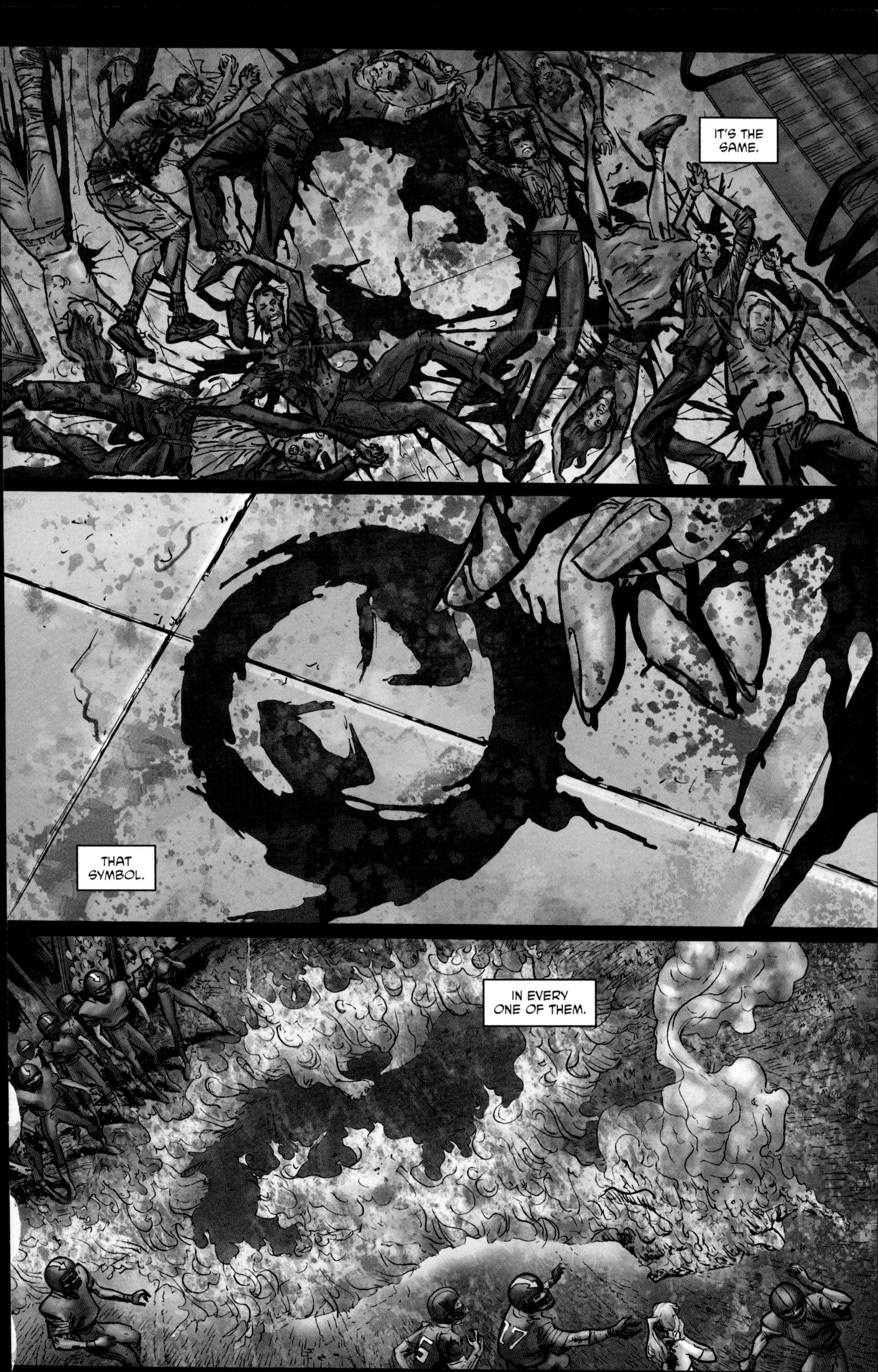
IT'S THE SAME.
THAT SYMBOL.
IN EVERY ONE OF THEM.

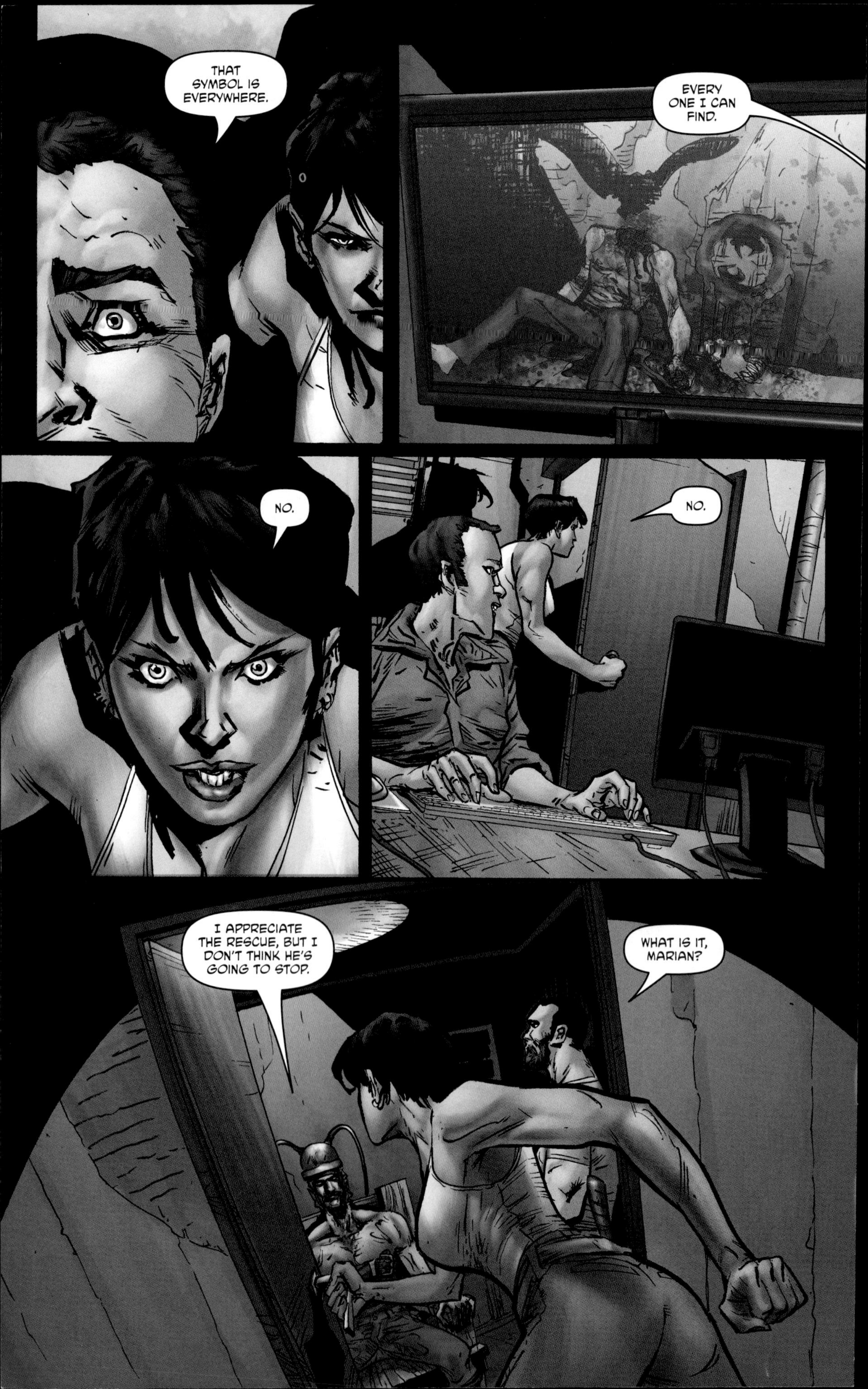
THAT SYMBOL IS EVERYWHERE.
EVERY ONE I CAN FIND.
NO.
NO.
I APPRECIATE THE RESCUE, BUT I DON'T THINK HE'S GOING TO STOP.
WHAT IS IT, MARIAN?

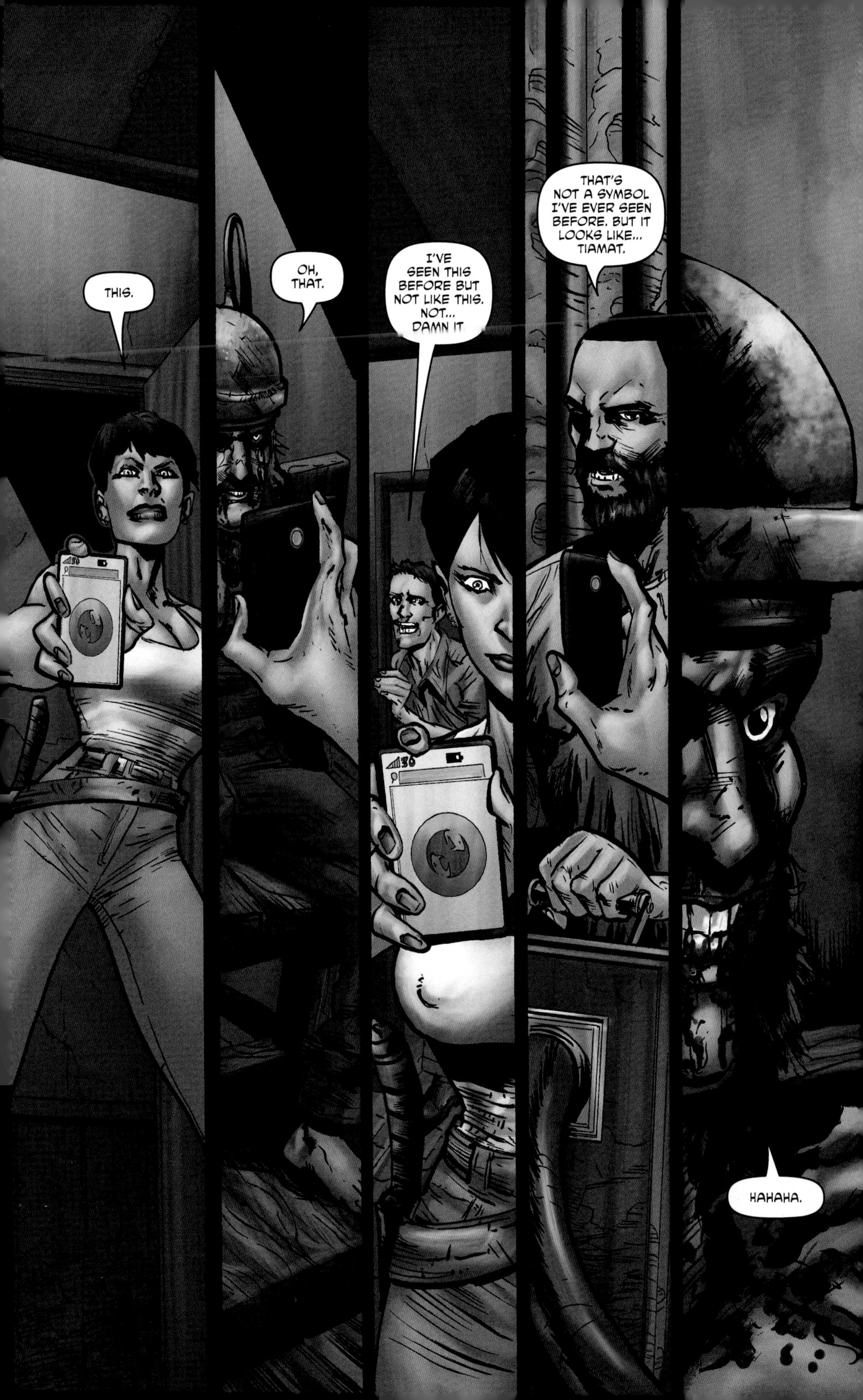
THIS.
OH, THAT.
I'VE SEEN THIS BEFORE BUT NOT LIKE THIS. NOT... DAMN IT
THAT'S NOT A SYMBOL I'VE EVER SEEN BEFORE. BUT IT LOOKS LIKE... TIAMAT.
HAHAHA.

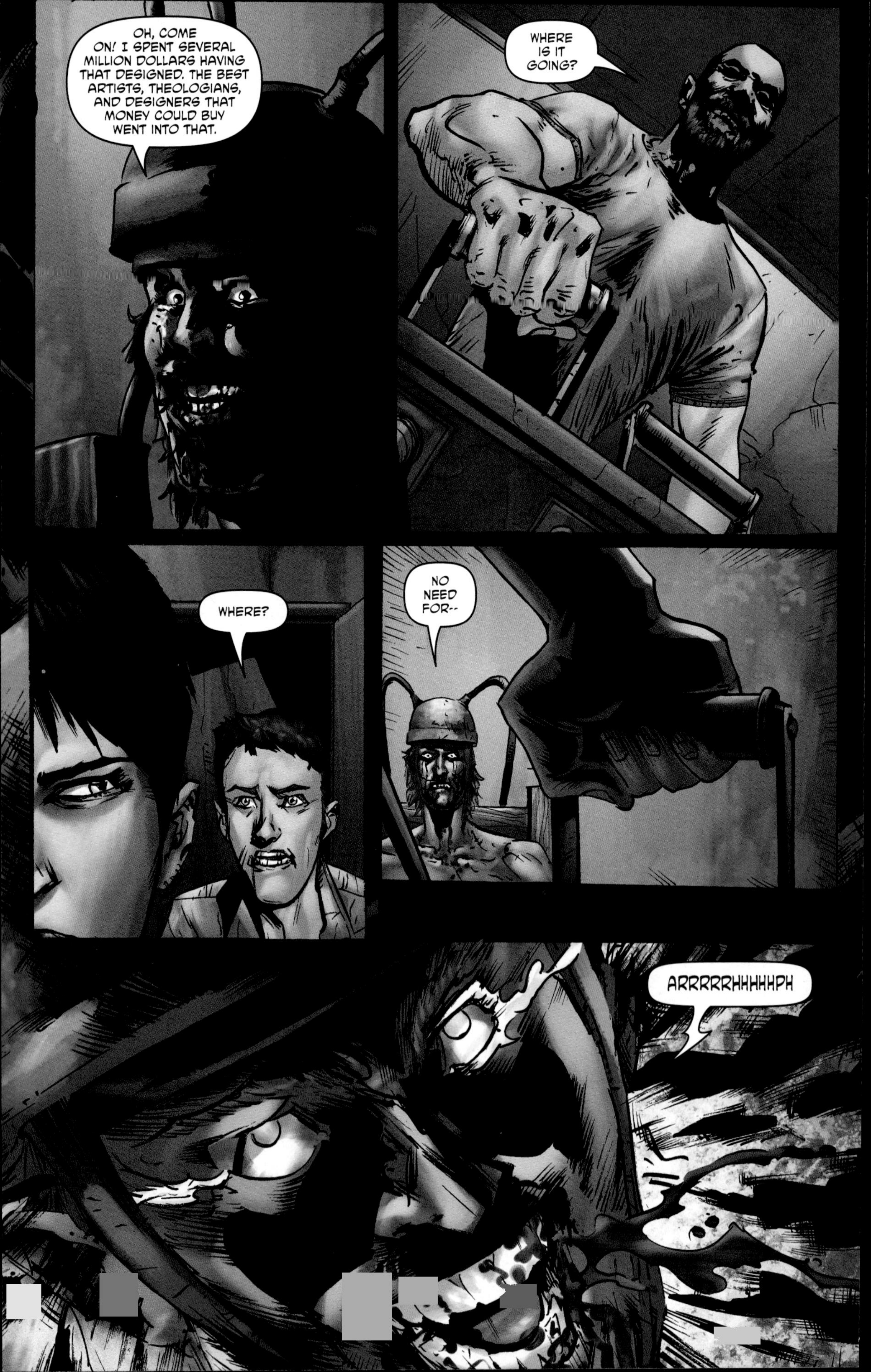
OH, COME ON! I SPENT SEVERAL MILLION DOLLARS HAVING THAT DESIGNED. THE BEST ARTISTS, THEOLOGIANS, AND DESIGNERS THAT MONEY COULD BUY WENT INTO THAT.
WHERE IS IT GOING?
WHERE?
NO NEED FOR--
ARRRRRHHHHHPH

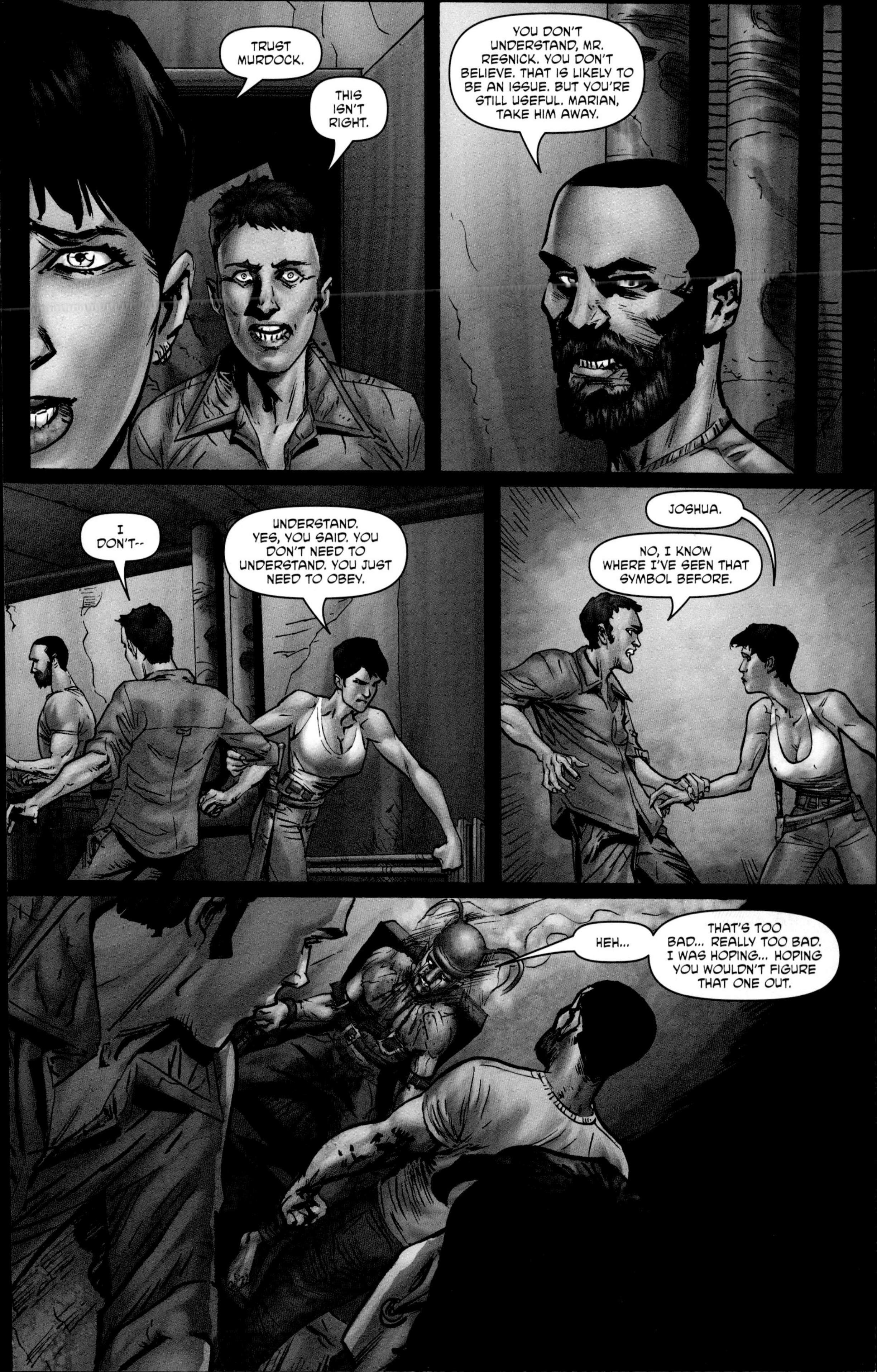
TRUST MURDOCK.
THIS ISN'T RIGHT.
YOU DON'T UNDERSTAND, MR. RESNICK. YOU DON'T BELIEVE. THAT IS LIKELY TO BE AN ISSUE. BUT YOU'RE STILL USEFUL. MARIAN, TAKE HIM AWAY.
I DON'T--
UNDERSTAND. YES, YOU SAID. YOU DON'T NEED TO UNDERSTAND. YOU JUST NEED TO OBEY.
JOSHUA.
NO, I KNOW WHERE I'VE SEEN THAT SYMBOL BEFORE.
HEH...
THAT'S TOO BAD... REALLY TOO BAD. I WAS HOPING... HOPING YOU WOULDN'T FIGURE THAT ONE OUT.

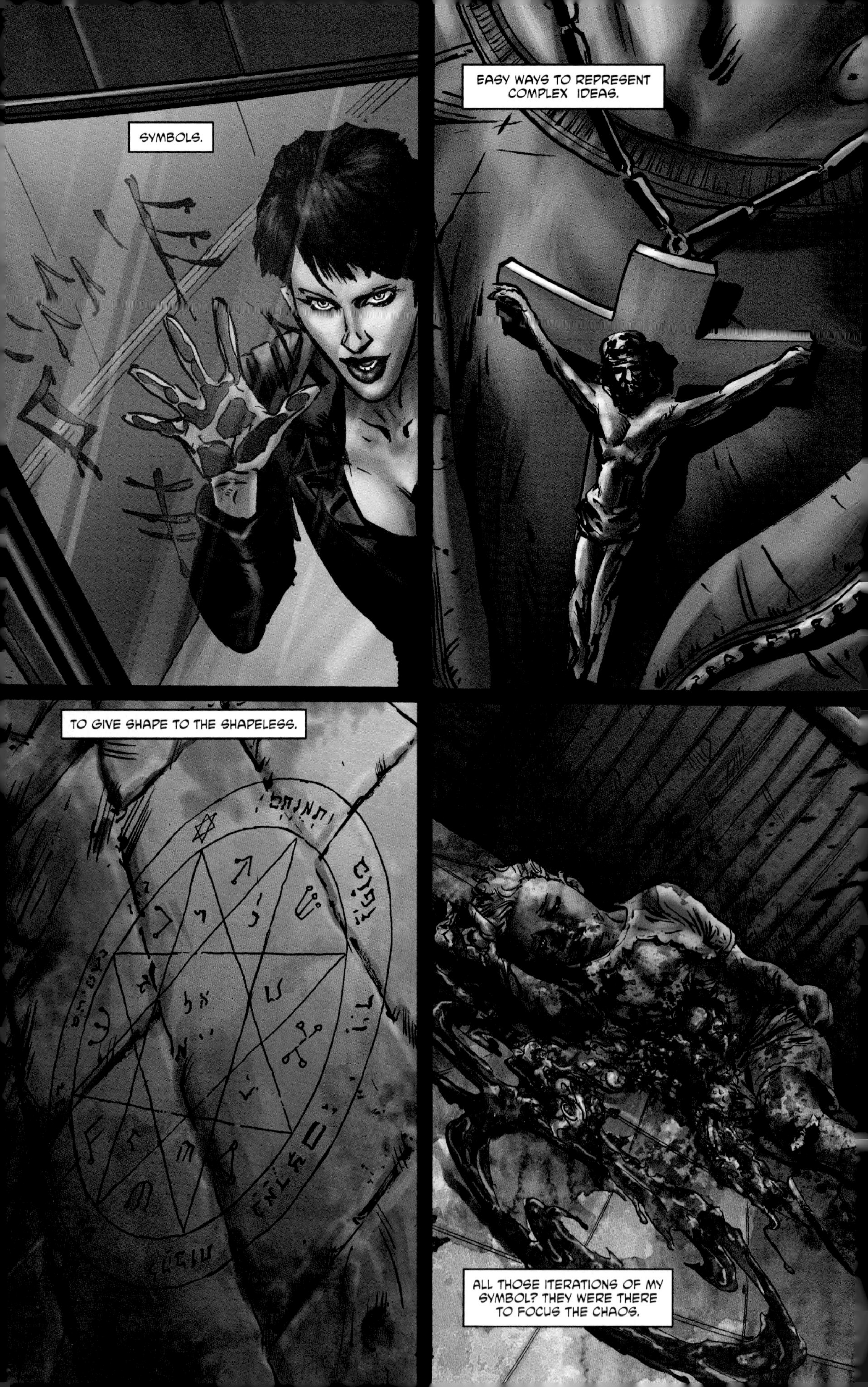
SYMBOLS.
EASY WAYS TO REPRESENT COMPLEX IDEAS.
TO GIVE SHAPE TO THE SHAPELESS.
ALL THOSE ITERATIONS OF MY SYMBOL? THEY WERE THERE TO FOCUS THE CHAOS.

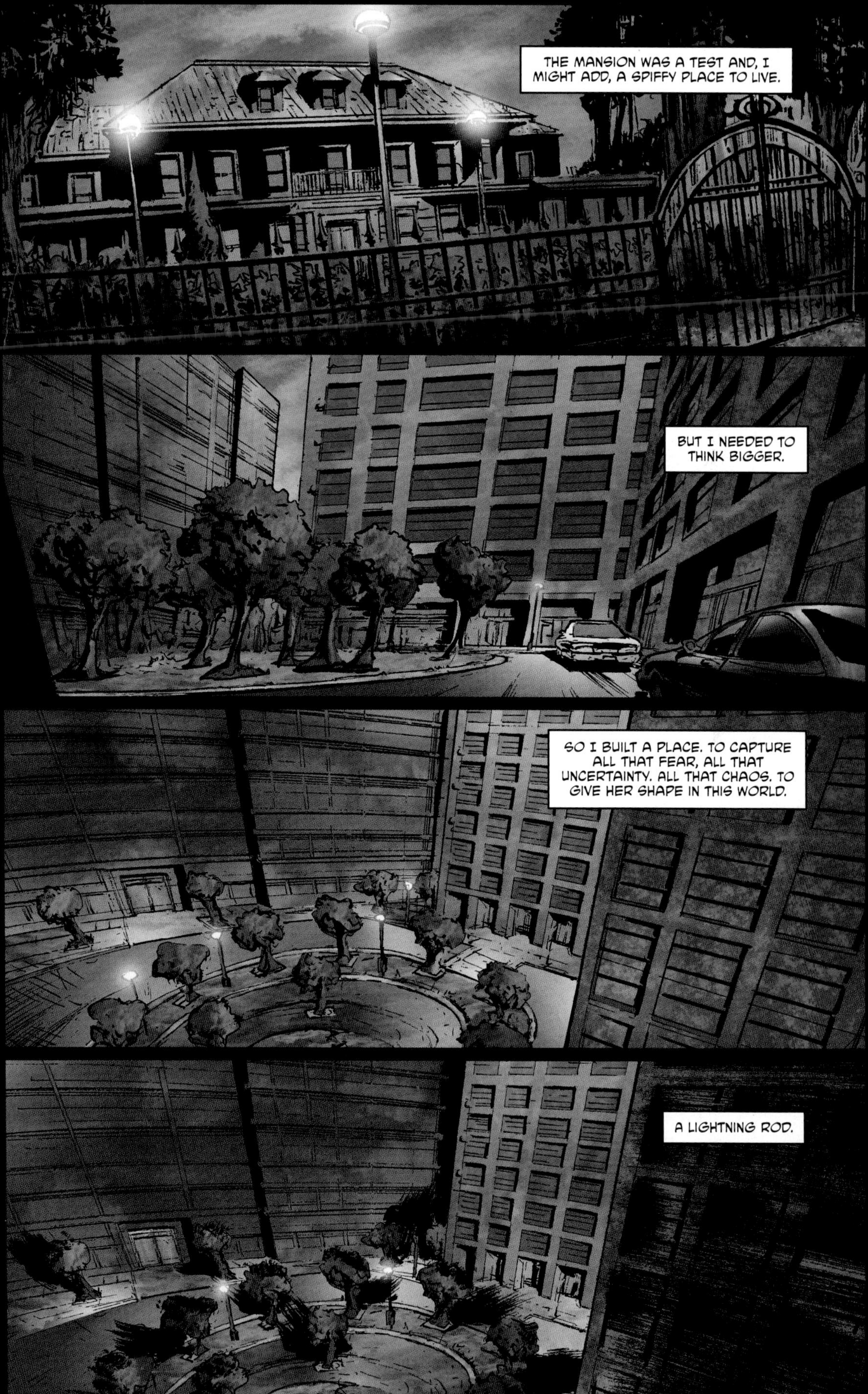
THE MANSION WAS A TEST AND, I MIGHT ADD, A SPIFFY PLACE TO LIVE.
BUT I NEEDED TO THINK BIGGER.
SO I BUILT A PLACE. TO CAPTURE ALL THAT FEAR, ALL THAT UNCERTAINTY. ALL THAT CHAOS. TO GIVE HER SHAPE IN THIS WORLD.
A LIGHTNING ROD.

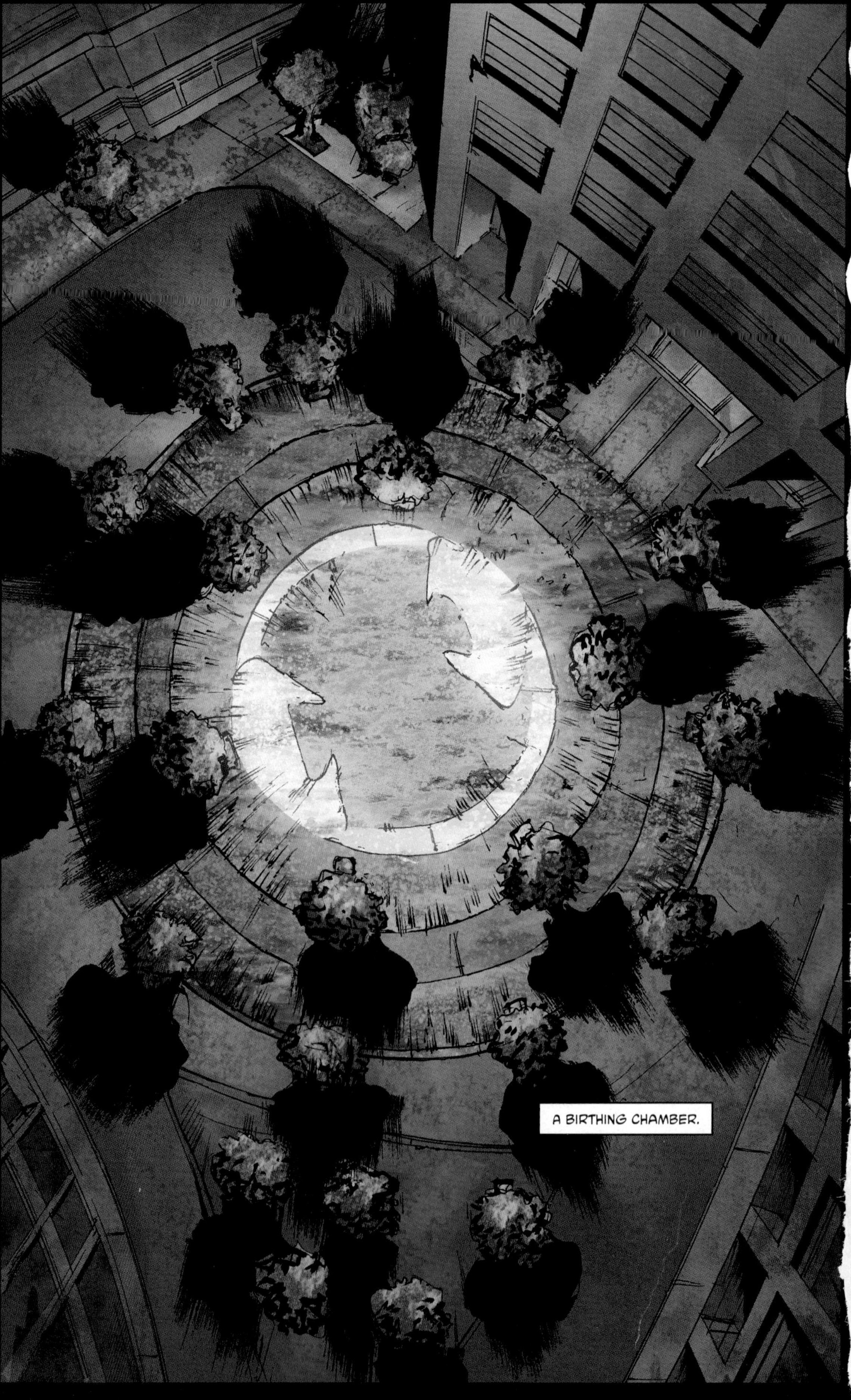
A BIRTHING CHAMBER.

**CHAPTER 5**

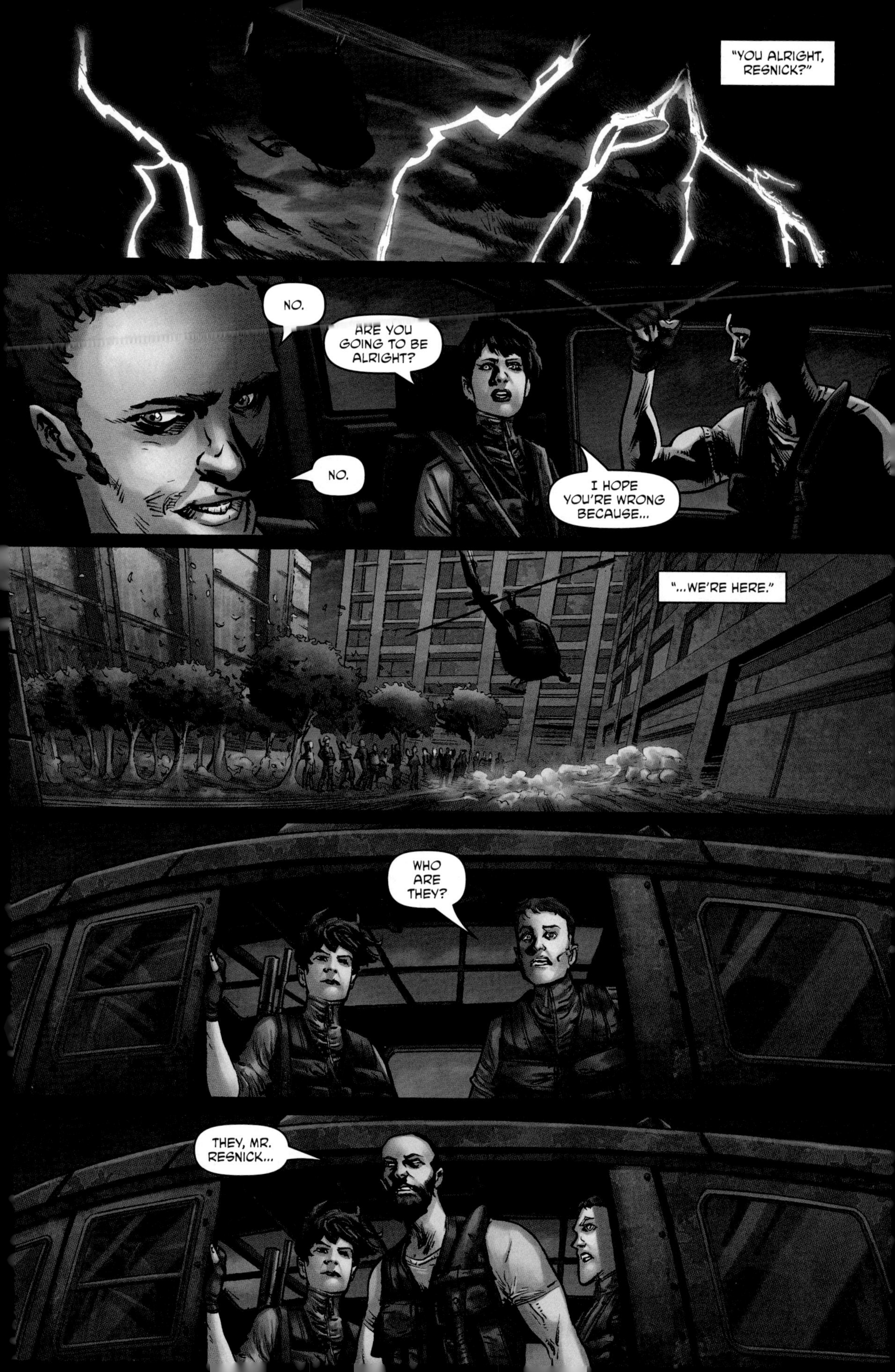
"YOU ALRIGHT, RESNICK?"
NO.
ARE YOU GOING TO BE ALRIGHT?
NO.
I HOPE YOU'RE WRONG BECAUSE...
"...WE'RE HERE."
WHO ARE THEY?
THEY, MR. RESNICK...

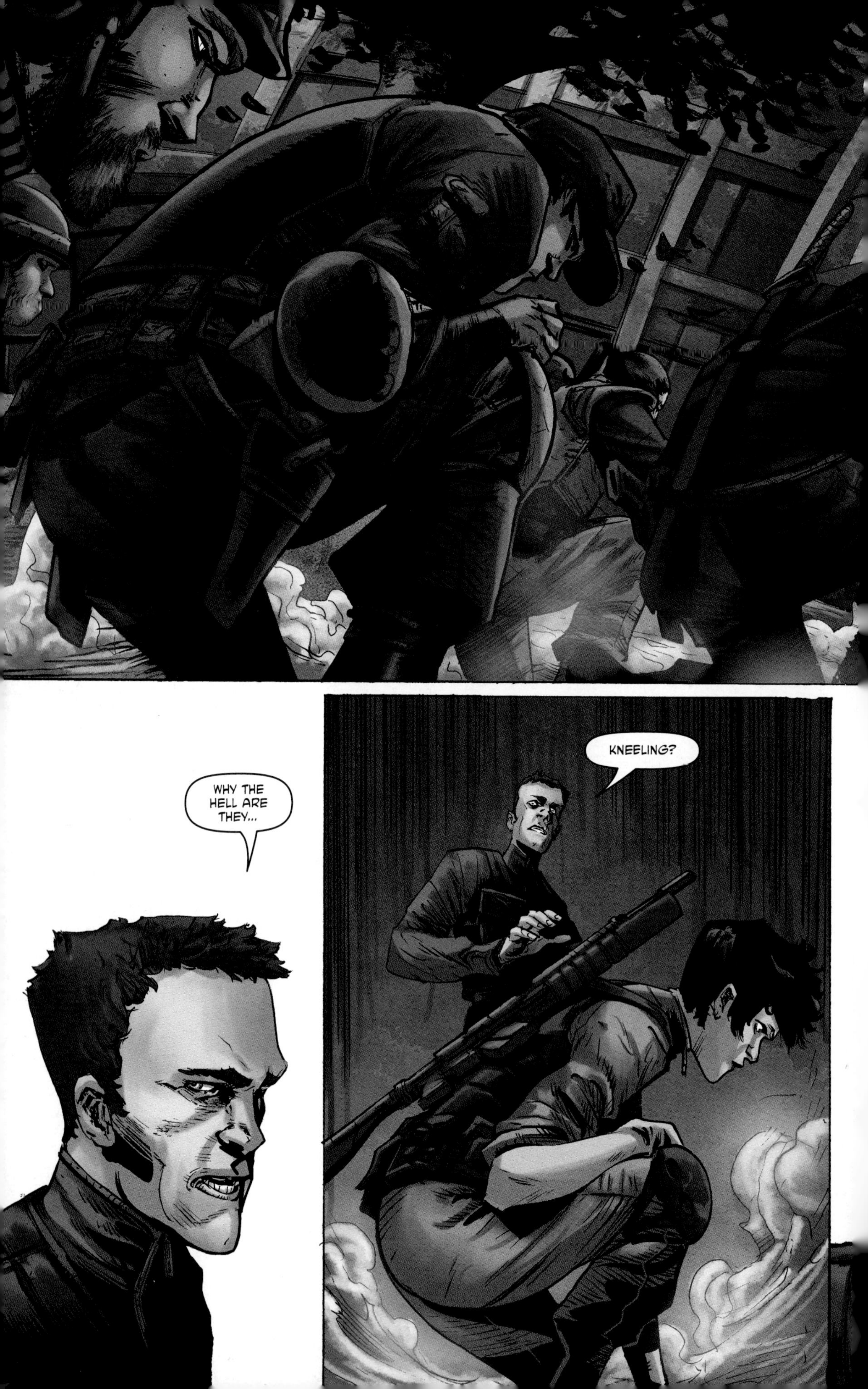
WHY THE HELL ARE THEY...
KNEELING?

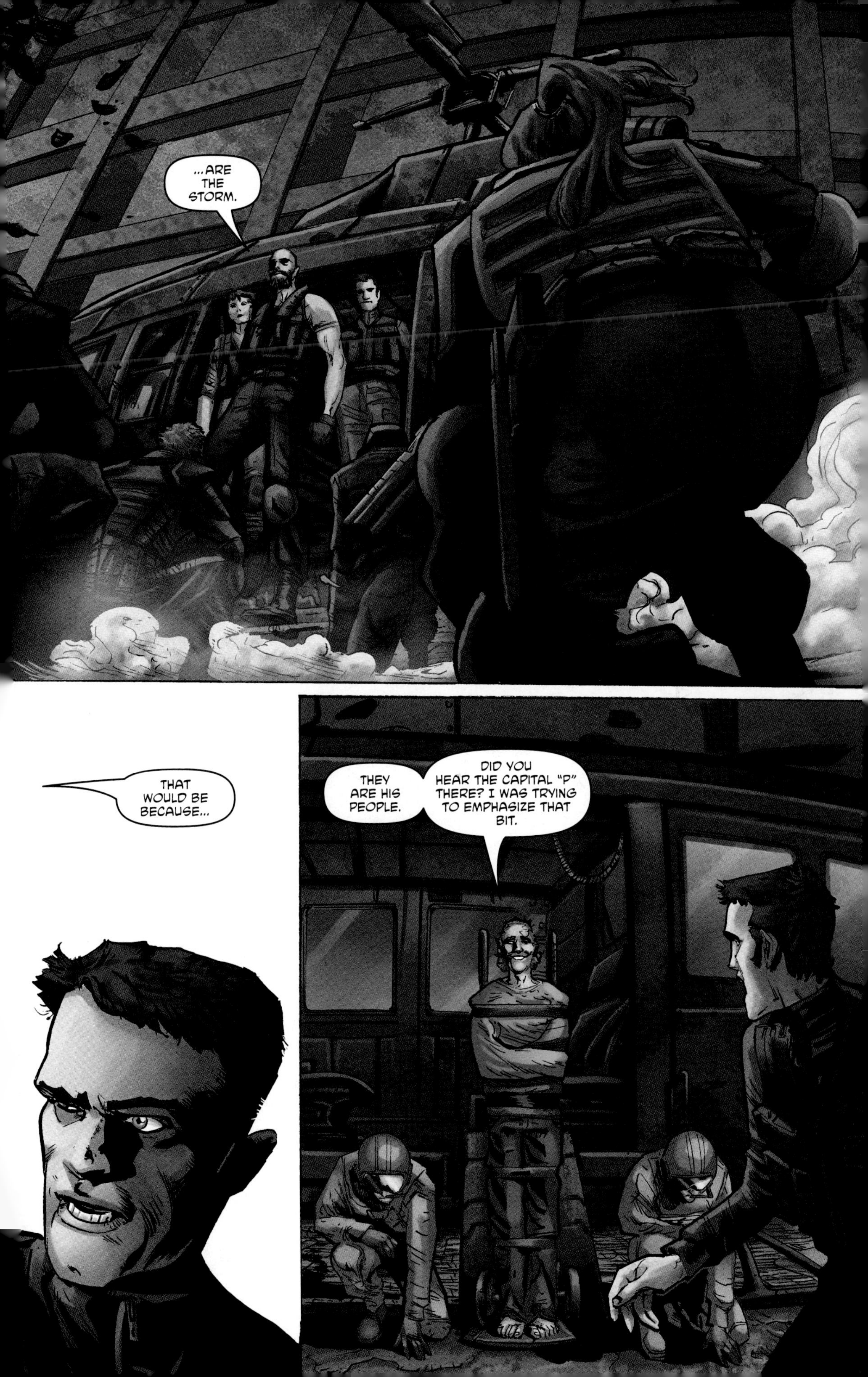
...ARE THE STORM.
THAT WOULD BE BECAUSE...
THEY ARE HIS PEOPLE.
DID YOU HEAR THE CAPITAL "P" THERE? I WAS TRYING TO EMPHASIZE THAT BIT.

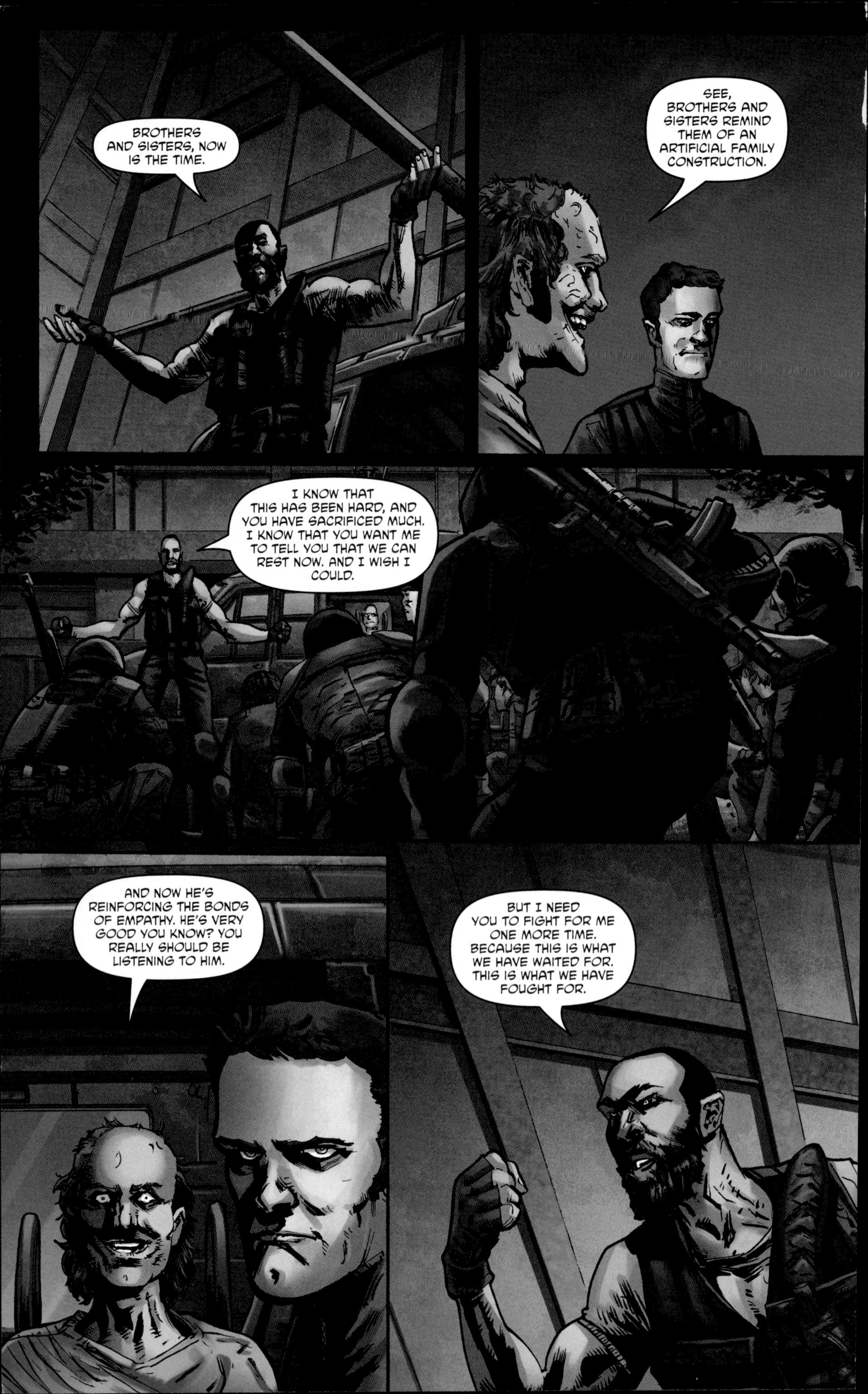
BROTHERS AND SISTERS, NOW IS THE TIME.
SEE, BROTHERS AND SISTERS REMIND THEM OF AN ARTIFICIAL FAMILY CONSTRUCTION.
I KNOW THAT THIS HAS BEEN HARD, AND YOU HAVE SACRIFICED MUCH. I KNOW THAT YOU WANT ME TO TELL YOU THAT WE CAN REST NOW. AND I WISH I COULD.
AND NOW HE'S REINFORCING THE BONDS OF EMPATHY. HE'S VERY GOOD YOU KNOW? YOU REALLY SHOULD BE LISTENING TO HIM.
BUT I NEED YOU TO FIGHT FOR ME ONE MORE TIME. BECAUSE THIS IS WHAT WE HAVE WAITED FOR. THIS IS WHAT WE HAVE FOUGHT FOR.

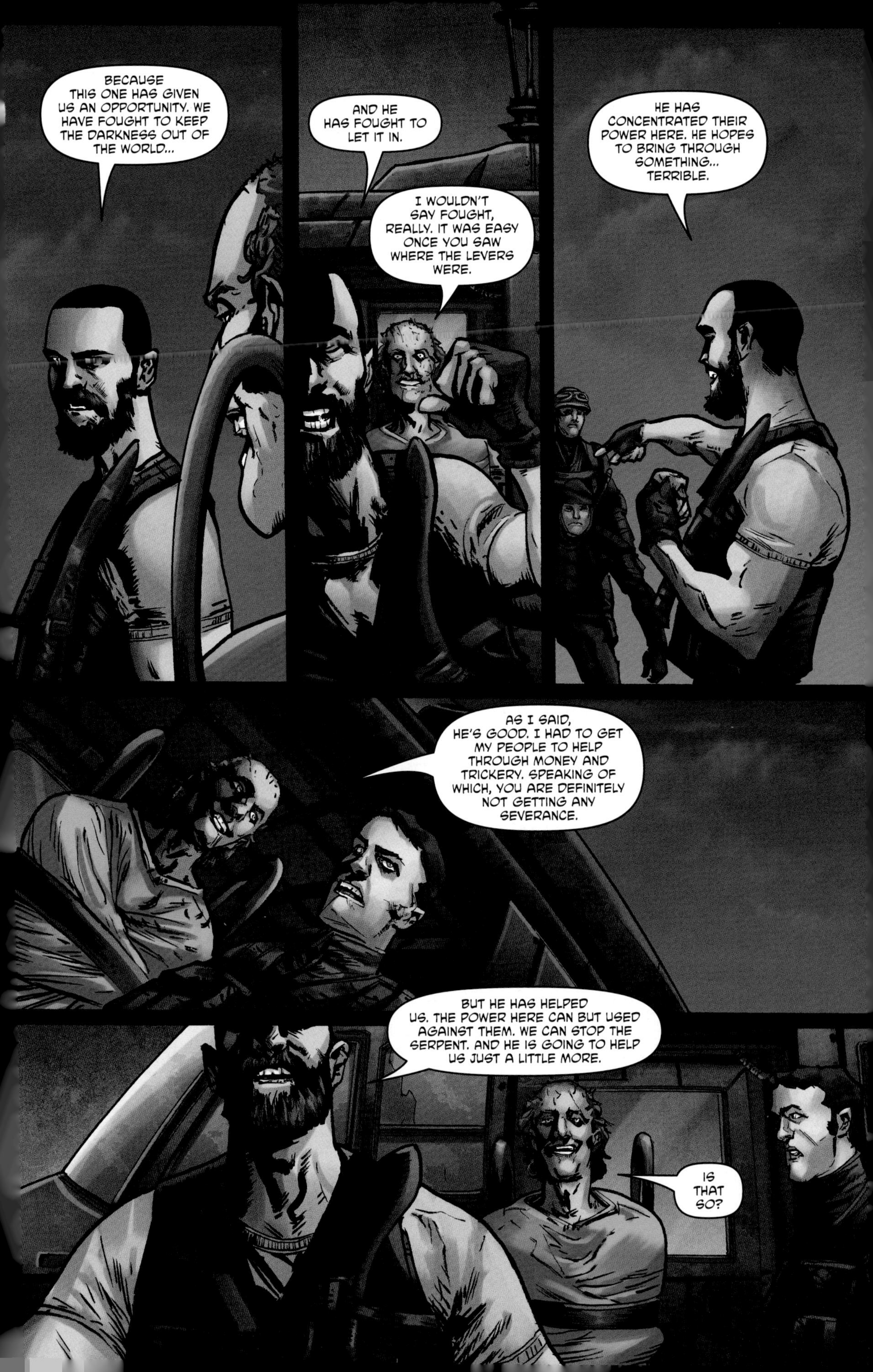
BECAUSE THIS ONE HAS GIVEN US AN OPPORTUNITY. WE HAVE FOUGHT TO KEEP THE DARKNESS OUT OF THE WORLD...
AND HE HAS FOUGHT TO LET IT IN.
I WOULDN'T SAY FOUGHT, REALLY. IT WAS EASY ONCE YOU SAW WHERE THE LEVERS WERE.
HE HAS CONCENTRATED THEIR POWER HERE. HE HOPES TO BRING THROUGH SOMETHING... TERRIBLE.
AS I SAID, HE'S GOOD. I HAD TO GET MY PEOPLE TO HELP THROUGH MONEY AND TRICKERY. SPEAKING OF WHICH, YOU ARE DEFINITELY NOT GETTING ANY SEVERANCE.
BUT HE HAS HELPED US. THE POWER HERE CAN BUT USED AGAINST THEM. WE CAN STOP THE SERPENT. AND HE IS GOING TO HELP US JUST A LITTLE MORE.
IS THAT SO?

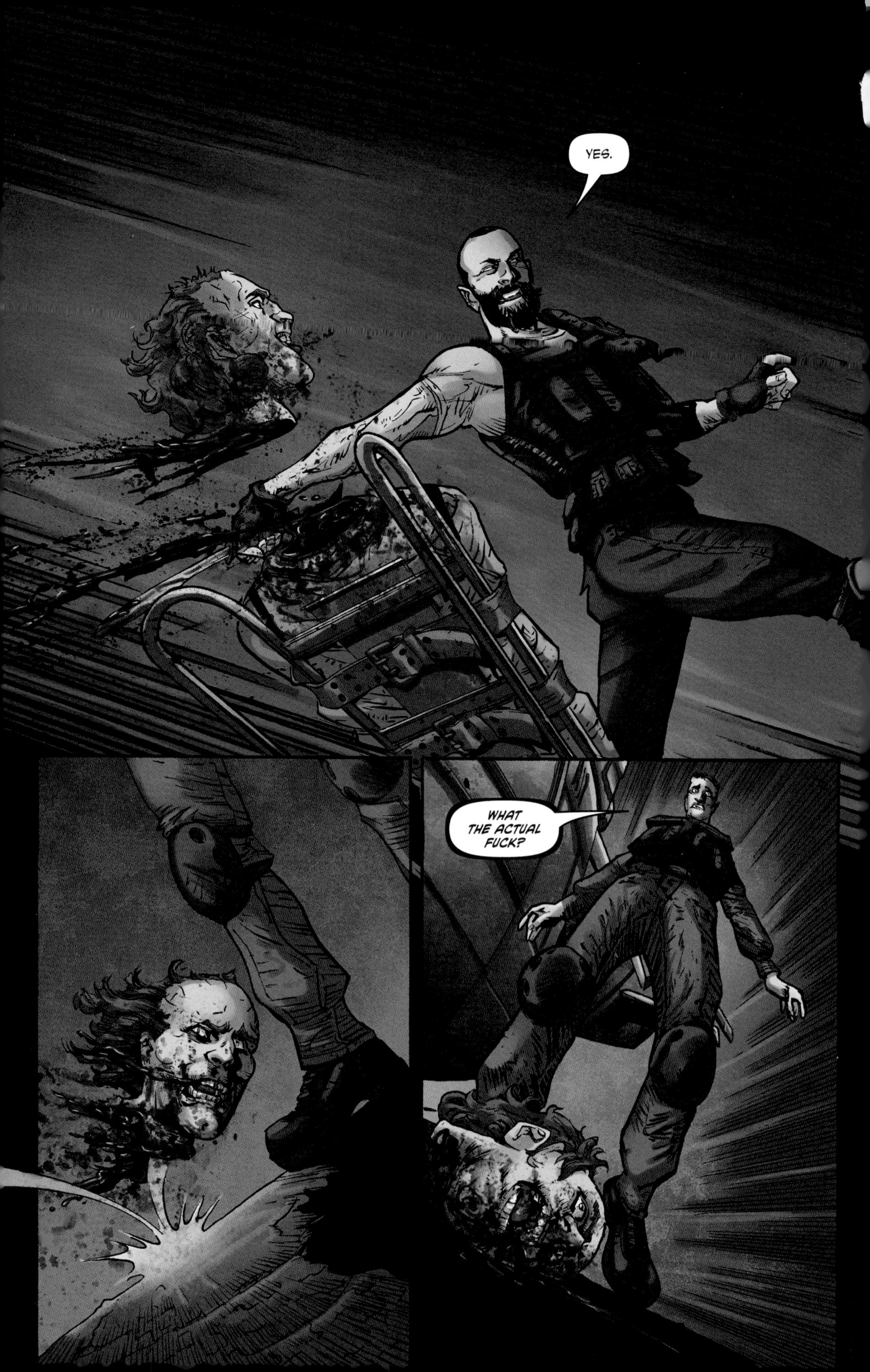
YES.
WHAT THE ACTUAL FUCK?

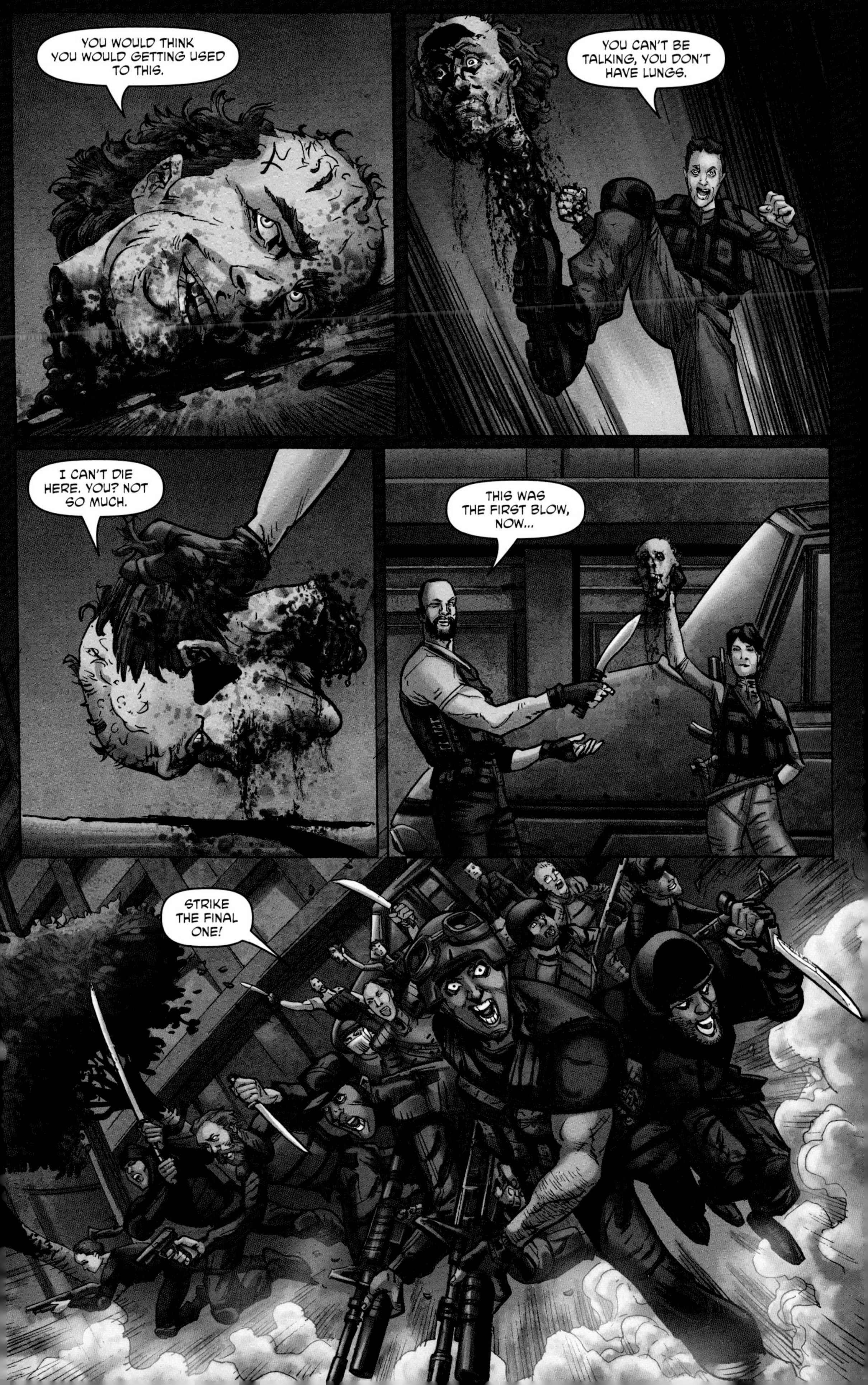
YOU WOULD THINK YOU WOULD GETTING USED TO THIS.
YOU CAN'T BE TALKING, YOU DON'T HAVE LUNGS.
I CAN'T DIE HERE. YOU? NOT SO MUCH.
THIS WAS THE FIRST BLOW, NOW...
STRIKE THE FINAL ONE!

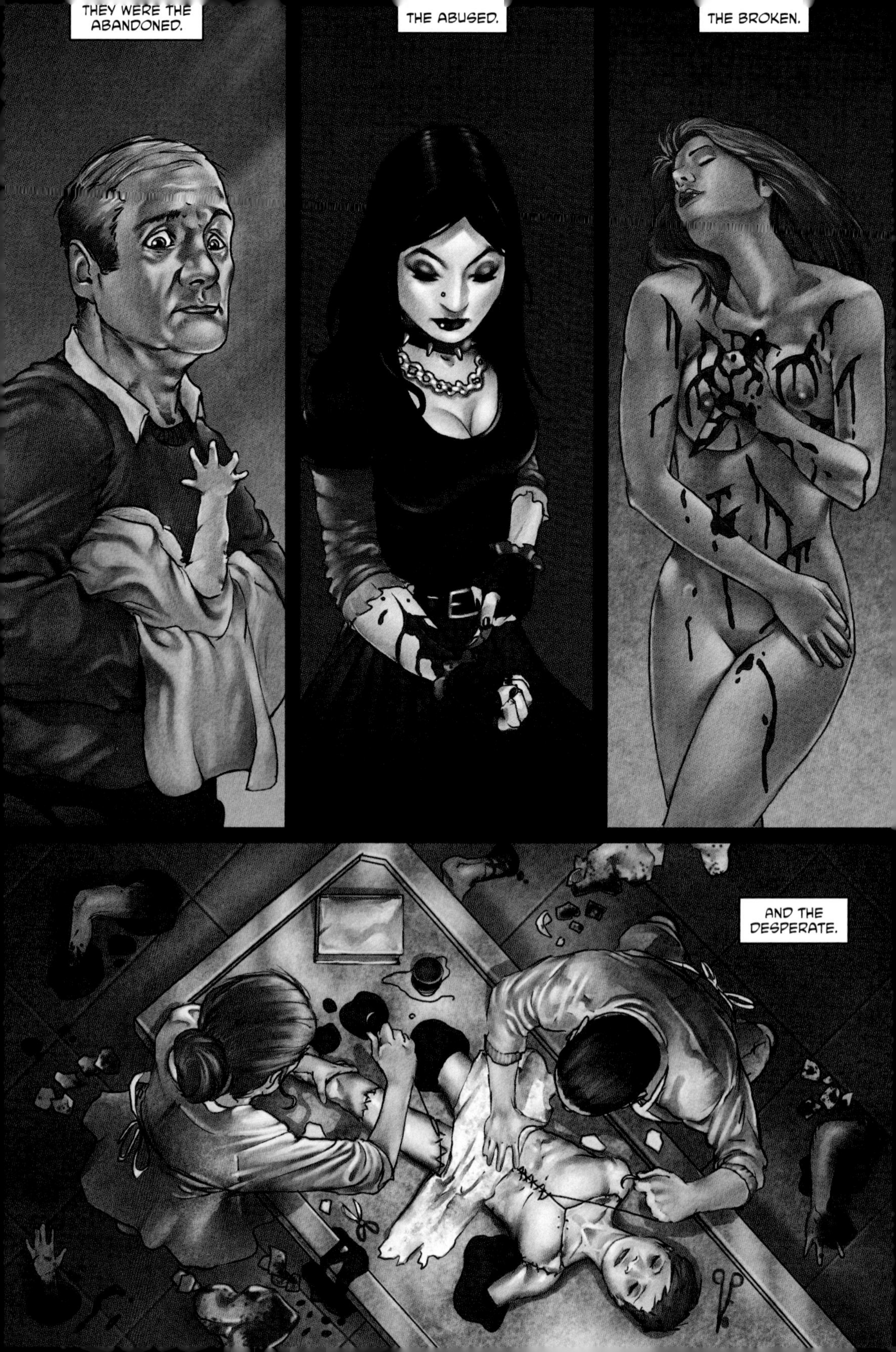
THEY WERE THE ABANDONED.
THE ABUSED.
THE BROKEN.
AND THE DESPERATE.

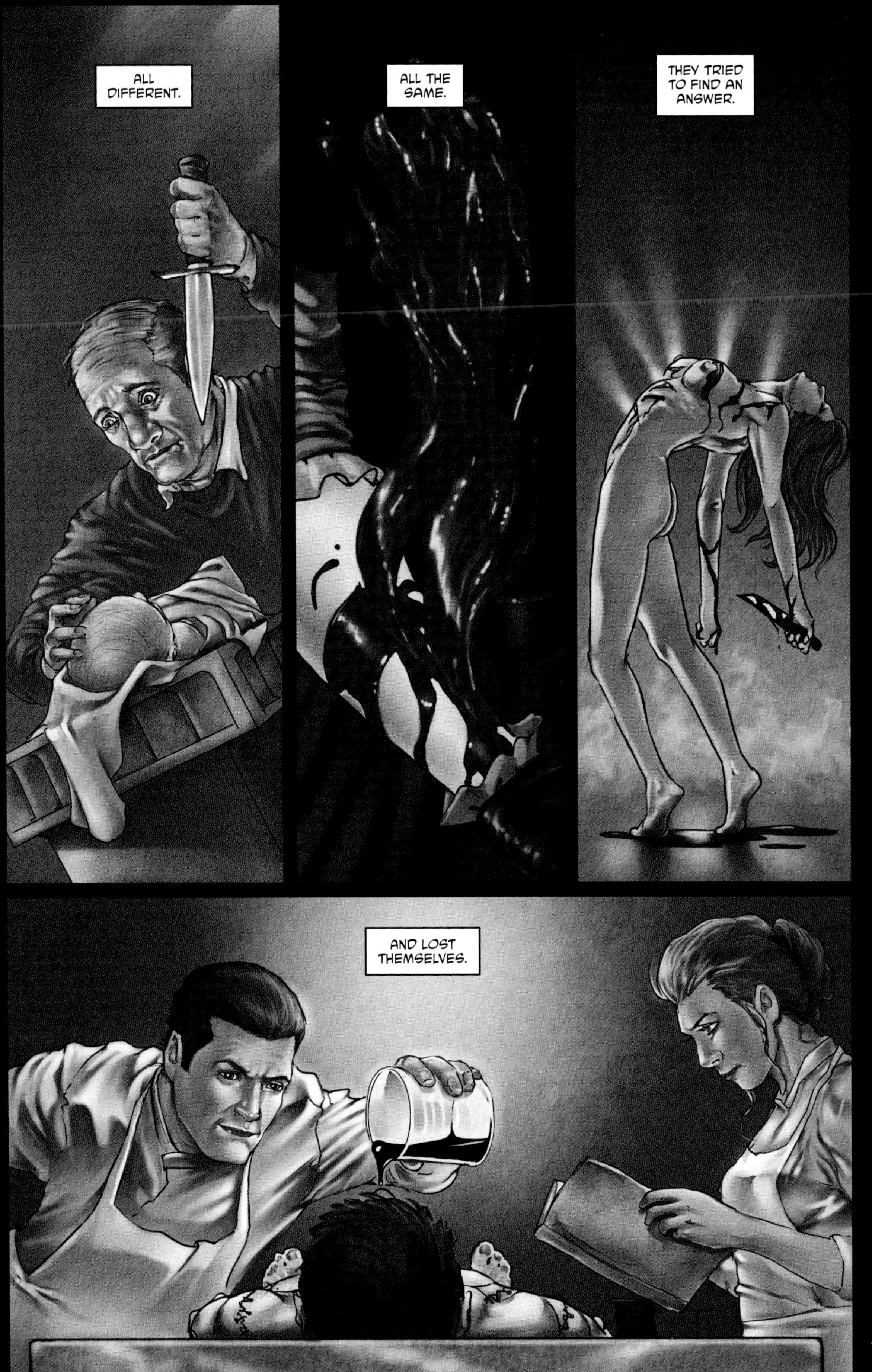
ALL DIFFERENT.
ALL THE SAME.
THEY TRIED TO FIND AN ANSWER.
AND LOST THEMSELVES.

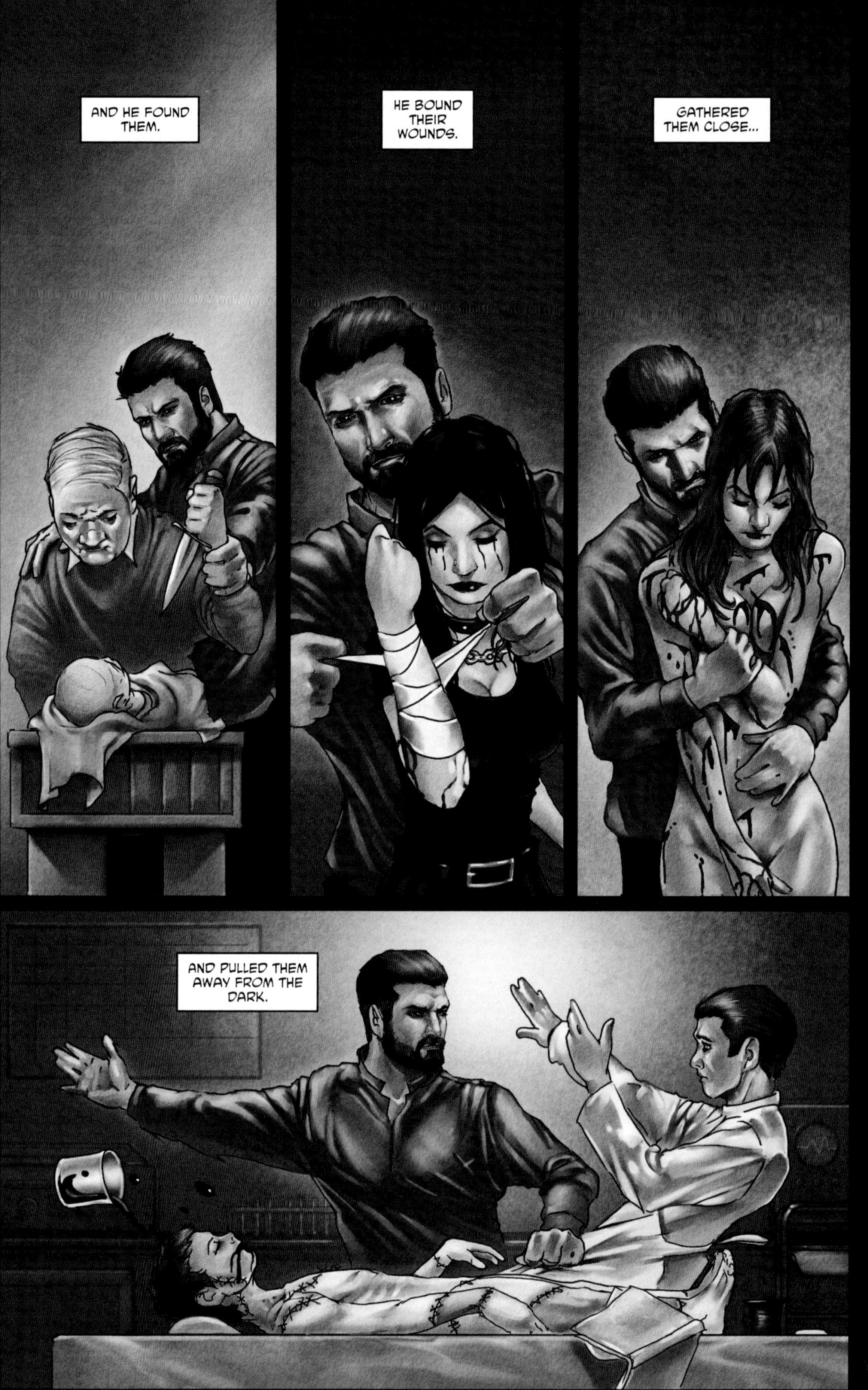
AND HE FOUND THEM.
HE BOUND THEIR WOUNDS.
GATHERED THEM CLOSE...
AND PULLED THEM AWAY FROM THE DARK.

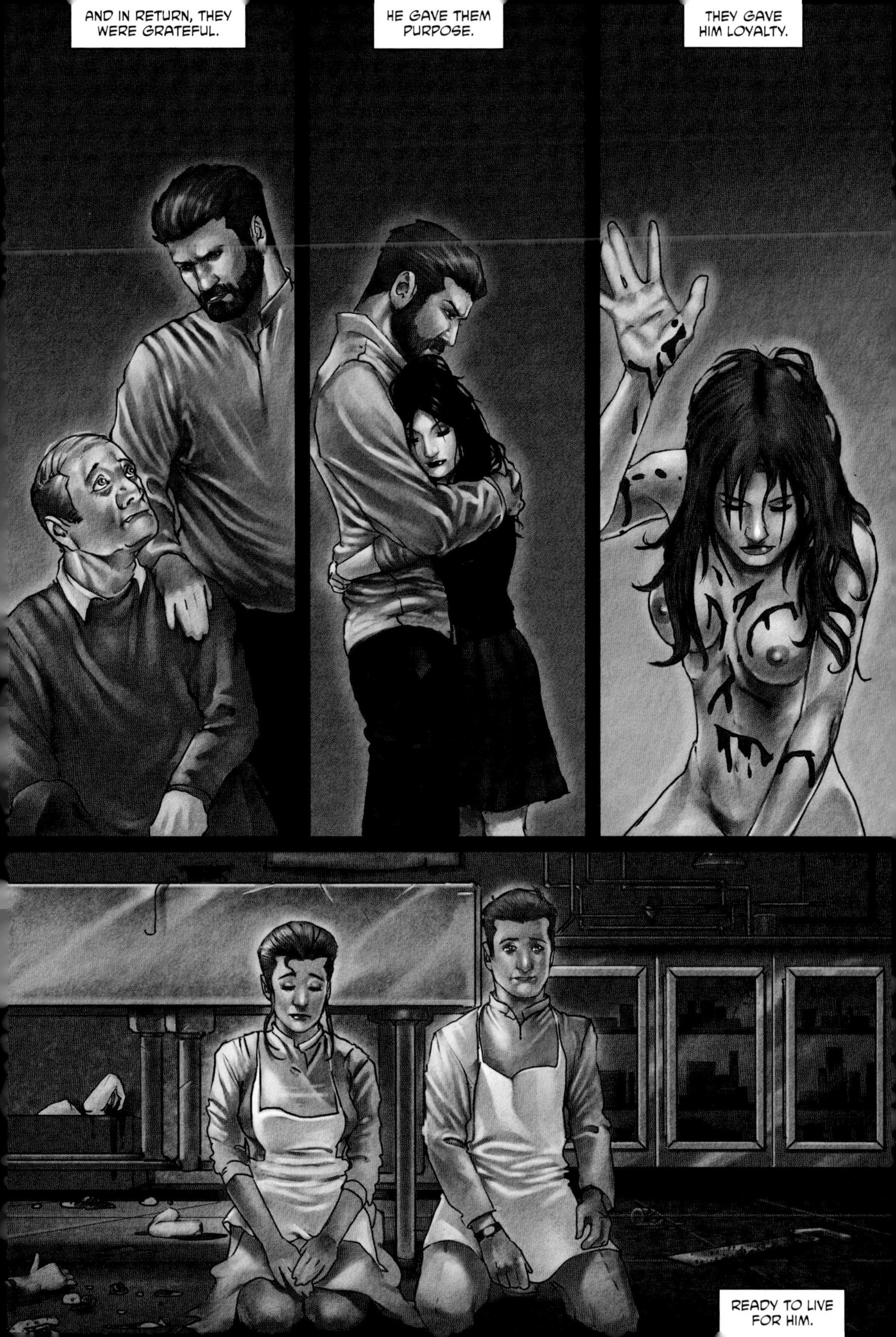
AND IN RETURN, THEY WERE GRATEFUL.
HE GAVE THEM PURPOSE.
THEY GAVE HIM LOYALTY.
READY TO LIVE FOR HIM.

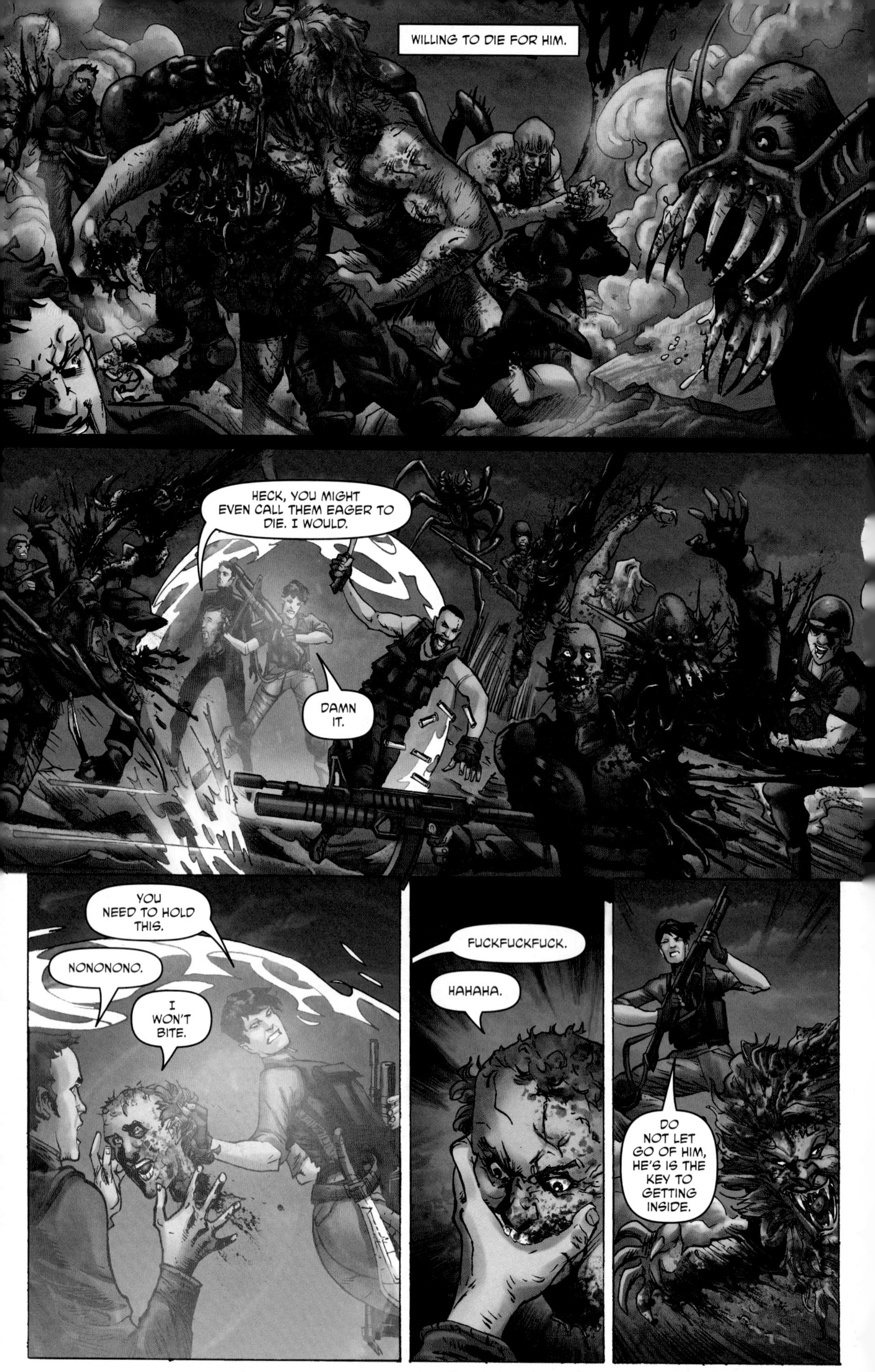
WILLING TO DIE FOR HIM.
HECK, YOU MIGHT EVEN CALL THEM EAGER TO DIE. I WOULD.
DAMN IT.
YOU NEED TO HOLD THIS.
NONONONO.
I WON'T BITE.
FUCKFUCKFUCK.
HAHAHA.
DO NOT LET GO OF HIM, HE'S IS THE KEY TO GETTING INSIDE.

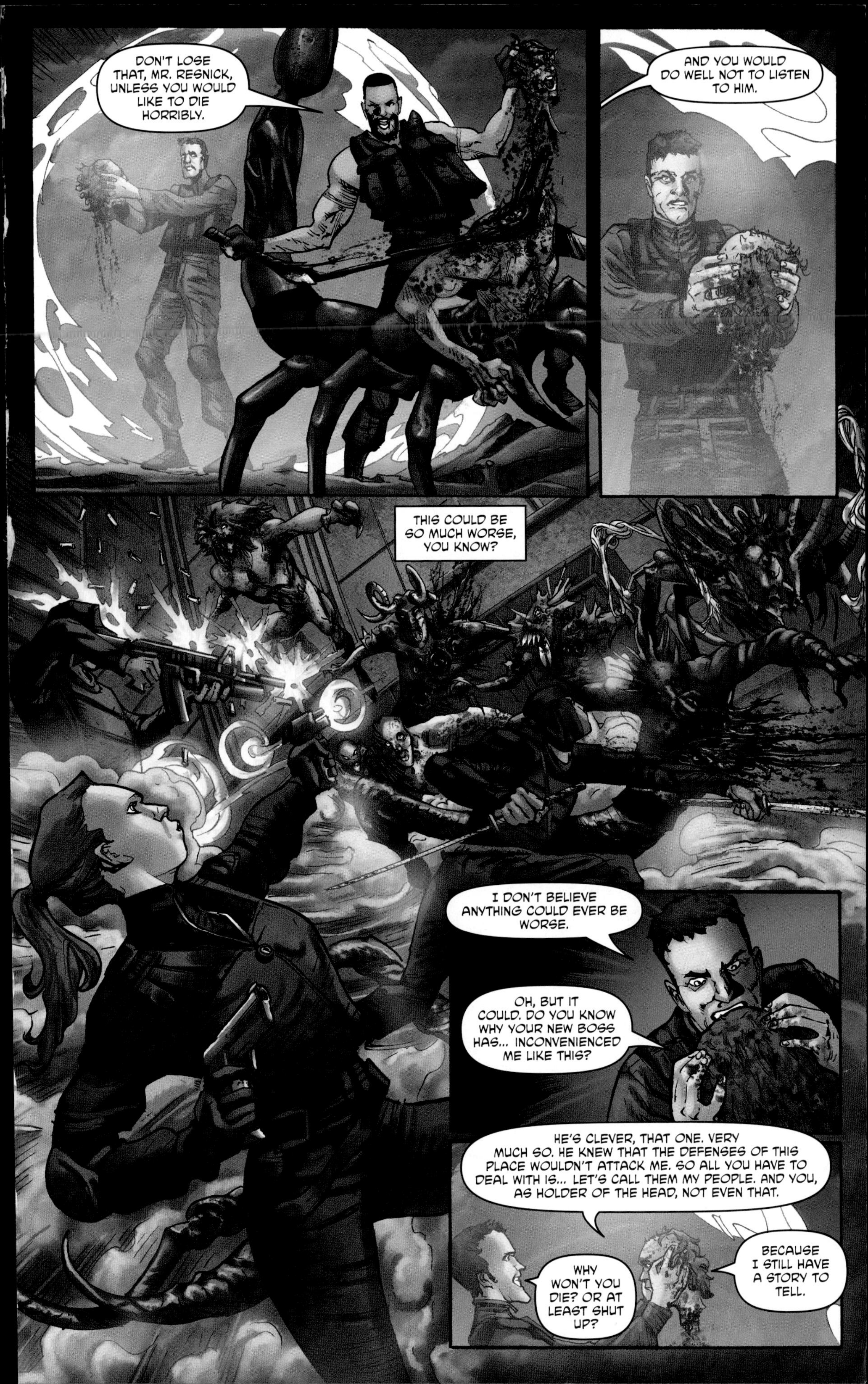
DON'T LOSE THAT, MR. RESNICK, UNLESS YOU WOULD LIKE TO DIE HORRIBLY.
AND YOU WOULD DO WELL NOT TO LISTEN TO HIM.
THIS COULD BE SO MUCH WORSE, YOU KNOW?
I DON'T BELIEVE ANYTHING COULD EVER BE WORSE.
OH, BUT IT COULD. DO YOU KNOW WHY YOUR NEW BOSS HAS... INCONVENIENCED ME LIKE THIS?
HE'S CLEVER, THAT ONE. VERY MUCH SO. HE KNEW THAT THE DEFENSES OF THIS PLACE WOULDN'T ATTACK ME. SO ALL YOU HAVE TO DEAL WITH IS... LET'S CALL THEM MY PEOPLE. AND YOU, AS HOLDER OF THE HEAD, NOT EVEN THAT.
WHY WON'T YOU DIE? OR AT LEAST SHUT UP?
BECAUSE I STILL HAVE A STORY TO TELL.

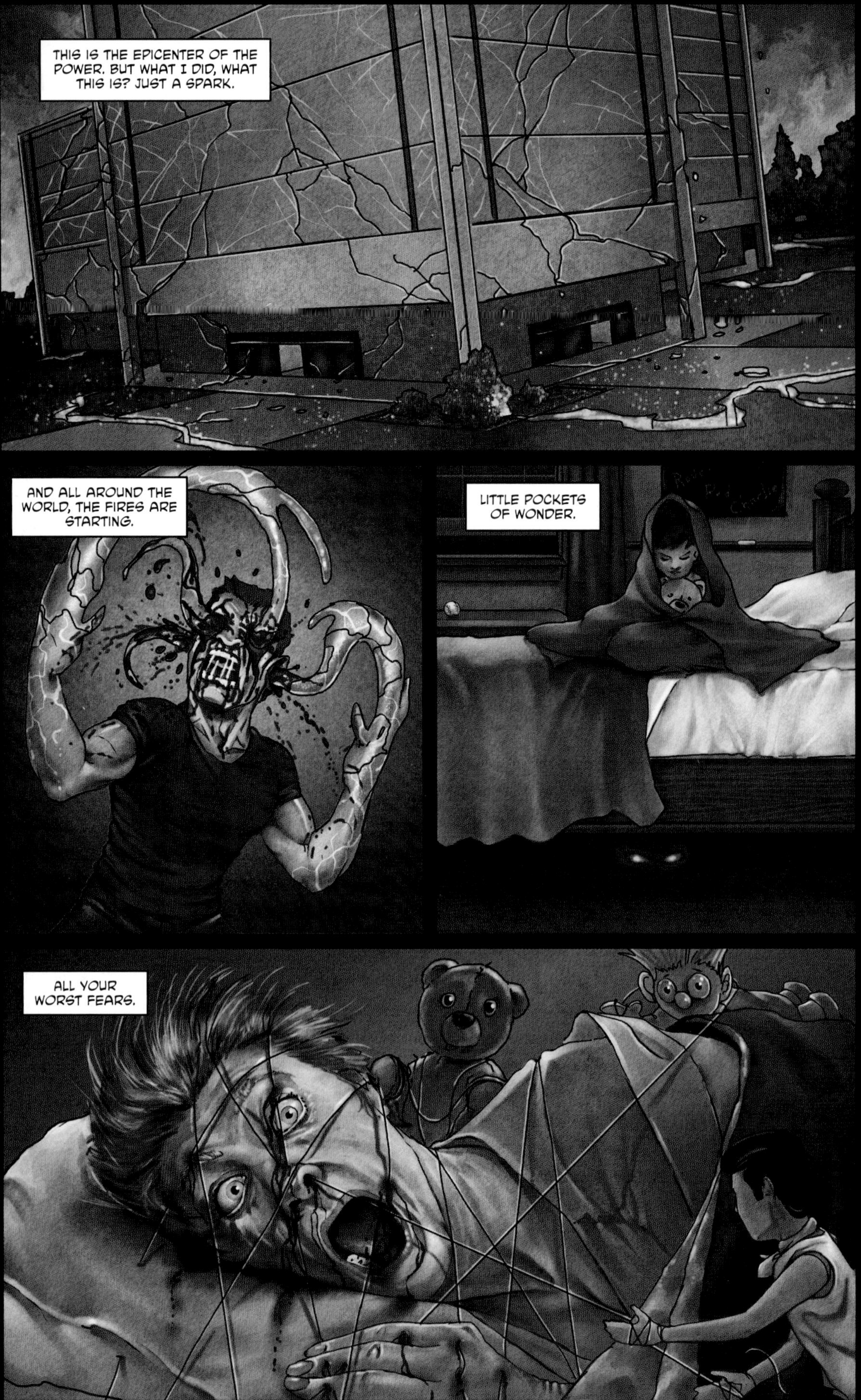
THIS IS THE EPICENTER OF THE POWER. BUT WHAT I DID, WHAT THIS IS? JUST A SPARK.
AND ALL AROUND THE WORLD, THE FIRES ARE STARTING.
LITTLE POCKETS OF WONDER.
ALL YOUR WORST FEARS.

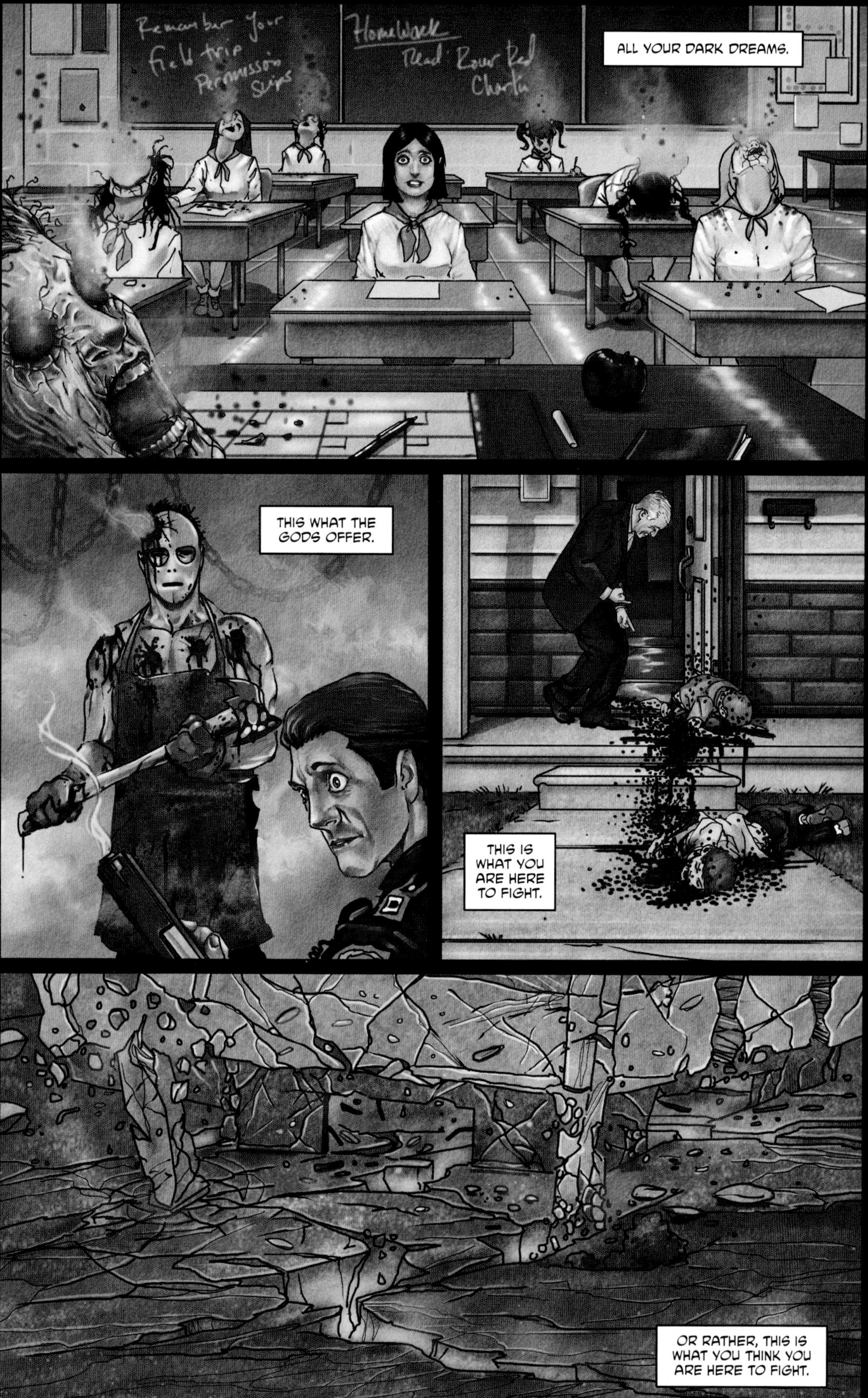
Remember your field trip Permission slips
Homework
ALL YOUR DARK DREAMS.
THIS WHAT THE GODS OFFER.
THIS IS WHAT YOU ARE HERE TO FIGHT.
OR RATHER, THIS IS WHAT YOU THINK YOU ARE HERE TO FIGHT.

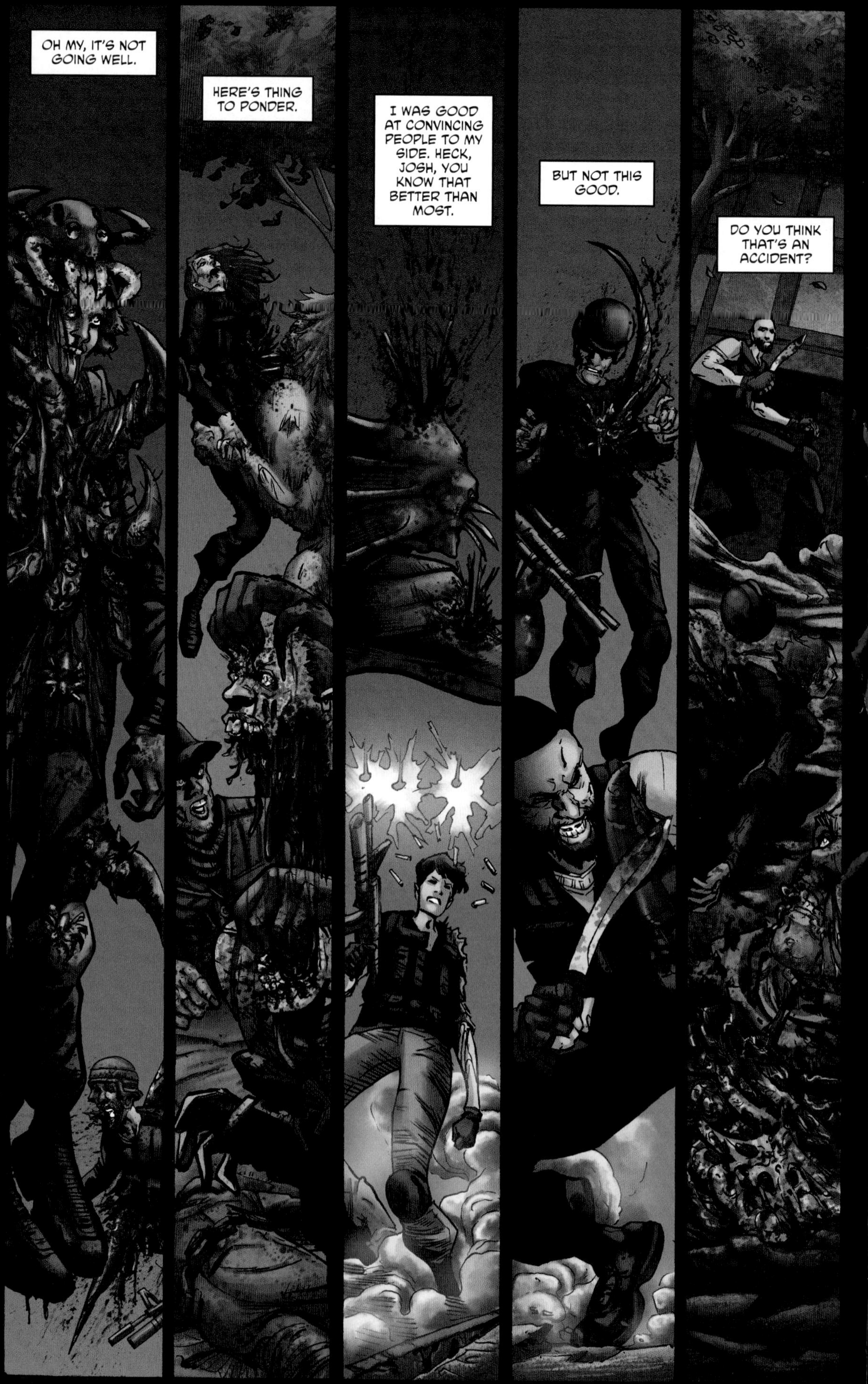
OH MY, IT'S NOT GOING WELL.
HERE'S THING TO PONDER.
I WAS GOOD AT CONVINCING PEOPLE TO MY SIDE. HECK, JOSH, YOU KNOW THAT BETTER THAN MOST.
BUT NOT THIS GOOD.
DO YOU THINK THAT'S AN ACCIDENT?

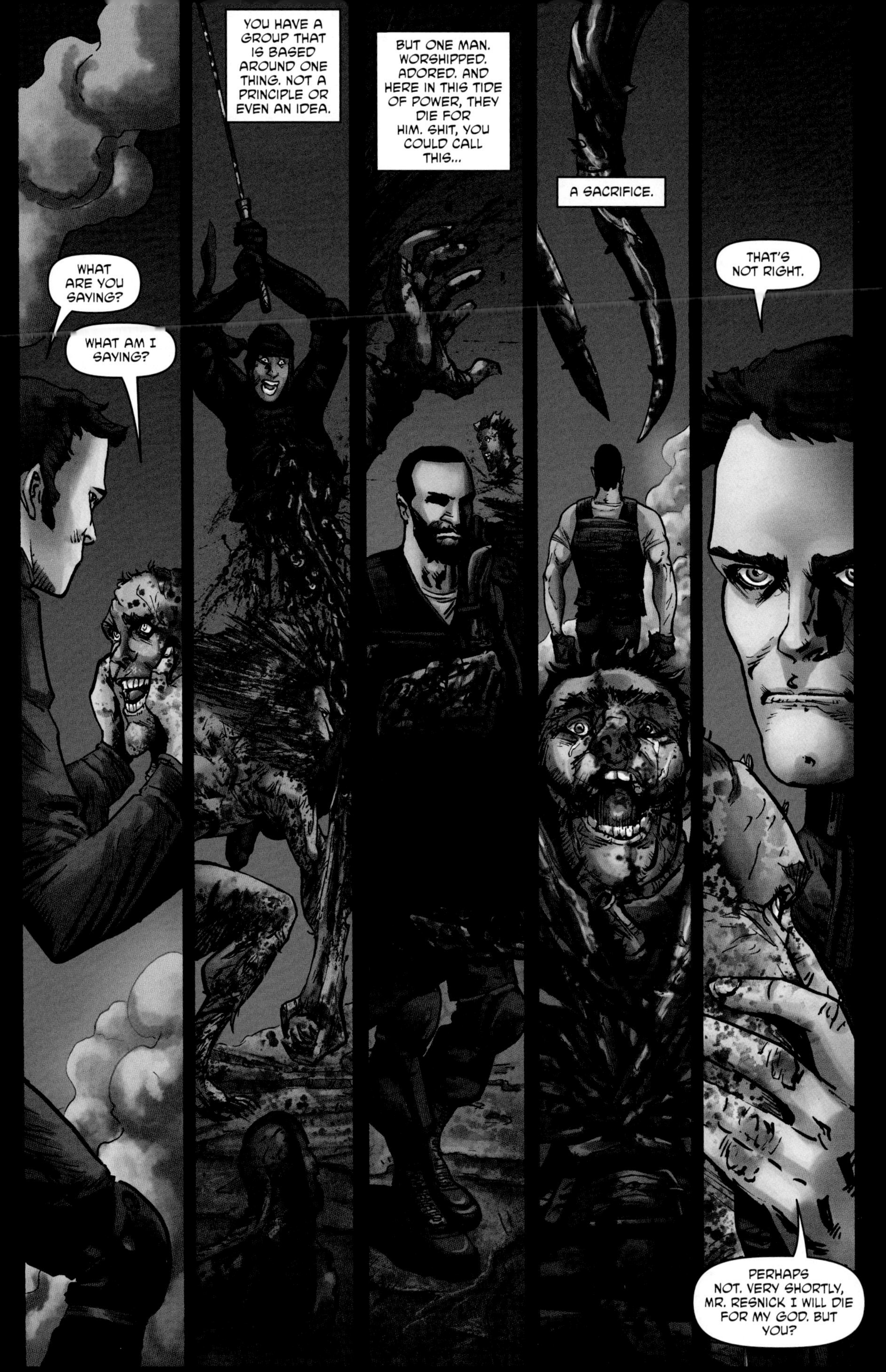
WHAT ARE YOU SAYING?
WHAT AM I SAYING?
YOU HAVE A GROUP THAT IS BASED AROUND ONE THING. NOT A PRINCIPLE OR EVEN AN IDEA.
BUT ONE MAN. WORSHIPPED. ADORED. AND HERE IN THIS TIDE OF POWER, THEY DIE FOR HIM. SHIT, YOU COULD CALL THIS...
A SACRIFICE.
THAT'S NOT RIGHT.
PERHAPS NOT. VERY SHORTLY, MR. RESNICK I WILL DIE FOR MY GOD. BUT YOU?

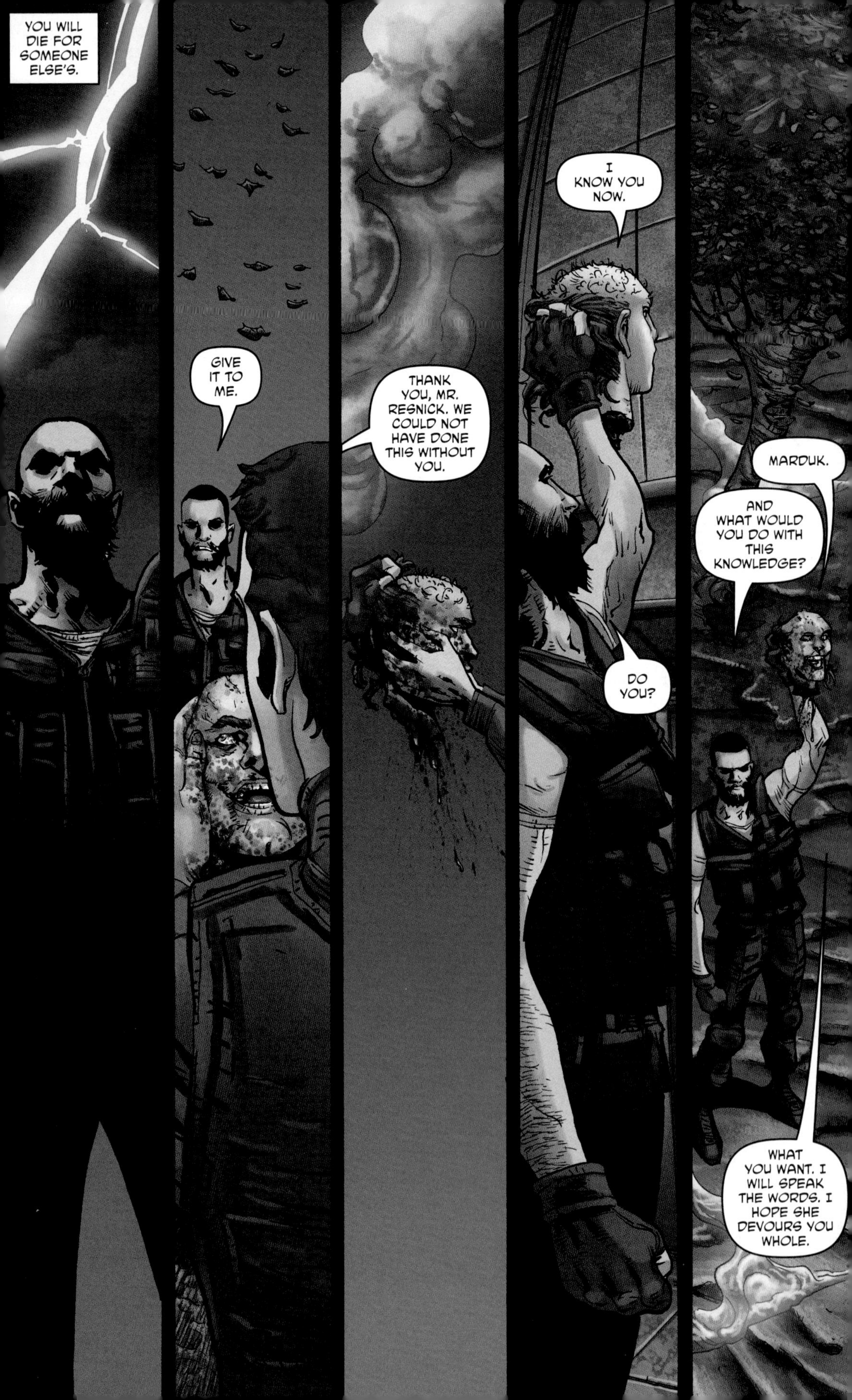
YOU WILL DIE FOR SOMEONE ELSE'S.
GIVE IT TO ME.
THANK YOU, MR. RESNICK. WE COULD NOT HAVE DONE THIS WITHOUT YOU.
I KNOW YOU NOW.
DO YOU?
MARDUK.
AND WHAT WOULD YOU DO WITH THIS KNOWLEDGE?
WHAT YOU WANT. I WILL SPEAK THE WORDS. I HOPE SHE DEVOURS YOU WHOLE.

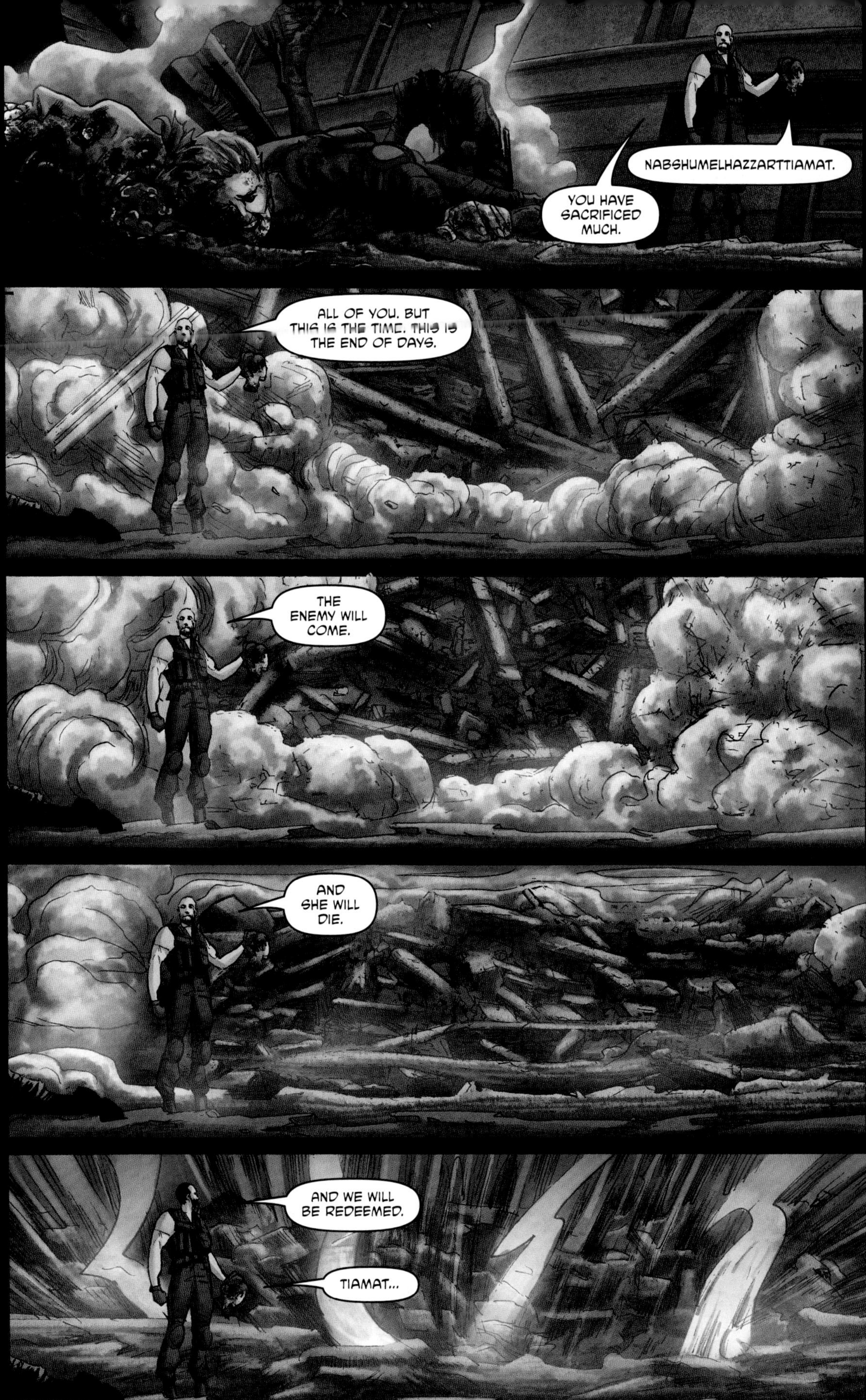
NABSHUMELHAZZARTTIAMAT.
YOU HAVE SACRIFICED MUCH.
ALL OF YOU. BUT THIS IS THE TIME. THIS IS THE END OF DAYS.
THE ENEMY WILL COME.
AND SHE WILL DIE.
AND WE WILL BE REDEEMED.
TIAMAT...

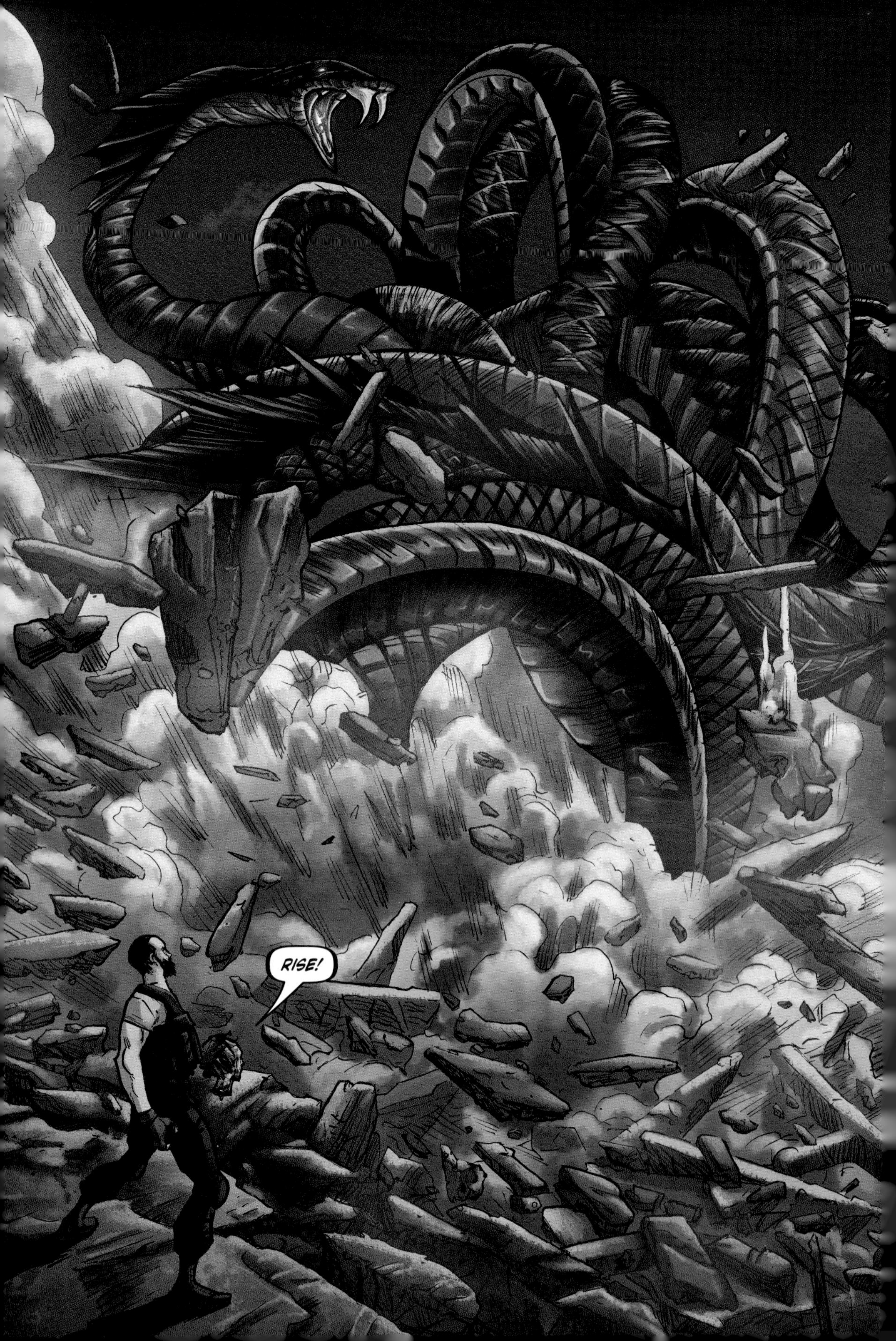
RISE!

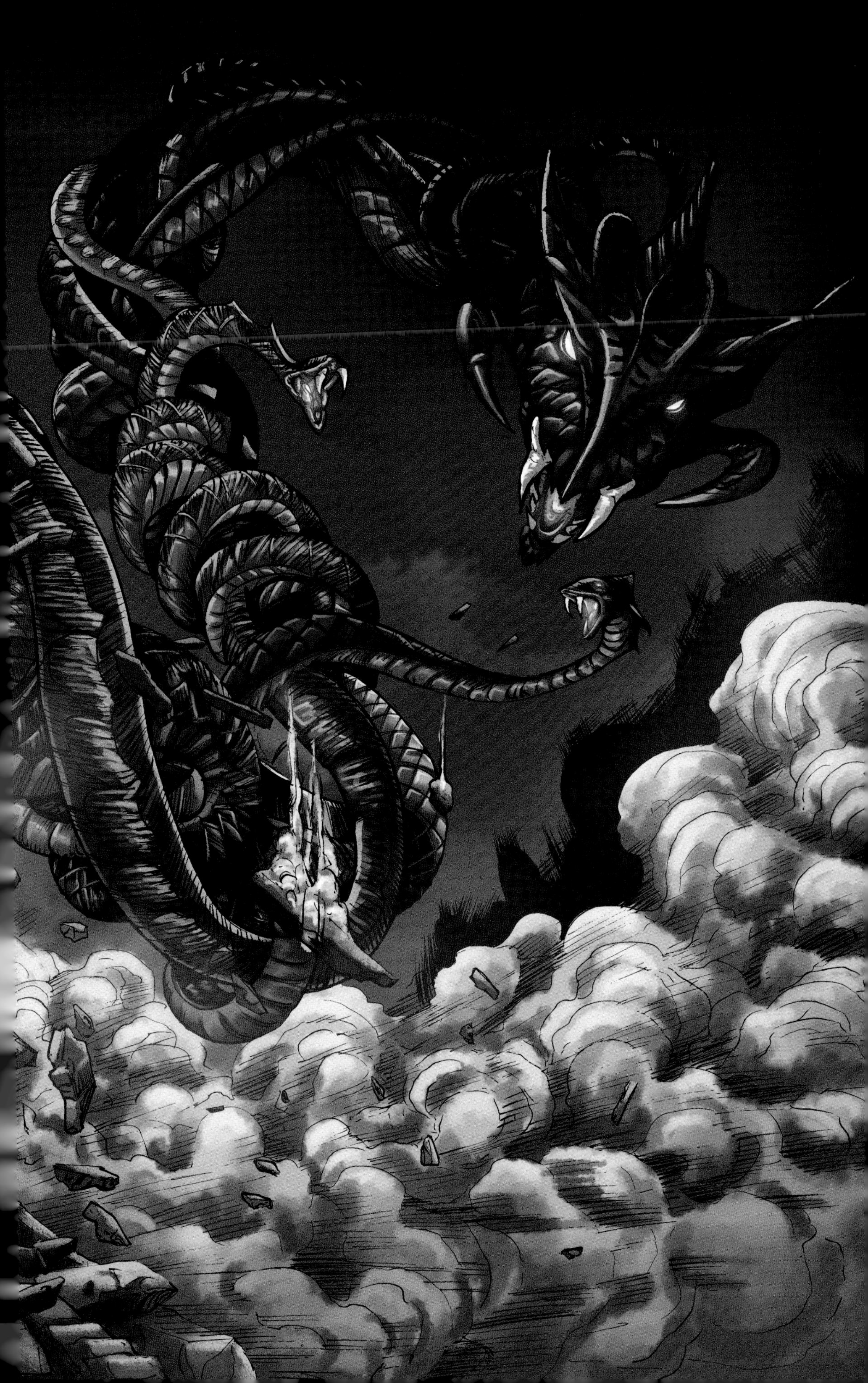

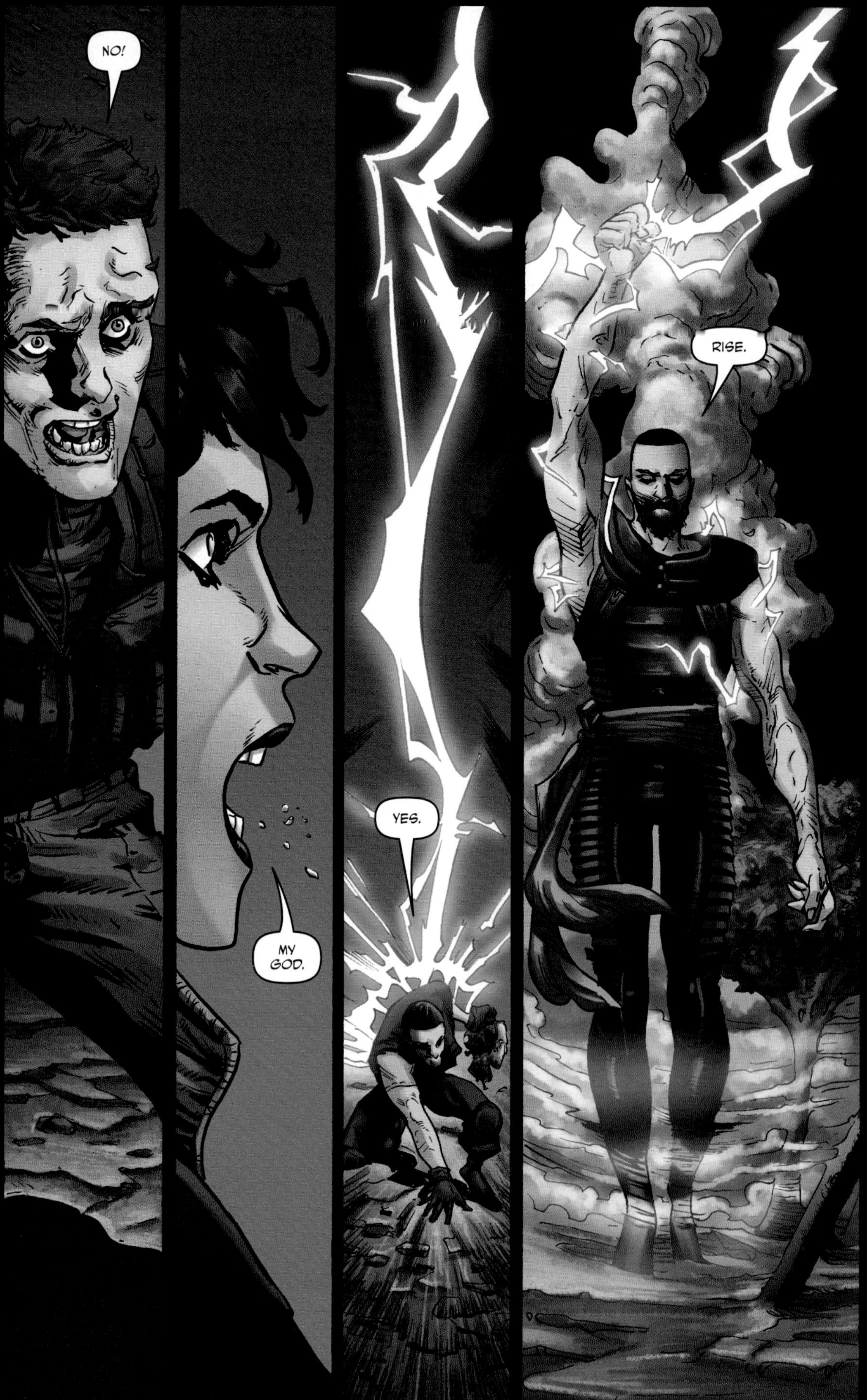
NO!
MY GOD.
YES.
RISE.

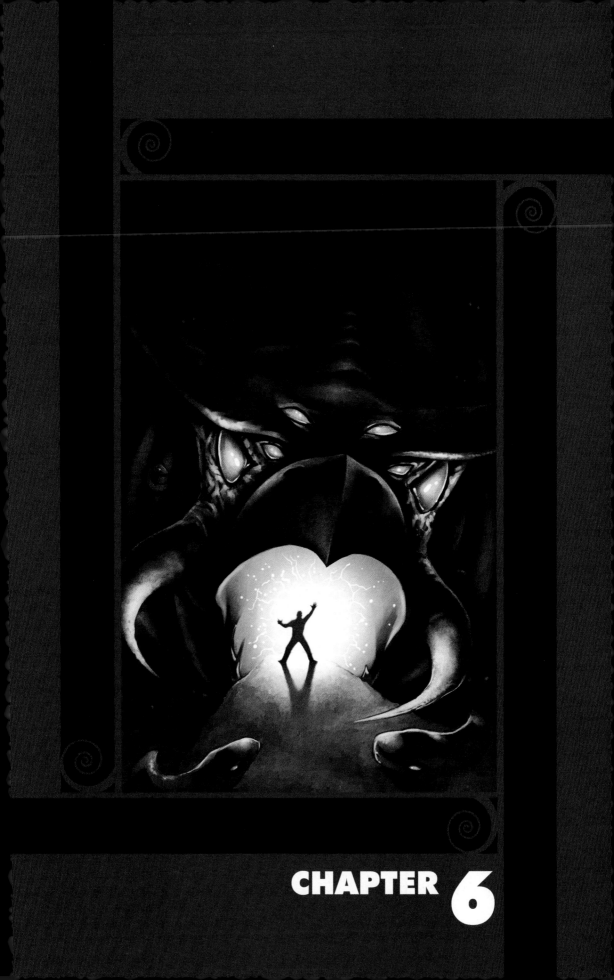

**CHAPTER 6**

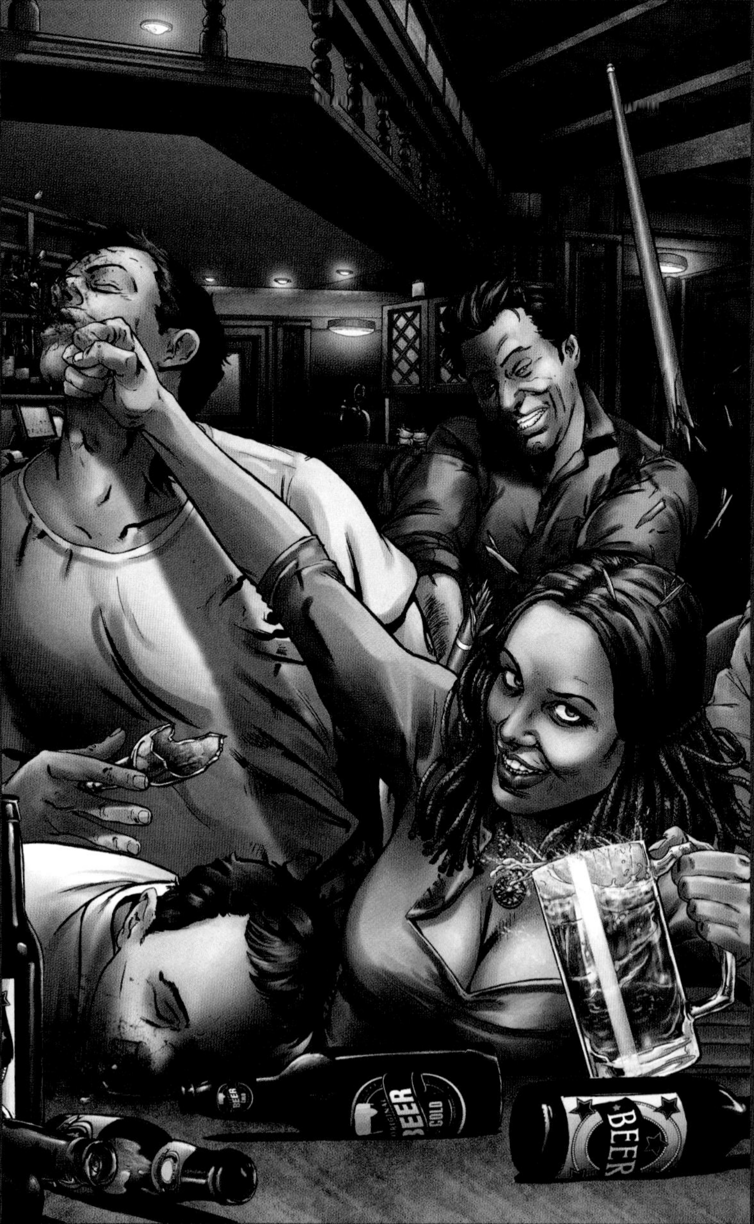
BEER
BEER
COLD
BEER

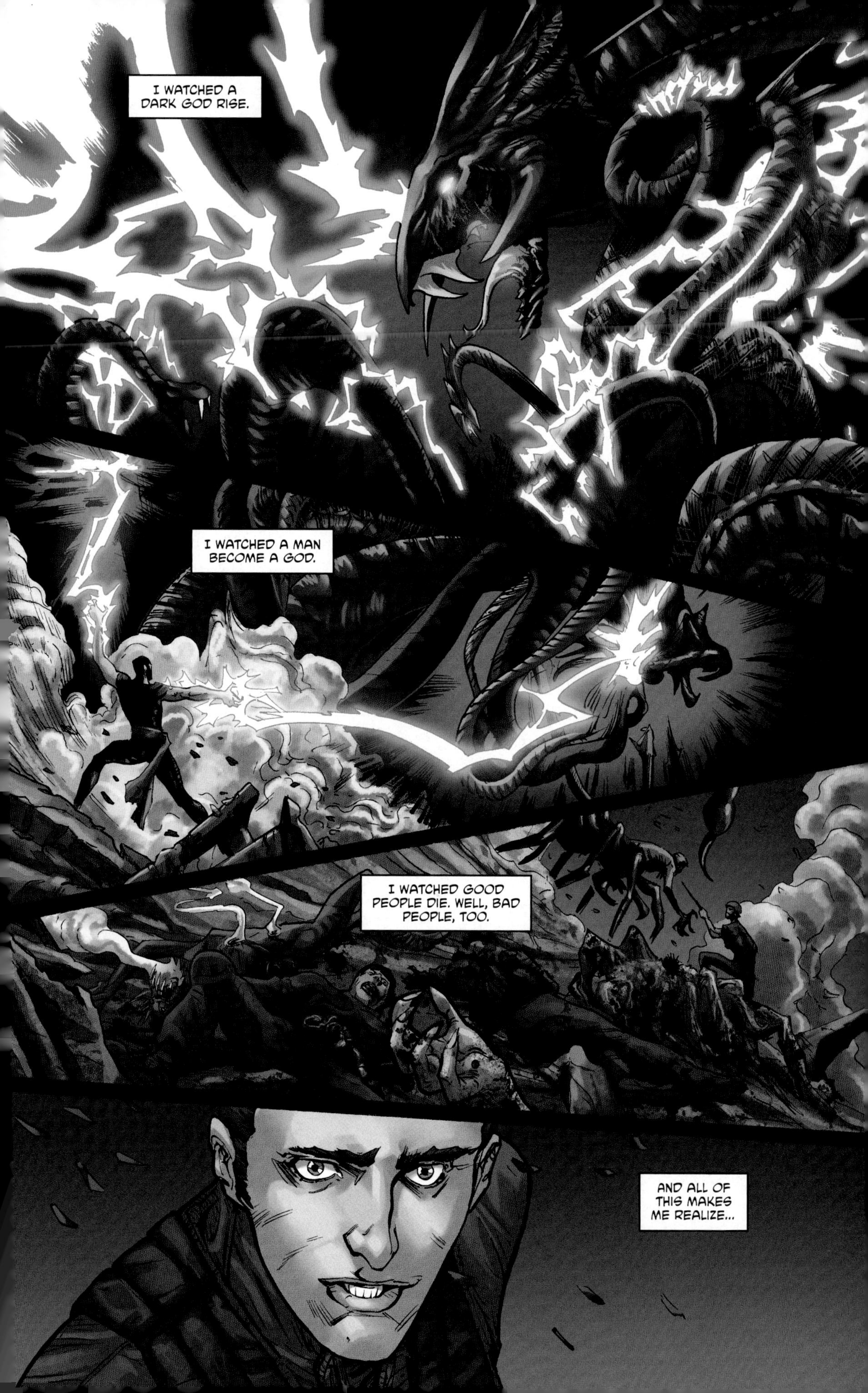
I WATCHED A DARK GOD RISE.
I WATCHED A MAN BECOME A GOD.
I WATCHED GOOD PEOPLE DIE. WELL, BAD PEOPLE, TOO.
AND ALL OF THIS MAKES ME REALIZE...

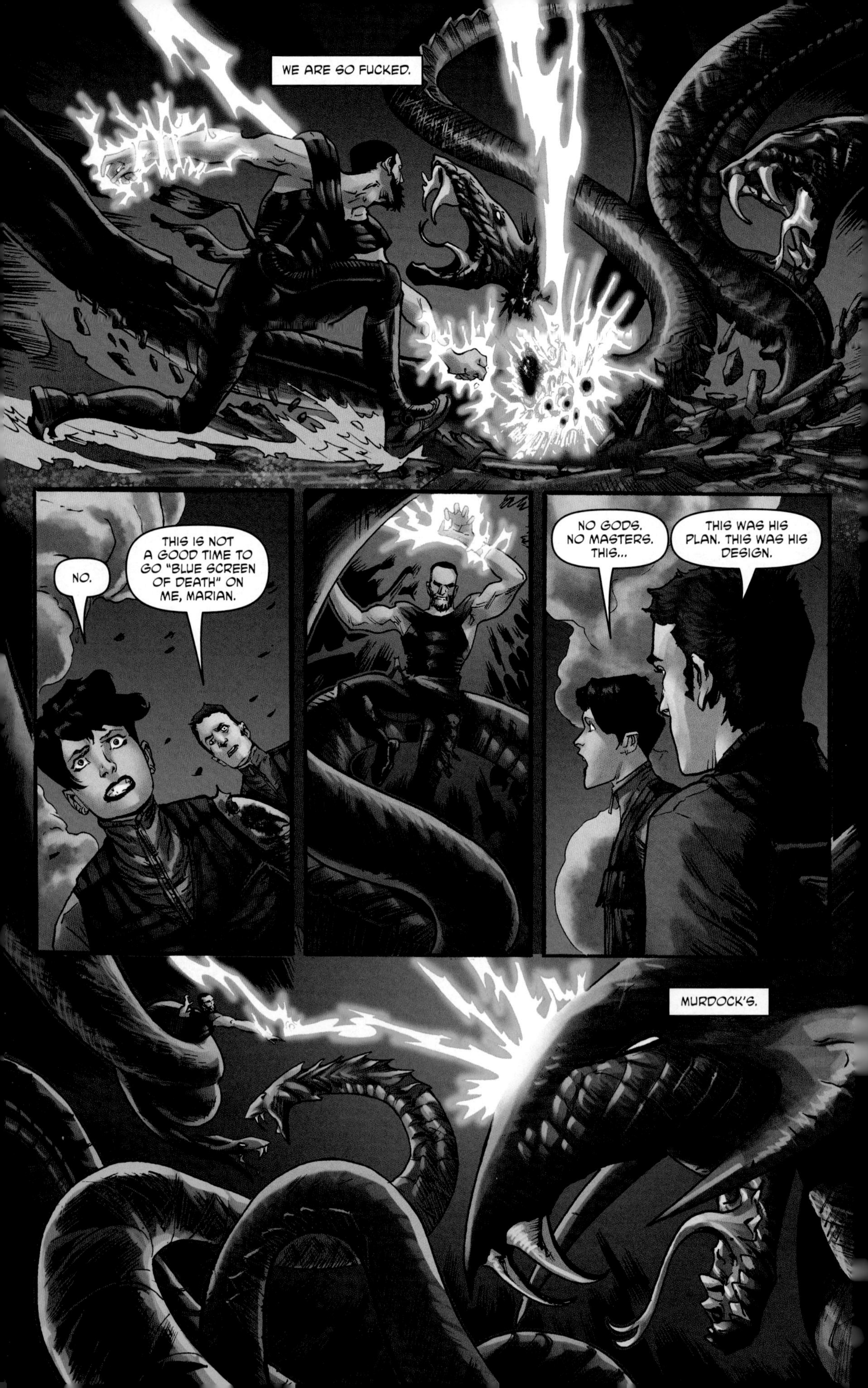
WE ARE SO FUCKED.
NO.
THIS IS NOT A GOOD TIME TO GO "BLUE SCREEN OF DEATH" ON ME, MARIAN.
NO GODS. NO MASTERS. THIS...
THIS WAS HIS PLAN. THIS WAS HIS DESIGN.
MURDOCK'S.

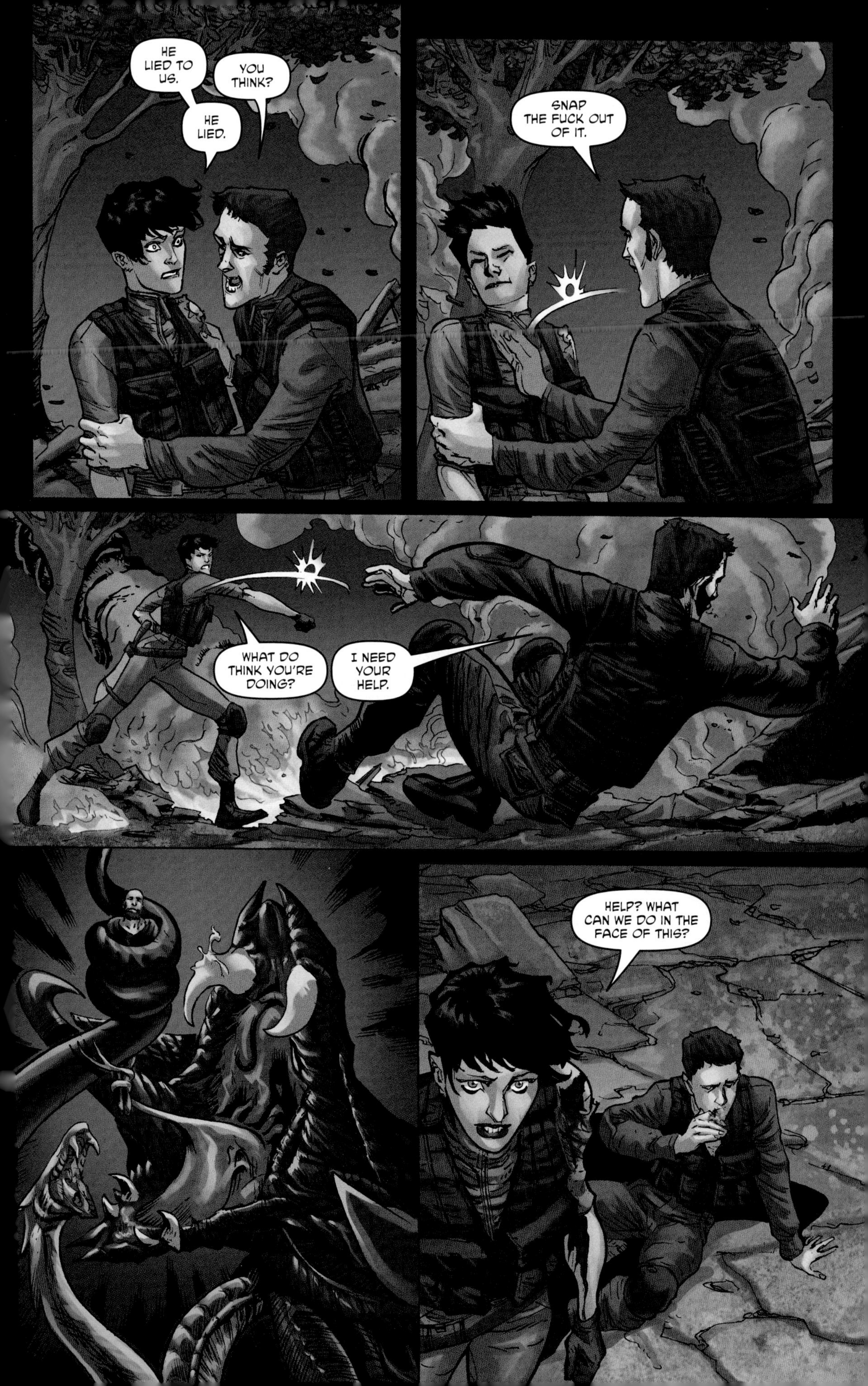
HE LIED TO US.
YOU THINK?
HE LIED.
SNAP THE FUCK OUT OF IT.
WHAT DO THINK YOU'RE DOING?
I NEED YOUR HELP.
HELP? WHAT CAN WE DO IN THE FACE OF THIS?

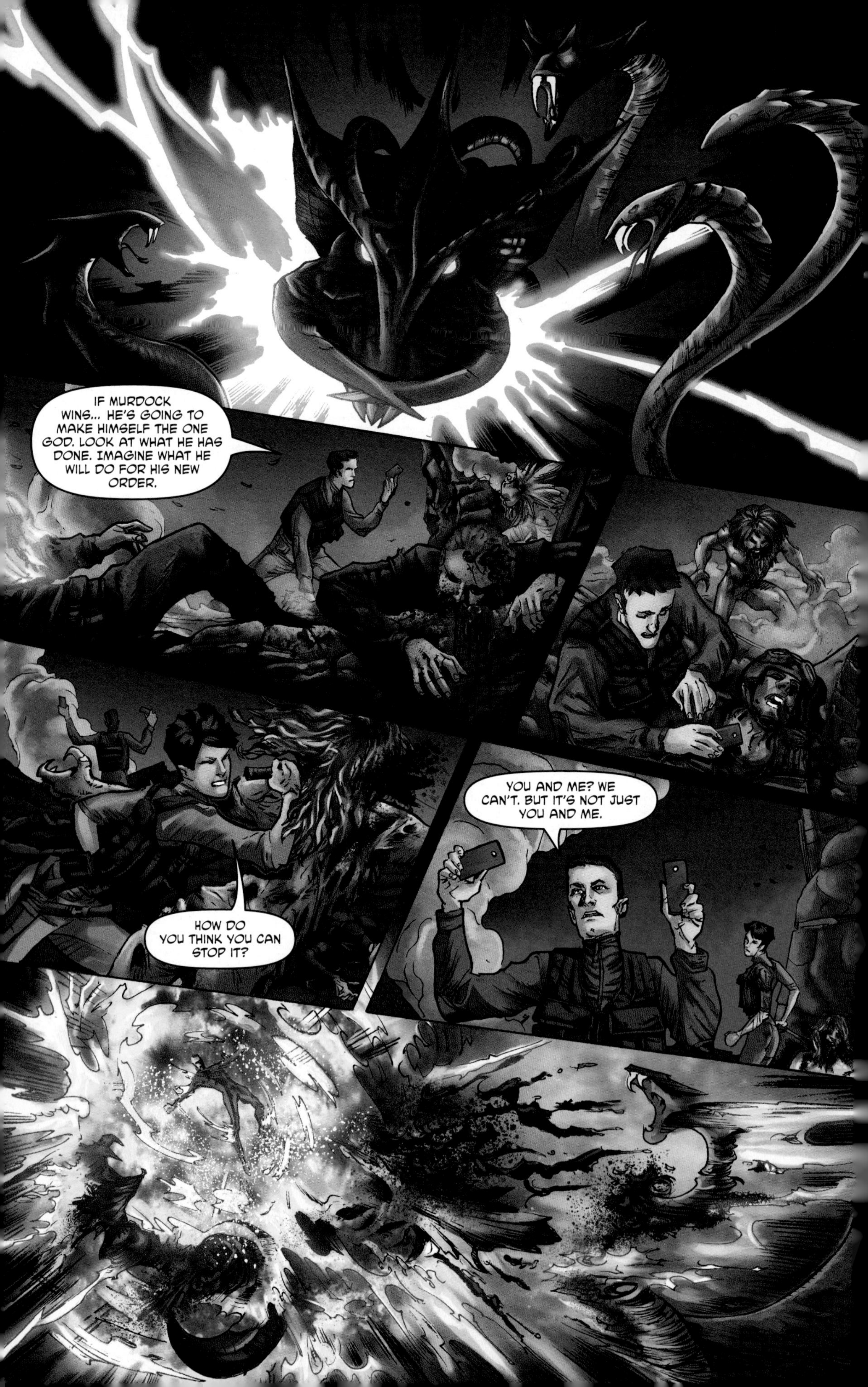
IF MURDOCK WINS... HE'S GOING TO MAKE HIMSELF THE ONE GOD. LOOK AT WHAT HE HAS DONE. IMAGINE WHAT HE WILL DO FOR HIS NEW ORDER.
HOW DO YOU THINK YOU CAN STOP IT?
YOU AND ME? WE CAN'T. BUT IT'S NOT JUST YOU AND ME.

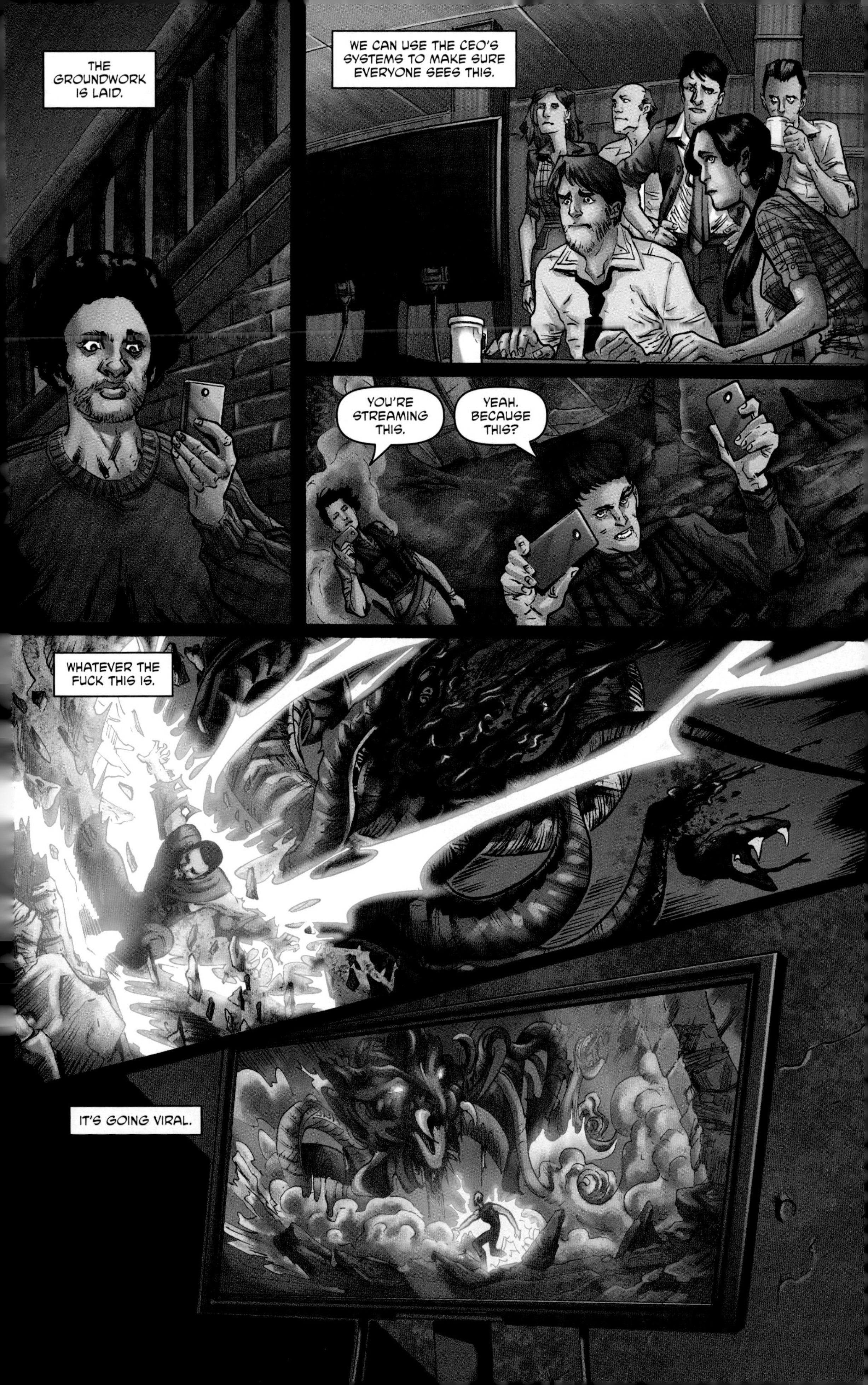
THE GROUNDWORK IS LAID.
WE CAN USE THE CEO'S SYSTEMS TO MAKE SURE EVERYONE SEES THIS.
YOU'RE STREAMING THIS.
YEAH. BECAUSE THIS?
WHATEVER THE FUCK THIS IS.
IT'S GOING VIRAL.

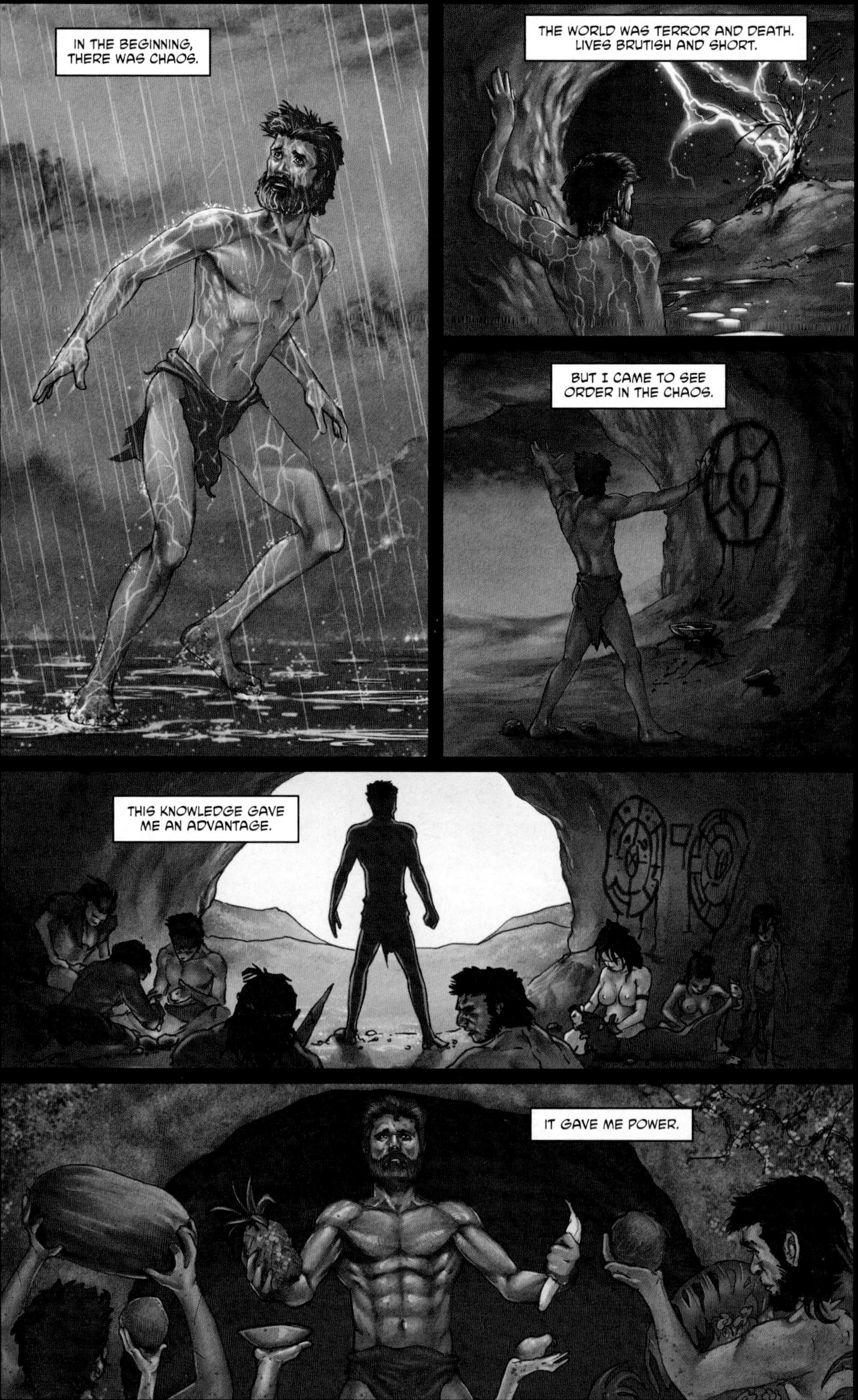
IN THE BEGINNING, THERE WAS CHAOS.
THE WORLD WAS TERROR AND DEATH. LIVES BRUTISH AND SHORT.
BUT I CAME TO SEE ORDER IN THE CHAOS.
THIS KNOWLEDGE GAVE ME AN ADVANTAGE.
IT GAVE ME POWER.

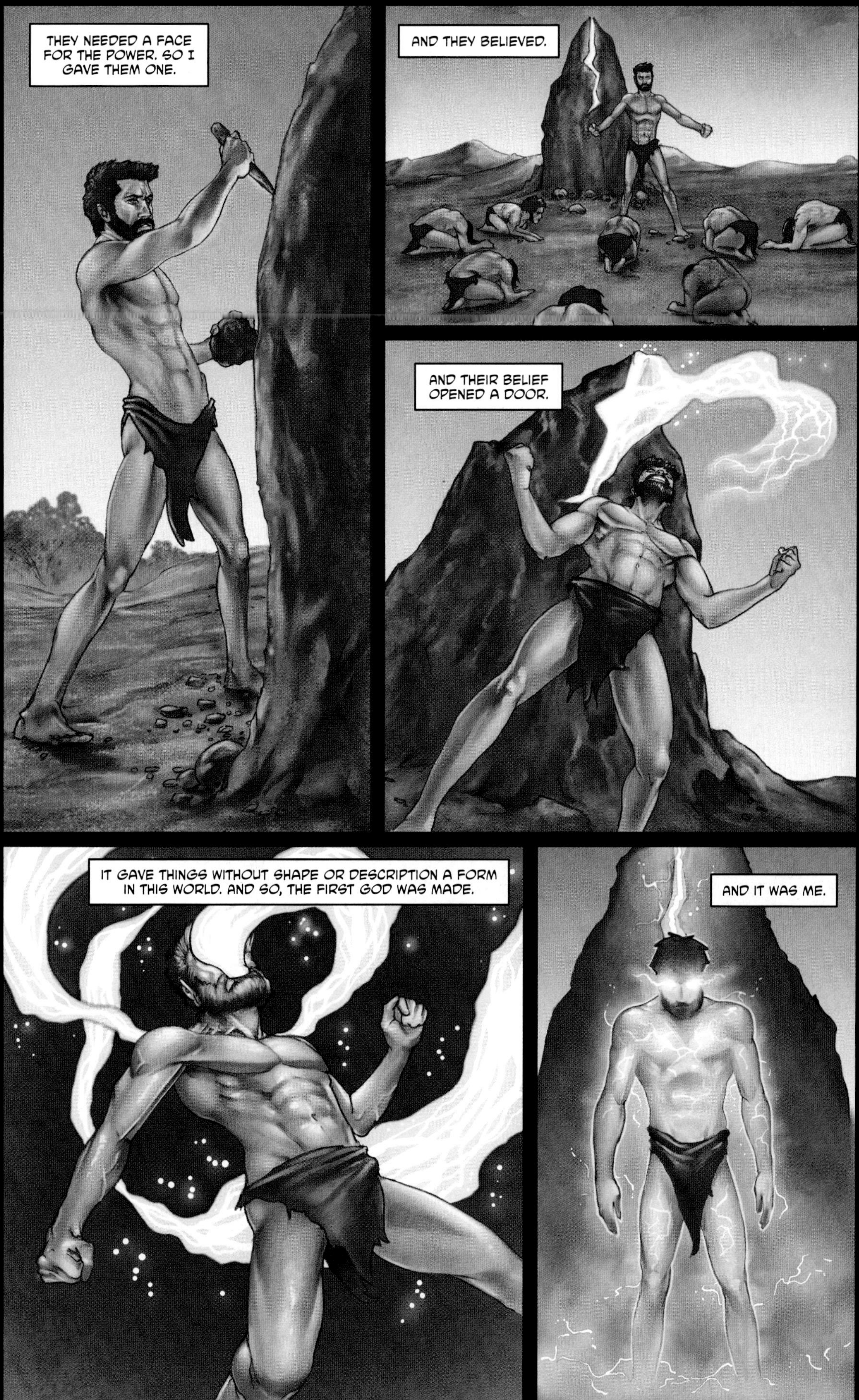
THEY NEEDED A FACE FOR THE POWER. SO I GAVE THEM ONE.
AND THEY BELIEVED.
AND THEIR BELIEF OPENED A DOOR.
IT GAVE THINGS WITHOUT SHAPE OR DESCRIPTION A FORM IN THIS WORLD. AND SO, THE FIRST GOD WAS MADE.
AND IT WAS ME.

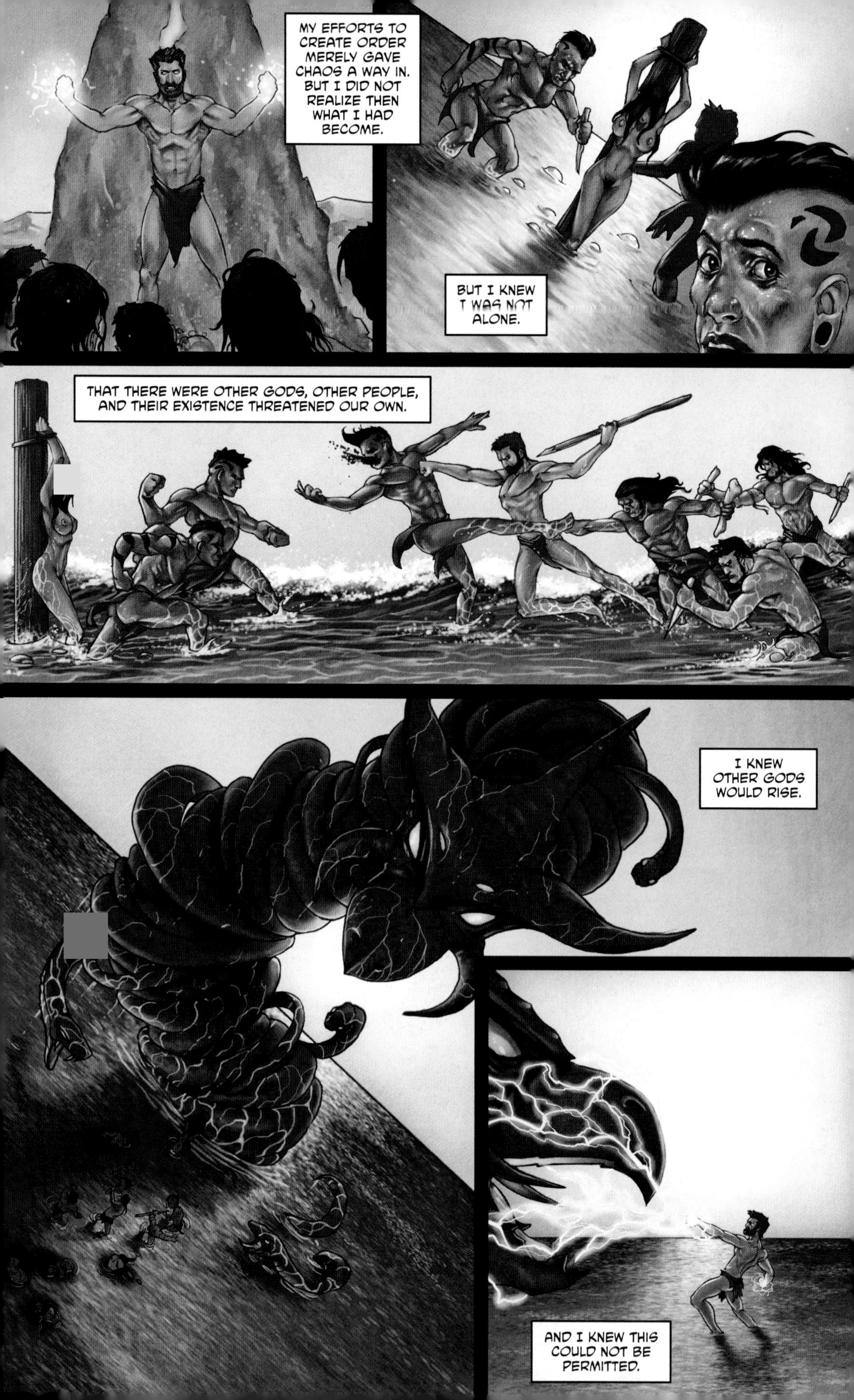
MY EFFORTS TO CREATE ORDER MERELY GAVE CHAOS A WAY IN. BUT I DID NOT REALIZE THEN WHAT I HAD BECOME.
BUT I KNEW I WAS NOT ALONE.
THAT THERE WERE OTHER GODS, OTHER PEOPLE, AND THEIR EXISTENCE THREATENED OUR OWN.
I KNEW OTHER GODS WOULD RISE.
AND I KNEW THIS COULD NOT BE PERMITTED.

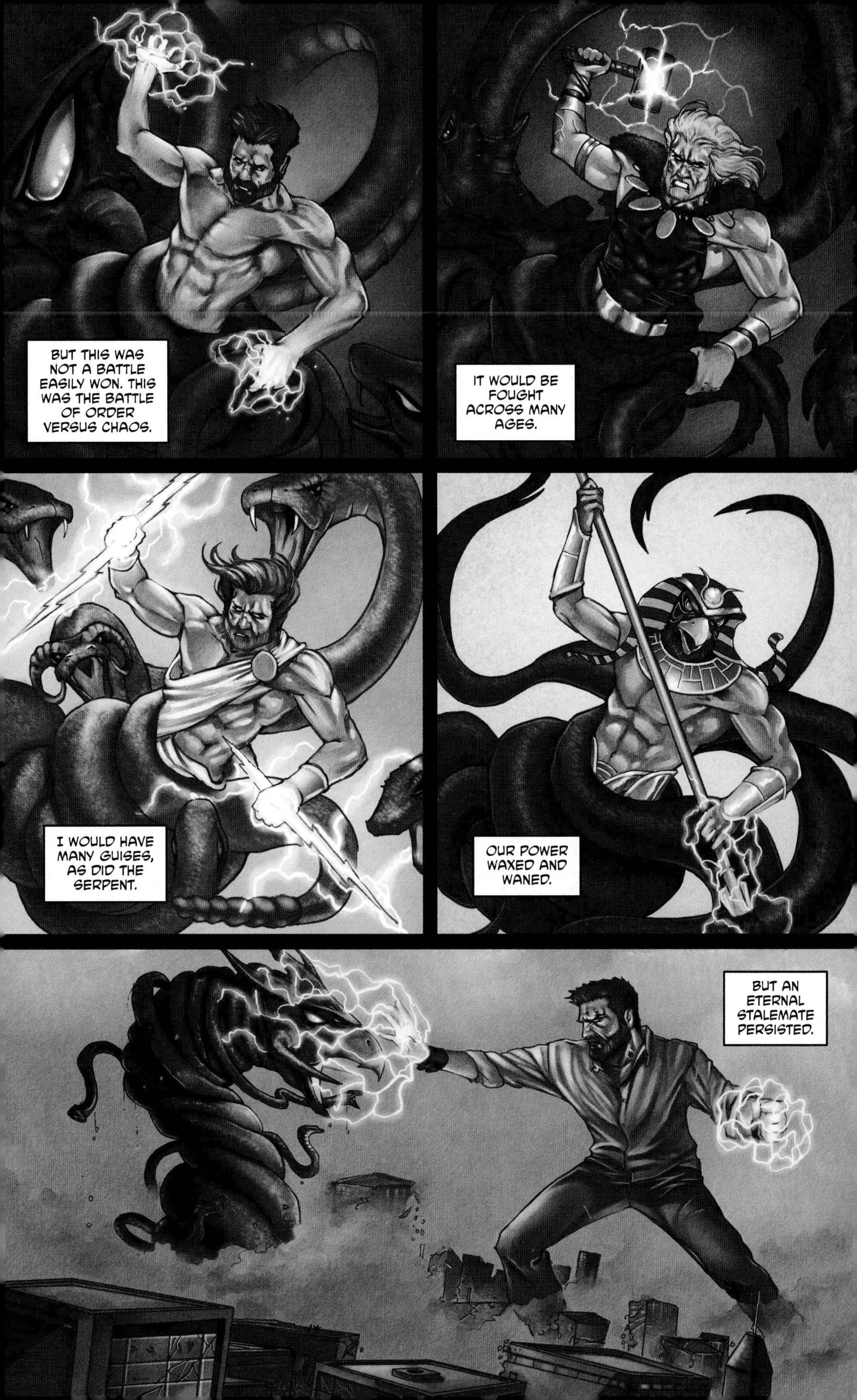
BUT THIS WAS NOT A BATTLE EASILY WON. THIS WAS THE BATTLE OF ORDER VERSUS CHAOS.
IT WOULD BE FOUGHT ACROSS MANY AGES.
I WOULD HAVE MANY GUISES, AS DID THE SERPENT.
OUR POWER WAXED AND WANED.
BUT AN ETERNAL STALEMATE PERSISTED.

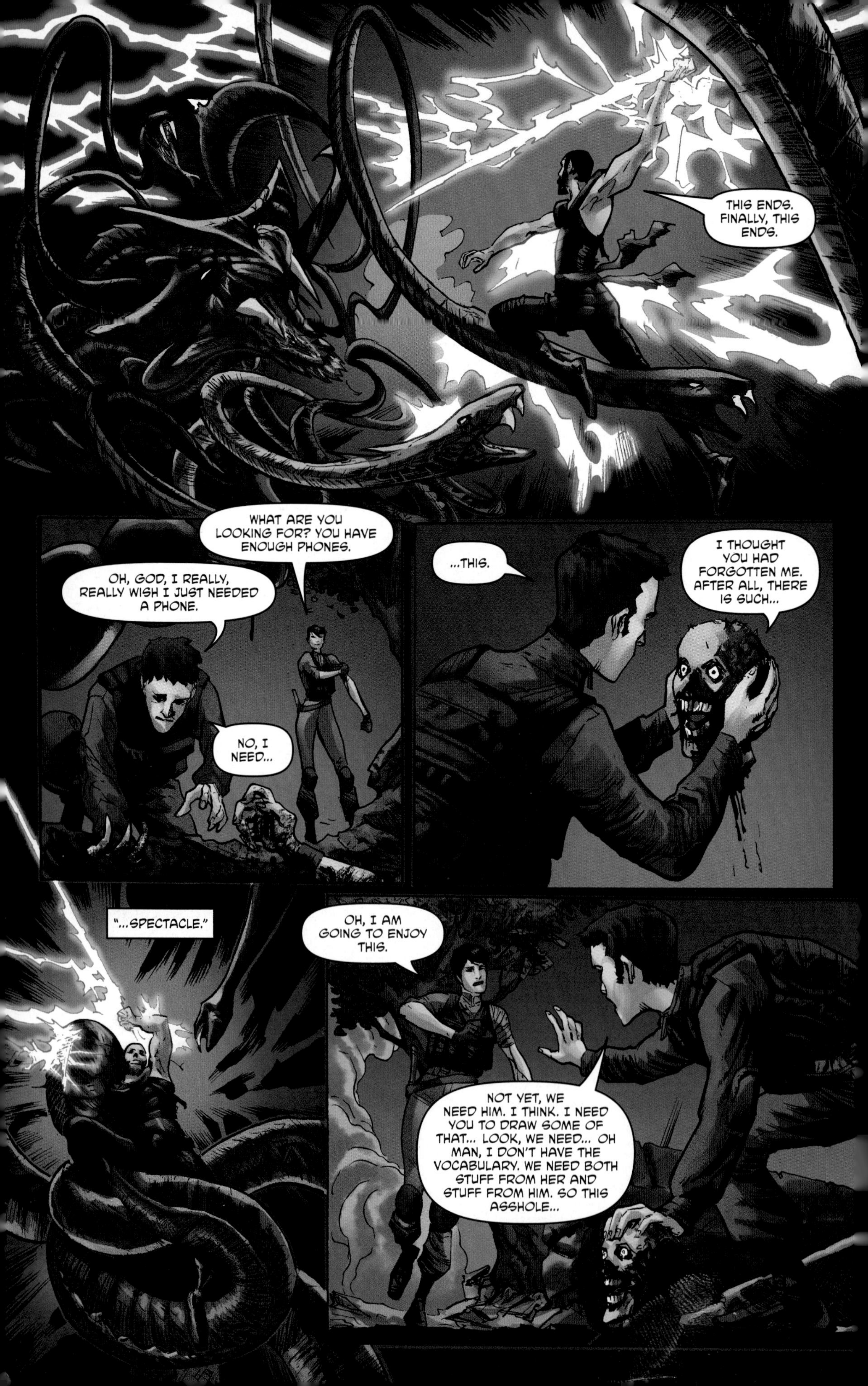
THIS ENDS. FINALLY, THIS ENDS.
WHAT ARE YOU LOOKING FOR? YOU HAVE ENOUGH PHONES.
OH, GOD, I REALLY, REALLY WISH I JUST NEEDED A PHONE.
NO, I NEED...
...THIS.
I THOUGHT YOU HAD FORGOTTEN ME. AFTER ALL, THERE IS SUCH...
"...SPECTACLE."
OH, I AM GOING TO ENJOY THIS.
NOT YET, WE NEED HIM. I THINK. I NEED YOU TO DRAW SOME OF THAT... LOOK, WE NEED... OH MAN, I DON'T HAVE THE VOCABULARY. WE NEED BOTH STUFF FROM HER AND STUFF FROM HIM. SO THIS ASSHOLE...

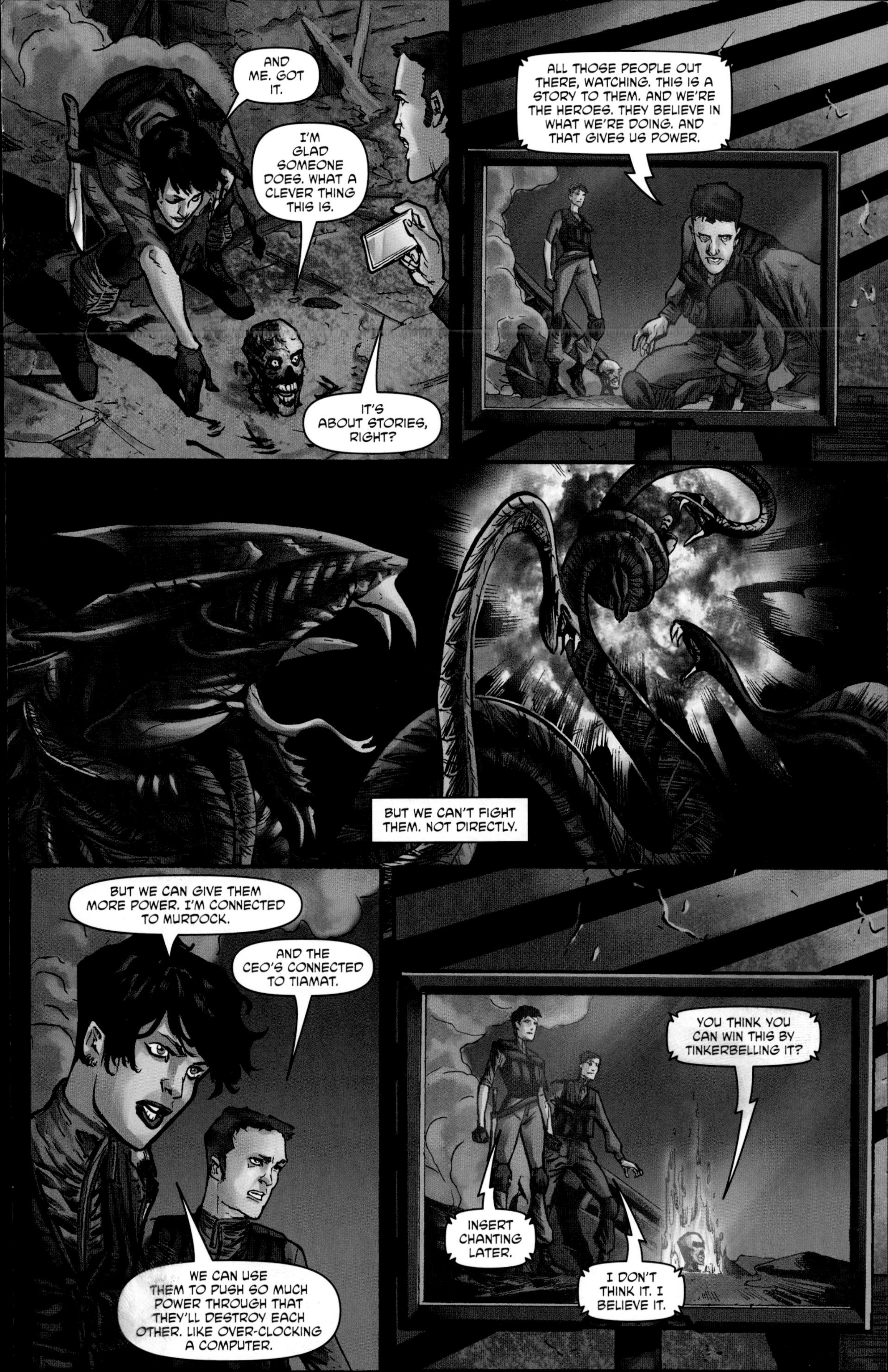
AND ME. GOT IT.
I'M GLAD SOMEONE DOES. WHAT A CLEVER THING THIS IS.
IT'S ABOUT STORIES, RIGHT?
ALL THOSE PEOPLE OUT THERE, WATCHING. THIS IS A STORY TO THEM. AND WE'RE THE HEROES. THEY BELIEVE IN WHAT WE'RE DOING. AND THAT GIVES US POWER.
BUT WE CAN'T FIGHT THEM. NOT DIRECTLY.
BUT WE CAN GIVE THEM MORE POWER. I'M CONNECTED TO MURDOCK.
AND THE CEO'S CONNECTED TO TIAMAT.
WE CAN USE THEM TO PUSH SO MUCH POWER THROUGH THAT THEY'LL DESTROY EACH OTHER. LIKE OVER-CLOCKING A COMPUTER.
YOU THINK YOU CAN WIN THIS BY TINKERBELLING IT?
INSERT CHANTING LATER.
I DON'T THINK IT. I BELIEVE IT.

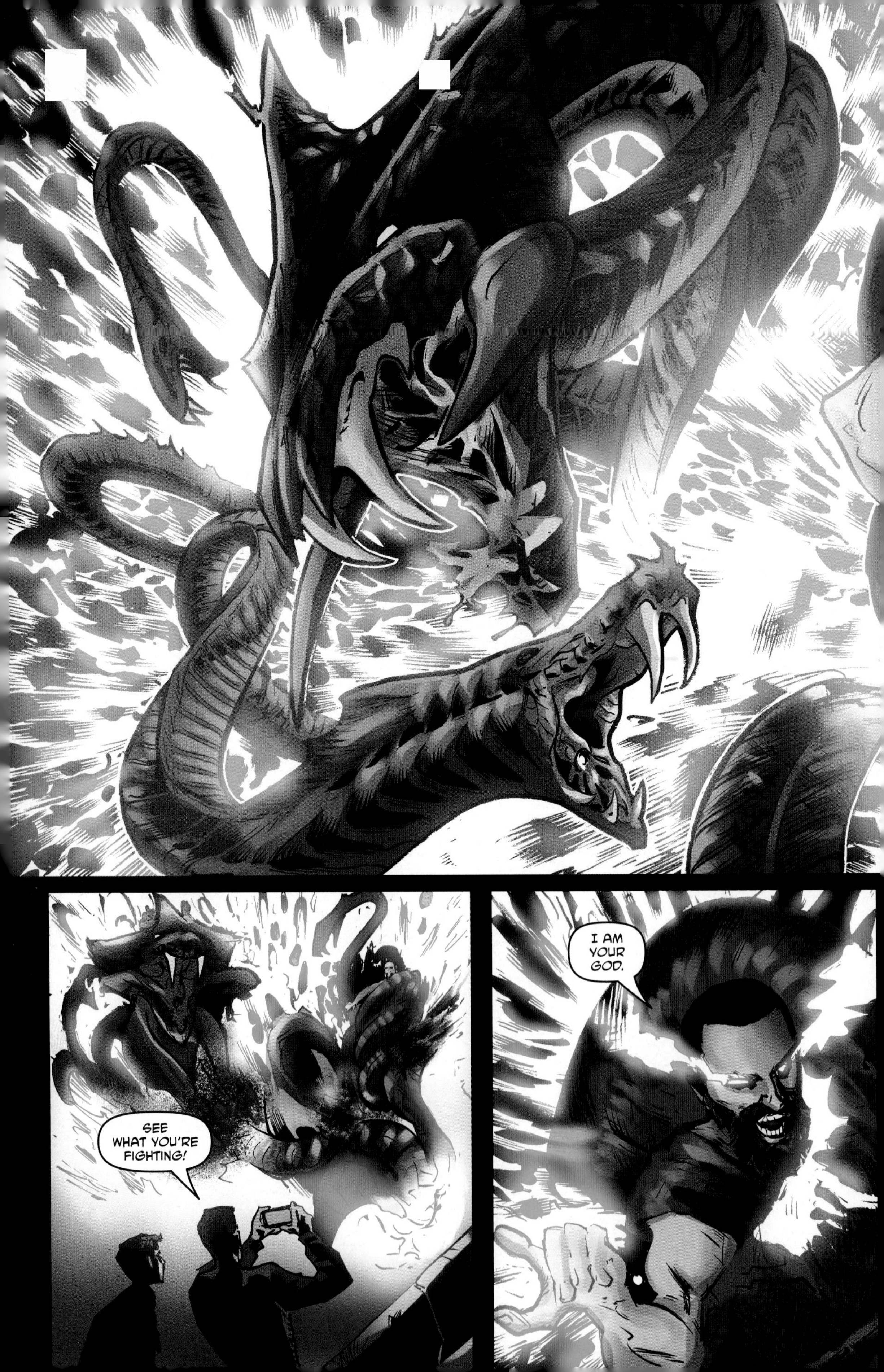
SEE WHAT YOU'RE FIGHTING!
I AM YOUR GOD.

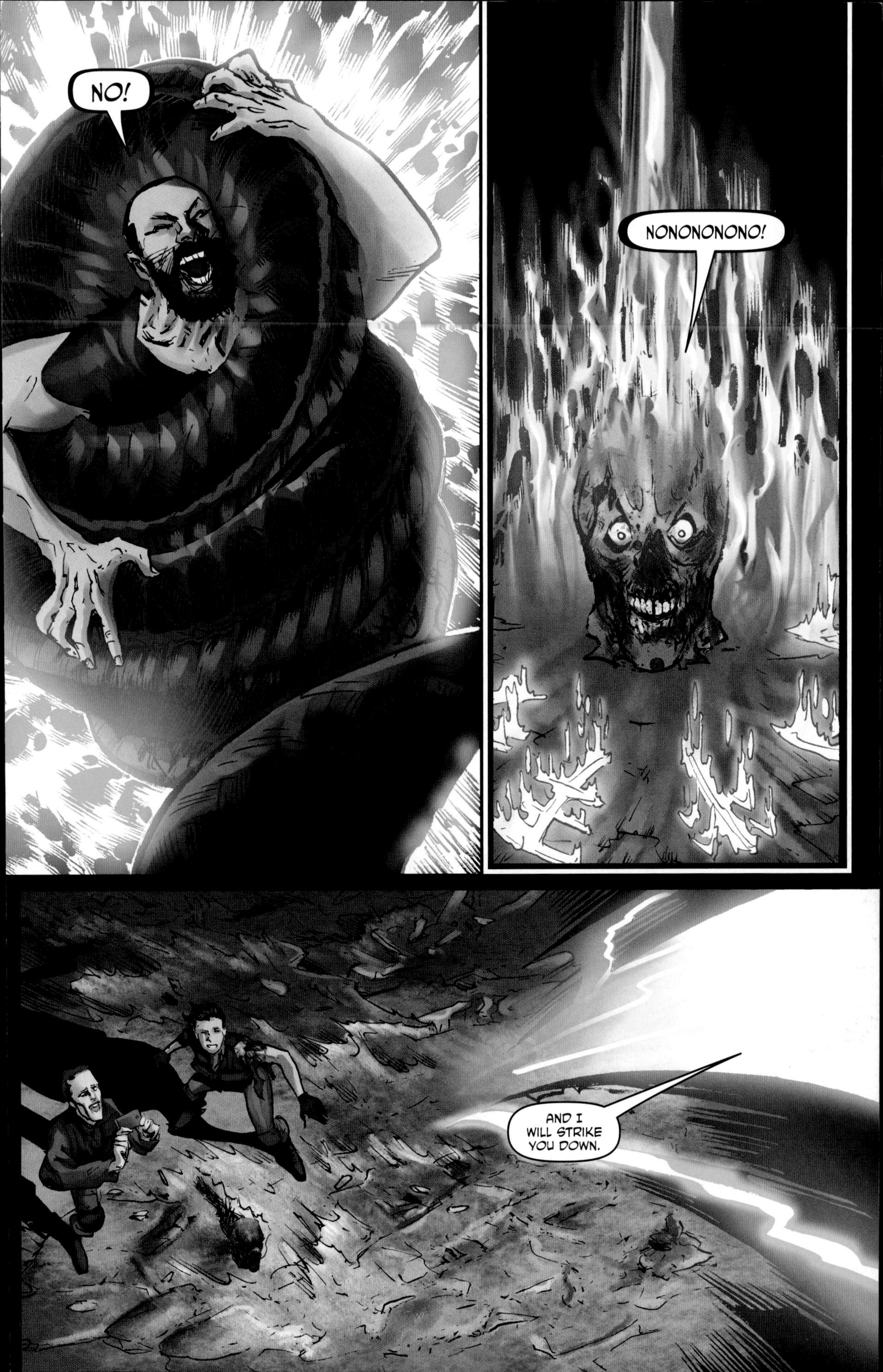
NO!
NONONONONO!
AND I WILL STRIKE YOU DOWN.

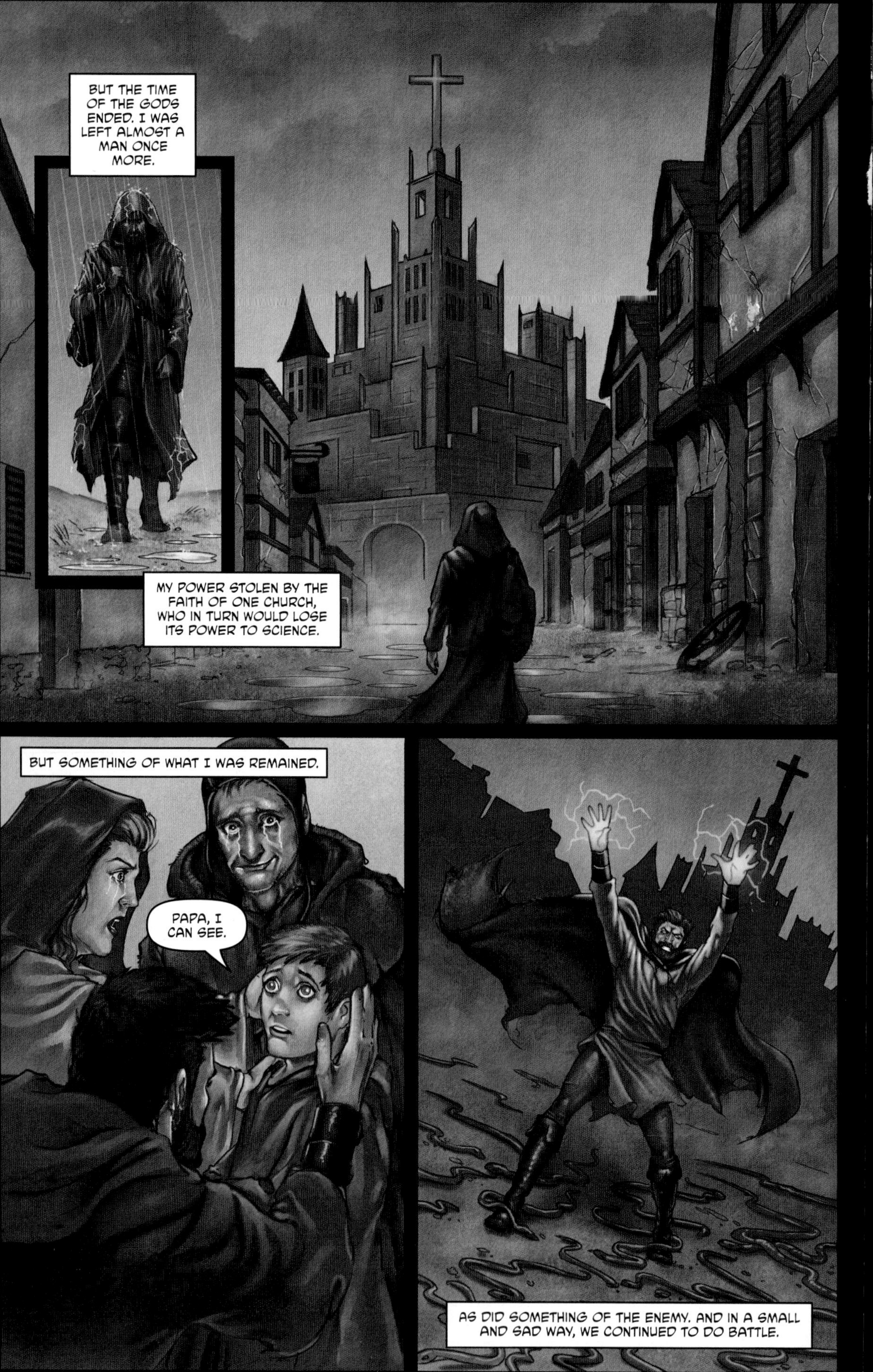
BUT THE TIME OF THE GODS ENDED. I WAS LEFT ALMOST A MAN ONCE MORE.
MY POWER STOLEN BY THE FAITH OF ONE CHURCH, WHO IN TURN WOULD LOSE ITS POWER TO SCIENCE.
BUT SOMETHING OF WHAT I WAS REMAINED.
PAPA, I CAN SEE.
AS DID SOMETHING OF THE ENEMY. AND IN A SMALL AND SAD WAY, WE CONTINUED TO DO BATTLE.

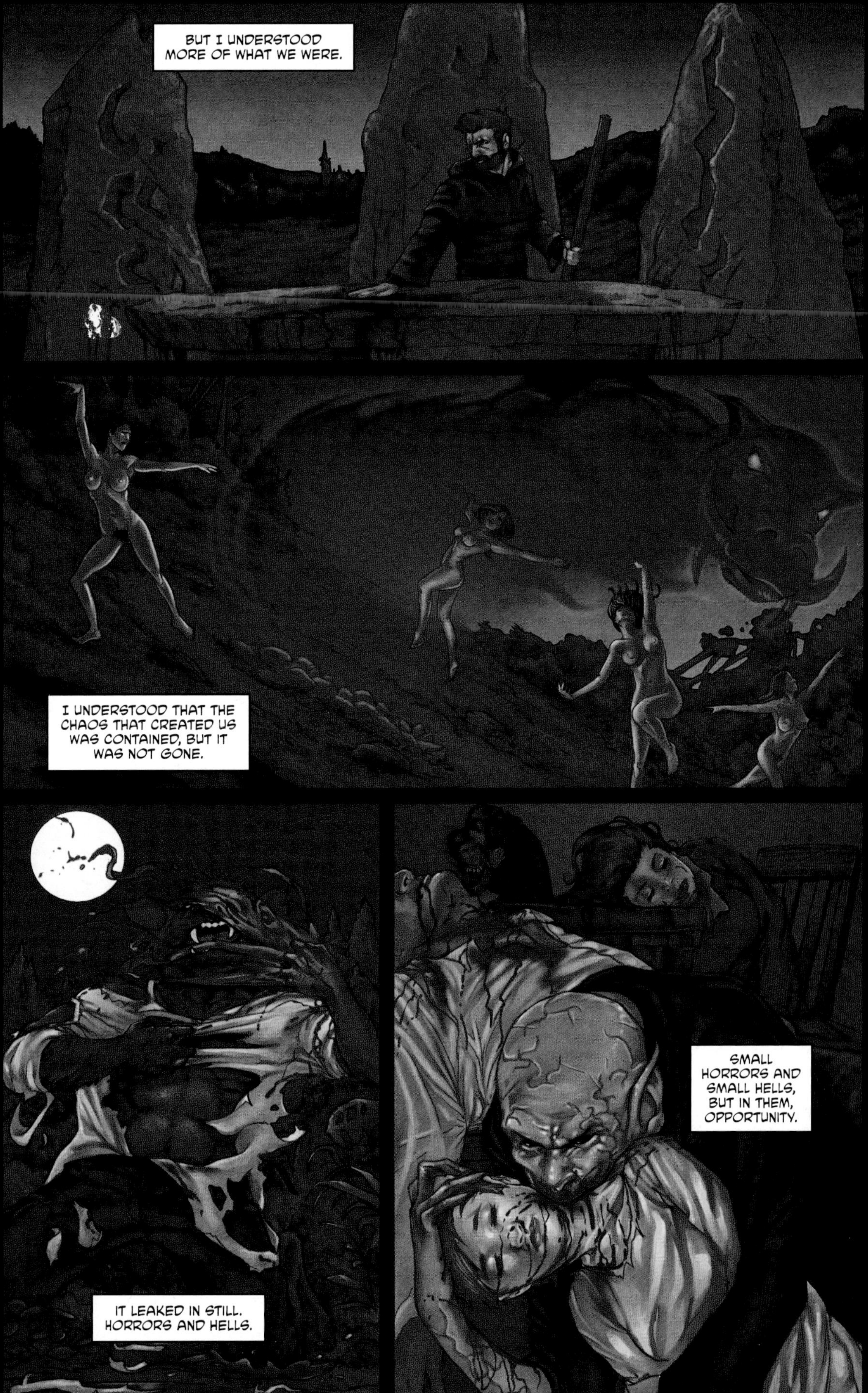
BUT I UNDERSTOOD MORE OF WHAT WE WERE.
I UNDERSTOOD THAT THE CHAOS THAT CREATED US WAS CONTAINED, BUT IT WAS NOT GONE.
IT LEAKED IN STILL. HORRORS AND HELLS.
SMALL HORRORS AND SMALL HELLS, BUT IN THEM, OPPORTUNITY.

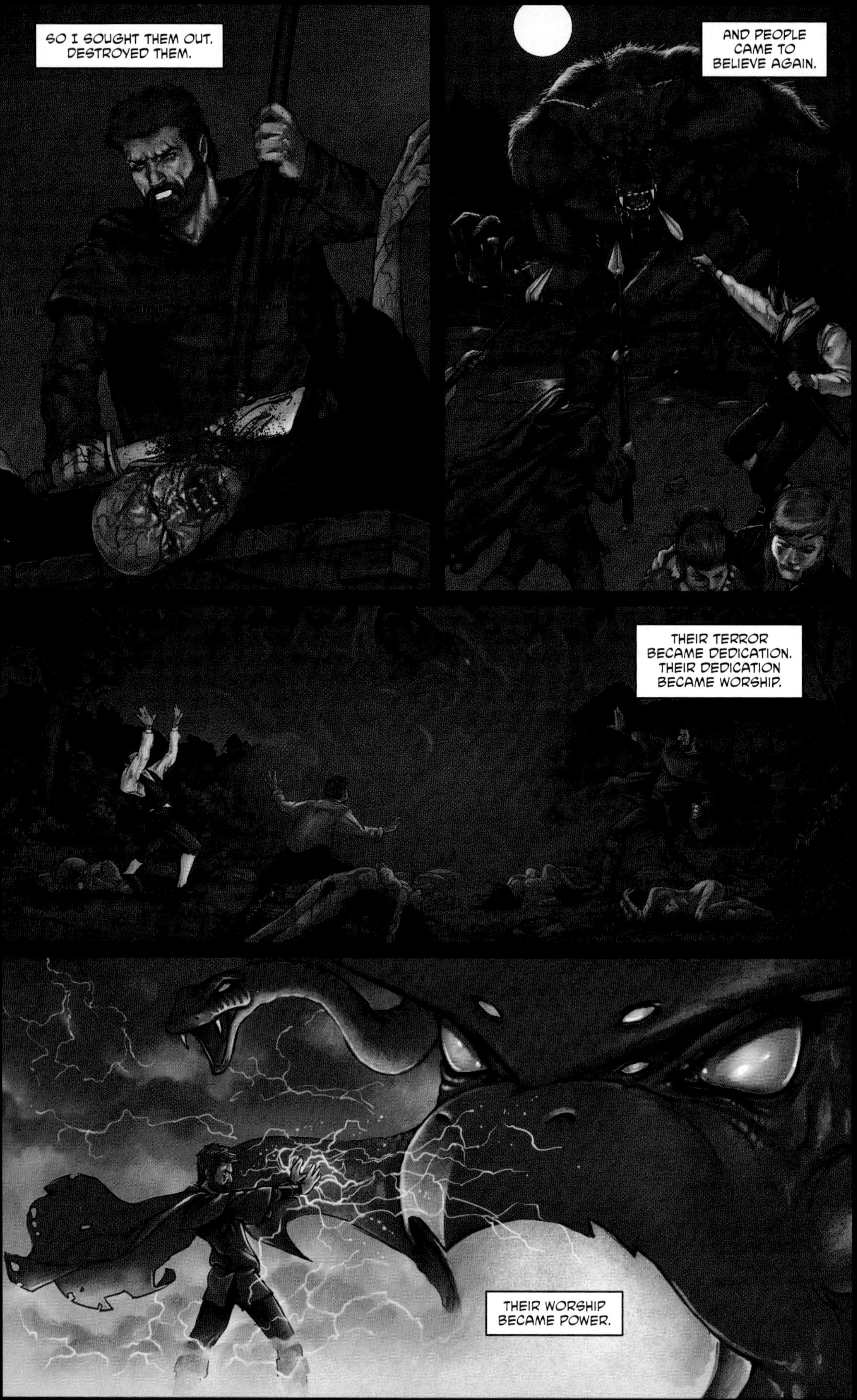
SO I SOUGHT THEM OUT. DESTROYED THEM.
AND PEOPLE CAME TO BELIEVE AGAIN.
THEIR TERROR BECAME DEDICATION. THEIR DEDICATION BECAME WORSHIP.
THEIR WORSHIP BECAME POWER.

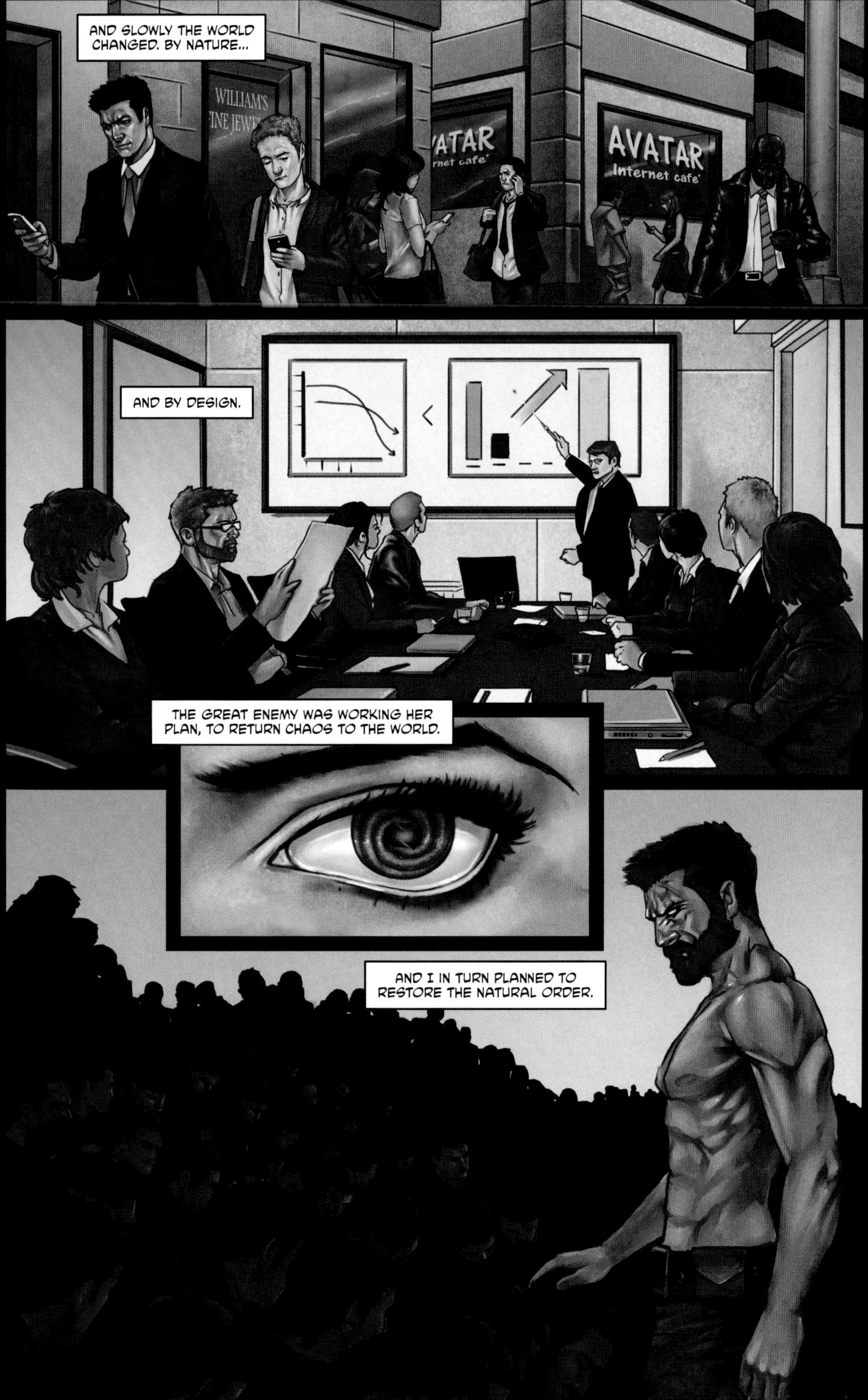
AND SLOWLY THE WORLD CHANGED. BY NATURE...
WILLIAM'S
AVATAR
Internet cafe'
AND BY DESIGN.
THE GREAT ENEMY WAS WORKING HER PLAN, TO RETURN CHAOS TO THE WORLD.
AND I IN TURN PLANNED TO RESTORE THE NATURAL ORDER.

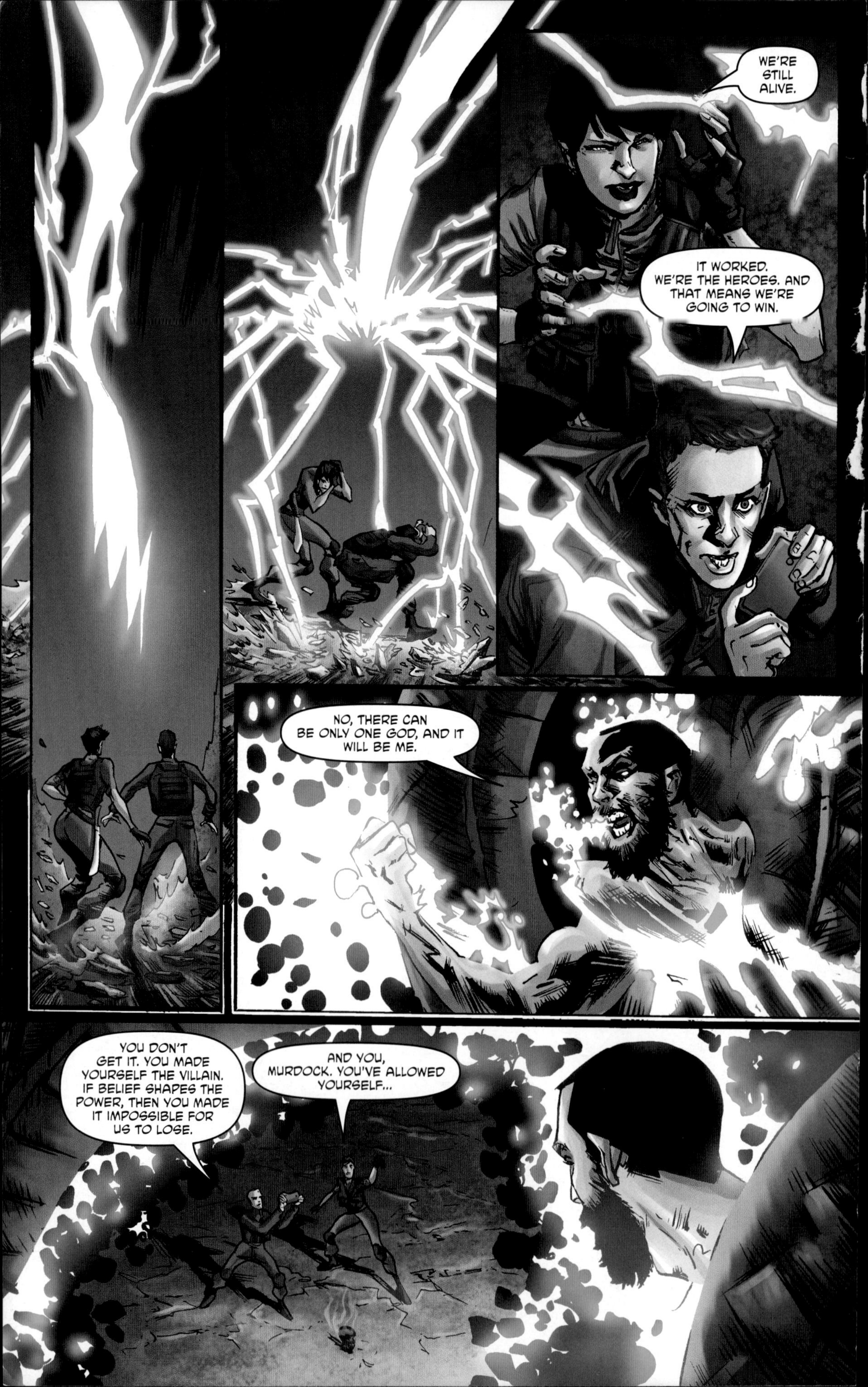
WE'RE STILL ALIVE.
IT WORKED. WE'RE THE HEROES. AND THAT MEANS WE'RE GOING TO WIN.
NO, THERE CAN BE ONLY ONE GOD, AND IT WILL BE ME.
YOU DON'T GET IT. YOU MADE YOURSELF THE VILLAIN. IF BELIEF SHAPES THE POWER, THEN YOU MADE IT IMPOSSIBLE FOR US TO LOSE.
AND YOU, MURDOCK. YOU'VE ALLOWED YOURSELF...

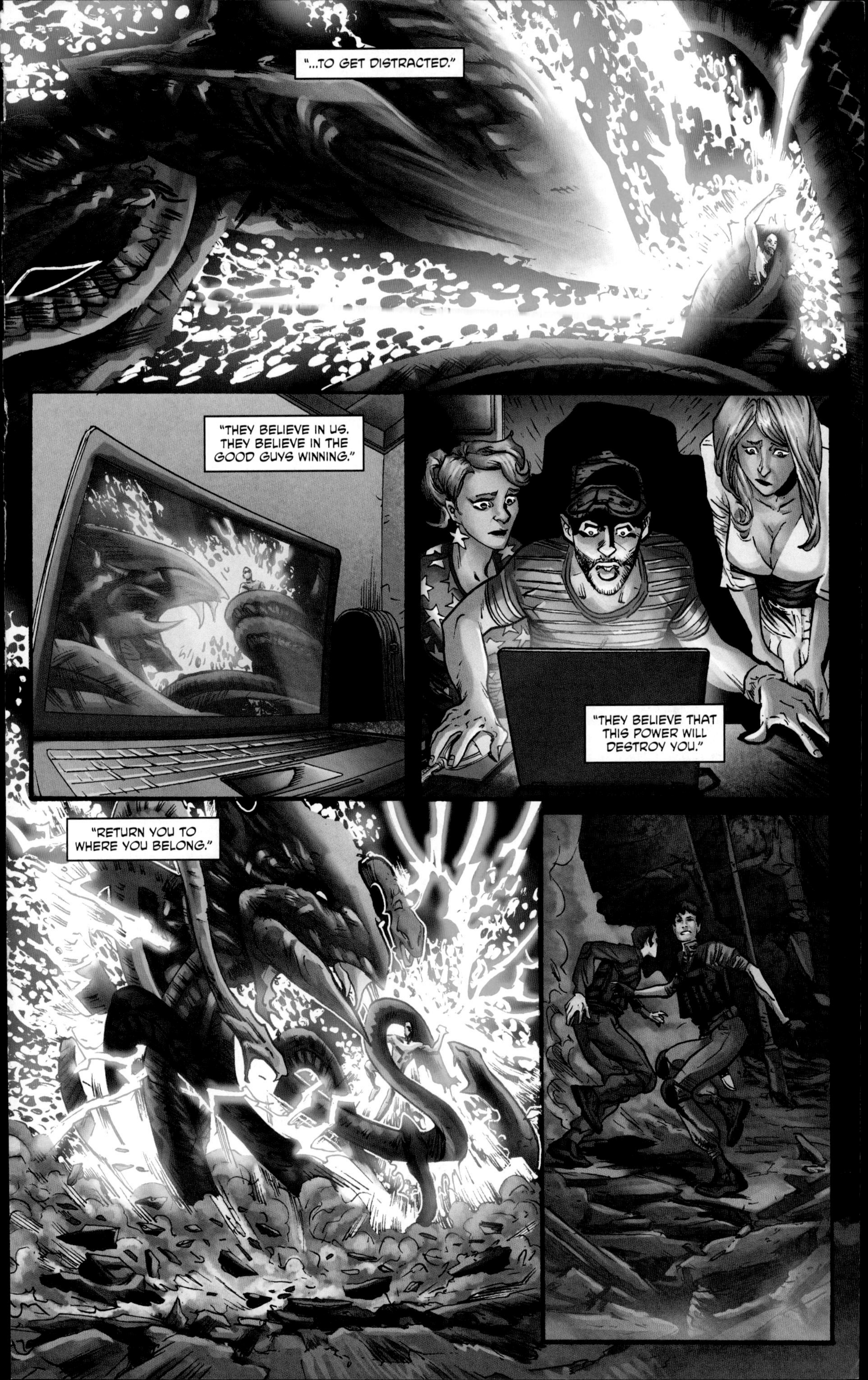
"...TO GET DISTRACTED."
"THEY BELIEVE IN US. THEY BELIEVE IN THE GOOD GUYS WINNING."
"THEY BELIEVE THAT THIS POWER WILL DESTROY YOU."
"RETURN YOU TO WHERE YOU BELONG."

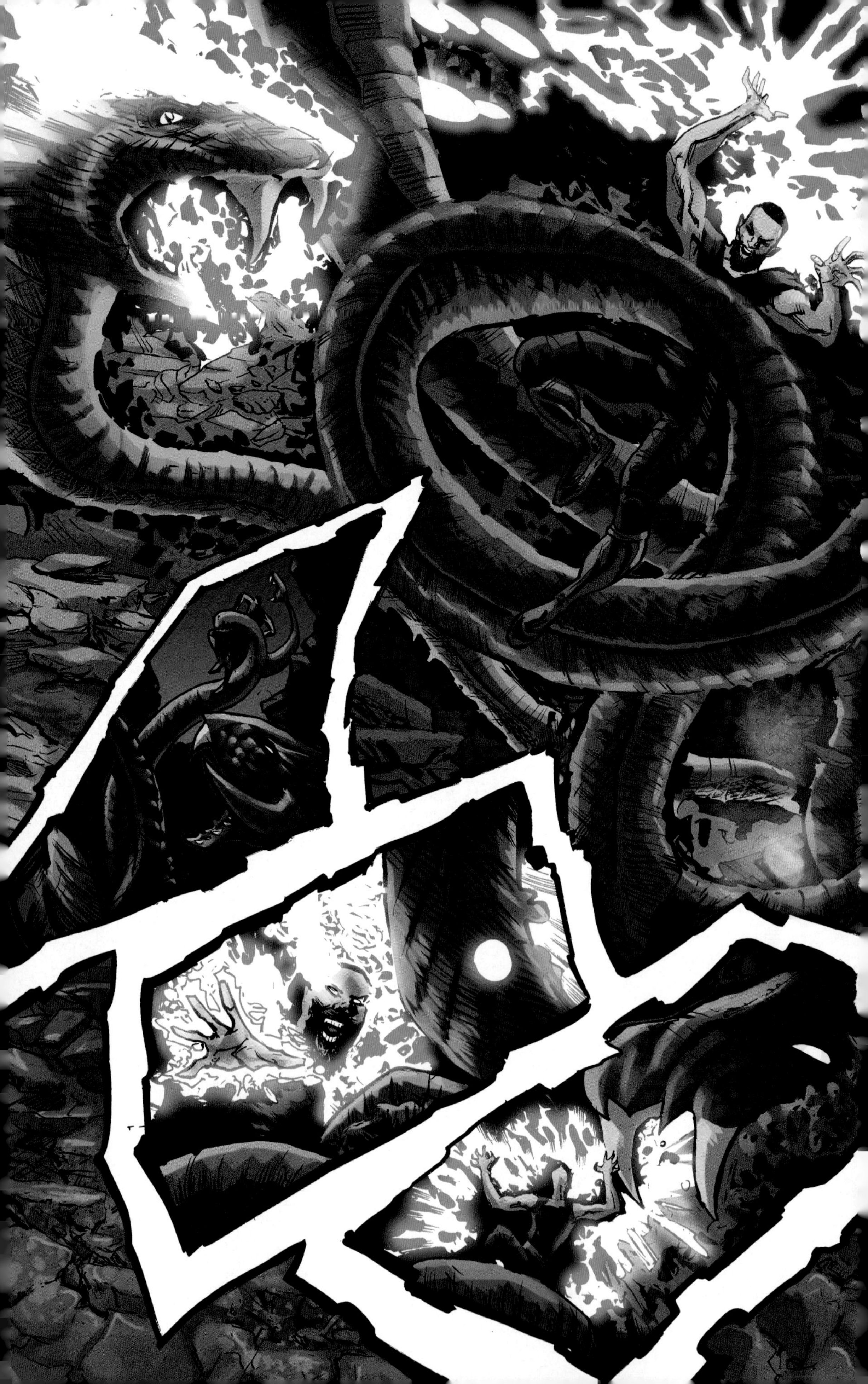

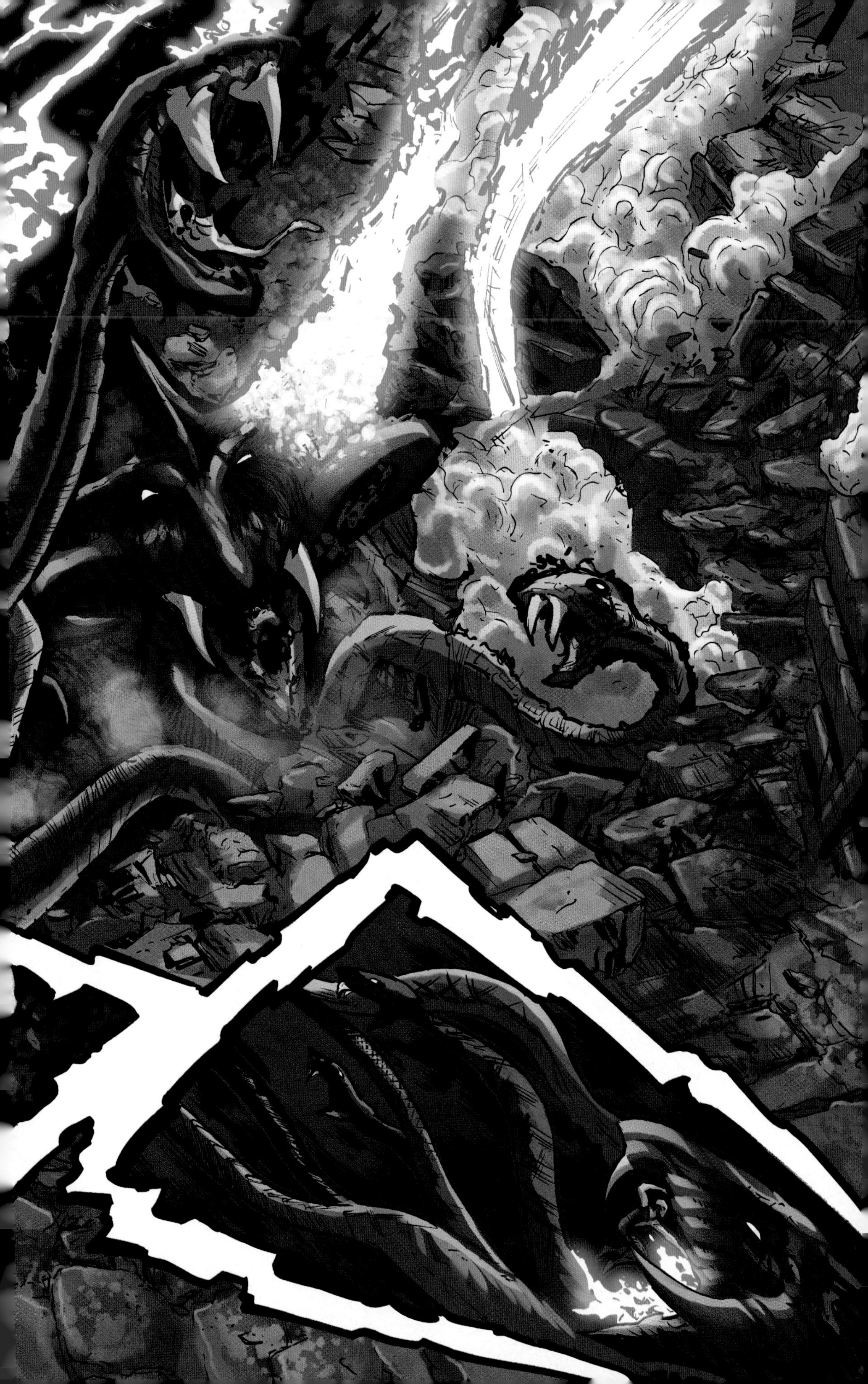

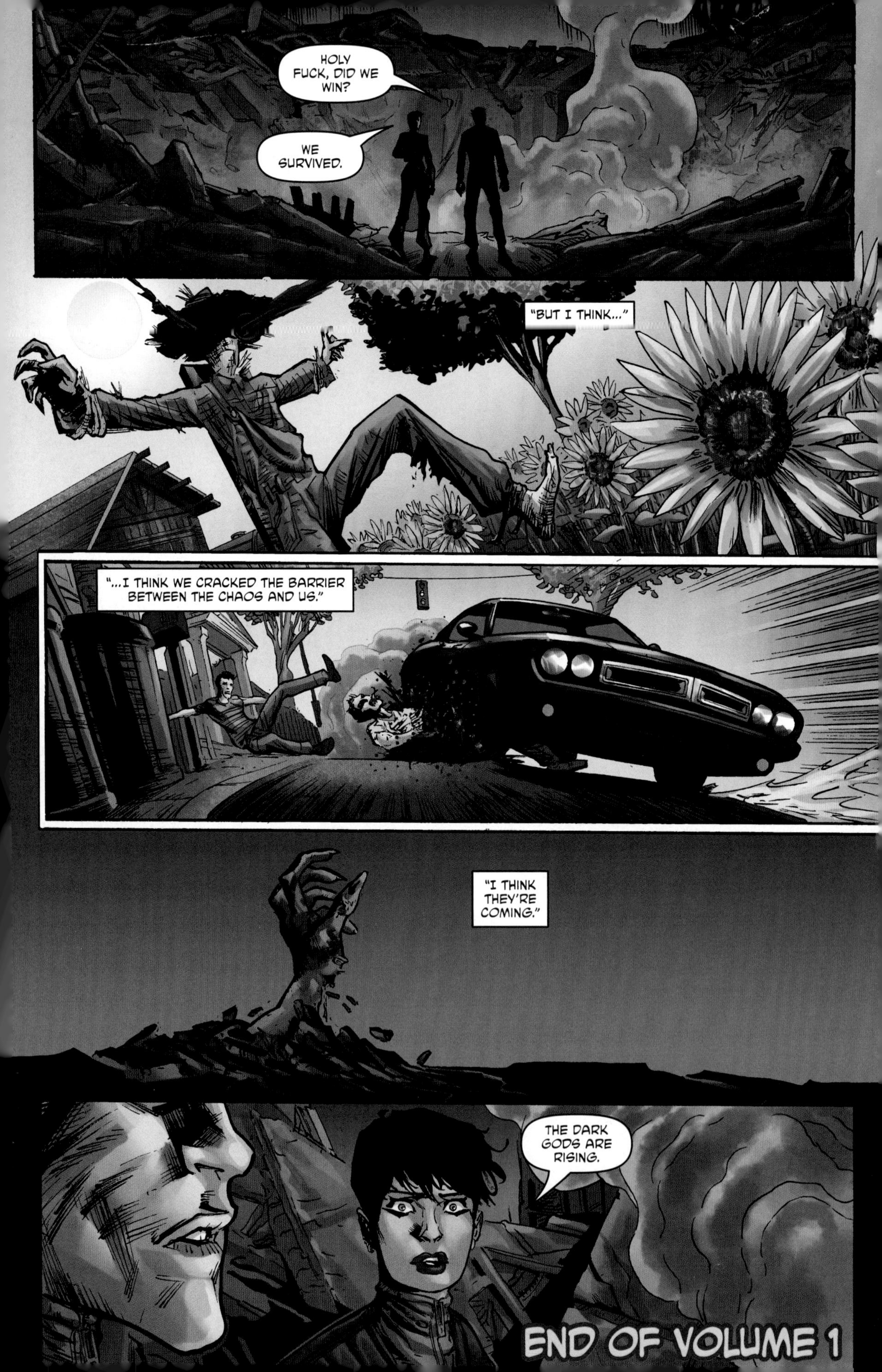
HOLY FUCK, DID WE WIN?
WE SURVIVED.
"BUT I THINK..."
"...I THINK WE CRACKED THE BARRIER BETWEEN THE CHAOS AND US."
"I THINK THEY'RE COMING."
THE DARK GODS ARE RISING.
END OF VOLUME 1

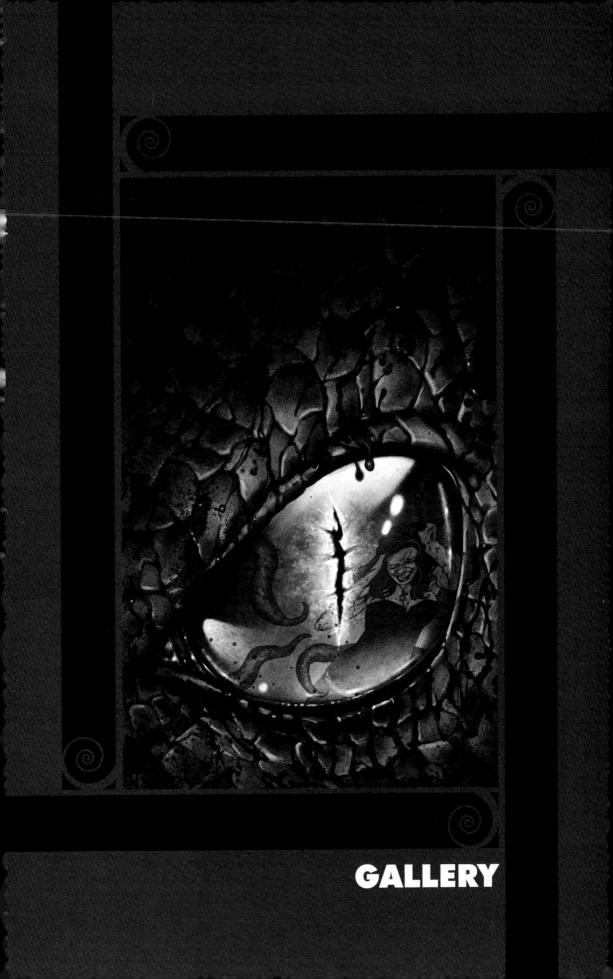

**GALLERY**

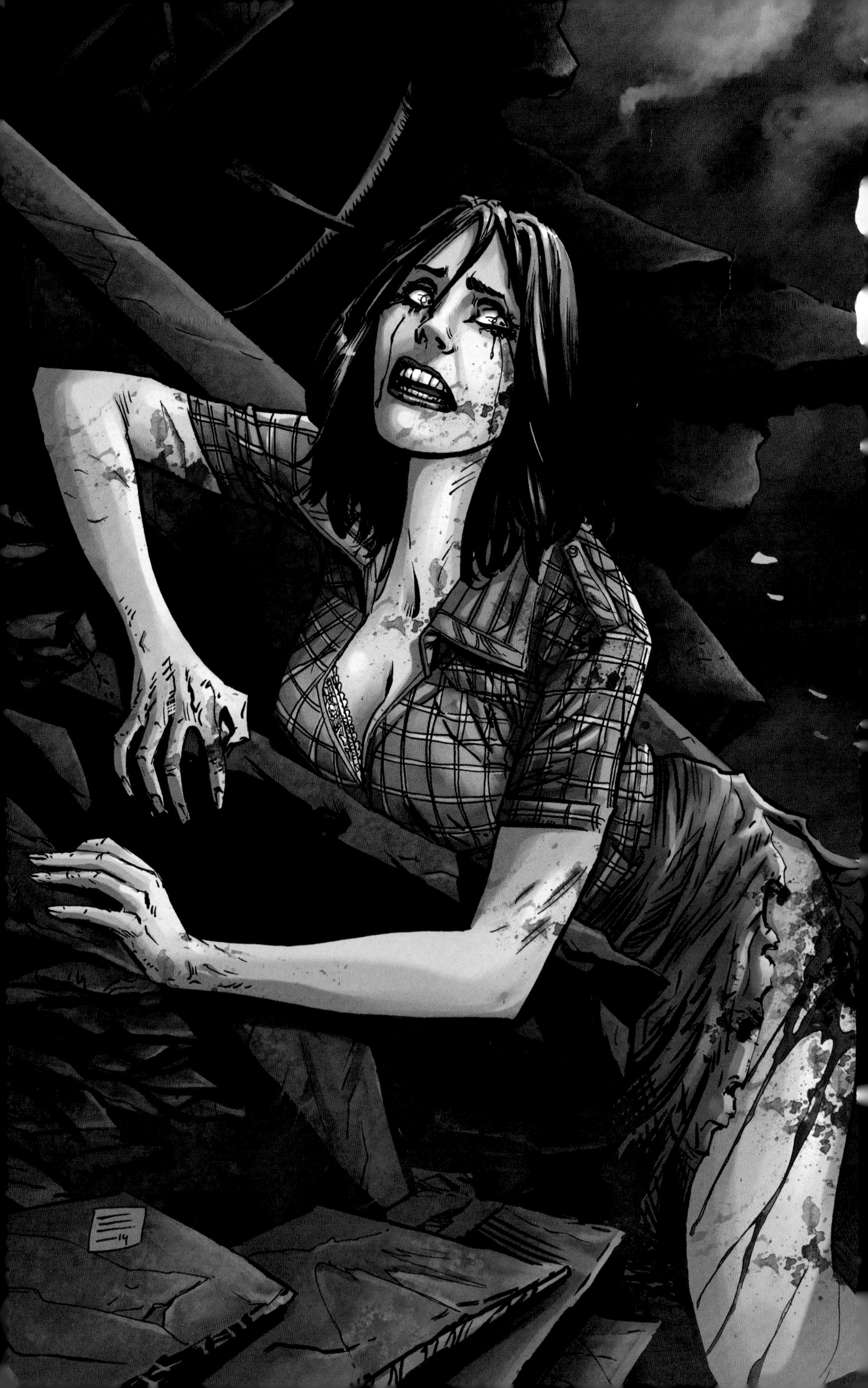

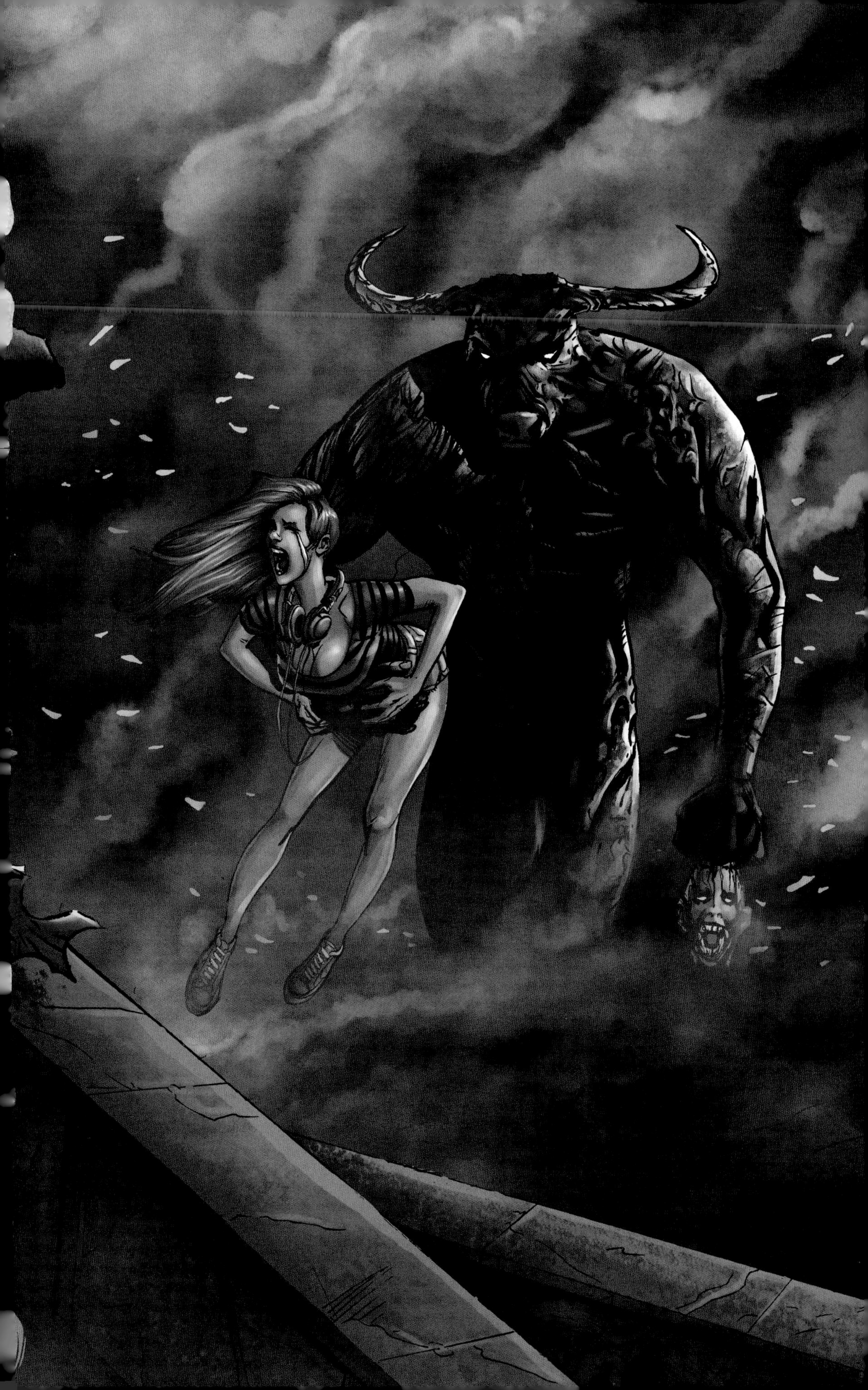

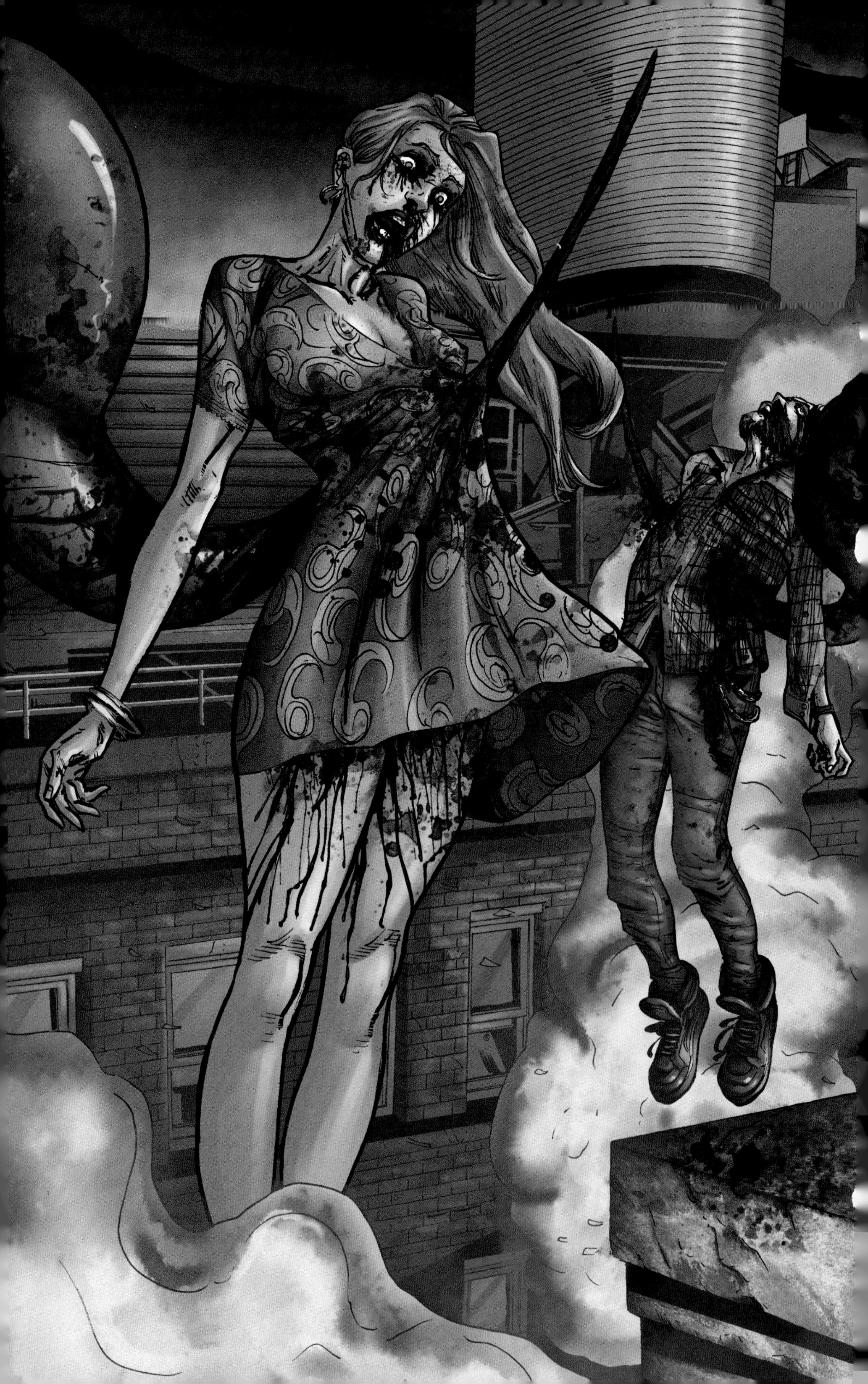

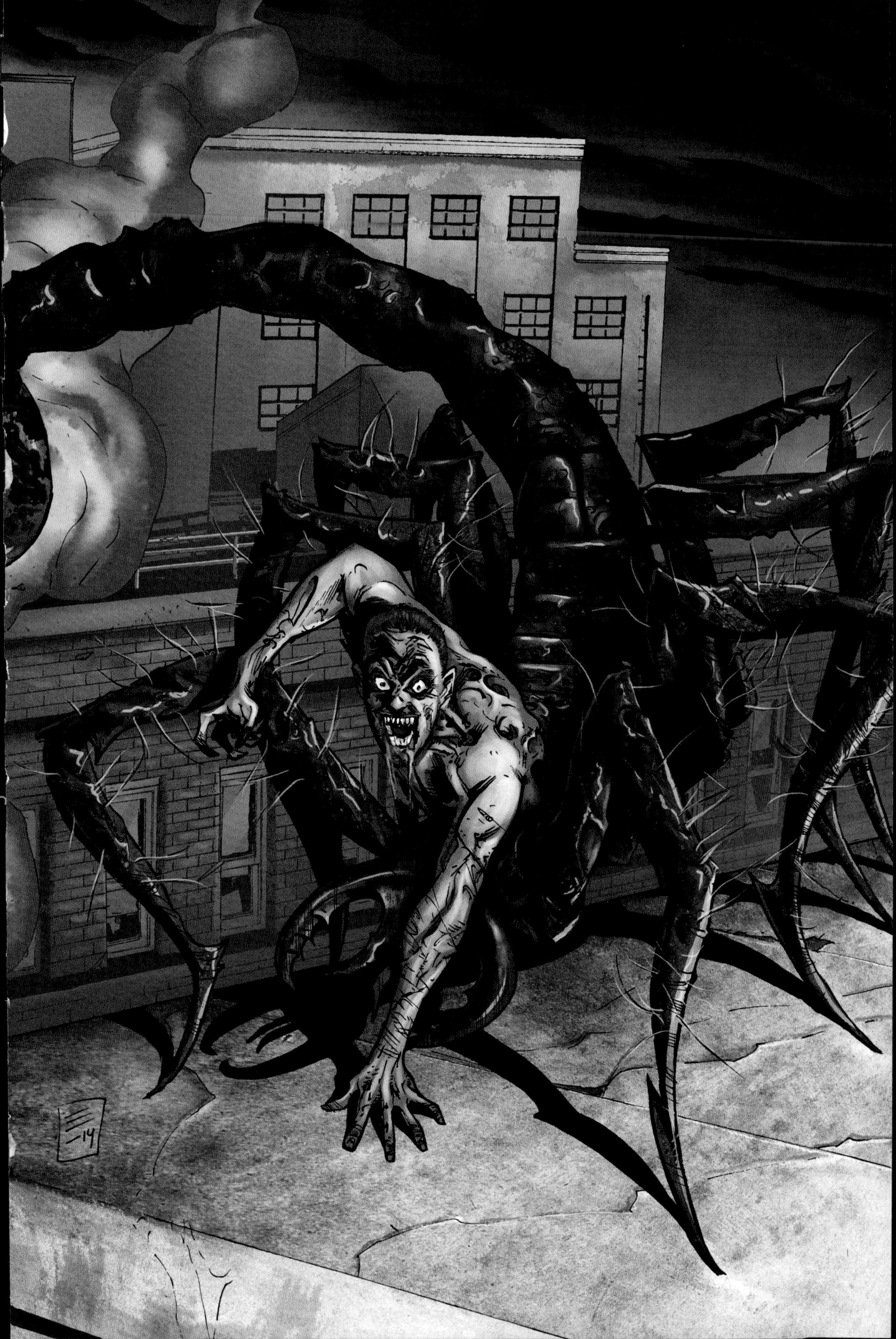

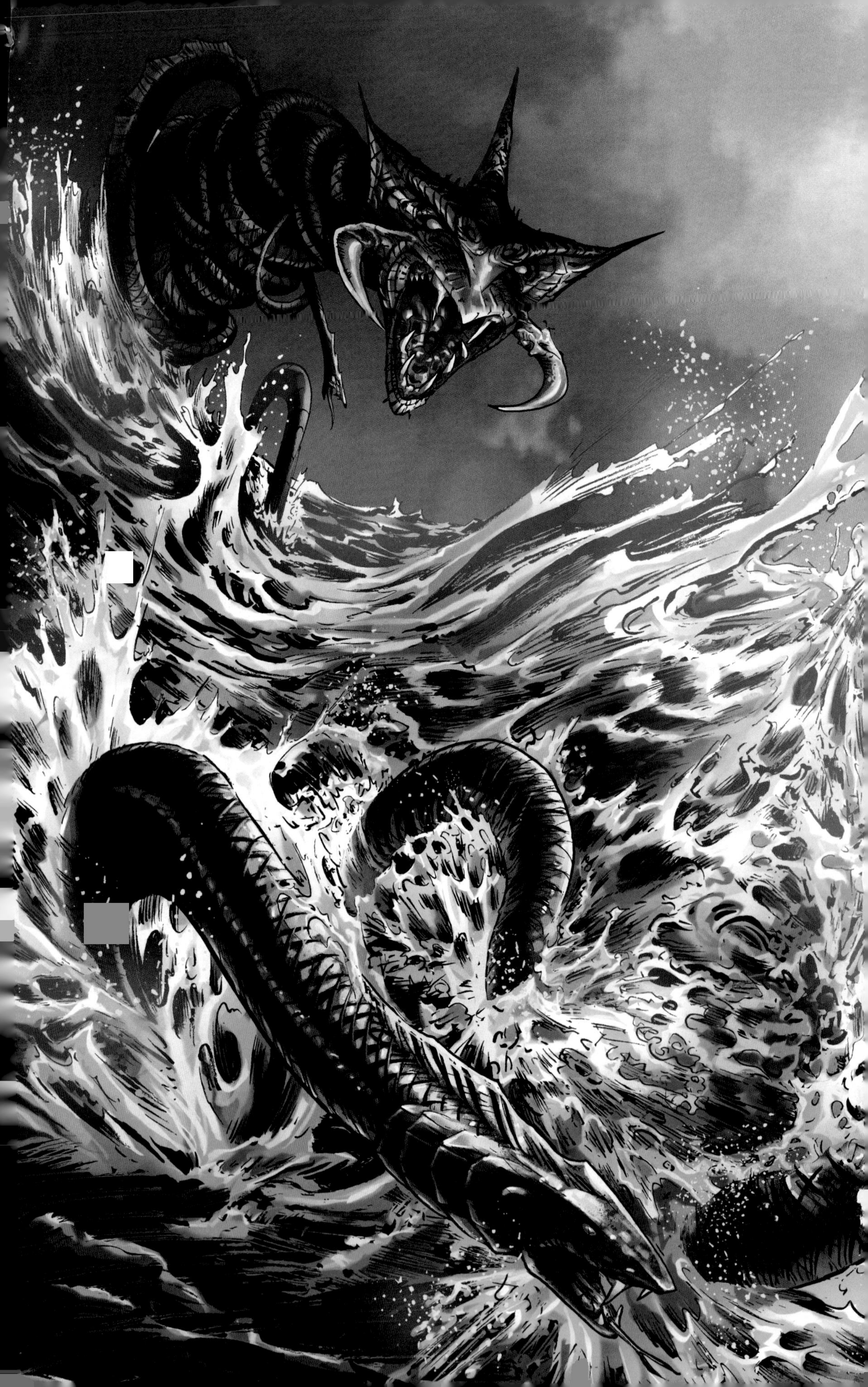

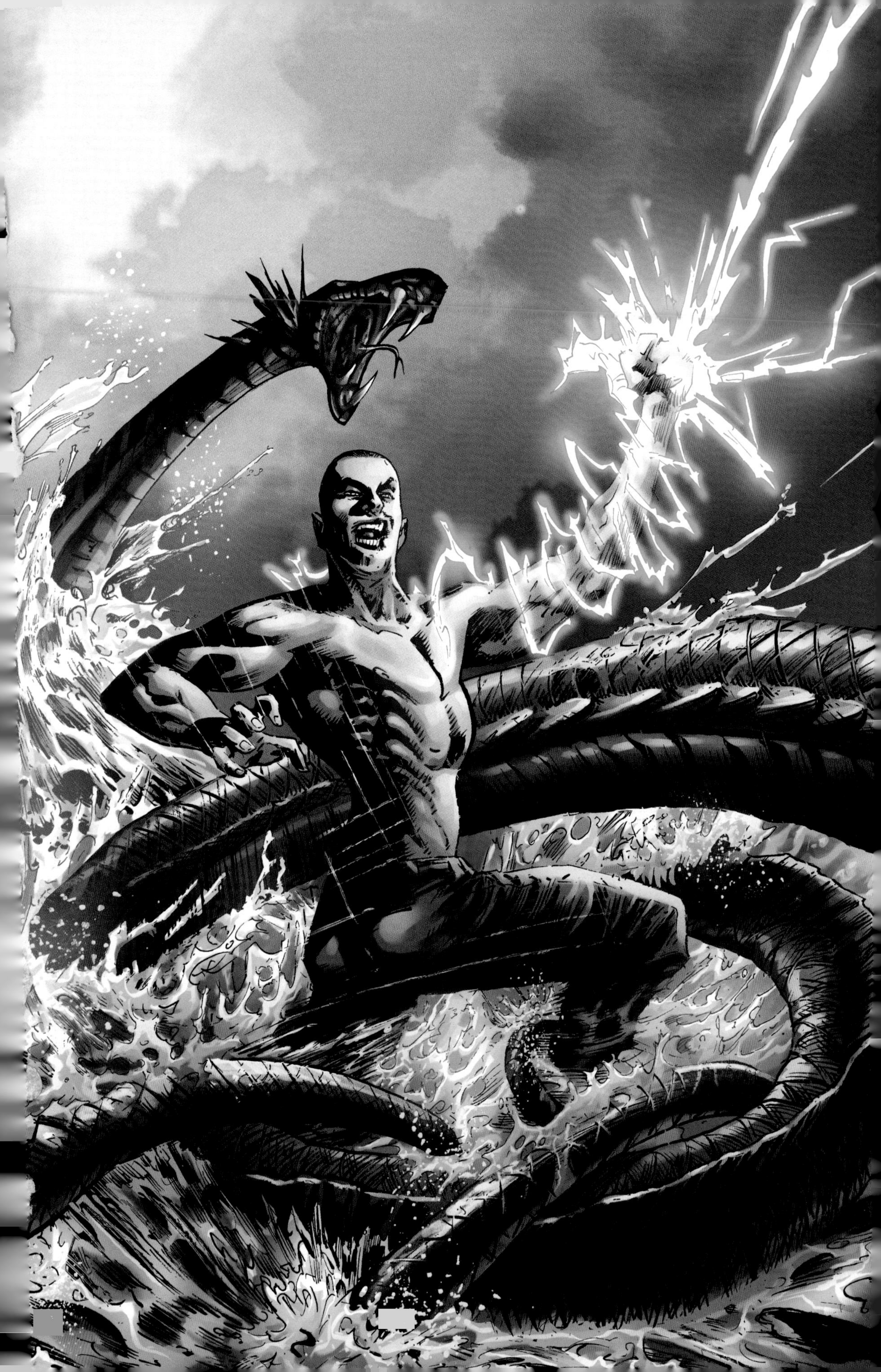

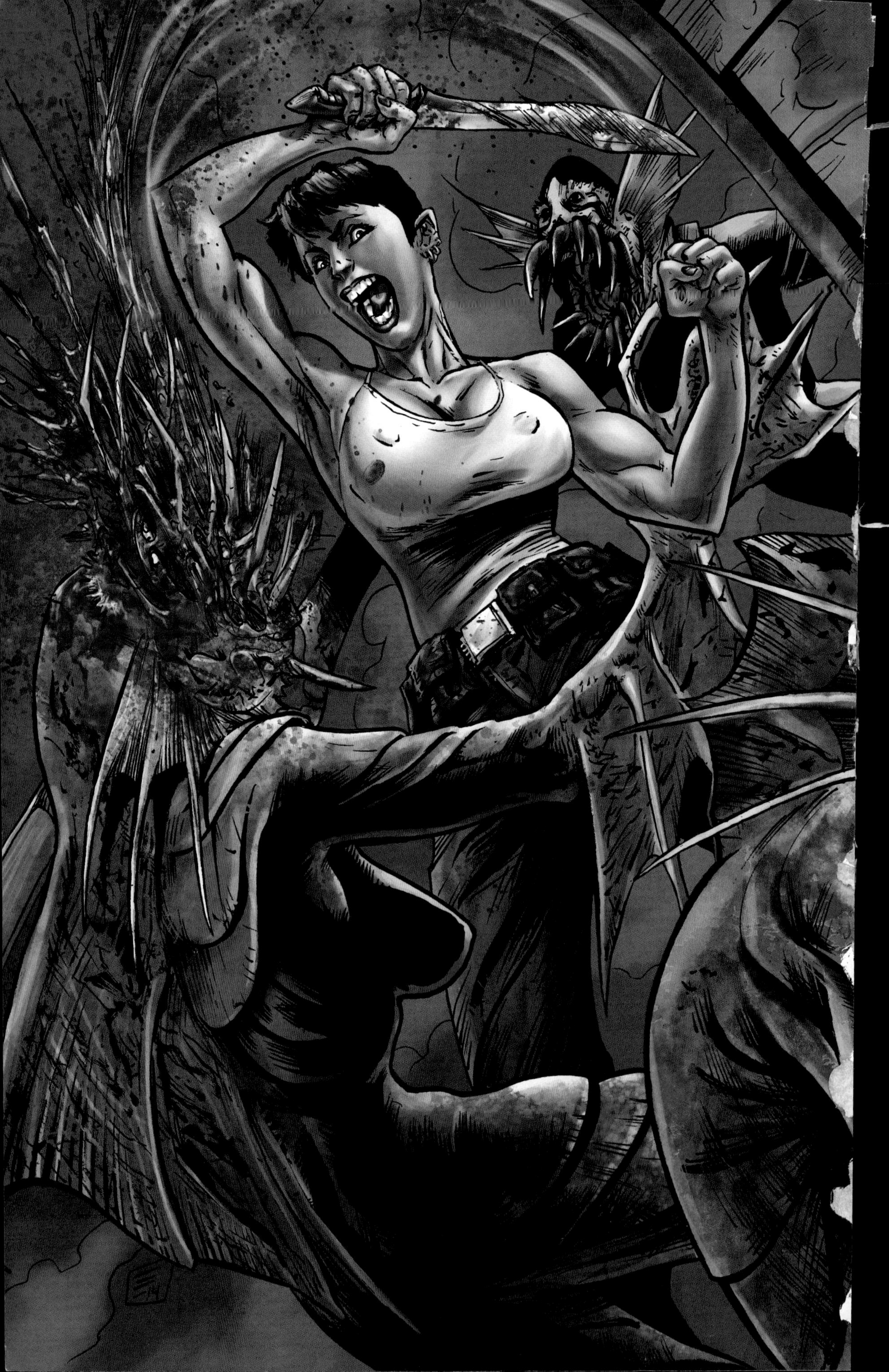

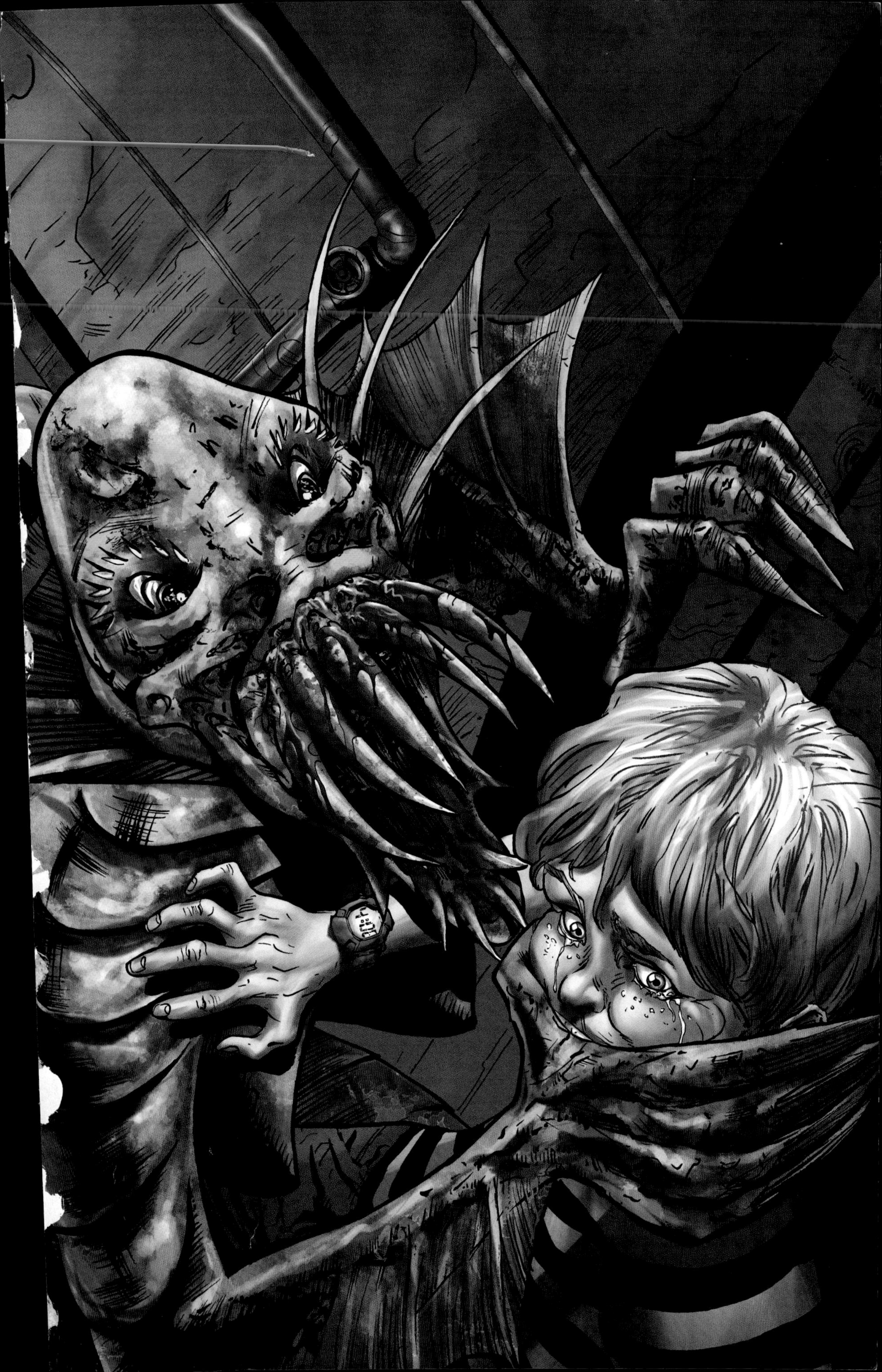

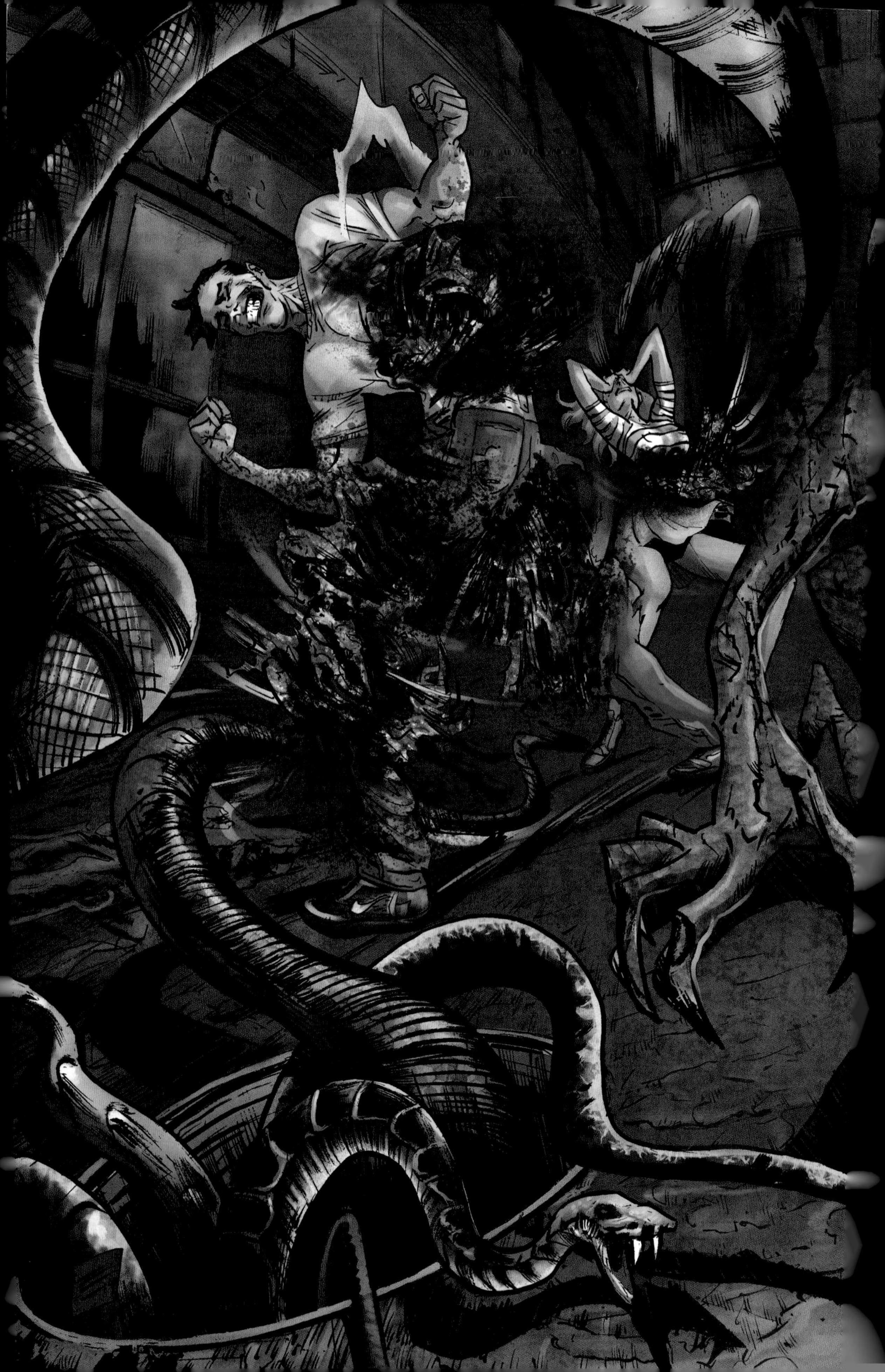

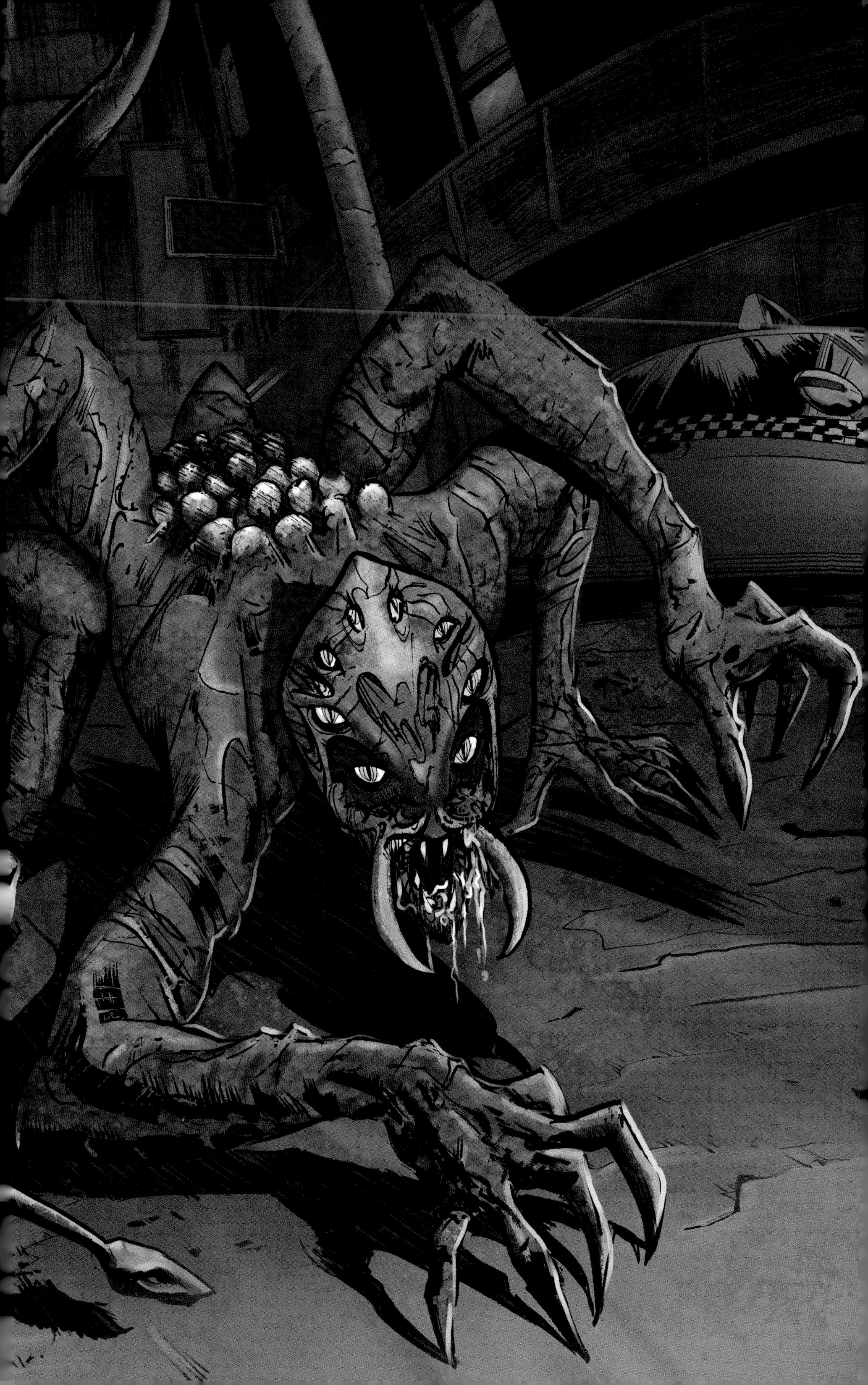

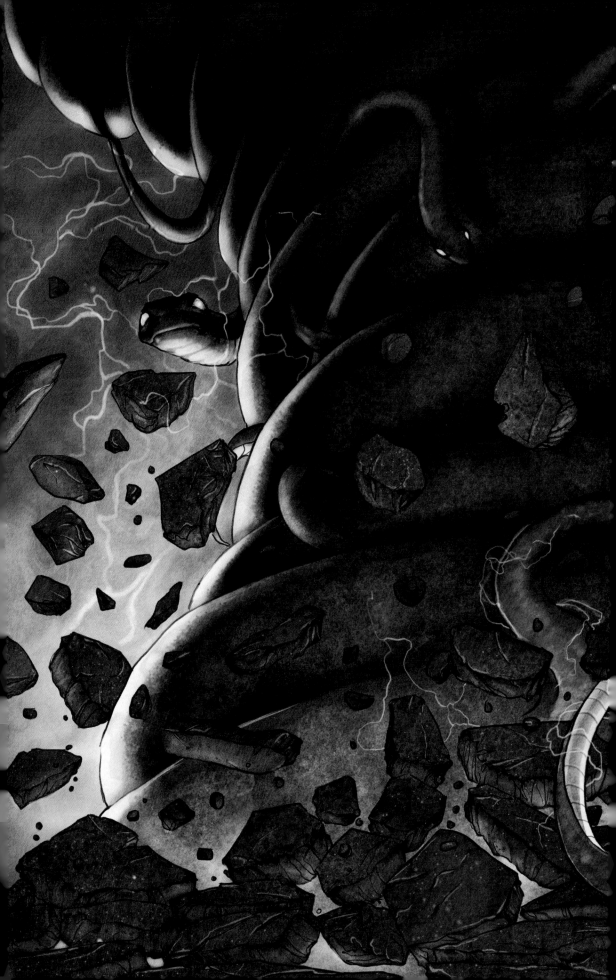

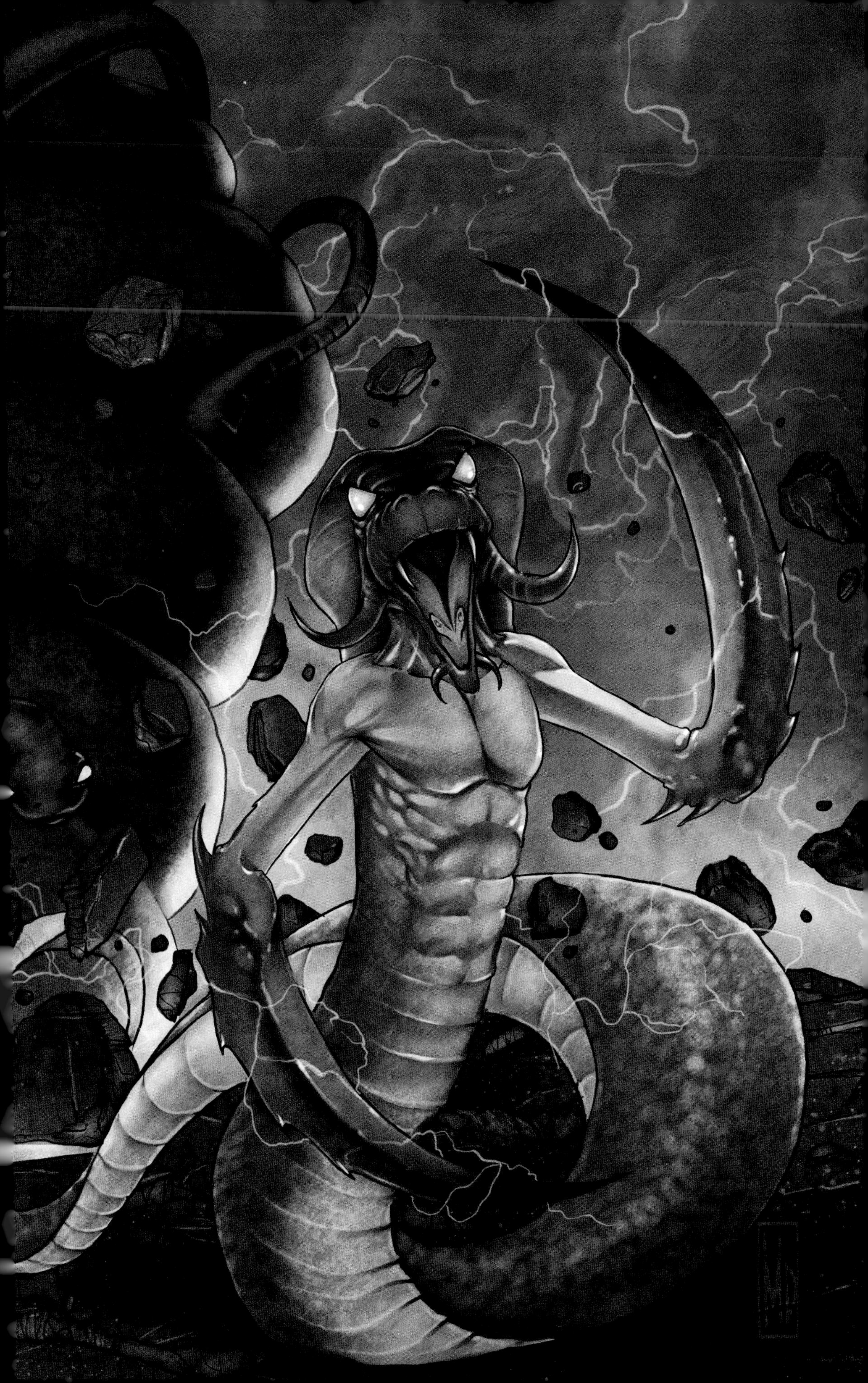

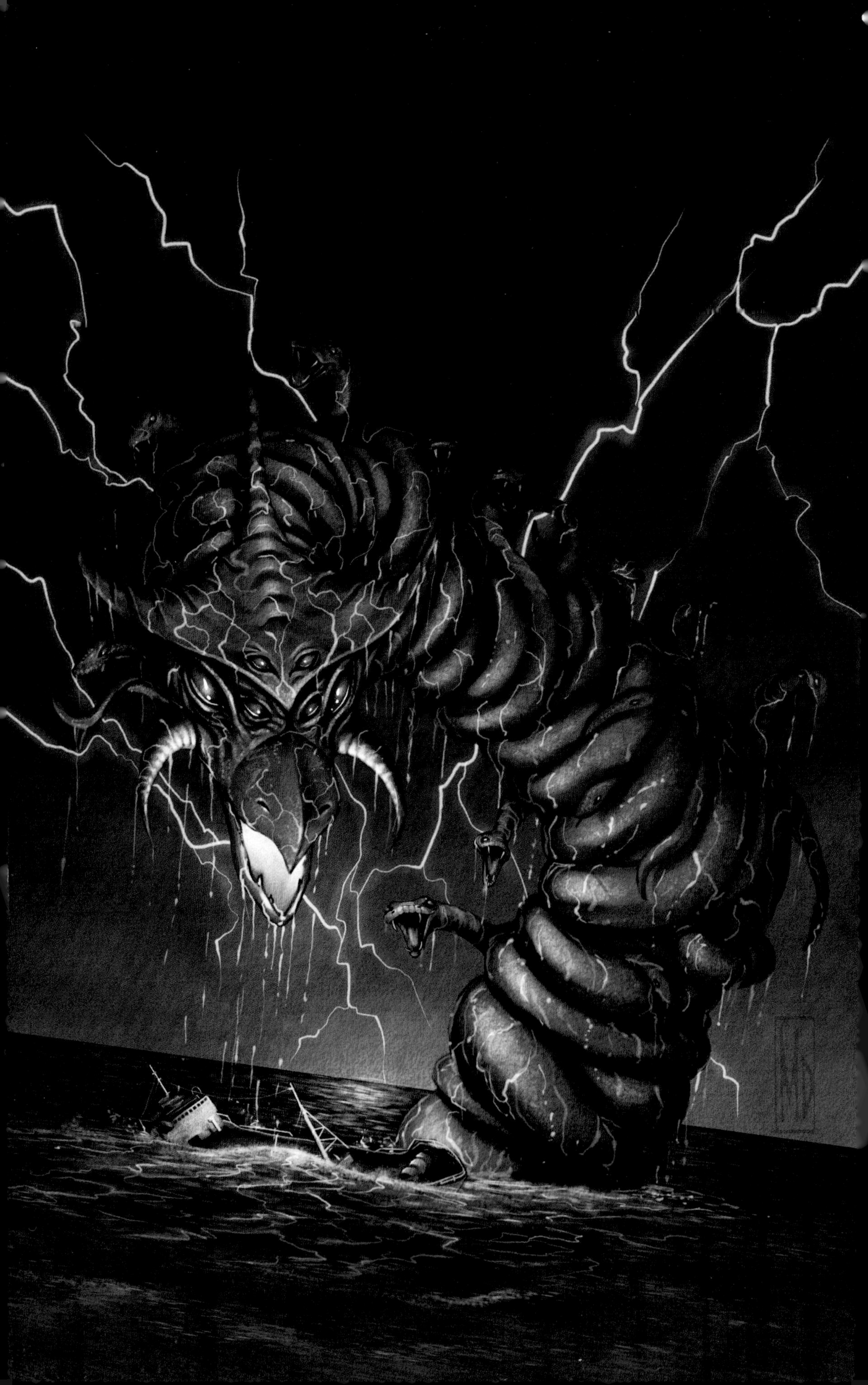

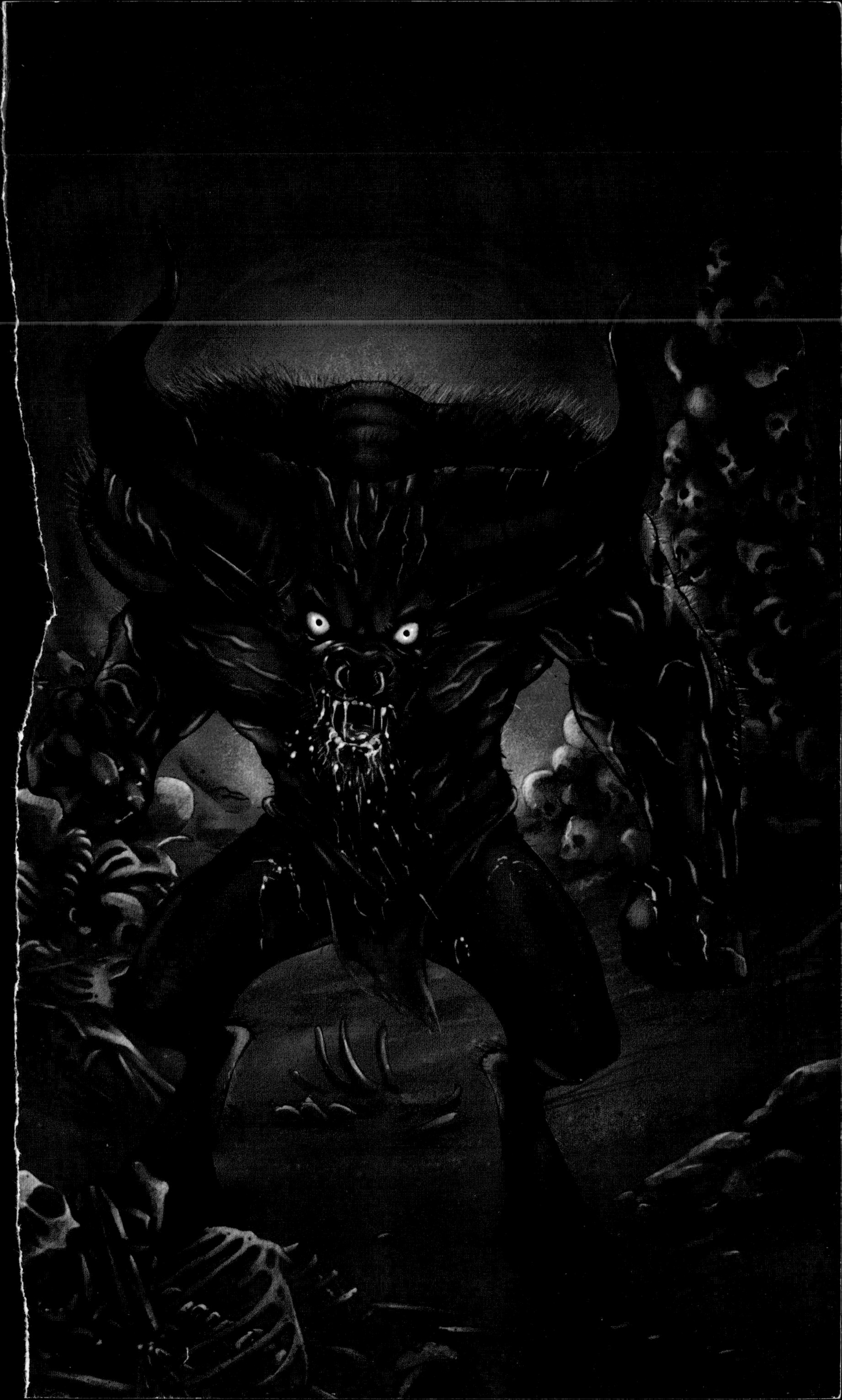

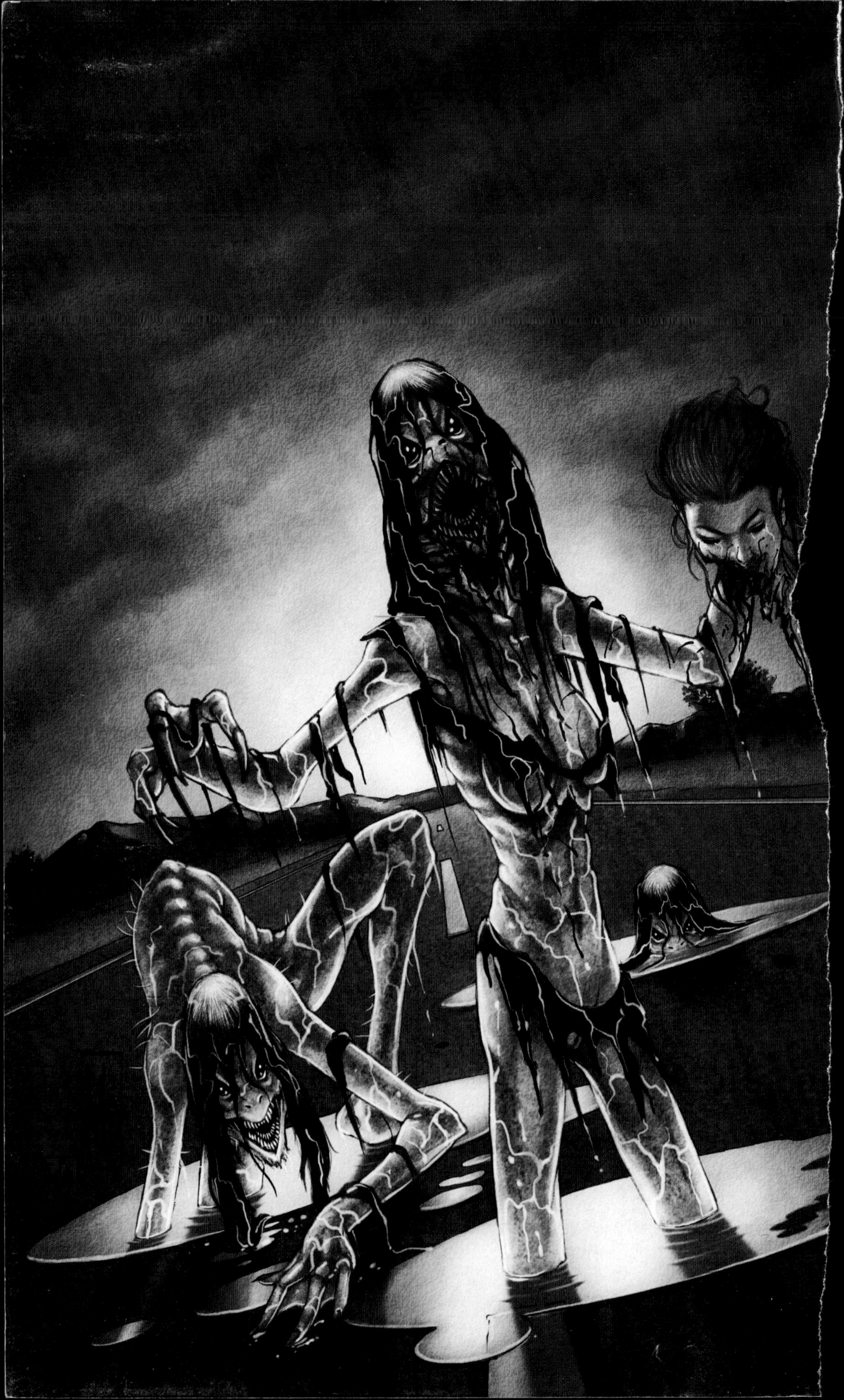